International Monetary Economics

BENNETT T. MCCALLUM

New York   Oxford
Oxford University Press
1996

Oxford University Press

Oxford   New York
Athens   Auckland   Bangkok   Bombay
Calcutta   Cape Town   Dar es Salaam   Delhi
Florence   Hong Kong   Istanbul   Karachi
Kuala Lumpur   Madras   Madrid   Melbourne
Mexico City   Nairobi   Paris   Singapore
Taipei   Tokyo   Toronto

and associated companies in
Berlin   Ibadan

Published by Oxford University Press, Inc.,
198 Madison Avenue New York, New York 10016

Oxford is a registered trademark of Oxford University Press

Library of Congress Cataloging-in-Publication Data
McCallum, Bennett T.
International monetary economics/Bennett T. McCallum.
p. cm.   Includes bibliographical references and index.
ISBN 0-19-509494-8
1. International finance.   2. Foreign exchange.   I. Title.
HG3881.M392   1995
332'.042—dc20   94-45731

9 8 7 6 5 4 3 2 1

Printed in the United States of America
on acid-free paper

PREFACE

There are several ways in which this book differs substantially from almost all existing texts in international economics. First, the present work is designed specifically for the study of international monetary economics, an area alternatively known as open-economy macroeconomics. The main concerns, accordingly, are exchange rate behavior, balance of payments considerations, macroeconomic policies, and international monetary arrangements.

Second, the book is relatively short—brief enough to be covered in a realistic one-semester course. This implies that some traditional topics must be treated quickly with others omitted entirely. I believe, however, that this is not a limitation, but instead a positive virtue. The reason is that a crucial ingredient of effective instruction is the careful determination of those topics that are of fundamental and/or essential importance. In my view, it is not very helpful to merely hand a student a comprehensive encyclopedia.

Most importantly, however, the book's analytical material is presented in terms of a single unified framework. Most textbooks on the subject present a bewildering sequence of special-purpose models, each one involving its own combination of simplifying restrictions or "assumptions" such as limited capital mobility, constant real exchange rates, fixed price levels, and so on. Indeed, considerable attention is, in many cases, devoted to models of the most extreme Keynesian multiplier type, in which investment spending is treated as exogenous and interest rates are ignored completely. In the present work, by contrast, the emphasis is on a single setup—usable with fixed or floating exchange rates—in which capital mobility is complete, real exchange rates are variable, and investment spending is endogenous. Variants are utilized for short-run and long-run comparative static analysis, i.e., assuming fixed and fully-adjusted commodity prices. Indeed, steady-state as well as stationary-state applications of the latter are explored, thereby lending additional realism to the analysis in a manner that is not present in existing texts. The simplifying assumption that makes possible a unified and compact graphical treatment of all these cases, with both fixed and floating exchange rates, is that the perspective taken is (in most places) that of a small open economy.

In addition to these comparative static exercises, the book devotes one sizable chapter to proper dynamic analysis with rational expectations, something rarely found in textbook presentations. There the technical demands on the reader are somewhat greater. But except in this one chapter—which can be skipped without major consequences in subsequent portions—the expositional technique is predominantly graphical rather than algebraic.

Some additional features of the book that are moderately unusual include the following: an analytical model of the gold standard or other commodity-money arrangements; an integrated discussion of historical developments and recent data; explicit recognition that interest rates are used as operating instruments by actual central banks; and the presentation of empirical evidence concerning the validity of each component of the basic analytical model. This latter presentation includes a proposed rationalization of uncovered interest parity with well-known evidence that seems superficially to be inconsistent with that crucial relation. In a more standard vein, the book's concluding chapters feature extended discussions of the European Monetary System and the theory and practice of international macroeconomic cooperation.

Valuable comments or discussions have been provided by a number of friends and colleagues including Michael Bordo, Marvin Goodfriend, Albert Marcet, Allan Meltzer, and Gary Quinlivan. In addition, helpful advice was provided by several anonymous reviewers. For logistical help, I am especially indebted to Patricia Niber, who expertly and cheerfully typed the entire manuscript.

Pittsburgh   *B. T. M*
February 1995

CONTENTS

PART III APPLICATIONS

I

BASIC CONCEPTS

1

Introduction

1.1 Preliminary Remarks

International monetary topics such as exchange rate adjustments, balance-of-payments crises, and the possible reconstruction of international institutions have long been considered among the most fascinating in all of economics. In recent years, however, these topics have moved even more strongly into the forefront of consciousness ofr analysts, practitioners, policy makers, and students alike. As the next two sections will document, the behavior of exchange rates and balance-of-payments accounts departed sharply from their historical patterns during the 1980s. That decade, moreover, witnessed an impressive effort by members of the European Monetary System in maintaining their exchange rate arrangements of 1979, an effort that led to a volatile situation in which a full-fledged European Monetary Union—previously almost inconceivable—first appeared likely to blossom forth within a very few years, and then suffered severe setbacks during 1992 and 1993 from currency crises reminiscent of earlier eras. In addition, the emergence of the nations of eastern Europe as newly activated participants in the world marketplace has given rise to a host of new issues pertaining to their monetary relationships with western nations and with the former USSR, whose own market (and political!) arrangements have been changing too erratically even to permit characterization. Accordingly, it seems entirely possible that the area of international monetary economics has never been richer in terms of fascinating but challenging and difficult issues.

The object of the present work is to provide a brief introduction to the major topics of the subject area together with an analytical framework that is designed to facilitate their understanding. In particular, the text will concentrate on (1) concepts and relationships involving exchange rates and balance-of-payments magnitudes, (2) the construction and manipulation of a small but versatile model of exchange rate and balance-of-payments behavior, and (3) a description of current and prospective arrangements for multicountry cooperation in Europe and elsewhere. These three main topics are the focus of the book's three main parts. Before turning to an outline, it may be useful to begin with a quick description of two of the striking recent developments mentioned, presented from the perspective of the United States. Accordingly, Sections 1.2

3

and 1.3 will feature recent U.S. experience in terms of exchange rate and balance-of-payments measures, respectively.

1.2 U.S. Exchange Rates, 1947–1993

International exchange rates are fundamentally, of course, prices of one nation's currency in terms of another's, such as 100 Japanese yen per U.S. dollar or 2.4 German marks per British pound. But while these *bilateral* rates provide the basic ingredients, it is often useful to work with aggregative or average measures for some nation under special consideration. For the United States, the most widely cited measure of this type is an index published by the Board of Governors of the Federal Reserve System, which is a weighted average of the exchange value of the dollar relative to each of 10 important currencies.[1] These weights are based on the relative magnitudes of each nation's volume of international trade, so the measure could reasonably referred to as a *trade-weighted index*.[2] A somewhat more common practice, however, is to refer to it and other such indexes as "effective exchange rates" for the country in question.

Be that as it may, the Fed's index for the U.S. dollar over the postwar (i.e., post-World War II) period is plotted in Figure 1–1. As with all such indexes, the absolute level is arbitrarily specified as of some reference or base period; in this case the base is such as to make the index value equal 100 in March 1973. Since the Fed's published series actually dates back only to 1967, approximate values for 1947–1966 have been estimated by the present author.[3]

Straightforward inspection of Figure 1–1 shows clearly the extensive changes in value that the dollar has undergone since the advent of floating or market-determined exchange rates in August 1971.[4] After a near decade of irregular downward movements, the dollar's value climbed rapidly from

[1] The precise weights assigned to the 10 national currencies are specified in Chapter 2.

[2] That term is not unambiguous, however. The weights could be based on the various nations' shares in international trade globally or their shares in trade with the United States (or whatever country to which the average is designed to pertain).

[3] The procedure was to splice on values of another index that is based on only the subset of nations with exchange rate data available for the entire span of years 1947 to 1993. These include Belgium, Canada, Italy, the Netherlands, and the United Kingdom. The weights were obtained from a least-squares regression equation designed to explain the Fed's index value over the sample period 1967–1986.

[4] Most readers will be aware that a system of fixed exchange rates relative to the U.S. dollar was agreed upon, at a conference held at Bretton Woods in 1944, by many of the world's nations. This same conference established the International Monetary Fund to coordinate and oversee the system of fixed rates. For various reasons, including the failure of the United States to conduct a monetary policy consistent with its obligation to sell gold to other nations at $35 per ounce, the system began to break down in the 1960s. Unilateral action by the United States in August 1971 effectively ended the fixed-rate arrangement, but floating rates were not considered the norm until March 1973. Additional discussion will be provided in Chapter 4. For alternative treatments, see Kenen (1994) and Yeager (1976).

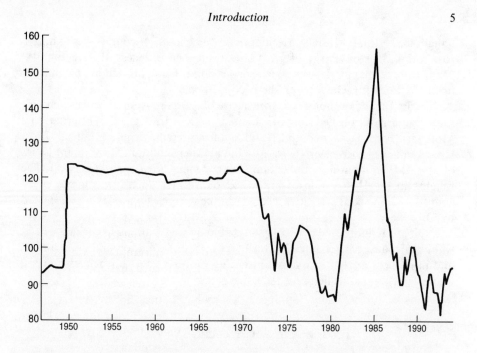

Figure 1–1 Foreign exchange value of U.S. dollar, 1947–1993. Base—index equals 100 in March 1973. *Source*: Board of Governors of the Federal Reserve System; pre-1967 values estimated by author.

1980 through 1984, with the peak occurring in February 1985, and then plunged even more rapidly over the three-year span of 1985–1987. Also apparent is the relative stability of the dollar's value, in comparison with other currencies, during the Bretton Woods period of fixed exchange rates (1947–1971), during which other nations pledged to intervene in currency markets so as to maintain their exchange rates against the dollar within tight limits around specified par values. The one major change during that span resulted from the United Kingdom's devaluation of the pound in 1949, which was accompanied by realignments of several other currencies traditionally tied to the pound.[5]

It is of course the case that any basic bilateral exchange rate, such as that between the dollar and the Japanese yen, can be expressed in two ways: as the dollar price of a yen ($/¥) or as the yen price of a dollar (¥/$). The latter can also be described as the value of a dollar in terms of yen. Clearly, then, an average or effective exchange rate index can be reported either as the foreign exchange value of a currency—as with the Fed's index for the dollar—or as the price (in terms of that currency) of foreign exchange. The latter convention is often used by practitioners in European nations (except for the United Kingdom); the former is more common in the United States and the United

[5] This effect is perhaps overstated by the weights in the 1947–1966 index and therefore in Figure 1–1.

Kingdom. Nothing of substance hinges on the choice, of course; it is simply a convention. It is obviously of great importance, nevertheless, that the analyst or practitioner be clear about which convention is being utilized in any analysis or discussion with which he or she is concerned.[6]

The Fed's index is not the only measure of the average or effective exchange rate regularly published for the United States. In fact, the International Monetary Fund (IMF) compiles and publishes trade-weighted indexes for a large number of currencies. (Currently the number is about 75; see recent issues of the IMF's monthly publication *International Financial Statistics*.) The weights in the IMF's indexes are based on worldwide trade volumes of 17 countries. Some considerations relevant in the design of an index are discussed by Ott (1987).

Numerous additional concepts and distinctions pertaining to exchange rates will be introduced in Chapter 2, which focuses more attention on bilateral rates and introduces analytical issues concerning *forward* rates (for delivery several weeks later) and so-called *real* exchange rates.

1.3 U.S. Current Account, 1947–1993

Turning now to the topic of a nation's balance of payments (BOP), our aim will be merely to illustrate a dramatic change in the United States's foreign trade performance that took place in the middle 1980s. The change will be described in terms of only one measure of a nation's payments behavior, the *current-account* balance, with our main discussion of BOP concepts more generally reserved for Chapter 3.

The current-account balance for any country (over any year or other specified time span) may be defined as the value of its net exports—that is, exports minus imports—of goods and services plus net transfers (i.e., gifts) received. It will be emphasized in Chapter 3 that with this definition "services exported" must include some nonobvious items such as capital services paid for by interest and dividend income from abroad. But here our object is only to examine the U.S. record for the current-account balance without yet putting much emphasis on the precise meaning of the measure.

Numerical figures pertaining to that record are reported in the second column of Table 1–1, where positive values reflect current-account surpluses—exports in excess of imports—and negative values imply deficits. From those figures it is clear that the United States traditionally maintained a surplus in its current account before 1983, but has recorded a sizable deficit in each subsequent year. To put the contrast in a dramatic manner, one could say that the United States never experienced a current-account deficit of more than $16 billion prior to 1983, but then recorded one in excess of $100 billion for each of six consecutive years, 1984–1989. Since then the deficit magnitudes have

---

[6] In formal analytical models it is fairly standard to express rates in terms of the European convention, that is, as the "home-country" price of foreign exchange.

Table 1-1 U.S. Current-Account Balance, 1947–1993

Year	Current-account balance ($ bil)	GDP ($ bil)	Current-account balance (% of GDP)
1947	8.99	234.3	3.84
1948	2.42	260.3	0.93
1949	0.87	259.3	0.33
1950	−1.84	287.0	−0.64
1951	0.88	331.6	0.26
1952	0.61	349.7	0.17
1953	−1.29	370.0	0.35
1954	0.22	370.9	0.06
1955	0.43	404.3	0.11
1956	2.73	426.2	0.64
1957	4.76	448.6	1.06
1958	0.78	454.7	0.17
1959	−1.28	494.2	−0.26
1960	2.82	513.3	0.55
1961	3.82	531.8	0.72
1962	3.39	571.6	0.59
1963	4.41	603.1	0.73
1964	6.82	648.0	1.05
1965	5.43	702.7	0.77
1966	3.03	769.8	0.39
1967	2.58	814.3	0.32
1968	0.61	889.3	0.07
1969	0.40	959.5	0.04
1970	2.33	1010.7	0.23
1971	−1.43	1097.2	−0.13
1972	−5.79	1207.0	−0.48
1973	7.14	1349.6	0.53
1974	1.96	1458.6	0.13
1975	18.12	1585.9	1.14
1976	4.29	1768.4	0.24
1977	−14.33	1974.1	−0.73
1978	−15.14	2232.7	−0.68
1979	−0.29	2488.6	−0.01
1980	2.37	2708.0	0.09
1981	5.03	3030.6	0.16
1982	−11.44	3149.6	−0.36
1983	−44.46	3405.0	−1.30
1984	−100.33	3777.2	−2.66
1985	−123.87	4038.7	−3.07
1986	−150.20	4268.6	−3.52
1987	−167.31	4539.9	−3.68
1988	−127.17	4900.4	−2.59
1989	−101.62	5250.8	−1.93
1990	−91.86	5546.1	−1.66
1991	−8.32	5722.9	−0.14
1992	−66.40	6038.5	−1.10
1993	−109.24	6374.0	−1.71

Source: Economic Report of the President (Feb. 1994).

remained high through 1993 except for 1991, when the figure was distorted by the war in the Persian Gulf.[7]

The foregoing statement may dramatize the 1983–1984 shift in behavior excessively, however, since the size of the U.S. economy has grown substantially over the postwar period. A more reasonable picture may then be provided by a standardized measure of the deficit, such as its magnitude relative to the nation's gross domestic product (GDP). Accordingly, GDP magnitudes for each year are reported in column 3 of Table 1–1, with current-account surpluses (or deficits, if negative) as a percentage of GDP then appearing in column 4. Use of this preferred measure does not eliminate the indication of a substantial shift in behavior during 1983–1984, but it does make that shift appear somewhat less drastic. Standardization makes a bigger difference when applied to the nation's earlier history. Indeed, historical statistics suggest that the current-account deficits of 1984–1989 may have been exceeded, as a percentage of GDP, during the 1800s before the economy matured.

Whether current-account deficits (or surpluses) are per se undesirable is a question that we will not attempt to answer at this time. Indeed, it should be stressed that there are several other BOP measures that deserve attention as indicators of current payments imbalances.[8] These other concepts will be introduced in Chapter 3 and then employed in discussions in subsequent portions of the book.

1.4 Alternative International Arrangements

An altert reader of the previous two sections will have noticed that U.S. exchange rate fluctuations became much more extensive after the 1971–1973 breakdown of the Bretton Woods fixed-rate system, that is, after the advent of floating (market-determined) rates. That fact itself is hardly surprising, though the *extent* of the difference arguably is. But floating rates were expected by some proponents to reduce or virtually eliminate BOP deficits and surpluses, so the recent magnitude of U.S. imbalances might be considered as inconsistent with their views.[9] It is not only the United States that has experienced large imbalances during recent years, moreover. Table 1–2 shows that the same is true for the United Kingdom, Germany, and Japan, but with surplus rather than deficit imbalances for the latter two.

But whatever the significance of major BOP imbalances, the extent of exchange rate fluctuations since 1973 has led several prominent economists to

[7] Specifically, the United States received large payments from several nations as their contributions toward the U.N.-sponsored action. For BOP purposes, these contributions were classified as transfers, one component of the current-account balance.

[8] During 1993 and 1994, much attention was directed to the U.S. *bilateral* current-account deficit with Japan. That topic will be briefly treated in Chapter 3.

[9] This type of argument has been made by Rolnick and Weber (1989). It should be noted, however, that the current-account magnitude is *not* the balance concept that should be kept close to zero by floating rates, according to the criticized argument. See Chapters 3 and 7.

Table 1–2 Current-Account Imbalances (% of GDP) for United Kingdom, Germany, and Japan

Year	U.K.	Germany	Japan
1973	−1.3	1.5	0.0
1974	−3.8	2.8	−1.0
1975	−1.4	1.1	−0.1
1976	−0.6	0.8	0.7
1977	0.1	0.8	1.6
1978	0.7	1.4	1.7
1979	−0.2	−0.7	−0.9
1980	1.3	−1.7	−1.0
1981	2.8	−0.5	0.4
1982	1.6	0.8	0.6
1983	1.2	0.8	1.8
1984	0.5	1.5	2.8
1985	0.9	2.7	3.7
1986	0.0	4.5	4.3
1987	−1.1	4.2	3.6
1988	−3.4	4.2	2.7
1989	−4.2	4.8	2.0
1990	−3.0	3.1	1.2
1991	−1.1	−1.2	2.2
1992	−2.1	−1.5	3.2

Source: IMF, *International Financial Statistics Yearbook* (1993).

call for a return to some system with fixed rates.[10] These economists have suggested that fluctuations in exchange rates of the magnitude experienced during the 1980s are undesirable for the world economy as a whole, as well as for individual nations, because they discourage trade and investment among nations and also lead to inappropriate investment patterns (e.g., too many export goods) within national boundaries.

It should be explained, in this context, that a tendency to favor (rather than deplore) floating exchange rates does not imply disapproval of regional arrangements with fixed rates. Almost all economists believe that the case for a single monetary unit for Belgium and Luxembourg is convincing, for example, and possibly so for the nations of the European Monetary System (EMS), though some analysts are dubious with regard to inclusion of the United Kingdom.[11] Indeed, a fairly typical opinion would view with approval developments toward an arrangement featuring three major regional currency unions—ones in which the leading nations are those of Europe, the United States, and Japan—with exchange rates fixed within each region but floating

[10] See, for example, McKinnon (1988) or Rolnick and Weber (1989).

[11] As of September 1994 the EMS includes the following nations: Belgium-Luxembourg, Denmark, France, Germany, Greece, Ireland, Italy, the Netherlands, Spain, and the United Kingdom. Austria, Finland, and Sweden are scheduled to join in 1995.

across the three groups. The fixed-rate proponents referred to earlier would, by contrast, disapprove of the three-region scheme with rates floating across regions.

On top of the venerable fixed- versus floating-rate controversy, a new dimension has been added in recent years by the European Commission's proposal to abolish national currencies in favor of a single money for all of Europe. Such a proposal is of particular analytical interest because it represents the logical extension of the fixed-rate point of view, yet would clearly amount to a truly drastic development with numerous political and emotional ramifications for the citizens of participating nations. The proposal was warmly received by most of the member nations of the European Community,[12] and plans for monetary unification were agreed to by the governments of all member nations at the Maastricht conference of December 1991. But Danish voters denied approval to the agreement in a referendum in June 1992,[13] and shortly thereafter speculative activity in the foreign exchange markets put the fixed exchange rates of the EMS under severe pressure. As a result, Britain and Italy withdrew from the exchange rate mechanism in September 1992. Then in July 1993 a new wave of speculative attacks led the EMS to drastically widen the exchange rate limits, virtually eliminating their fixed-rate arrangement. How this historic attempt to form a monetary union will finally be resolved remains to be seen.

1.5 A Look Ahead

In the chapters that follow we shall explore in depth the three major subject areas indicated by the three foregoing sections. The object will be to develop the factual and theoretical knowledge necessary to reach reasoned conclusions regarding issues relating to the conduct of national monetary policy and to the design of international monetary institutions. The intention will be more to enhance the reader's skills than to reach specific conclusions, but the author's opinions will nevertheless be apparent in several places.

The material begins in Chapter 2 with a detailed look at bilateral exchange rates, including forward rates (for future delivery), and an introduction to important relationships involving these rates and national interest rates— relationships known as covered and uncovered interest parity. In addition, the concept of *real* exchange rates is introduced, as is the doctrine of purchasing-power parity. Next, Chapter 3 considers the fundamental ideas and concepts of BOP accounting with the presentation proceeding by means of an approach that is designed to eliminate laborious memorization of accounting rules in favor of a simple but flexible analytical framework.

The final chapter in Part I of the book is intended to convey some historical perspective, with emphasis on the evolution of international monetary institu-

---

[12] Subsequently renamed the European Union.
[13] A second vote led to approval in Denmark.

tions since about 1800. That 200-year span of time is divided into six distinct periods, each of which receives some attention. Because of the enormous historical importance of the gold standard, a simplified model of an economy that maintains a commodity money standard is presented and its use illustrated.

Chapter 5 begins the book's analytical core (Part II) by introducing five relationships that are included in all variants of a basic model that is developed for the purpose of explaining exchange rate and BOP behavior. As the model has six endogenous variables, one additional relationship is needed to complete the system, but completion can be effected in different ways for different modes of analysis. In Chapter 6, accordingly, variants of the model are presented that are appropriate for long-run and short-run analysis of the comparative static type under floating exchange rates. In the case of long-run analysis, the home economy's rate of output is assumed to equal its capacity or natural-rate value, which is determined exogenously, whereas short-run analysis treats the price level as temporarily fixed at its historically given level. Two types of long-run analysis are developed, one pertaining to stationary states (with unchanging values of all variables) and the other to steady states (in which values may be growing at constant rates). It is noted that most of the book's analysis pertains to economies that are "small," in the sense that their conditions do not appreciably affect those abroad, but Section 6.6 considers a pair of economies that are large enough to affect world conditions.

In Chapter 7 the basic model is modified so as to become applicable to an economy with *fixed* (rather than floating) exchange rates. The discussion emphasizes that adoption of a fixed-rate regime renders monetary policy unavailable for the pursuit of other, possibly conflicting, macroeconomic objectives. Issues relating to monetary and fiscal policy "effectiveness" under alternative exchange rate regimes are discussed, and attention is devoted to effects on the current-account balance. In this chapter, as in the one preceding it, the limitations of comparative static analysis are apparent. More satisfactory in principle is proper dynamic analysis, which proceeds by adoption of an additional behavioral relation specifying output supply behavior. In such analysis expectations become crucial, so Chapter 8 is concerned with expectational behavior as well as supply responses. The chapter includes, accordingly, an introduction to one method for conducting dynamic analysis in linear systems with rational expectations. Because of the nature of the material, this chapter is more technically demanding than others in the course. Its mastery is desirable but is not necessary for the material that follows.

The final chapter of Part II, Chapter 9, is concerned with empirical evidence relating to the model deployed in Chapters 5 to 8. Studies of the validity of the model's various behavioral relations are reviewed, with special attention devoted to evidence often taken to indicate that the uncovered interest parity (UIP) relation does not hold in reality. An argument developed in Section 9.4 suggests that the usual interpretation is incorrect; that UIP actually holds (on average), with the anomalous evidence arising because of monetary policy behavior by central banks.

Part III begins in Chapter 10 with a consideration of one of the classic topics of international economics—the choice between fixed and floating exchange rates. The emphasis is on the comparative merits of these two arrangements from the perspective of a single nation, but the factors involved are also relevant from a multicountry perspective. The range of choice for an exchange rate regime is actually broader than the simple two-way categorization suggests, of course, but consideration of these "pure" extremes is analytically useful. The discussion in Chapter 10 includes an exposition of the "rules versus discretion" distinction that is of extreme importance in monetary policy analysis of closed as well as open economies.

Chapter 11 is devoted to the past, present, and future of the European Monetary System (EMS). It reviews earlier cooperative efforts within Europe as well as experience since the founding of the EMS in 1979. Features of the Delors Report and the Maastricht Treaty are summarized, and some scrutiny of the case for a single-currency monetary union is offered. The nature of the private Ecu as well as the official European currency unit (ECU) is explored.

The book's concluding unit, Chapter 12, is concerned with both analytical and practical aspects of international policy cooperation. Here some of the issues considered in Chapter 10 are relevant again, but now with the multi-country perspective predominant. A brief review of the analysis of optimal currency areas is included.

References

Council of Economic Advisers, Annual Report. With *Economic Report of the President.* Washington, D.C.: U.S. Government Printing Office, 1994.

International Monetary Fund, *International Financial Statistics Yearbook.* Washington, D.C.: International Monetary Fund, 1993.

Kenen, P. B., *The International Economy,* 3rd ed. New York: Cambridge University Press, 1994.

McKinnon, R. I., "Monetary and Exchange Rate Policies for International Financial Stability: A Proposal," *Journal of Economic Perspectives* **2** (Winter 1988), 83–104.

Ott, M., "The Dollar's Effective Exchange Rate: Assessing the Impact of Alternative Weighting Schemes," *Federal Reserve Bank of St. Louis Review* **69** (Feb. 1987), 5–14.

Rolnick, A. J., and W. E. Weber, "A Case for Fixing Exchange Rates," *Federal Reserve Bank of Minneapolis 1989 Annual Report.*

Yeager, L. B., *International Economic Relations: Theory, History, and Policy,* 2nd ed. New York: Harper and Row, 1976.

Problems

1. Bring up to date the statistics reported in Tables 1–1 and 1–2.
2. Problem 1 is intended in part to acquaint the reader with two useful data sources, the *Economic Report of the President* and *International Financial*

Statistics. (Note that the latter is published monthly, as well as in the annual Yearbook version referenced in Table 1–2.) While in the library, the reader should also locate and examine the *Survey of Current Business* (U.S. Commerce Department), the *Federal Reserve Bulletin* (Board of Governors of the Federal Reserve System), and *Main Economic Indicators* (Organization for Economic Cooperation and Development).

2

Exchange Rate Concepts

2.1 Bilateral Rates: Spot and Forward

The purpose of this chapter is to introduce several concepts involving international exchange rates, starting with ordinary bilateral exchange rates involving two national currencies. It will be convenient to begin the discussion by referring to Figure 2–1, which was taken from the *Wall Street Journal* of July 28, 1994. (A table of this type appears there each Monday through Friday.) It will be noted that in this publication values are presented for the dollar price of each foreign currency and also its inverse, the foreign-currency price of the dollar. That rather extravagant practice is not universal, however. It is not followed, for instance, by the influential British daily, the *Financial Times*. That publication's main tabulation of July 27, 1994, exchange rates vis-à-vis the dollar is given for comparison in Figure 2–2. In both of these tabulations the rates reported are those for large interbank transactions involving sums in excess of one million dollars.

Inspection of the two tabulations shows that the reported values are very close but not identical. In part this is due to different reporting conventions, since the *Financial Times* features the midpoint between bid and offer rates— that is, rates at which banks are willing to buy and sell foreign exchange— whereas the *Wall Street Journal* simply reports the offer (selling) rates.[1] But even if the reporting conventions were alike, one would expect to find somewhat different values, since the two tabulations refer to transactions in New York and in London, respectively, and the latter's market is inactive for all but the early part of the trading day in New York. The "markets" in these two cities, incidentally, are not ones of the formally organized type with a specified place for face-to-face meetings of buyers and sellers. They are, rather, computer- and telephone-based networks connecting trading desks at major banks with each other and with brokers. The volume of trade on these markets is very large. Some idea of a typical day's magnitude is given by the figures in Table 2–1. There the reported values pertain to the listed nations, but in each of these

---

[1] These are, to be precise, dealers' quoted dollar prices at which they will sell foreign currency, prevailing at 3:00 P.M. Similar practices are followed by the *New York Times*, which presents a tabulation much like the *Wall Street Journal*'s each Tuesday through Saturday.

CURRENCY TRADING

EXCHANGE RATES

Wednesday, July 27, 1994

The New York foreign exchange selling rates below apply to trading among banks in amounts of $1 million and more, as quoted at 3 p.m. Eastern time by Bankers Trust Co., Dow Jones Telerate Inc. and other sources. Retail transactions provide fewer units of foreign currency per dollar.

Country	U.S. $ equiv. Wed.	Tues.	Currency per U.S. $ Wed.	Tues.
Argentina (Peso)	1.01	1.01	.99	.99
Australia (Dollar)	.7393	.7430	1.3526	1.3459
Austria (Schilling)	.09024	.08961	11.08	11.16
Bahrain (Dinar)	2.6522	2.6522	.3771	.3771
Belgium (Franc)	.03086	.03066	32.40	32.62
Brazil (Real)	1.0695187	1.0729614	.94	.93
Britain (Pound)	1.5325	1.5245	.6525	.6560
30-Day Forward	1.5316	1.5236	.6529	.6563
90-Day Forward	1.5308	1.5228	.6533	.6567
180-Day Forward	1.5306	1.5226	.6533	.6568
Canada (Dollar)	.7246	.7250	1.3801	1.3793
30-Day Forward	.7239	.7243	1.3815	1.3807
90-Day Forward	.7224	.7228	1.3843	1.3835
180-Day Forward	.7191	.7195	1.3907	1.3899
Czech. Rep. (Koruna) Commercial rate	.0353282	.0351630	28.3060	28.4390

Country	U.S. $ equiv. Wed.	Tues.	Currency per U.S. $ Wed.	Tues.
Chile (Peso)	.002427	.002427	411.99	411.99
China (Renminbi)	.11521	.11521	8.6790	8.6790
Colombia (Peso)	.001225	.001225	816.00	816.00
Denmark (Krone)	.1615	.1606	6.1913	6.2256
Ecuador (Sucre) Floating rate	.000457	.000457	2190.00	2190.00
Finland (Markka)	.19303	.19171	5.1804	5.2163
France (Franc)	.18575	.18481	5.3835	5.4110
30-Day Forward	.18559	.18465	5.3882	5.4157
90-Day Forward	.18541	.18447	5.3933	5.4210
180-Day Forward	.18533	.18439	5.3958	5.4233
Germany (Mark)	.6351	.6307	1.5746	1.5855
30-Day Forward	.6348	.6304	1.5754	1.5863
90-Day Forward	.6348	.6304	1.5754	1.5863
180-Day Forward	.6357	.6313	1.5731	1.5840
Greece (Drachma)	.004201	.004174	238.05	239.55
Hong Kong (Dollar)	.12945	.12945	7.7250	7.7250
Hungary (Forint)	.0098542	.0098203	101.4800	101.8300
India (Rupee)	.03212	.03212	31.13	31.13
Indonesia (Rupiah)	.0004613	.0004613	2168.00	2168.02
Ireland (Punt)	1.5175	1.5115	.6590	.6616
Israel (Shekel)	.3298	.3298	3.0320	3.0320
Italy (Lira)	.0006300	.0006301	1587.20	1587.10
Japan (Yen)	.010151	.010191	98.51	98.13

Country	U.S. $ equiv. Wed.	Tues.	Currency per U.S. $ Wed.	Tues.
30-Day Forward	.010173	.010212	98.30	97.92
90-Day Forward	.010219	.010259	97.86	97.48
180-Day Forward	.010304	.010344	97.05	96.67
Jordan (Dinar)	1.404	1.404	.6801	.6801
Kuwait (Dinar)	3.3585	3.3585	.2978	.2978
Lebanon (Pound)	.000596	.000596	1677.00	1677.00
Malaysia (Ringgit)	.3857	.3856	2.5930	2.5935
Malta (Lira)	2.8810	2.8810	.3730	.3730
Mexico (Peso) Floating rate	.2939879	.2938152	3.4015	3.4035
Netherland (Guilder)	.5660	.5622	1.7667	1.7786
New Zealand (Dollar)	.6020	.6050	1.611	1.6529
Norway (Krone)	.1456	.1448	6.8660	6.9049
Pakistan (Rupee)	.0328	.0328	30.52	30.52
Peru (New Sol)	.4683	.4683	2.14	2.14
Philippines (Peso)	.03870	.03870	25.84	25.84
Poland (Zloty)	.0004374	.0004382	22862.00	22819.01
Portugal (Escudo)	.006214	.006171	160.92	162.04
Saudi Arabia (Riyal)	.26664	.26664	3.7504	3.7504
Singapore (Dollar)	.6623	.6619	1.5100	1.5108
Slovak Rep. (Koruna)	.0317158	.0317158	31.5300	31.5500
South Africa (Rand) Commercial rate	.2726	.2714	3.6690	3.6850
Financial rate	.2181	.2193	4.5860	4.5600
South Korea (Won)	.0012460	.0012460	802.60	802.60
Spain (Peseta)	.007715	.007670	129.62	130.38
Sweden (Krona)	.1293	.1288	7.7321	7.7610
Switzerland (Franc)	.7496	.7424	1.3341	1.3470
30-Day Forward	.7497	.7425	1.3339	1.3468
90-Day Forward	.7504	.7432	1.3327	1.3456
180-Day Forward	.7524	.7452	1.3290	1.3419
Taiwan (Dollar)	.037552	.037552	26.63	26.63
Thailand (Baht)	.03997	.03997	25.02	25.02
Turkey (Lira)	.0000322	.0000321	31088.88	31174.79
United Arab (Dirham)	.2723	.2723	3.6725	3.6725
Uruguay (New Peso) Financial	.199860	.199860	5.00	5.00
Venezuela (Bolivar)	.00588	.00588	170.00	170.00
SDR	1.45522	1.44987	.68718	.68972
ECU	1.21300	1.20660		

Special Drawing Rights (SDR) are based on exchange rates for the U.S., German, British, French and Japanese currencies. Source: International Monetary Fund. European Currency Unit (ECU) is based on a basket of community currencies.

Figure 2–1 Exchange rates from *Wall Street Journal* of July 28, 1994.

Source: "Reprinted by permission of *Wall Street Journal*, © 1994 Dow Jones & Company, Inc. All Rights Reserved Worldwide."

Basic Concepts

DOLLAR SPOT FORWARD AGAINST THE DOLLAR

Jul 27		Closing mid-point	Change on day	Bid/offer spread	Day's mid high	low	One month Rate	%PA	Three months Rate	%PA	One year Rate	%PA	J.P Morgan index
Europe													
Austria	(Sch)	11.0895	-0.076	870 - 920	11.1380	11.0750	11.0922	-0.3	11.0858	0.1	11.0078	0.7	104.0
Belgium	(BFr)	32.4500	-0.22	300 - 700	32.6000	32.4000	32.47	-0.7	32.5075	-0.7	32.57	-0.4	105.5
Denmark	(DKr)	6.1943	-0.0414	933 - 953	6.2224	6.1870	6.2003	-1.2	6.2113	-1.1	6.2483	-0.9	105.0
Finland	(FM)	5.1819	-0.0396	769 - 869	5.2233	5.1744	5.1849	-0.7	5.1874	-0.4	5.2264	-0.9	77.0
France	(FFr)	5.3858	-0.03	840 - 875	5.4090	5.3745	5.3906	-1.1	5.3965	-0.8	5.3743	0.2	106.1
Germany	(D)	1.5760	-0.0105	755 - 764	1.5847	1.5740	1.5767	-0.5	1.5768	-0.2	1.5667	0.6	106.3
Greece	(Dr)	238.400	-1.4	200 - 600	239.120	238.200	238.75	-1.8	239.52	-1.9	242.9	-1.9	69.1
Ireland	(I£)	1.5130	+0.006	122 - 137	1.5162	1.5078	1.5118	1.0	1.5095	0.9	1.5007	0.8	—
Italy	(L)	1585.90	+4.2	500 - 680	1588.00	1582.33	1590.95	-3.8	1599.75	-3.5	1637.9	-3.3	76.3
Luxembourg	(LFr)	32.4500	-0.22	300 - 700	32.6000	32.4000	32.47	-0.7	32.515	-0.8	32.57	-0.4	105.5
Netherlands	(Fl)	1.7690	-0.0107	687 - 692	1.7775	1.7667	1.7696	-0.4	1.7683	0.1	1.7612	0.4	105.2
Norway	(NKr)	6.8696	-0.0413	686 - 706	6.9019	6.8631	6.8731	-0.6	6.8776	-0.5	6.8531	0.2	98.4
Portugal	(Es)	161.250	-1.05	100 - 400	162.400	160.950	162.48	-9.2	164.52	-8.1	171.65	-6.4	94.6
Spain	(Pta)	129.750	-0.65	700 - 800	130.400	129.600	130.115	-3.4	130.77	-3.1	133.14	-2.6	81.3
Sweden	(SKr)	7.7231	-0.0213	193 - 268	7.7715	7.7193	7.7401	-2.6	7.7766	-2.8	7.9311	-2.7	79.3
Switzerland	(SFr)	1.3370	-0.0105	365 - 375	1.3455	1.3348	1.3367	0.3	1.3353	0.5	1.3228	1.1	105.2
UK	(£)	1.5309	+0.005	305 - 312	1.5325	1.5247	1.5299	0.8	1.5289	0.5	1.5248	0.4	86.9
Ecu		1.2115	+0.005	112 - 117	1.2133	1.2057	1.21	1.4	1.2079	1.2	1.2198	-0.7	—
SDR†		1.44987	—										
Americas													
Argentina	(Peso)	0.9986	-0.0009	985 - 986	0.9986	0.9983							
Brazil	(R)	0.9350	+0.002	340 - 360	0.9360	0.9340							
Canada	(C$)	1.3791	-0.0007	788 - 793	1.3837	1.3788	1.3807	-1.4	1.3839	-1.4	1.4049	-1.9	82.6
Mexico	(New Peso)	3.4045	-0.0009	020 - 070	3.4020	3.4070	3.4055	-0.4	3.4073	-0.3	3.4147	-0.3	—
USA	($)												97.1
Pacific/Middle East/Africa													
Australia	(A$)	1.3529	+0.008	524 - 534	1.3539	1.3463	1.3531	-0.2	1.3538	-0.3	1.3612	-0.6	87.9
Hong Kong	(HK$)	7.7250	-0.0001	245 - 255	7.7255	7.7232	7.7248	0.0	7.7255	0.0	7.7405	-0.2	—
India	(Rs)	31.3675	-0.0013	625 - 725	31.3750	31.3625	31.4525	-3.3	31.5975	-2.9			—
Japan	(Y)	98.0100	+0.01	700 - 500	98.2300	97.7500	97.805	2.5	97.36	2.7	94.955	3.1	153.0
Malaysia	(M$)	2.5930	-0.0003	925 - 935	2.5935	2.5905	2.5838	4.3	2.5725	3.2	2.646	-2.0	—
New Zealand	(NZ$)	1.6635	+0.0094	628 - 642	1.6642	1.6556	1.6644	-0.7	1.6663	-0.7	1.6716	-0.5	—
Philippines	(Peso)	26.3500	—	000 - 000	26.6000	26.1000							
Saudi Arabia	(SR)	3.7504	—	501 - 506	3.7506	3.7501	3.7517	-0.4	3.7558	-0.6	3.7744	-0.6	—
Singapore	(S$)	1.5099	-0.0003	096 - 101	1.5103	1.5096	1.5085	1.1	1.5066	0.9	1.4999	0.7	—
S Africa (Com.)	(R)	3.6695	-0.014	680 - 710	3.6885	3.6670	3.685	-5.1	3.7133	-4.8	3.79	-3.3	—
S Africa (Fin.)	(R)	4.5550	+0.01	450 - 650	4.5800	4.5600	4.5887	-8.9	4.6475	-8.1			—
South Korea	(Won)	802.450	—	400 - 500	802.500	802.400	805.45	-4.5	808.95	-3.2	827.45	-3.1	—
Taiwan	(T$)	26.5988	-0.0152	965 - 010	26.6020	26.5965	26.6188	-0.9	26.6588	-0.9			—
Thailand	(Bt)	24.9500	-0.01	400 - 600	24.9700	24.9400	25.0225	-3.5	25.15	-3.2	25.63	-2.7	—

†SDR rate for Jul 26. Bid/offer spreads in the Dollar Spot table show only the last three decimal places. Forward rates are not directly quoted to the market but are implied by current interest rates. UK, Ireland & ECU are quoted in US currency. J.P. Morgan nominal indices Jul 26. Base average 1990=100

Figure 2–2 Exchange rates from *Financial Times* of July 28, 1994.

Table 2–1 Foreign Exchange Market
Turnover ($ bil/day)

Location	April 1989	April 1992
United Kingdom	187	300
United States	129	192
Japan	115	128
Singapore	55	74
Switzerland	57	68
Hong Kong	49	61
Germany		57
France	26	35
Australia	30	30
Canada	15	22

Source: Goldstein et al. (1993).

virtually all of the foreign exchange trading takes place in one major city such as London or New York. About 30 percent of all transactions on the interbank markets are mediated through brokers; the remainder are conducted directly by major banks on their own accounts or for their customers, which include small banks and other business organizations.[2]

One might wonder about exchange rates in the New York market pertaining to pairs of currencies not including the dollar. What about, for instance, the pound sterling price of a Swiss franc (£/SF)? One could in principle exchange pounds for Swiss francs either directly or by buying dollars with the pounds and then using these dollars to purchase Swiss francs. If there were an active market for the direct exchange of pounds and francs, the price would have to be close to that implied by the indirect exchange, the possible difference being limited to transaction costs. Otherwise, an energetic transactor could become rich quickly by trading to exploit the difference. In actuality, there is extremely little of the direct form of trading; almost all exchanges in New York utilize the dollar as a "vehicle" currency (see Table 2–2). This is so because the markets involving dollars are so competitive that transaction charges are extremely low. Thus going from pounds into dollars and then into francs is cheaper to the dealer, in terms of transaction charges, than the single direct pound-for-francs purchase. It would be adequate, consequently, for the *Wall Street Journal* to publish only dollar rates. In fact, it also reports a table of "cross rates," but the figures given are simply those implied by the dollar rates appearing in its first column. This role of the dollar as a vehicle currency is important, incidentally, even in locations other than New York (again, see Table 2–2). That role has been gradually diminishing in recent years, however, with the use of DM and yen increasing.

Most of the rates reported in Figure 2–1 are ordinary *spot* rates, that is,

[2] For readable descriptions of the trading institutions, the reader is referred to Chrystal (1984), Kubarych (1983), and Goldstein et al. (1993).

Table 2–2 Fraction of Foreign
Exchange Activity Involving Dollars*

Location	1986	1989	1992
United Kingdom	96	89	76
United States	87	85	89
Japan		90	
Singapore		81	77
Switzerland			73
Hong Kong		93	90
France			59
Australia		87	87
Canada	99	99	96

* Blanks indicate figures are unavailable.
Source: Goldstein et al. (1993).

rates applicable to current transactions.[3] It is these rates that are typically
referred to, in the absence of indications to the contrary. For some of the more
widely traded currencies, however, the table also includes reported values for
30-day, 90-day, and 180-day *forward* contracts. Thus we see, for example, that
while a British pound traded for $1.5325 on July 27, 1994, a contract to purchase
a pound 90 days in the future could be obtained (on July 27) for only $1.5308.
The difference, involving a slightly lower dollar price for future pounds, might
suggest that market participants believed that pounds were likely to fall in spot
value over the coming three months—a suggestion that will be explored in
subsequent chapters.

Forward rates are reported by the *Wall Street Journal* in a straightforward
manner, as $/currency unit and as currency units/$. In the tabulation from the
Financial Times, only currency unit/$ values are given, as with the spot rates
(except for the U.K. and Irish currencies and the European currency unit
(ECU), which have the units of $/currency unit). Some additional information
is included, however, under the heading of %PA. What these values indicate is
whether the currency in question stands at a premium (no sign) or at a discount
(minus sign) in the forward market and what the percentage magnitude is on
an annualized basis. Thus, for example, the −2.7 value for Sweden indicates
that on July 27 the Swedish krona stood at a 2.7 percent discount (relative to
the dollar) in the one-year forward market. That figure may be verified by
noting that 7.9311 is 2.69 percent larger than 7.7231 and rounding. For the
three-month forward krona we see that 7.7766 is 0.692 percent larger than
7.7231; then multiplying that 3-month value by 4.0 will put it on an annualized
basis of 2.8 percent. Each of the figures represents a discount for the krona, on
the forward market, because the value of the krona is lower in the forward
market—more kroner are needed to purchase one dollar—than in the spot
market. In the case of the U.K. and Irish currencies and the ECU, the numerical

---

[3] These "current" transactions normally take two working days to be completed.

calculations are similar, but a larger reported figure in the forward market column would mean that the currency is more valuable than in the spot market and so stands at a premium.

The existence of the forward market in foreign exchange makes it possible for businesses engaged in international trade to avoid the risk of exchange rate changes over the next several months, if this avoidance is desired. An American exporter may, for example, make a sale to a German firm that will result in payment in marks (DM) in one month's time. If the exporter wishes to avoid the risk that marks might become less valuable in terms of dollars before he receives payment, he could trade DM for dollars on the forward market so that the number of dollars he receives for his sale will be determined at the time of the sale, even though payment will be made in DM a month later.

It should be mentioned that in addition to the forward contract, there are also *futures* and *options* contracts in foreign exchange. Futures are basically similar to forward contracts but are less flexible, being available only for certain specified volumes of currency to be delivered on specified days in March, June, September, or December. They also differ from forward contracts in involving advance margin payments that might require augmentation if the currency being sold falls in value. Since the volume of futures contracts is relatively small, however, they will be ignored throughout the remainder of this book. It will be assumed, that is, that foreign exchange dealings pertaining to future dates are conducted in terms of forward contracts. Options are, as their name suggests, contracts giving the purchaser the right to buy or sell a currency at some specified data in the future, with the price (and the charge for purchasing the option) specified at the time the contract is entered into. A brief guide to the *Wall Street Journal*'s daily table of options prices is given as an appendix to this chapter. Also worthy of mention is the fact that most forward contracts are made in conjunction with another contract (spot or forward) that is designed to limit the parties' exposure to risk from exchange rate changes. Such combination contracts are termed *swaps*. Table 2–3 shows the fraction of foreign

Table 2–3 Distribution of Foreign Exchange Market Turnover by Type of Transaction (percent)

Location	Spot		Forward		Swaps		Futures and options	
	1989	1992	1989	1992	1989	1992	1989	1992
United Kingdom	64	50		6	35	41	1	3
United States	62	51	5	6	25	31	8	12
Japan	40		6		51		4	6
Singapore	54		5		38		1	
Switzerland	53	54	5	9	40	33	2	4
Hong Kong	61	52		3	39	44	0	1
France	58	52		4	36	38	6	6
Australia	61	42	5	4	32	51	3	3
Canada	41	35	5	4	54	61	0	0

Source: Goldstein et al. (1993).

exchange turnover accounted for by the various types of contracts—spot, pure forward, swaps, and other (futures and options).

2.2 Interest Parity

The existence of the forward market in foreign exchange was shown to provide a mechanism for exporters and importers to avoid certain risks implied by the possibility of exchange rate changes. But clearly the same scope for risk avoidance will be available also to other participants in the market. In particular, the existence of forward contracts makes it possible for a holder of American securities—say, U.S. Treasury bills—to hold his wealth in the form of foreign-currency securities instead, without risk of losses due to exchange rate movements, if the promised yield is greater. Indeed, because of this possibility, a particular relationship should prevail (if transaction costs were negligible) in terms of spot and forward rates for any pair of currencies,[4] relating them to interest rates on low-risk securities denominated in those currencies.

To develop this relationship we need to introduce some notation. Accordingly, let us use the symbols S_t and F_t to denote the spot and (one-period) forward exchange rates in period t, with these expressed as the home-country price of the foreign currency.[5] If the United States were the home country, for example, and the Swiss franc were the foreign currency, then S_t and F_t would have the units of \$/SF. This convention, with exchange rate variables expressed as the home-country currency price of foreign exchange, will be used extensively in this chapter and most of those that follow. Often, but not invariably, the home-country currency will be called "dollars."

Next let R_t and R_t^* denote the home-country and foreign-country interest rates on riskless or low-risk one-period securities, that is, loans from period t to $t + 1$. Let these rates be expressed in fractional form (so that 0.02 represents a rate of two percent per period, for example). Then a dollar invested[6] in a home-country security will result in a gross return of $1 + R_t$ dollars in period $t + 1$. But alternatively a U.S. investor could use the dollar to purchase $1/S_t$ Swiss francs, and investment of these in Swiss (foreign) securities would result in a gross return of $(1/S_t)(1 + R_t^*)$ in period $t + 1$. Furthermore, these could be converted into dollars in $t + 1$ at a rate of F_t dollars per SF, with that conversion contracted for in period t. So the home-country (e.g., U.S.) investor could guarantee himself or herself a gross return of $(F_t/S_t)(1 + R_t^*)$ by holding Swiss francs and making use of the spot and forward exchange markets.

---

[4] For any pair, that is, for which there is an active forward market. The tabulation from the *Wall Street Journal* (Figure 2–1) suggests that in New York forward markets exist for only a limited set of currencies.

[5] One might use the symbol F_t^j to denote the period t rate for delivery j periods in the future. Then F_t^1 would be equivalent to F_t.

[6] Here we are using the term "invest" in the financial sense, indicating that wealth is held in some particular form rather than another. The economist's meaning, which implies the creation of new capital goods or other productive assets, is of course quite different.

Clearly, then, there will be a strong tendency for the *covered interest parity* relationship

$$1 + R_t = \frac{F_t}{S_t}(1 + R_t^*) \tag{1}$$

to prevail, for if the expression on either side of the equality is greater than the other, then an opportunity for riskless gain is being missed by market participants. In today's financial markets, few such opportunities are missed for long. Of course the existence in actuality of transaction costs will keep Equation (1) from holding *precisely* at every point of time, but existing evidence suggests that it holds to a very good approximation.[7] That it does can be exemplified, roughly, by means of interest rates for July 27, 1994, reported in Figure 2–3, taken from the *Financial Times*. As a sample calculation, note that $R_t = 0.0475$ and $R_t^* = 0.083125$ for Italy, where we have taken the midpoint of the range of values for three-month eurocurrency[8] interest rates prevailing on July 27. Thus the value of $(1 + R_t)/(1 + R_t^*)$ is $1.0475/1.083125 = 0.9671$ when Italy is taken as the foreign country. That figure should, according to Equation (1), agree with the value of F_t/S_t. But F_t/S_t can be obtained quite directly from the %PA figures in Figure 2–2 as $1 - 0.0350 = 0.9650$. The two numbers are not exactly equal, of course, but the disagreement is less than one-fourth of one percent. Proceeding similarly for a few other currencies for which there are active forward markets, we obtain the results listed in Table 2–4.

Agreement is quite impressive for each of the five other bilateral rates, and the rank ordering is exactly the same for F_t/S_t and $(1 + R_t)/(1 + R_t^*)$ values. All in all, therefore, agreement with the covered interest parity relationship (1) is quite good for the data of July 27, 1994.

In fact, the foregoing demonstration does not actually compare interest rates with observed forward market rates. Instead, it compares interest rates with calculated forward market rates that are determined by interest rates and a covered interest parity formula. So if the two sets of interest rates were the same, and were observed at the same point of time, the foregoing calculations would result in precise agreement. That they do not is presumably because one (or both) of these two conditions does not prevail. That Table 2–4 refers to calculated, not observed forward rates is apparent from the third sentence in the footnotes to the *Financial Times* tabulation of Figure 2–2. The reason why such values are reported is that actual interbank traders quote forward rates determined by computer programs that relate them to the interest rates being quoted by the bank in question.

[7] Extensive studies have been performed by a number of researchers. See Fratianni and Wakeman (1982) and Frenkel and Levich (1977) for two examples and MacDonald (1988, pp. 206–208) or Thornton (1989) for recent reviews of the evidence. Also see Section 9-3.

[8] Eurocurrency rates apply to eurocurrency deposits, which are bank deposits denominated in currency units that are not those of the nation within which the bank is located (e.g., yen-denominated deposits in a London bank). The term evolved from "eurodollars," which refers to dollar accounts in European banks. Eurocurrencies are quite different from the European Currency Unit (ECU), which is discussed in Chapter 11. For more on eurocurrencies, see McKenzie (1992).

WORLD INTEREST RATES

MONEY RATES

July 27	Over night	One month	Three mths	Six mths	One year	Lomb. inter.	Dis. rate	Repo rate
Belgium	$4\frac{7}{8}$	$5\frac{1}{8}$	$5\frac{3}{8}$	$5\frac{3}{4}$	6	7.40	4.50	–
week ago	5	$5\frac{1}{8}$	$5\frac{1}{2}$	$5\frac{7}{8}$	$6\frac{1}{8}$	7.40	4.50	–
France	$5\frac{3}{8}$	$5\frac{7}{16}$	$5\frac{9}{16}$	$5\frac{5}{8}$	$5\frac{15}{16}$	5.10	–	6.75
week ago	$5\frac{3}{8}$	$5\frac{7}{16}$	$5\frac{5}{8}$	$5\frac{3}{4}$	$5\frac{15}{16}$	5.10	–	6.75
Germany	5.03	4.97	4.93	4.93	5.08	6.00	4.50	4.85
week ago	4.85	4.97	4.85	4.85	4.95	6.00	4.50	4.91
Ireland	$5\frac{15}{16}$	$5\frac{5}{16}$	$5\frac{5}{8}$	$6\frac{1}{16}$	$6\frac{1}{2}$	–	–	6.25
week ago	5	$5\frac{5}{16}$	$5\frac{5}{8}$	$6\frac{1}{16}$	$6\frac{1}{2}$	–	–	6.25
Italy	$8\frac{3}{16}$	$8\frac{1}{4}$	$8\frac{1}{2}$	$8\frac{15}{16}$	$9\frac{7}{16}$	–	7.00	7.95
week ago	$8\frac{3}{8}$	$8\frac{1}{4}$	$8\frac{5}{16}$	$8\frac{11}{16}$	$9\frac{3}{16}$	–	7.00	8.15
Netherlands	4.85	4.91	4.93	5.02	5.21	–	5.25	–
week ago	4.85	4.91	4.82	4.94	5.12	–	5.25	–
Switzerland	$4\frac{1}{8}$	$4\frac{5}{16}$	$4\frac{3}{8}$	$4\frac{7}{16}$	$4\frac{5}{8}$	6.625	3.50	–
week ago	4	$4\frac{5}{16}$	$4\frac{1}{4}$	$4\frac{5}{16}$	$4\frac{1}{2}$	6.625	3.50	–
US	$4\frac{3}{16}$	$4\frac{7}{16}$	$4\frac{3}{4}$	$5\frac{3}{16}$	$5\frac{11}{16}$	–	3.50	–
week ago	$4\frac{3}{16}$	$4\frac{7}{16}$	$4\frac{11}{16}$	$5\frac{1}{8}$	$5\frac{9}{16}$	–	3.50	–
Japan	2	$2\frac{1}{16}$	$2\frac{3}{16}$	$2\frac{1}{4}$	$2\frac{1}{2}$	–	1.75	–
week ago	2	$2\frac{1}{16}$	$2\frac{1}{8}$	$2\frac{3}{16}$	$2\frac{3}{8}$	–	1.75	–
■ $ LIBOR FT London								
Interbank Fixing	–	$4\frac{1}{2}$	$4\frac{13}{16}$	$5\frac{1}{4}$	$5\frac{3}{4}$	–	–	–
week ago	–	$4\frac{1}{2}$	$4\frac{11}{16}$	$5\frac{1}{8}$	$5\frac{9}{16}$	–	–	–
US Dollar CDs	–	4.23	4.59	5.01	5.58	–	–	–
week ago	–	4.23	4.60	4.90	5.44	–	–	–
SDR Linked Ds	–	$3\frac{1}{2}$	$3\frac{9}{16}$	$3\frac{3}{4}$	4	–	–	–
week ago	–	$3\frac{1}{2}$	$3\frac{9}{16}$	$3\frac{3}{4}$	4	–	–	–

ECU Linked Ds mid rates: 1 mth: $5\frac{3}{4}$; 3 mths: $5\frac{7}{8}$; 6 mths: $6\frac{1}{16}$; 1 year: $6\frac{5}{16}$. $ LIBOR Interbank fixing rates are offered rates for $10m quoted to the market by four reference banks at 11am each working day. The banks are: Bankers Trust, Bank of Tokyo, Barclays and National Westminster.
Mid rates are shown for the domestic Money Rates, US $ CDs and SDR Linked Deposits (Ds).

EURO CURRENCY INTEREST RATES

Jul 27	Short term	7 days notice	One month	Three months	Six months	One year
Belgian Franc	$5 - 4\frac{7}{8}$	$5 - 4\frac{7}{8}$	$5\frac{1}{8} - 5$	$5\frac{3}{8} - 5\frac{1}{4}$	$5\frac{3}{4} - 5\frac{3}{8}$	$6 - 5\frac{7}{8}$
Danish Krone	$5\frac{3}{8} - 5\frac{1}{8}$	$5\frac{3}{4} - 5\frac{1}{2}$	$5\frac{13}{16} - 5\frac{9}{16}$	$6\frac{1}{4} - 6$	$6\frac{5}{8} - 6\frac{3}{8}$	$6\frac{13}{16} - 6\frac{9}{16}$
D-Mark	$5\frac{1}{16} - 4\frac{15}{16}$	$5\frac{3}{16} - 5\frac{1}{16}$	$5\frac{1}{16} - 4\frac{15}{16}$	$5 - 4\frac{7}{8}$	$5\frac{1}{16} - 4\frac{15}{16}$	$5\frac{1}{8} - 5$
Dutch Guilder	$4\frac{15}{16} - 4\frac{13}{16}$	$4\frac{15}{16} - 4\frac{13}{16}$	$4\frac{31}{32} - 4\frac{29}{32}$	$4\frac{15}{16} - 4\frac{13}{16}$	$5\frac{1}{16} - 4\frac{15}{16}$	$5\frac{1}{4} - 5\frac{1}{8}$
French Franc	$5\frac{7}{16} - 5\frac{5}{16}$	$5\frac{7}{16} - 5\frac{5}{16}$	$5\frac{1}{2} - 5\frac{3}{8}$	$5\frac{9}{16} - 5\frac{7}{16}$	$5\frac{11}{16} - 5\frac{9}{16}$	$6 - 5\frac{7}{8}$
Portuguese Esc.	$12\frac{1}{8} - 11\frac{7}{8}$	$11\frac{3}{4} - 11\frac{3}{8}$	$12\frac{3}{8} - 12\frac{1}{8}$	$12\frac{3}{8} - 12\frac{1}{8}$	$12\frac{3}{8} - 12\frac{1}{8}$	$12\frac{1}{4} - 11\frac{3}{4}$
Spanish Peseta	$7\frac{5}{8} - 7\frac{7}{16}$	$7\frac{5}{8} - 7\frac{7}{16}$	$7\frac{13}{16} - 7\frac{11}{16}$	$7\frac{15}{16} - 7\frac{3}{4}$	$8\frac{3}{16} - 8$	$8\frac{1}{2} - 8\frac{5}{16}$
Sterling	$5\frac{1}{8} - 4\frac{7}{8}$	$5\frac{1}{16} - 4\frac{15}{16}$	$5\frac{5}{32} - 5\frac{3}{32}$	$5\frac{3}{8} - 5\frac{1}{4}$	$5\frac{11}{16} - 5\frac{9}{16}$	$6\frac{3}{8} - 6\frac{1}{4}$
Swiss Franc	$4\frac{1}{4} - 4$	$4\frac{1}{4} - 4$	$4\frac{1}{4} - 4\frac{1}{8}$	$4\frac{5}{16} - 4\frac{3}{16}$	$4\frac{7}{16} - 4\frac{5}{16}$	$4\frac{9}{16} - 4\frac{7}{16}$
Can. Dollar	$5\frac{5}{16} - 5\frac{1}{16}$	$5\frac{1}{2} - 5\frac{1}{4}$	$5\frac{1}{2} - 5\frac{3}{8}$	$5\frac{15}{16} - 5\frac{13}{16}$	$6\frac{11}{16} - 6\frac{9}{16}$	$7\frac{5}{8} - 7\frac{1}{2}$
US Dollar	$4\frac{5}{16} - 4\frac{3}{16}$	$4\frac{5}{16} - 4\frac{3}{16}$	$4\frac{1}{2} - 4\frac{3}{8}$	$4\frac{13}{16} - 4\frac{11}{16}$	$5\frac{1}{4} - 5\frac{1}{8}$	$5\frac{3}{4} - 5\frac{5}{8}$
Italian Lira	$9 - 7\frac{1}{2}$	$8\frac{1}{8} - 8$	$8\frac{1}{8} - 8$	$8\frac{3}{8} - 8\frac{1}{4}$	$8\frac{11}{16} - 8\frac{9}{16}$	$9\frac{1}{4} - 9\frac{1}{8}$
Yen	$2\frac{3}{32} - 2\frac{1}{32}$	$2\frac{1}{8} - 2\frac{1}{16}$	$2\frac{1}{8} - 2\frac{1}{16}$	$2\frac{7}{32} - 2\frac{5}{32}$	$2\frac{1}{4} - 2\frac{3}{16}$	$2\frac{1}{2} - 2\frac{7}{16}$
Asian $Sing	$3\frac{7}{8} - 3\frac{3}{4}$	$3\frac{7}{8} - 3\frac{3}{4}$	$4\frac{7}{16} - 4\frac{5}{16}$	$4\frac{3}{4} - 4\frac{5}{8}$	$5\frac{3}{16} - 5\frac{1}{16}$	$5\frac{13}{16} - 5\frac{11}{16}$

Short term rates are call for the US Dollar and Yen, others: two days' notice.

Figure 2–3 Interest rates from *Financial Times* of July 28, 1994.

Table 2–4

Currency	R_t^*	$(1 + R_t)/(1 + R_t^*)$	F_t/S_t
United Kingdom	0.053125	0.9947	0.9950
Canada	0.058755	0.9894	0.9860
Germany	0.049375	0.9982	0.9980
Japan	0.021875	1.0251	1.0270
Switzerland	0.04250	1.0048	1.0050

There is an alternative version of Equation (1)—actually, an approximation—that warrants discussion at this point. To derive it, we begin with $F_t/S_t = (1 + R_t)/(1 + R_t^*)$ and then take (natural) logarithms of both sides of that equation, obtaining

$$\log F_t - \log S_t = \log(1 + R_t) - \log(1 + R_t^*). \tag{2}$$

But for values of any variable z that are small in relation to 1.0, it is the case that $\log(1 + z)$ is approximately equal to z. Thus the right-hand side of Equation (2) is approximately equal to $R_t - R_t^*$ as long as interest rates are of the magnitude normally observed in industrial nations. If we use the symbols $f_t = \log F_t$ and $s_t = \log S_t$, then, we can rewrite Equation (2) as

$$f_t - s_t = R_t - R_t^*. \tag{3}$$

The latter is a version of the covered interest parity relationship that is very clean and simple in appearance. It is, accordingly, frequently employed by researchers in place of the more cumbersome Equation (1), and it will therefore be used to a considerable extent in this book.

It should also be noted that F_t/S_t is definitionally equal to 1.0 plus the forward premium on the foreign currency or the forward discount on the domestic currency, with the (foreign) premium expressed in fractional form as $(F_t - S_t)/S_t$ (and the discount being the negative of the premium for any currency). Therefore, $\log(F_t/S_t) = f_t - s_t$ is approximately equal to this foreign premium or domestic discount. Thus Equation (3) can be interpreted as saying that the forward discount on the domestic currency tends to equal the interest differential (domestic minus foreign rates). Also, although we have derived this relationship in fractional terms, it will obviously continue to hold in percentage terms and in annualized percentage terms such as those reported by the *Financial Times*. Thus the %PA forward premium values in the *Financial Times* table will equal the interest differential (in per-annum units) if covered interest parity holds. That equality provides an easy way of making parity calculations.

It should be further mentioned, as a digression, that other formulas based on the approximation $\log(1 + z) = z$ will be utilized below. It may be useful, accordingly, to recall from elementary calculus that the Taylor series expression for $\log(1 + z)$ is $z - z^2/2 + z^3/3 - z^4/4 + \cdots$. Thus our expression $\log(1 + z) \doteq z$ is just a first-order Taylor series approximation. An important and quite useful application of this approximation occurs in expressions involving growth rates. For a variable Z that takes on the value Z_t in period t, the growth rate between periods t and $t + 1$ is often defined as $(Z_{t+1} - Z_t)/Z_t$, from which we see that $Z_{t+1}/Z_t = 1 +$ growth rate of Z. But then we can take logs of both sides of the latter and see that to an approximation the growth rate equals $\log(Z_{t+1}/Z_t)$. Since the latter also equals $\log Z_{t+1} - \log Z_t$, we have that the growth rate of Z_t equals

$$\frac{Z_{t+1} - Z_t}{Z_t} \doteq \log Z_{t+1} - \log Z_t = \Delta \log Z_{t+1} = \Delta z_{t+1} = z_{t+1} - z_t \qquad (4)$$

where z_t is defined as $\log Z_t$.

There is a second relationship similar in form to Equation (1) or Equation (3) that involves the concept of *uncovered* interest parity. In this case, the forward rate F_t (or its log, f_t) is replaced by the value of the spot rate S_{t+1} (or its log, s_{t+1}) that is *expected* to prevail one period in the future (i.e., in $t + 1$). Clearly, this relationship would hold—since Equations (1) and (3) do—if it were true that forward rates always agreed with current expectations of future spot rates. But that could possibly fail to be the case without leaving open any possibilities for *riskless* exchanges—any arbitrage possibilities. Consequently, there is a greater chance that uncovered interest parity might not hold in actual markets than is the case with covered interest parity. Indeed, there exists considerable evidence suggesting that the former is badly violated in the data. But most formal models of exchange rate behavior are nevertheless based on the assumption that uncovered parity does prevail. We shall go more deeply into this matter in Chapters 5 and 9. Our purpose at this point is simply to call the reader's attention to this second interest parity relationship, and to stress the distinction between the two.

2.3 Average Exchange Rates

While bilateral rates form the fundamental building blocks for exchange rate analysis, it is for several purposes convenient and appropriate to focus attention on an *average* measure for some nation of interest. That fact was mentioned in Section 1.2, where reference was made to the Federal Reserve's effective exchange rate for the U.S. dollar relative to 10 other national currencies. It was also mentioned in Section 1.2 that the IMF compiles and publishes exchange rate indexes for a large number of nations. In fact, the IMF publishes three different indexes (as well as several others pertaining to "real" exchange rates, a concept discussed in the next section). All of these indexes are constructed as weighted averages of the more important of a nation's bilateral rates, but

Table 2–5 Weights Used in Fed and IMF
MERM Effective Exchange Rate Indexes
for United States

Nation	Fed index	MERM index
Germany	0.208	0.1302
Japan	0.136	0.2125
France	0.131	0.1011
United Kingdom	0.119	0.0506
Canada	0.091	0.2028
Italy	0.090	0.0747
Netherlands	0.083	0.0324
Belgium	0.064	0.0244
Sweden	0.042	0.0273
Switzerland	0.036	0.0169
Australia	—	0.0486
Spain	—	0.0244
Denmark	—	0.0140
Norway	—	0.0121
Austria	—	0.0113
Finland	—	0.0111
Ireland	—	0.0058
Total	1.000	1.0002

Source: Belongia (1986).

different criteria are used in determining the weights assigned to the various
constituent bilateral rates. For example, the Fed's index has weights based on
the various nations' relative sizes in *world* trade, whereas the intermediate (in
terms of complexity) of the IMF's three indexes for the United States bases its
weights on the various nations' volume of trade with the United States. The
more complex IMF index uses weights that are derived from the properties of
an econometric model (their multilateral exchange rate model, called MERM)
by a procedure that takes account of import and export elasticities as well as
country-specific volumes. The IMF computes this MERM index only for 18
countries; its intermediate index is currently reported for about 75 different
economies and its simplest index for about 150.

The precise weights used in the Fed's and the IMF's MERM indexes for
the U.S. exchange rate are presented in Table 2–5. There it can be seen that
Germany, Belgium, and the United Kingdom have smaller weights when U.S.
rather than world trade flows (and elasticities) are taken into account (i.e., in
the MERM index), whereas in the Fed's index the weights are smaller for
Canada and Japan. For additional information concerning these indexes, as
well as others compiled by Morgan Guaranty Bank and the U.S. Department
of Agriculture, the reader could consult articles by Belongia (1986), Ott (1987),
and Pauls (1987).

2.4 Real Exchange Rates

In courses in macroeconomics much emphasis is placed on the distinction between "nominal" and "real" variables, that is, between variables measured in terms of monetary units and those measured as physical quantities (or as nominal variables *deflated* by some appropriate price index). Students become familiar, for example, with concepts such as real GDP, real wages, and even real interest rates.[9] The reason for making these adjustments is, of course, that standard economic analysis presumes that rational consumers, workers, and business people basically care about the quantities of goods and services that they consume or supply, not the volume measured in terms of dollars or any other monetary unit.

For several purposes, similarly, it is more appropriate to utilize so-called real exchange rates, rather than their nominal counterparts. This will be the case, for instance, if an exchange rate measure is supposed to represent the home-country real price of foreign goods rather than the home-country money price of foreign money. To obtain such a measure, a real exchange rate will be calculated by beginning with the nominal rate—the home-country price of foreign exchange—then dividing by a home-country price index for the class of goods in question, and finally multiplying by the corresponding foreign price index.

Suppose, for example, that we take the U.S. price of Japanese currency—the $/Y rate—denoted by S_t and multiply it by P_t^*/P_t, where P_t^* and P_t represent consumer price indexes for Japan and the United States, respectively. These steps give the real exchange rate for period t,

$$Q_t = \frac{S_t P_t^*}{P_t}, \qquad (5)$$

that expresses the price of Japanese consumer goods in terms of U.S. consumer goods. The real exchange rate Q then measures how many typical bundles of U.S. goods would be equivalent in exchange value to one typical bundle of Japanese goods. The absolute level of such an index is entirely arbitrary, and thus of no significance, but *movements* over time in the index would provide useful indications of whether the U.S. goods price of Japanese goods was rising or falling.

There is a certain air of artificiality about such movements, admittedly, as it is not possible actually to exchange typical U.S. consumption bundles for typical Japanese consumption bundles, since both bundles include services that

---

[9] Real interest rates are conceptually different from the other examples, principally because nominal interest rates are measured in dimensions that are not expressed in monetary units. In particular, a real interest rate is a nominal rate minus the rate of (price-level) inflation expected to prevail over the life of the relevant loan.

are inherently nontradeable.[10] A more interesting real exchange rate index may, therefore, be one that uses *producer* price indexes for P_t^* and P_t. Such an index would give the price of Japanese produced good in terms of U.S. produced goods.[11] Or, P_t and P_t^* might be taken to refer to narrower classes of goods—say, manufactured goods or goods from industries specializing in exports.

Real, like nominal, exchange rates may be of the average or "effective" variety rather than bilateral in coverage. Thus it is possible to calculate a real-rate counterpart to the Fed's 10-country effective rate by making P_t^* a weighted average of the price index values for the various countries. Indeed, the Fed computes and reports values for just such an index. Since the Fed's convention is to refer to the value of U.S. currency or goods relative to those abroad, however, this index will be the reciprocal of our Q_t concept given in Equation (5). Values of the Fed's index for the years 1973–1993 are presented as the last item in Figure 2–4, which also includes annual average values of the Fed's nominal effective index and several bilateral rates.

One special example of a real effective exchange rate measure is that in which P_t and P_t^* refer to a particular nation's export and import goods, respectively. The inverse of such a measure was frequently discussed in the older (prewar) literature under the title of "terms of trade." An increase in export prices relative to import prices was referred to as an "improvement" in the terms of trade, indicating that fewer goods needed to be exported in order to pay for a given quantity of imports.

2.5 Purchasing Power Parity

Consider now a version of Equation (5) that is rewritten with S_t as the left-hand side variable,

$$S_t = \frac{Q_t P_t}{P_t^*}. \tag{6}$$

Viewed merely as a rearranged version of the *definition* of Q_t, this equation can have no explanatory power of its own. But the equation shows that *if* an analyst had a model that would explain the behavior of the real exchange rate Q_t and the relative price level ratio P_t/P_t^*, then he or she would also have an explanation of the behavior of S_t, the nominal exchange rate. In fact, there is a famous and controversial theory of exchange rate behavior, known as the purchasing power parity (PPP) theory, which utilizes that general approach.

---

[10] The usual example is haircuts. Strictly speaking, such services are not literally impossible to trade—one *could* fly from Pittsburgh to Tokyo for a haircut and return immediately—but the transportation cost is so high in relation to the value of the service as to render the trade almost inconceivable.

[11] Moving even farther away from consumer prices, the IMF reports real exchange rates that use as deflators nations' indexes of normal labor costs per unit of output in manufacturing industry.

Period	Belgium (franc)	Canada (dollar)	France (franc)	Germany (mark)	Ital; (lira)	Japan (yen)
March 1973	39.408	0.9967	4.5156	2.8132	568.17	261.90
1969	50.142	1.0769	5.1999	3.9251	627.32	358.36
1970	49.656	1.0444	5.5288	3.6465	627.12	358.16
1971	48.598	1.0099	5.5100	3.4830	618.34	347.79
1972	44.020	.9907	5.0444	3.1886	583.70	303.13
1973	38.955	1.0002	4.4535	2.6715	582.41	271.31
1974	38.959	.9780	4.8107	2.5868	650.81	291.84
1975	36.800	1.0175	4.2877	2.4614	653.10	296.78
1976	38.609	.9863	4.7825	2.5185	833.58	296.45
1977	35.849	1.0633	4.9161	2.3236	882.78	268.62
1978	31.495	1.1405	4.5091	2.0097	849.13	210.39
1979	29.342	1.1713	4.2567	1.8343	831.11	219.02
1980	29.238	1.1693	4.2251	1.8175	856.21	226.63
1981	37.195	1.1990	5.4397	2.2632	1138.58	220.63
1982	45.781	1.2344	6.5794	2.4281	1354.00	249.06
1983	51.123	1.2325	7.6204	2.5539	1519.32	237.55
1984	57.752	1.2952	8.7356	2.8455	1756.11	237.46
1985	59.337	1.3659	8.9800	2.9420	1908.88	238.47
1986	44.664	1.3896	6.9257	2.1705	1491.16	168.35
1987	37.358	1.3259	6.0122	1.7981	1297.03	144.60
1988	36.785	1.2306	5.9595	1.7570	1302.39	128.17
1989	39.409	1.1842	6.3802	1.8808	1372.28	138.07
1990	33.424	1.1668	5.4467	1.6166	1198.27	145.00
1991	34.195	1.1460	5.6468	1.6610	1241.28	134.59
1992	32.148	1.2085	5.2935	1.5618	1232.17	126.78
1993	34.581	1.2902	5.6669	1.6545	1573.41	111.08
1992: I	33.347	1.1775	5.5137	1.6204	1218.54	128.77
II	33.220	1.1940	5.4416	1.6146	1217.23	130.37
III	30.170	1.2016	4.9628	1.4643	1135.18	124.93
IV	31.915	1.2617	5.2671	1.5509	1362.89	123.02
1993: I	33.686	1.2608	5.5463	1.6349	1547.37	120.67
II	33.311	1.2703	5.4635	1.6198	1506.55	110.05
III	35.447	1.3039	5.8180	1.6776	1586.56	105.65
IV	35.857	1.3251	5.8368	1.6851	1653.17	108.35

Period	Netherlands (guilder)	Sweden (krona)	Switzerland (franc)	United Kingdom (pound) [1]	Multilateral trade-weighted value of the U.S. dollar (March 1973=100)	
					Nominal	Real [2]
March 1973	2.8714	4.4294	3.2171	2.4724	100.0	100.0
1969	3.6240	5.1701	4.3131	2.3901	122.4	
1970	3.6166	5.1862	4.3106	2.3959	121.1	
1971	3.4953	5.1051	4.1171	2.4442	117.8	
1972	3.2098	4.7571	3.8186	2.5034	109.1	
1973	2.7946	4.3619	3.1688	2.4525	99.1	98.9
1974	2.6879	4.4387	2.9805	2.3403	101.4	99.4
1975	2.5293	4.1531	2.5839	2.2217	98.5	94.1
1976	2.6449	4.3580	2.5002	1.8048	105.7	97.6
1977	2.4548	4.4802	2.4065	1.7449	103.4	93.3
1978	2.1643	4.5207	1.7907	1.9184	92.4	84.4
1979	2.0073	4.2893	1.6644	2.1224	88.1	83.2
1980	1.9875	4.2310	1.6772	2.3246	87.4	84.9
1981	2.4999	5.0660	1.9675	2.0243	103.4	100.9
1982	2.6719	6.2839	2.0327	1.7480	116.6	111.8
1983	2.8544	7.6718	2.1007	1.5159	125.3	117.3
1984	3.2085	8.2708	2.3500	1.3368	138.2	128.8
1985	3.3185	8.6032	2.4552	1.2974	143.0	132.4
1986	2.4485	7.1273	1.7979	1.4677	112.2	103.6
1987	2.0264	6.3469	1.4918	1.6398	96.9	90.9
1988	1.9778	6.1370	1.4643	1.7813	92.7	88.2
1989	2.1219	6.4559	1.6369	1.6382	98.6	94.4
1990	1.8215	5.9231	1.3901	1.7841	89.1	86.0
1991	1.8720	6.0521	1.4356	1.7674	89.8	86.5
1992	1.7587	5.8258	1.4064	1.7663	86.6	83.4
1993	1.8585	7.7956	1.4781	1.5016	93.2	89.9
1992: I	1.8243	5.8854	1.4573	1.7692	88.2	84.8
II	1.8182	5.8302	1.4780	1.8070	88.0	84.4
III	1.6506	5.3523	1.3041	1.9030	81.9	78.9
IV	1.7448	6.2581	1.3888	1.5781	88.5	85.4
1993: I	1.8387	7.5299	1.5063	1.4769	93.3	90.0
II	1.8180	7.4130	1.4628	1.5331	90.9	87.6
III	1.8861	8.0151	1.4768	1.5037	93.7	90.2
IV	1.8907	8.2185	1.4676	1.4914	94.9	91.7

[1] Value is U.S. dollars per pound.
[2] Adjusted by changes in consumer prices.
Source: Board of Governors of the Federal Reserve System.

Figure 2–4 Exchange rate data from Economic Report of the President, 1994. (Currency units per U.S. dollar, except as noted).

What the PPP theory contends is that Q_t can be taken as an exogenously determined constant,

$$Q_t = \bar{Q}. \tag{7}$$

That is an extremely simple model or theory of the behavior of Q_t, but it is one with refutable content, nevertheless. Then with $Q_t = \bar{Q}$, the PPP theory notes that

$$S_t = \frac{\bar{Q}P}{P_t^*}, \tag{8}$$

implying that the exchange rate moves over time in proportion to movements in the ratio of price levels, P_t/P_t^*. This proposition could be applied to bilateral exchange rates or to a nation's effective exchange rate, depending on the price indexes used for P_t and P_t^*. Also worth noting is that a logarithmic version could be written, as follows:

$$s_t = \bar{q} + p_t - p_t^*. \tag{9}$$

In the latter, p_t and p_t^* are logs of the relevant price levels and the constant $\bar{q}$ equals log $\bar{Q}$. Taking differences, we readily obtain

$$\Delta s_t = \Delta p_t - \Delta p_t^*, \tag{10}$$

where the three variables can all be thought of as fractional changes (i.e., percentage changes divided by 100). Equation (10) provides the most readily usable formulation of the PPP hypothesis.

The PPP theory was put forth during the 1920s, which was a decade that witnessed several extremely large movements in national price levels, including a few hyperinflationary experiences. In these experiences, national price levels rose at extremely rapid rates: the (arbitrary) definition of a hyperinflation is an inflation that proceeds at a pace of 50 percent *per month* or faster. Consequently, movements in P_t/P_t^* for those experiences were much greater in magnitude than movements in real exchange rates, since the latter reflect relative values of real commodity bundles (the exact bundles depending on the precise specification chosen for the index numbers P_t and P_t^*). The PPP relationship (8) or (9) holds fairly accurately, then, when applied to the experiences of the 1920s.[12]

Perhaps of more interest today, however, is whether the PPP relationship of proportionality between exchange rates S_t and relative price levels P_t/P_t^* is valid more generally. Would it, for example, be helpful in understanding the sizable exchange rate movements of the 1980s? In answering that question it is necessary to be clear about the time perspective involved—quarter to quarter, year to year, or decade to decade. If one's concern is with either of the first two, then the accumulated evidence must be viewed as highly inconsistent with

[12] For documentation, see Frenkel (1978).

the PPP theory. That conclusion can be justified very easily, simply by showing that real exchange rates exhibit a lot of variability in the quarterly or annual data, in comparison with the variability of relative price levels. Even more convincing evidence can be provided by plots of nominal and real exchange rates, such as Figure 2–5. If movements of nominal rates are closely matched by movements of real rates, then it is clear that, in terms of Equation (6), (9), or (10), nominal-rate variations are *not* being explained by relative price levels (as posited by PPP). Figure 2–5 shows real and nominal exchange rates over the floating-rate years of 1973–1993 for the pound and the DM, each relative

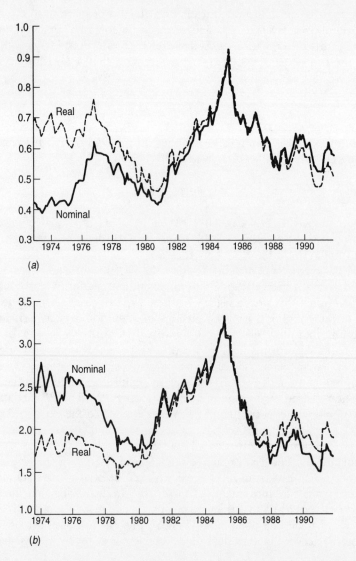

Figure 2–5 Movements in real and nominal exchange rates. (*a*) – £/$. (*b*) DM/$.

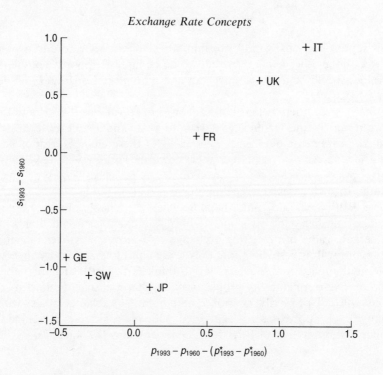

Figure 2–6 Long-term PPP conformity.

to the dollar. In both cases it is clear that most of the quarter-to-quarter or year-to-year variability in the nominal rate is coming from movements in the real rate, not the relative price level.

Over a matter of decades, by contrast, the ups and downs of real rates will tend to cancel out and nominal-rate movements may be secularly dominated by relative price-level changes. That type of effect shows up to some extent even in the relatively short time span covered in Figure 2–5. Thus in the case of the £/$ rate, Britain's higher rate of inflation in comparison with the United States moves the nominal rate index from below the real-rate curve in 1973 to above it in 1993, whereas the opposite movement holds for the DM/$ rate since Germany has had a lower rate of inflation than the United States.

More systematically, let us consider exchange rate and relative price level statistics over the time span of 1960–1993 for various countries. In Figure 2–6, values of $s_{1993} - s_{1960}$ are plotted against $p_{1993} - p_{1960} - (p^*_{1993} - p^*_{1960})$ for the following countries, with the United States being taken as the reference (or foreign) country in each case: Germany, Japan, France, Italy, Switzerland, and the United Kingdom. It will be seen that agreement with the PPP prediction, namely, that the points should lie on a line with slope of unity, would be fairly impressive if the point for Japan were excluded. The Japanese data do not conform well to the theory because real productivity has grown much more rapidly in Japan than in the United States, causing the real exchange rate (U.S.

goods/Japanese goods) to fall substantially.[13] If one were to add a point for
Mexico, on the other hand, the result would be highly supportive of the theory:
the values would be approximately 5.5 and 5.6 on the horizontal and vertical
axes, respectively.

What we see, then, is that real exchange rates vary to a substantial extent
from quarter to quarter and from year to year, and may even exhibit some
trendlike movements over time. The extent of these changes cannot be more
than a few percentage points per year, however, so they will be swamped by
relative price-level changes if one country experiences rapid or sustained
inflation. In such cases, the PPP predictions will be borne out.[14]

The PPP idea does not, therefore, yield a reliable theory of nominal
exchange rate behavior on a quarterly or annual time frame. It may be of
considerable value in predicting exchange rate movements over longer spans
of time, but will at best constitute only a portion of a satisfactory theory even
for decadal application. A better way to think of the PPP idea, perhaps, is as
a kind of long-run neutrality proposition: long-term effects of monetary policy
actions will fall primarily on prices and nominal exchange rates, with real
exchange rates approximately unaffected. This proposition is presented as the
"proper" interpretation of PPP doctrine by Niehans (1984, ch. 2).

2.6 PPP and Nontraded Goods

It was suggested in connection with Figure 2–6 that unusually rapid productivity
growth in a country will tend to induce an appreciation in its real exchange
rate and therefore a deviation from the PPP relationship. This section will be
devoted to an introductory exposition of one theory designed to explain that
tendency. As a background to this explanation, consider the situation pertaining
to a single good that is actively traded among nations, with transportation
costs (and imposed taxes) that are negligible in relation to its value. In this
case, one would expect that good's price to be the same everywhere—this is
the "law of one price"—when expressed in terms of a single currency. If good
k costs P_k dollars in the United States and P_k^* yen in Japan, then its dollar price
in Japan would be SP_k^*, where S is the \$/¥ exchange rate. And if this price were
lower than P_k, it would pay to buy the good in Japan and ship it to the United
States—this activity would yield easy profits since transportation costs are (by
assumption) negligible. But then as purchasers shift their demands toward
Japan and away from the United States, they will tend to bid SP_k^* upward and
P_k downward. Thus there is a strong tendency for SP_k^* and P_k to be equalized,
that is, for $P_k = SP_k^*$ to prevail for goods with low transportation costs.

Next suppose that transportation costs (and duties) were low for *all* goods.
Then it would be the case that

$$P = SP^* \qquad (11)$$

[13] The mechanism by which rapid real productivity growth induces a nation's real exchange
rate to appreciate will be discussed in the next section of this chapter.

[14] Some evidence will be described in Chapter 9.

would tend to prevail in terms of general price indexes if their weights and index base years were the same in both countries. Thus we would have that $Q = 1$ always, implying that $\Delta q = 0$ over any selected period of time, so the PPP condition (10) would hold. Of course actual index weights will not be exactly the same in different countries, but they will not be vastly different among groups of countries at roughly similar stages of development. And the effect of different index base years is unimportant, for it would merely be to make Q equal to some constant other than 1.0, which would still imply that $\Delta q = 0$ and thus that Equation (10) would hold as before.

But now let us consider a more realistic case in which some goods have extremely high transportation costs and consequently do not enter into international trade at all. For simplicity, we pretend that there is a clear line of demarcation between two classes of goods, traded goods (with negligible transport costs) and nontraded goods (with prohibitive transport costs). Let p_t^T and p_t^N denote logs of price indexes for these two classes in the home country, with p_t^{*T} and p_t^{*N} pertaining to the foreign country under consideration. Then the general price levels in the two countries, p_t and p_t^*, can plausibly be regarded as being given (in logs) by

$$p_t = ap_t^N + (1 - a)p_t^T \tag{12}$$

and

$$p_t^* = ap_t^{*N} + (1 - a)p_t^{*T}. \tag{13}$$

Here a denotes the weight of nontraded goods in the home country's overall price index and $1 - a$ the weight of traded goods. To make the point at hand, it will be satisfactory to assume that these weights are the same at home and in the foreign country, an assumption that does not imply that the nature of the nontraded goods is the same in both nations.

In addition, let us suppose that the law of one price holds for the traded goods, so that

$$\Delta s_t = \Delta p_t^T - \Delta p_t^{*T}. \tag{14}$$

No such condition holds, however, for the nontraded goods. Now $\Delta q_t = \Delta s_t - \Delta p_t + \Delta p_t^*$, by definition, so we can insert Equations (12), (13), and (14) into this definition and obtain

$$\Delta q_t = (\Delta p_t^T - \Delta p_t^{*T}) - a\Delta p_t^N - (1 - a)\Delta p_t^T + a\Delta p_t^{*N} + (1 - a)\Delta p_t^{*T}. \tag{15}$$

Rearranging terms, we then have

$$\Delta q_t = a(\Delta p_t^T - \Delta p_t^N) - a(\Delta p_t^{*T} - \Delta p_t^{*N}). \tag{16}$$

But this last expression shows that Δq_t will be nonzero, and the PPP equation (10) will not hold, if $\Delta p_t^T - \Delta p_t^N$ is not equal to $\Delta p_t^{*T} - \Delta p_t^{*N}$. So if the relative price of traded versus nontraded goods grows at different rates at home and abroad, Δq_t will be nonzero and PPP will not hold.

The foregoing conclusion follows from little more than algebra plus the assumption that $\Delta s_t = \Delta p_t^T - \Delta p_t^{*T}$ for traded goods. But there exist plausible theories about conditions that will make $\Delta p_t^N - \Delta p_t^T$ different in different nations. The most prominent of these, promoted by Balassa (1964) and Kravis and Lipsey (1983), is based on the hypothesis that productivity growth causes Δp_t^N to exceed Δp_t^T, with higher growth rates leading to higher $\Delta p_t^N - \Delta p_t^T$ differentials. The rationale for this hypothesis is that tradables are mostly tangible *goods*—manufactures or raw materials—whereas nontradables are largely *services*. This distinction is significant because technological progress usually brings about rapid growth in labor productivity in the production of manufactures and other tangible goods, whereas there is comparatively little scope for productivity increases in the service industries. And rapid productivity tends, of course, to hold down production cost increases and therefore product price increases. So, the faster the growth of productivity (and per-capita income levels), the larger will be the value of $\Delta p_t^N - \Delta p_t^T$ for any nation.

Referring back to Equation (16), finally, we see that if in the home country productivity and income growth are rapid (relative to abroad), then the value of $\Delta p_t^T - \Delta p_t^N$ will be lower than abroad, and Δq_t will be negative. In other words, the home country's real exchange rate will appreciate. Conversely, if productivity growth is lower at home than abroad, then the home country's real exchange rate will depreciate (Δq_t will be positive).

The foregoing argument accords with the points plotted in Figure 2–6 in the following manner. It is common knowledge that productivity and income growth have been especially high in Japan over the past few decades—higher than in the United States or in most European nations. So if one viewed Japan as the home country, one would conclude that its average Δq_t value would be low when the United States is viewed as the foreign country. So for Japan it would be the case that Δs_t would be smaller on average than $\Delta p_t - \Delta p_t^*$ since $\Delta s_t = \Delta p_t - \Delta p_t^* + \Delta q_t$ by definition. Thus the point pertaining to Japan in Figure 2–6 should lie below the relationship pertaining to other economies and below the line that would represent conformity with the PPP equation (10), namely, a line with slope 1.0 that passes through the (0, 0) origin. In fact, the point for Japan clearly satisfies both of these conditions.

It is interesting to note that essentially the same line of argument can be used to explain why the average level of prices tends to be noticeably higher in countries with high levels of income, in comparison with poorer nations, even after conversion into common currency units. The basic point is that if a nation has high incomes, then it has experienced rapid productivity growth and so its value of q_t will have fallen relative to other nations. But from the definitional identity $q_t = s_t - p_t + p_t^*$, we have

$$p_t = s_t + p_t^* - q_t. \tag{17}$$

From the latter we see that if q_t is low, p_t will be high in relation to $s_t + p_t^*$. Thus Equation (17) implies that prices in the home country will be high relative to $p_t^* + s_t$, that is, to foreign prices expressed in home-country currency.

2.7 U.S. Spot Rates, 1947–1993

We conclude this chapter by presenting, in Figures 2–7 through 2–12, time plots covering the period of 1947–1993 for U.S. dollar exchange rates relative to the currencies of Canada, France, Germany, Italy, Japan, Switzerland, and the United Kingdom. These spot rates are all reported as foreign-currency prices of one dollar. The values for the German mark and the Swiss franc are plotted on the same diagram because their movements have been so similar. It should be noted that the vertical scales are different, even on a percentage basis, in the different figures.

In these figures it will be seen that most of the bilateral rates against the dollar were virtually constant from 1949 to 1971, the main exceptions being France, which devalued twice, and Canada, which had a floating rate over the time span 1950–1962. It will also be seen that the value of the dollar rose sharply over 1980–1984 relative to each of the other currencies, and then fell over the period of 1985–1987. These cyclical movements are superimposed on longer term trends, which show the dollar depreciating relative to the yen, DM, and Swiss franc and appreciating relative to the lira, pound, and French franc.

Appendix: Foreign Exchange Options

Here we provide a description of the table in Figure 2–13, which reports quotations from the Philadelphia foreign exchange *options* market as of July 27, 1994. Developing an understanding of the various entries in this table will provide the reader with a reasonble comprehension of the nature of foreign exchange options contracts.

On any date there will be options contracts available that will expire in each of the next two months (August and September in our example) plus the next March, June, September, and December. The main contracts expire on the Saturday before the third Wednesday of each month, although a few are traded whose expiration dates are the end of the month. As a typical example, consider the option quotations given for contracts each of which involves 62,500 German DM in the lower middle of the second column. (Several such bundles can be combined, of course, but each contract involves at least one.) Note the entry that reports "64" and "Sep" in the first two columns. Here 64, in the units of $ per 100 DM, is the *strike* price, that is, the price at which the option transaction will be settled (on September 21, the month's third Wednesday) if the purchaser of the option chooses. The volume figures for this contract indicate that during the day there were 120 call options purchased and 7 put options, these being options to buy or sell DM, respectively, at the strike price when the expiration date (September 17) comes around. Finally, there is the price paid for this option—for the right to buy (or sell) 62,500 DM at the price of $0.64/DM on September 17. For a call (buy) option the price was 0.88 cent per DM (or $0.88 per 100 DM). So the call option buyer pays ($0.0088)62,500 = $550 for the option of purchasing 62,500 DM at a price of 0.64 $/DM on

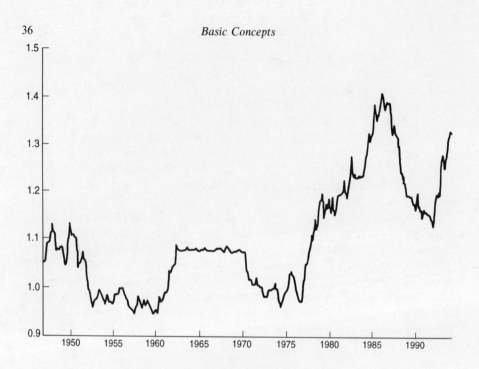

Figure 2–7 Canadian exchange rate, Can$/$.

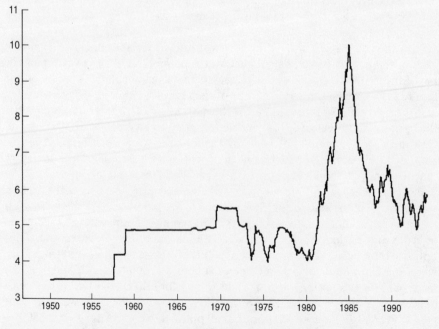

Figure 2–8 French exchange rate, FF/$.

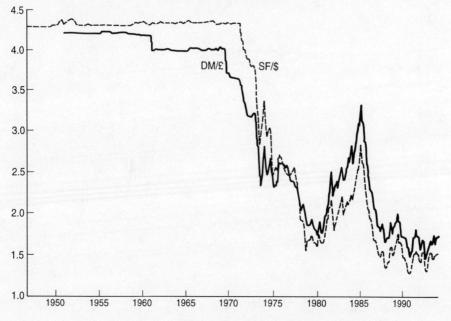

Figure 2-9 German and Swiss exchange rates, DM/$ and SF/$.

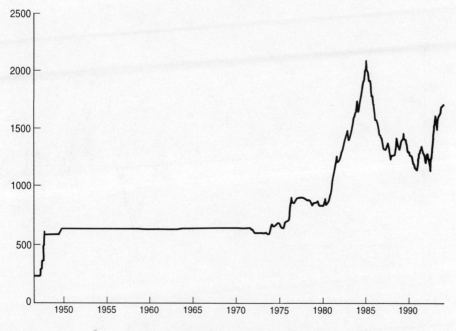

Figure 2-10 Italian exchange rate, L/$.

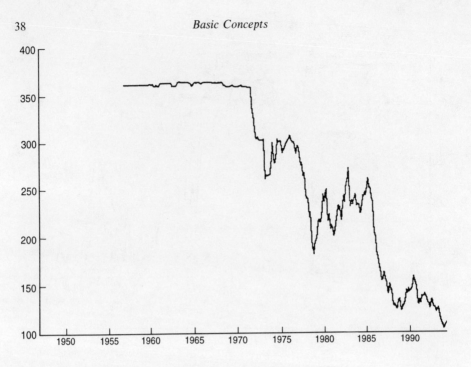

Figure 2–11 Japanese exchange rate, Y/$.

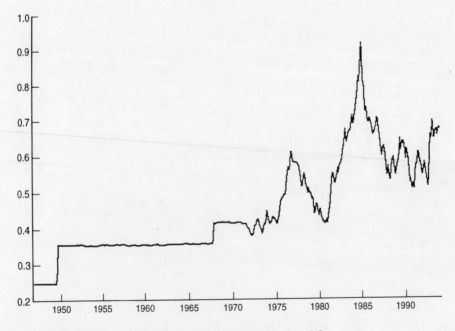

Figure 2–12 British exchange rate, £/$.

```
                      OPTIONS
                PHILADELPHIA EXCHANGE

              Calls     Puts                              Calls     Puts                                 Calls     Puts
              Vol. Last Vol. Last                         Vol. Last Vol. Last                            Vol. Last Vol. Last
FFranc                185.85                                                          102  Jul   750 0.33   ...  ...
250,000 French Franc EOM-European style.                                             103  Jul    16 0.14   ...  ...
  18½ Jul  500 0.90 500 0.66                                                         6,250,000 Japanese Yen EOM.
DMark                  63.54          18¾ Aug 1000 0.88  ...  ...                      102½ Jul  16 0.30   ...  ...
62,500 German Mark EOM-European style. 18¾ Sep 6870 2.04  ...  ...                    6,250,000 Japanese Yen-100ths of a cent per unit.
  65  Jul  200 0.01  ...  ...         German Mark          63.54                       91  Dec   ...  ...    5 0.18
  68  Aug   25 0.04  ...  ...         62,500 German Marks EOM-cents per unit.          94  Dec   ...  ...  100 0.40
  69  Aug  275 0.02  ...  ...           62  Jul 200 1.38 255 0.03                       94½ Sep  ...  ...    2 0.07
62,500 German Marks EOM-European style.  62½ Jul   5 0.90 380 0.06                      95  Sep  ...  ...    4 0.09
  61½ Jul   50 1.98  ...  ...            63  Jul 555 0.58 530 0.14                       98  Sep  ...  ...    5 0.44
  62½ Jul  ...  ...  15 0.06             63½ Jul 496 0.31  50 0.38                       98  Dec  ...  ...    7 1.29
  62½ Aug  ...  ...  16 0.48             64  Jul 280 0.08 130 0.65                       98½ Sep  ...  ...    2 0.47
  63½ Jul    5 0.30  ...  ...         62,500 German Marks-European Style.               99  Aug   20 3.33  23 0.11
  64½ Jul  200 0.05  ...  ...           57  Dec   6 6.38  ...  ...                       99  Sep   20 3.83   2 0.58
  64½ Aug  150 0.45  ...  ...           57½ Sep   4 5.90  ...  ...                       99  Dec  ...  ...  102 1.53
  68½ Aug  150 0.02  ...  ...           60  Sep  ...  ...   4 0.16                      100  Aug   12 2.28  10 0.44
  69½ Aug  275 0.02  ...  ...           61½ Aug  50 2.04  ...  ...                      100  Sep    1 2.84  ...  ...
Australian Dollar      73.94            61½ Sep  ...  ...   8 0.43                     100½ Aug  ...  ...   50 0.39
50,000 Australian Dollars-European Style. 62½ Sep ...  ...  8 0.77                     100½ Sep  ...  ...    4 0.96
  74  Aug   20 0.63  ...  ...           64  Dec 337 1.60  ...  ...                     101  Sep  ...  ...   10 1.11
50,000 Australian Dollars-cents per unit. 62,500 German Marks-cents per unit.         101½ Aug  ...  ...    5 0.90
  73  Sep    5 1.54   1 0.62            60  Aug  ...  ...  58 0.01                     102  Aug  ...  ...    7 1.00
  75  Sep   50 0.66  ...  ...           61  Sep  ...  ...  10 0.30                     102  Sep  ...  ...    7 1.54
British Pound         153.18            62  Aug  ...  ...  50 0.18                     102  Dec  ...  ...    4 2.61
31,250 British Pounds-European Style.   62  Sep  ...  ...  60 0.54                     102½ Aug  20 0.94  ...  ...
  152½ Aug  ...  ...  32 0.99           62  Dec  ...  ...  71 1.17                     102½ Sep  ...  ...    8 1.96
31,250 British Pounds-cents per unit.   62½ Aug  27 0.27  20 0.35                     103½ Sep  ...  ...    5 2.53
  150  Aug  ...  ...  20 0.16           62½ Sep  ...  ...  92 0.71                     104  Aug   12 0.34  ...  ...
  152½ Aug  58 1.45   1 0.80            63  Aug  25 0.85 120 0.40                      104  Sep   16 1.07  ...  ...
  155  Aug  20 0.45  ...  ...           63  Sep   6 1.27  19 0.88                      105½ Sep   5 0.60  ...  ...
  155  Sep 100 1.00  ...  ...           63  Dec   1 2.00 660 1.66                     Swiss Franc          75.00
British Pound-GMark   241.26            63½ Aug  25 0.58  13 0.70                     62,500 Swiss Francs EOM.
31,250 British Pound-German Mark cross. 63½ Sep 142 1.07 400 1.11                      73½ Jul  ...  ...   20 0.06
  238  Sep  ...  ...  10 1.16           64  Aug 185 0.44   5 0.93                       75½ Jul   3 0.08  ...  ...
  242  Aug   8 1.04  ...  ...           64  Sep 120 0.88   7 1.40                     62,500 Swiss Francs-European Style.
Canadian Dollar        72.49            64  Dec  ...  ...  10 2.15                      72½ Aug  ...  ...  435 0.14
50,000 Canadian Dollars-cents per unit. 64½ Aug  40 0.27  ...  ...                      72½ Sep  ...  ...   40 0.44
  71  Dec   ...  ...  10 0.60           64½ Sep   2 0.69  ...  ...                      76½ Aug  ...  ...   64 1.93
  71½ Sep   ...  ...  27 0.30           65  Dec  49 1.17  ...  ...                     62,500 Swiss Francs-cents per unit.
French Franc          185.85            65½ Sep 390 0.37  ...  ...                      70½ Sep  22 4.26  ...  ...
250,000 French Franc-European Style.    66  Aug 390 0.04  ...  ...                      71  Dec  ...  ...   75 0.77
  16½ Sep   ...  ...   8 0.32           66  Sep  30 0.30  ...  ...                      73  Sep  ...  ...   34 0.63
  17  Dec    8 15.72 ...  ...           68  Sep 1500 0.10 ...  ...                      73  Dec  ...  ...   88 1.48
  17½ Dec   ...  ...   8 1.40         Japanese Yen         101.45                       73½ Aug  ...  ...   20 0.35
250,000 French Francs-10ths of a cent per unit. 6,250,000 Japanese Yen EOM-100ths of a cent per unit.  74  Aug ... ... 10 0.51
  19  Dec   ...  ...  10 7.48           99  Jul  ...  ... 100 0.03                       76  Aug   20 0.28  ...  ...
250,000 French Francs-European Style.   99  Aug  ...  ...  50 0.33                       76  Sep    6 0.86   5 2.03
  18¼ Aug   ...  ... 1000 0.60          101 Jul  20 1.30  ...  ...                     Call Vol ...... 26,725  Open Int ... 671,299
  18½ Sep  6870 3.16 ...  ...                                                         Put Vol ....... 6,399   Open Int ... 533,995
```

Figure 2–13 Foreign exchange options prices from *Wall Street Journal* of July 28, 1994. *Source*: "Reprinted by permission of *Wall Street Journal*, © 1994 Dow Jones & Company, Inc. All Rights Reserved Worldwide."

September 21, 1994. Also, on that day there were 7 contracts purchased to "put" (sell) 62,500 DM at 0.64 $/DM on September 21. The price of one of these put contracts was ($0.014)62,500 = $875.

Some of the contracts are labeled "European style," indicating that they can only be exercised on the final or expiration day of the contract. The others are "American style" contracts, which can be exercised (at the buyer's discretion) anytime before the expiration date.

References

Balassa, B., "The Purchasing-Power Parity Doctrine: A Reappraisal," *Journal of Political Economy* **72** (Dec. 1964), 584–596.

Belongia, M. T., "Estimating Exchange Rate Effects on Exports: A Cautionary Note," *Federal Reserve Bank of St. Louis Review* **68** (Jan. 1986), 5–16.

Chrystal, K. A., "A Guide to Foreign Exchange Markets," *Federal Reserve Bank of St. Louis Review* **66** (Mar. 1984), 5–18.

Fratianni, M., and L. M. Wakeman, "The Law of One Price in the Eurocurrency Market," *Journal of International Money and Finance* **1** (Dec. 1982), 307–323.

Frenkel, J. A., and R. M. Levich, "Transaction Costs and Interest Arbitrage: Tranquil versus Turbulent Periods," *Journal of Political Economy* **86** (Dec. 1977), 1209–1226.

Frenkel, J. A., "Purchasing Power Parity: Doctrinal Perspective and Evidence from the 1920s," *Journal of International Economics* 8 (May 1978).

Goldstein, M., D. Folkerts-Landau, P. Garber, L. Rojas-Suárez, and M. Spencer, *International Capital Markets, Part I. Exchange Rate Management and International Flows.* Washington, DC: International Monetary Fund, 1993.

Kravis, I., and R. Lipsey, *Toward an Explanation of National Price Levels*, Princeton Studies in International Finance no. 52, Princeton University Press, 1983.

Kubarych, R. M., *Foreign Exchange Markets in the United States*, rev. ed. New York: Federal Reserve Bank of New York, 1983.

MacDonald, R., *Floating Exchange Rates: Theories and Evidence*. London: Unwin Hyman, 1988.

McKenzie, G., "Eurocurrency Markets," in *The New Palgrave Dictionary of Money and Finance*, P. Newman, M. Milgate, and J. Eatwell, Eds. New York: Stockton Press, 1992.

Niehans, J., *International Monetary Economics*. Baltimore; MD: Johns Hopkins University Press, 1984.

Ott, M., "The Dollar's Effective Exchange Rate: Assessing the Impact of Alternative Weighting Schemes," *Federal Reserve Bank of St. Louis Review* **69** (Febr. 1987), 5–14.

Pauls, B. D., "Measuring the Foreign Exchange Value of the Dollar," *Federal Reserve Bulletin* **73** (June 1987), 411–422.

Thornton, D. L., "Tests of Covered Interest Rate Parity," *Federal Reserve Bank of St. Louis Review* **71** (July/Aug. 1989), 55–66.

Problems

1. What was the U.S.–Spain spot exchange rate reported in the most recent issue of the *Wall Street Journal*, expressed as $/peseta?

2. Find the comparable figure as reported in the *Financial Times*, and calculate the discrepancy in percentage terms.

3. What was the Mexican peso price of Austrian schillings according to the *Wall Street Journal*? What was the value of New Zealand dollars in terms of Australian dollars?

4. What was the $/peseta three-month forward rate? Was the peseta at a forward premium or discount?

5. Compare the percent per annum yield on three-month U.S. dollar securities in the London eurocurrency market with the covered yield in terms of dollars on three-month peseta securities in that market.

6. Did the Italian real exchange rate vis-à-vis Germany appreciate or depreciate over the time span of 1970–1990? By how much, in percentage terms? Answer also for the nominal exchange rate (see Figure 2–14).

Year or quarter	United States	Canada	Japan	European Community [1]	France	Germany [2]	Italy	United Kingdom
	Industrial production (1987 = 100) [3]							
1967	57.5	51.1	36.2	59.3	61	57.6	58.5	70.5
1968	60.7	54.3	41.7	63.7	62	62.9	61.9	75.9
1969	63.5	58.1	48.3	69.6	69	70.9	64.2	78.5
1970	61.4	58.8	55.0	73.1	72	75.5	68.3	78.9
1971	62.2	62.0	56.5	74.7	77	77.0	68.0	78.5
1972	68.3	66.7	59.6	78.0	81	79.9	70.8	79.9
1973	73.8	73.8	67.9	83.7	87	85.0	77.7	87.0
1974	72.7	76.1	66.4	84.3	90	84.8	81.2	85.4
1975	66.3	71.6	59.4	78.7	83	79.6	73.7	80.8
1976	72.4	76.0	66.0	84.5	90	86.8	82.9	83.4
1977	78.2	79.3	68.6	86.6	92	88.0	83.8	87.6
1978	82.6	82.1	73.0	95.4	94	90.4	85.4	90.1
1979	85.7	86.1	78.1	93.1	99	94.7	91.1	93.6
1980	84.1	82.8	81.7	92.8	98.9	95.0	96.2	86.9
1981	85.7	84.5	82.6	91.1	98.3	93.2	94.7	84.1
1982	81.9	76.2	82.9	89.9	97.3	90.3	91.7	85.7
1983	84.9	81.2	85.5	90.8	96.5	90.9	88.9	88.9
1984	92.8	91.0	93.4	92.8	97.1	93.5	91.8	89.0
1985	94.4	96.1	96.8	95.8	97.2	97.7	92.9	93.9
1986	95.3	95.4	96.6	98.0	98.0	99.6	96.2	96.2
1987	100.0	100.0	100.0	100.0	100.0	100.0	100.0	100.0
1988	104.4	105.3	109.3	104.2	104.6	103.9	105.9	104.8
1989	106.0	105.2	115.9	108.2	108.9	108.8	109.2	107.0
1990	106.0	101.8	121.4	110.3	111.0	114.1	109.4	106.7
1991	104.1	98.1	123.7	110.2	110.9	117.4	107.1	102.5
1992 p	106.5	98.5	116.5	108.9	109.8	116.0	106.5	102.0
1993 p	111.0							
1992: I	105.1	97.5	119.7	106.8	110.4	119.2	110.3	101.4
II	106.3	98.0	116.9	109.5	110.4	117.3	107.2	101.3
III	106.5	98.5	116.5	108.6	110.3	115.7	104.7	102.5
IV	108.3	100.0	113.5	106.6	107.3	110.3	104.0	103.1
1993: I	109.7	101.8	114.1	105.1	104.8	106.9	105.2	103.2
II	110.4	102.6	112.2		104.9	106.9	102.0	104.3
III	111.1	103.6	112.0			106.9	103.0	105.3
IV p	113.1							
	Consumer prices (1982–84 = 100)							
1967	33.4	31.3	32.2	23.5	24.6	49.3	16.0	18.5
1968	34.8	32.5	34.0	24.3	25.7	50.1	16.2	19.4
1969	36.7	34.0	35.8	25.3	27.4	51.0	16.6	20.4
1970	38.8	35.1	38.5	26.6	28.7	52.9	16.8	21.8
1971	40.5	36.1	40.9	28.3	30.3	55.6	17.6	23.8
1972	41.8	37.9	42.9	30.1	32.2	58.7	18.7	25.5
1973	44.4	40.7	47.9	32.7	34.5	62.8	20.6	27.9
1974	49.3	45.2	59.0	37.4	39.3	67.2	24.6	32.3
1975	53.8	50.1	65.9	42.8	43.9	71.2	28.8	40.2
1976	56.9	53.8	72.2	47.9	48.1	74.2	33.6	46.8
1977	60.6	58.1	78.1	53.8	52.7	76.9	40.1	54.2
1978	65.2	63.3	81.4	58.7	57.5	79.0	45.1	58.7
1979	72.6	69.1	84.4	65.1	63.6	82.3	52.1	66.6
1980	82.4	76.1	91.0	74.0	72.3	86.8	63.2	78.5
1981	90.9	85.6	95.3	83.2	82.0	92.2	75.4	87.9
1982	96.5	94.9	98.0	92.2	91.6	97.0	87.7	95.4
1983	99.6	100.4	99.8	100.2	100.5	100.3	100.8	99.8
1984	103.9	104.8	102.1	107.4	107.9	102.7	111.5	104.8
1985	107.6	108.9	104.1	114.0	114.2	104.8	121.1	111.1
1986	109.6	113.4	104.8	118.2	117.2	104.7	128.5	114.9
1987	113.6	118.4	104.9	122.2	120.9	104.9	134.4	119.7
1988	118.3	123.2	105.7	126.7	124.2	106.3	141.1	125.6
1989	124.0	129.3	108.0	133.3	128.6	109.2	150.4	135.4
1990	130.7	135.5	111.4	140.8	133.0	112.1	159.6	148.2
1991	136.2	143.1	115.0	147.9	137.2	116.0	169.8	156.9
1992	140.3	145.2	116.9	154.3	140.6	120.6	178.9	162.7
1993	144.5	147.9				125.5	186.4	165.3
1992: I	138.7	144.2	115.9	152.1	139.5	119.1	175.9	160.0
II	139.8	144.9	117.5	154.0	140.6	120.4	178.2	163.5
III	140.9	145.6	117.0	154.8	140.6	121.0	179.4	163.4
IV	141.9	146.1	117.4	156.2	141.3	122.1	181.7	164.0
1993: I	143.1	147.2	117.4	157.5	142.5	124.2	183.5	162.9
II	144.2	147.5	118.5	159.2	143.4	125.5	185.5	165.6
III	144.8	148.1	119.1	160.1	143.7	126.0	187.3	166.0
IV	145.8	148.8				126.6	189.2	166.6

[1] Consists of Belgium-Luxembourg, Denmark, France, Greece, Ireland, Italy, Netherlands, United Kingdom, Germany, Portugal, and Spain. Industrial production prior to July 1981 excludes data for Greece, which joined the EC in 1981. Data for Portugal and Spain, which became members on January 1, 1986 are excluded prior to 1982.
[2] Former West Germany.
[3] All data exclude construction. Quarterly data are seasonally adjusted.

Sources: National sources as reported by Department of Commerce (International Trade Administration, Office of Trade and Economic Analysis, Trade and Industry Statistics Division), Department of Labor (Bureau of Labor Statistics), and Board of Governors of the Federal Reserve System.

Figure 2–14 Industrial production and consumer prices, major industrial countries, 1967–1993.

7. From an examination of Figure 2–6, determine whether the U.S. real exchange rate appreciated or depreciated vis-à-vis European nations over 1960–1993. Explain briefly.

8. Would you expect China's real exchange rate vis-à-vis the United States to appreciate or depreciate over the next 20 years? Explain your reasoning.

3

Balance-of-Payments Accounts

3.1 Basic Concepts

This chapter's topic concerns a nation's balance-of-payments (BOP) accounts and their connection with its national income statistics. Accounting topics such as these are often unpopular with economists, but it is clear that some understanding is essential for anyone who wants to know about international monetary affairs or even purely domestic macroeconomic matters. And we already know from Section 1.3 that there have been some dramatic recent changes in the U.S. BOP accounts that cry out to be examined—the huge 1983–1984 jump in the current-account deficit, for example. Yet one cannot intelligently think about either causes or consequences unless one knows what it is that the current account measures.

The most straightforward way to gain an understanding of BOP concepts is to learn a lot of definitions and then work extensively with the accounts themselves until familiarity has been achieved. But a quicker and less painful way is to master a simple framework into which specific categories can be fit as needed. It is this latter approach that will be followed here.

Our framework requires the reader to begin by imagining a more primitive world in which the only type of international trade is straightforward importing and exporting of goods, with all payments made by means of an internationally accepted form of money, which we take to be gold. Then a summary set of BOP accounts might report only the period's net exports (exports minus imports) of goods and net exports (net payments) of gold:

Category	Net exports
Goods	100
Gold	− 100
Total	0

In the example, the nation in question had an excess of exports over imports to the extent of 100 monetary units, and as a result accumulated gold to that same extent—net exports of gold equal to − 100 implies a net importation and corresponding accumulation (addition to its stock of gold) of 100.

The world of that example is too primitive to be very useful, but suppose that we next imagine a world only slightly more complicated in which there are three categories: goods and services, financial claims, and gold. In this case there might be only one type of financial claim such as bonds or equity shares, or there might be many—stocks, bonds, bills, bank accounts, and so on. In any case, the BOP accounts for a period might then be as follows:

Category	Net exports
Goods and services	100
Financial claims	−80
Gold	−20
Total	0

Here the example again features a net export balance of 100 for the first category, which now pertains to services as well as goods. But in the postulated case the net buildup of gold—the net quantity of gold imported—is only 20, because financial-claim imports exceed exports by 80. The nation in question is exporting more goods and services than it imports, and is being paid for them largely by means of financial claims on the rest of the world, with only a fraction of the goods and services being paid for with gold. Any sort of mixture of the three net-export numbers is possible, it should be realized, so long as the total sums to zero. But it must be that the total does sum to zero, if the accounting is accurate, simply as a requirement that goods-and-service imbalances be either covered by financial-claim flows or paid for (with gold).

The only remaining step needed to convert the last system of accounts into one useful for our purposes is to relax the specification of the monetary medium that is used to settle accounts. But we can do so by recognizing that there are other assets besides gold that are internationally accepted as money. Let us then adopt the term "international reserves" to designate all of the acceptable settlement media, perhaps including gold as one type. In today's actual world, of course, most international reserves are simply claims on another country's central bank or treasury. Such claims are counted as reserves, however, only when held by or credited to the nation's official monetary authorities.

We are ready, at this point, to relate our three categories of net exports to three "balance" concepts that are of critical importance in BOP accounting. The relationship is as follows:

Net exports of:	BOP concept
Goods and services	Balance on current account
Financial claims	Balance on capital account
International reserves	−Balance on official reserve transactions

Thus "balance on current account" is used in actual BOP accounting to refer to a summation of items that essentially amounts to the nation's net exports of goods and services.[1] Similarly, "balance on capital account" will be used to mean basically the same thing as net exports of financial claims.[2] And the "balance on official reserve transactions" is equal to the sum of the previous two, a sum that also equals the net *imports* (negative of net exports) of international reserves. There are details that require discussion (some of these details will differ from country to country), but in basic outline, BOP accounts will accord with this three-way scheme.[3]

Before turning to a discussion that applies our framework to an actual set of accounts, it should be mentioned that, consistent with the principles of double-entry bookkeeping, every international transaction will involve two entries in our account categories. Most sales of goods to foreigners will, for example, involve an export item in the "goods and services" category and an import item in the "financial claims" category—the import of a financial claim being the acquisition of a claim on some foreign entity, such as an enhanced deposit balance with a foreign bank or the extension of a short-term loan to a foreign importing firm. Many transactions, however, involve the extension of two financial claims. These would be offsetting items and would therefore not show up in our simplified framework since it recognizes only *net* flows, as will be seen more clearly in the next section.

3.2 U.S. Accounts

Armed with our simplified three-item framework for thinking about BOP concepts, let us now turn to some actual tabulations for the United States, or, more precisely, for the residents of the United States. Figure 3–1 gives a reasonably brief and convenient presentation that appears annually in the *Economic Report of the President.*[4] There the balance on current account appears as the last column on the left-hand half of the tabulation, where it can be seen to comprise net exports of goods and services plus net receipt of investment income plus unilateral transfers. The latter component usually appears as a negative sum because transfers to foreigners normally exceed

[1] Here the qualifier "essentially" is needed for two reasons. First, services must be defined broadly so as to include net investment income, although this item is not now included in official U.S. tabulations. Second, the current account includes net receipts from unilateral transfers in addition to net exports of goods and services. But conceptually this is not actually much of an exception, since a unilateral transfer receipt can be thought of as a payment for a service of a highly intangible type.

[2] Unfortunately, it is also occasionally used in a different way, to refer to the sum of net exports of financial claims *and* reserves. That usage will be discussed later.

[3] An alternative presentation that is somewhat similar in spirit to ours is provided by Cumby and Levich (1992). It should be noted, however, that Cumby and Levich—and also some other writers including Caves, Frankel, and Jones (1990, p. 351)—define the official reserve transaction balance as the net *export* of reserves (i.e., the negative of our concept). When the term was (prior to 1976) used in the official U.S. accounts, however, it accorded with our definition.

[4] This particular tabulation appears as Table B-103 on pp. 386–387 of the 1994 *Economic Report of the President*. The latter publication is prepared once each year by the President's Council of Economic Advisers, to be used in his budget proposals to Congress.

Year or quarter	Merchandise [1] [2]			Services			Investment income			Balance on goods, services, and income	Unilateral transfers, net [4]	Balance on current account
	Exports	Imports	Net	Net military transactions [3] [4]	Net travel and transportation receipts	Other services, net	Receipts on U.S. assets abroad	Payments on foreign assets in U.S.	Net			
1946	11,764	−5,067	6,697	−424	733	310	772	−212	560	7,876	−2,991	4,885
1947	16,097	−5,973	10,124	−358	946	145	1,102	−245	857	11,714	−2,722	8,992
1948	13,265	−7,557	5,708	−351	374	175	1,921	−437	1,484	7,390	−4,973	2,417
1949	12,213	−6,874	5,339	−410	230	208	1,831	−476	1,355	6,722	−5,849	873
1950	10,203	−9,081	1,122	−56	−120	242	2,068	−559	1,509	2,697	−4,537	−1,840
1951	14,243	−11,176	3,067	169	298	254	2,633	−583	2,050	5,838	−4,954	884
1952	13,449	−10,838	2,611	528	83	309	2,751	−555	2,196	5,727	−5,113	614
1953	12,412	−10,975	1,437	1,753	−238	307	2,736	−624	2,112	5,371	−6,657	−1,286
1954	12,929	−10,353	2,576	902	−269	305	2,929	−582	2,347	5,861	−5,642	219
1955	14,424	−11,527	2,897	−113	−297	299	3,406	−676	2,730	5,516	−5,086	430
1956	17,556	−12,803	4,753	−221	−361	447	3,837	−735	3,102	7,720	−4,990	2,730
1957	19,562	−13,291	6,271	−423	−189	482	4,180	−796	3,384	9,525	−4,763	4,762
1958	16,414	−12,952	3,462	−849	−633	486	3,790	−825	2,965	5,431	−4,647	784
1959	16,458	−15,310	1,148	−831	−821	573	4,132	−1,061	3,071	3,140	−4,422	−1,282
1960	19,650	−14,758	4,892	−1,057	−964	639	4,616	−1,238	3,379	6,886	−4,062	2,824
1961	20,108	−14,537	5,571	−1,131	−978	732	4,999	−1,245	3,755	7,949	−4,127	3,822
1962	20,781	−16,260	4,521	−912	−1,152	912	5,618	−1,324	4,294	7,664	−4,277	3,387
1963	22,272	−17,048	5,224	−742	−1,309	1,036	6,157	−1,560	4,596	8,806	−4,392	4,414
1964	25,501	−18,700	6,801	−794	−1,146	1,161	6,824	−1,783	5,041	11,063	−4,240	6,823
1965	26,461	−21,510	4,951	−487	−1,280	1,480	7,437	−2,088	5,350	10,014	−4,583	5,431
1966	29,310	−25,493	3,817	−1,043	−1,331	1,497	7,528	−2,481	5,047	7,987	−4,955	3,031
1967	30,666	−26,866	3,800	−1,187	−1,750	1,742	8,021	−2,747	5,274	7,878	−5,294	2,583
1968	33,626	−32,991	635	−596	−1,548	1,759	9,367	−3,378	5,990	6,240	−5,629	611
1969	36,414	−35,807	607	−718	−1,763	1,964	10,913	−4,869	6,044	6,135	−5,735	399
1970	42,469	−39,866	2,603	−641	−2,038	2,330	11,748	−5,515	6,233	8,486	−6,156	2,331
1971	43,319	−45,579	−2,260	653	−2,345	2,649	12,707	−5,435	7,272	5,969	−7,402	−1,433
1972	49,381	−55,797	−6,416	1,072	−3,063	2,965	14,765	−6,572	8,192	2,749	−8,544	−5,795
1973	71,410	−70,499	911	740	−3,158	3,406	21,808	−9,655	12,153	14,053	−6,913	7,140
1974	98,306	−103,811	−5,505	165	−3,184	4,231	27,587	−12,084	15,503	11,210	[5] −9,249	1,962
1975	107,088	−98,185	8,903	1,461	−2,812	4,854	25,351	−12,564	12,787	25,191	−7,075	18,116
1976	114,745	−124,228	−9,483	931	−2,558	5,027	29,375	−13,311	16,063	9,982	−5,686	4,295
1977	120,816	−151,907	−31,091	1,731	−3,565	5,680	32,354	−14,217	18,137	−9,109	−5,226	−14,335
1978	142,075	−176,002	−33,927	857	−3,573	6,879	42,088	−21,680	20,408	−9,355	−5,788	−15,143
1979	184,439	−212,007	−27,568	−1,313	−2,935	7,251	63,834	−32,961	30,873	6,308	−6,593	−285
1980	224,250	−249,750	−25,500	−1,822	−997	8,912	72,606	−42,532	30,073	10,666	−8,349	2,317
1981	237,044	−265,067	−28,023	−844	144	12,552	86,529	−53,626	32,903	16,732	−11,702	5,030
1982	211,157	−247,642	−36,485	112	−992	13,209	86,200	−56,412	29,788	5,632	−17,075	−11,443
1983	201,799	−268,901	−67,102	−563	−4,227	14,095	84,778	−53,700	31,078	−26,719	−17,741	−44,460
1984	219,926	−332,418	−112,492	−2,547	−8,438	14,277	99,056	−69,572	29,483	−79,716	−20,612	−100,328
1985	215,915	−338,088	−122,173	−4,390	−9,798	14,266	89,489	−68,314	21,175	−100,920	−22,950	−123,870
1986	223,344	−368,425	−145,081	−5,181	−7,382	18,855	87,497	−74,736	12,761	−126,028	−24,176	−150,203
1987	250,208	−409,765	−159,557	−3,844	−6,481	17,900	95,129	−87,403	7,726	−144,256	−23,052	−167,308
1988	320,230	−447,189	−126,959	−6,315	−1,511	19,961	122,275	−109,653	12,621	−102,203	−24,965	−127,168
1989	362,116	−477,365	−115,249	−6,726	5,071	26,558	144,904	−130,091	14,813	−75,532	−26,092	−101,624
1990	389,303	−498,336	−109,033	−7,833	8,979	29,505	151,201	−130,853	20,348	−58,034	−33,827	−91,861
1991	416,937	−490,739	−73,802	−5,851	17,933	33,799	127,292	−114,272	13,021	−14,899	6,575	−8,324
1992	440,138	−536,276	−96,138	−2,751	19,718	39,444	110,612	−104,391	6,222	−33,505	−32,895	−66,400
1991:												
I	101,333	−120,123	−18,790	−2,532	2,926	7,935	36,018	−30,247	5,771	−4,690	14,096	9,406
II	104,206	−120,525	−16,319	−1,402	4,299	8,397	32,057	−29,147	2,910	−2,115	3,884	1,769
III	103,764	−123,404	−19,640	−1,164	5,228	8,660	30,074	−28,447	1,627	−5,289	−6,564	−11,853
IV	107,634	−126,687	−19,053	−755	5,481	8,809	29,144	−26,431	2,713	−2,805	−4,839	−7,644
1992:												
I	108,347	−126,110	−17,763	−571	5,011	9,608	29,028	−24,609	4,419	704	−7,389	−6,685
II	108,306	−133,107	−24,801	−727	5,201	9,177	28,641	−27,734	907	−10,243	−8,010	−18,253
III	109,493	−137,105	−27,612	−617	4,882	11,016	27,195	−25,492	1,703	−10,628	−7,147	−17,775
IV	113,992	−139,954	−25,962	−836	4,624	9,641	25,749	−26,555	−806	−13,339	−10,348	−23,687
1993:												
I	111,530	−140,839	−29,309	−145	5,014	9,755	26,078	−26,115	−37	−14,722	−7,586	−22,308
II	113,118	−147,502	−34,384	−226	5,372	9,313	27,876	−27,829	47	−19,878	−7,294	−27,172
III ᴾ	111,912	−148,191	−36,279	−341	5,279	9,169	28,695	−26,947	1,748	−20,424	−7,562	−27,986

[1] Excludes military.
[2] Adjusted from Census data for differences in valuation, coverage, and timing.
[3] Quarterly data are not seasonally adjusted.
[4] Includes transfers of goods and services under U.S. military grant programs.

See next page for continuation of table.

Figure 3–1 Balance-of-payments accounts from *Economic Report of the President,* 1994. (Millions of dollars; quarterly data seasonally adjusted, except as noted.)

Year or quarter	U.S. assets abroad, net [increase/capital outflow (−)]				Foreign assets in the U.S., net [increase/capital inflow (+)]			Allocations of special drawing rights (SDRs)	Statistical discrepancy	
	Total	U.S. official reserve assets [3][6]	Other U.S. Government assets	U.S. private assets	Total	Foreign official assets [3]	Other foreign assets		Total (sum of the items with sign reversed)	Of which: Seasonal adjustment discrepancy
1946		−623								
1947		−3,315								
1948		−1,736								
1949		−266								
1950		1,758								
1951		−33								
1952		−415								
1953		1,256								
1954		480								
1955		182								
1956		−869								
1957		−1,165								
1958		2,292								
1959		1,035								
1960	−4,099	2,145	−1,100	−5,144	2,294	1,473	821		−1,019	
1961	−5,538	607	−910	−5,235	2,705	765	1,939		−989	
1962	−4,174	1,535	−1,085	−4,623	1,911	1,270	641		−1,124	
1963	−7,270	378	−1,662	−5,986	3,217	1,986	1,231		−360	
1964	−9,560	171	−1,680	−8,050	3,643	1,660	1,983		−907	
1965	−5,716	1,225	−1,605	−5,336	742	134	607		−457	
1966	−7,321	570	−1,543	−6,347	3,661	−672	4,333		629	
1967	−9,757	53	−2,423	−7,386	7,379	3,451	3,928		−205	
1968	−10,977	−870	−2,274	−7,833	9,928	−774	10,703		438	
1969	−11,585	−1,179	−2,200	−8,206	12,702	−1,301	14,002		−1,516	
1970	−9,337	2,481	−1,589	−10,229	6,359	6,908	−550	867	−219	
1971	−12,475	2,349	−1,884	−12,940	22,970	26,879	−3,909	717	−9,779	
1972	−14,497	−4	−1,568	−12,925	21,461	10,475	10,986	710	−1,879	
1973	−22,874	158	−2,644	−20,388	18,388	6,026	12,362		−2,654	
1974	−34,745	−1,467	[5]366	−33,643	34,241	10,546	23,696		−1,458	
1975	−39,703	−849	−3,474	−35,380	15,670	7,027	8,643		5,917	
1976	−51,269	−2,558	−4,214	−44,498	36,518	17,693	18,826		10,455	
1977	−34,785	−375	−3,693	−30,717	51,319	36,816	14,503		−2,199	
1978	−61,130	732	−4,660	−57,202	64,036	33,678	30,358		12,236	
1979	−66,054	−1,133	−3,746	−61,176	38,752	−13,665	52,416	1,139	26,449	
1980	−86,967	−8,155	−5,162	−73,651	58,112	15,497	42,615	1,152	25,386	
1981	−114,147	−5,175	−5,097	−103,875	83,032	4,960	78,072	1,093	24,992	
1982	−122,335	−4,965	−6,131	−111,239	92,418	3,593	88,826		41,359	
1983	−58,735	−1,196	−5,006	−52,533	83,380	5,845	77,534		19,815	
1984	−29,654	−3,131	−5,489	−21,035	102,010	3,140	98,870		27,972	
1985	−34,687	−3,858	−2,821	−28,009	130,966	−1,119	132,084		27,592	
1986	−91,260	312	−2,022	−89,551	223,191	35,648	187,543		18,272	
1987	−61,254	9,149	1,006	−71,408	229,972	45,387	184,585		−1,410	
1988	−91,423	−3,912	2,967	−90,477	219,489	39,758	179,731		−899	
1989	−129,331	−25,293	1,259	−105,297	213,571	8,503	205,068		17,384	
1990	−44,132	−2,158	2,307	−44,280	105,173	34,198	70,975		30,820	
1991	−59,974	5,763	2,905	−68,643	83,439	17,564	65,875		−15,140	
1992	−50,961	3,901	−1,609	−53,253	129,579	40,684	88,895		−12,218	
1991:										
I	−5,555	−353	559	−5,761	−20	5,604	−5,624		−3,831	4,710
II	−875	1,014	−419	−1,470	7,120	−4,924	12,044		−8,014	−120
III	−15,672	3,877	3,224	−22,774	23,514	3,855	19,659		4,011	−6,506
IV	−37,870	1,225	−459	−38,637	52,826	13,029	39,798		−7,312	1,911
1992:										
I	−1,029	−1,057	−275	303	19,834	21,124	−1,290		−12,120	4,878
II	−8,695	1,464	−293	−9,866	44,450	21,008	23,442		17,502	653
III	−10,798	1,952	−305	−12,445	26,450	−7,378	33,828		2,123	−6,754
IV	−30,438	1,542	−737	−31,243	38,845	5,931	32,914		15,280	1,222
1993:										
I	−12,358	−983	535	−11,910	25,718	10,929	14,789		8,948	5,814
II	−29,341	822	−275	−29,888	42,380	17,699	24,681		14,133	681
III [p]	−43,961	−545	−86	−43,331	66,452	19,646	46,806		5,495	−7,605

[5] Includes extraordinary U.S. Government transactions with India.
[6] Consists of gold, special drawing rights, foreign currencies, and the U.S. reserve position in the International Monetary Fund (IMF).
Source: Department of Commerce, Bureau of Economic Analysis.

(*Figure 3–1 continued*)

transfer receipts from foreign to U.S. residents.[5] (1991 was an exceptional year for the reason mentioned in section 1.3.) Merchandise exports and imports are shown separately, with their net export sum appearing in the third column. Services then show up in the next three columns in three categories: military transactions, travel and transportation, and other services. Next, regarding investment income little explanation should be required, except to say that it comprises (net) interest earnings, profits repatriated, and so forth, and is similar to the export of services in that such flows can be regarded as payments for the services yielded by "capital" (i.e., invested wealth). Indeed, the column 10 "balance on goods, services, and income" was until recently labeled "balance on goods and services," with net investment income being treated as a part of the services category.

Turning now to the accounts in the right-hand half of the tabulation it becomes more difficult to identify the columns with our concepts of "balance on capital account" (net export of financial claims) and "balance on official reserve transactions" (net import of reserves). That identification can be made, however, by noting that the second and sixth column headings include the word "official." By adding these two columns together we total the change in foreign official assets (e.g., claims on the German government) held by the Fed (column 2) and dollar claims on the U.S. government held by foreign-country officials (column 6). The resulting figure will be analogous to net *exports* of gold since the figure in column 2 is negative when the U.S. buildup of claims on foreign officials is positive. So the sum of columns 2 and 6 consitutes the negative of the U.S. balance on official reserve transactions, sometimes referred to as the balance on "official settlements."[6]

The remainder of the columns of the right-hand side—columns 3, 4, 7, 8, and 9—can then be added to give the balance on capital account. Conceptually, it will be recalled, this account balance amounts to net exports of financial claims. Thus the large negative numbers in column 4 indicate that private U.S. firms have been importing claims on foreigners, that is, increasing their stock of claims. At the same time, the positive numbers in column 7 indicate that the United States has been exporting claims on assets located in the United States, such as land, office buildings in Los Angeles, or shares of U.S. corporations. During the period from 1970 through 1982, the negative figures in column 4 were larger than the positive figures in column 7, implying that the sum of the two was a net import item, in other words, that the United States was adding to its claims on foreigners faster than foreigners were adding to their claims on the United States. Since 1983, however, that situation has altered and for 1983 through 1992 these two columns indicate a net export of private financial

---

[5] Private and governmental transfers to Israel are a major component.

[6] Official presentations of the U.S. accounts were altered during the 1970s so as to deflect attention from the balance on official settlements, the justification being that this balance does not possess its usual meaning for the United States because of the special role of the dollar as a currency that is widely held by other nations as an international reserve. An account equivalent to our balance on official reserve transactions appears in the presentation currently used by the IMF under the designation "overall balance."

Table 3–1 BOP Summary

Net exports of	1965	1970	1975	1980	1985	1990
Goods and services (current-account balance)	5.4	2.3	18.1	2.3	−123.9	−91.9
Financial claims (capital-account balance)	−6.7	−11.7	−24.3	−9.7	128.8	59.8
International reserves (−official reserve transactions balance)	1.3	9.4	6.2	7.3	−5.0	32.0

claims—foreigners were adding to their claims on the United States faster than U.S. citizens were adding to their claims on foreigners. In blunt language, U.S. residents have recently been paying for a large excess of imports over exports by borrowing from abroad and selling off ownership rights to property.

Columns 8 and 9 require brief mention. The first refers to changes in (additions to) the U.S. allocation of special drawing rights (SDRs) with the IMF;[7] when any such allocation is assigned and payment made to the IMF, there is a counterpart entry (of negative sign) in column 2. The second of these columns, i.e., Column 9 appears in the tabulation because of accounting errors and omissions that would keep the sum of current account, capital account, and official reserve items from totalling to zero (as they should, conceptually). With the "statistical discrepancy" included, therefore, the sum of columns 1, 5, 8, and 9 from the right-hand page plus the current-account balance (left-hand page) will equal zero precisely. Alternatively, the total of the current account plus columns 1, 5, and 8 will equal the statistical discrepancy (with its sign reversed from that in column 9).

Let us now use the table in Figure 3–1 to compile, for a few selected years, accounts corresponding to the three-item framework outlined above. Doing so, including SDR allocations and the statistical discrepancy in with the capital account,[8] we obtain the values listed in Table 3–1.

In Table 3–1 the dramatic shift in both current- and capital-account totals beginning in 1983 is quite prominent. Readers should test their understanding of the material to this point by attempting to derive for themselves the entries in this simplified tabulation.

An alternative tabular arrangement that is sometimes used is attractive in some respects. This arrangement puts net exports of goods and services and financial claims "above the line" and equates their sum to net *imports* of international reserves entered "below the line," as shown in Table 3–2.

In Table 3–2 the totals above and below the line are equal, except for rounding discrepancies, and the sum below the line equals the balance on official

---

[7] The IMF was set up at the Bretton Woods Conference of 1944 to manage the system of fixed exchange rates that prevailed between 1948 and 1971. Some discussion will appear in Chapter 4.

[8] This choice is somewhat arbitrary, but is partially justified by the belief that records are much better for flows of reserves and goods and services than for financial claims. So the errors are apt to be largest in the capital account.

Table 3–2 BOP Summary, Alternative Arrangement

	1965	1970	1975	1980	1985	1990
Net exports of:						
Goods and services	5.4	2.3	18.1	2.3	−123.9	−91.9
Financial claims	−6.7	−11.7	−24.3	−9.7	128.8	59.8
Net import of:						
International reserves	−1.3	−9.4	−6.2	−7.3	5.0	−32.0

reserve transactions. Thus it measures the nation's gain in international reserves, net of official foreign claims on its own central bank, rather than its loss (exports) of reserves.

With this type of arrangement it is easy to devise many different "balance" measures by including different subsets of financial claims in the second category above the line and thereby affecting the contents of the total entered below the line. One example would be to include only long-term financial claims above the line, thereby adding net imports of short-term private and (non-reserve) official claims in with net imports of reserves below the line. This would give a total that was reported in the U.S. accounts for a number of years under the title of "basic balance." In general, many different measures of BOP "imbalance" can be devised by inclusion of different categories in the two groups located above the line. All such measures are, of course, somewhat arbitrary. The reason for placing emphasis on the current account and official settlements balance measures is that they result from two "natural" groupings. Specifically, the current-account balance results when we include *no* financial assets above the line; the result is a measure of the net imports of all types of financial claims (including reserves) below the line so that the balance on current account equals the change in the nation's net asset position vis-à-vis the rest of the world—clearly an important magnitude. The official settlements arrangement includes all financial claims except international reserves above the line, so the balance on official settlements pertains to the net increase in foreign reserves held by the central bank (or other officials), "net" meaning that account is taken of foreign-held official claims on the central bank. It should be noted that for most nations their currency (or claims to it) is held in small amounts if at all by other central banks, so their official settlements balance is virtually identical to the increase in their own holdings of international reserves—another important figure.

The tabulation from the *Economic Report of the President* given in Figure 3–1 is a very convenient one, but does not include much detail. Another version of the U.S. BOP accounts that includes somewhat more detail concerning transactions is presented in Figure 3–2. Clearly, this tabulation includes more entries, representing finer categories, than those recognized in Figure 3–1. As for the three main summary totals, the reader will find the current-account balance—the sum of lines 1, 15, and 29—on line 70. Totals corresponding to the capital and official reserve transaction (ORT) balances are not shown, but can readily be found. The quickest way is to calculate the ORT balance as the negative of the sum of lines 34 and 49, and then obtain the capital-account balance as the ORT value minus the current-account balance. For 1992, for example, we would have an ORT balance of −44.6 billion dollars (3.9 + 40.7 = 44.6) and a capital-account balance of −44.6 −(−66.4) = 21.8 billion dollars.

The foregoing representation of the ORT balance, as the negative of the sum of lines 34 and 49, corresponds to the one given previously that sums columns 2 and 6 of the right-hand half of Figure 3–1. It might be mentioned that there is a small correction that should actually be made, although we shall not typically do so. This correction would be to omit line 53, the change in "other U.S. government liabilities," when summing lines 34 and 49. That this small correction should be made, because the U.S. liabilities in question are not regarded as foreign exchange reserves by other nations, can be discovered by examining the version of Figure 3–2 that appeared in the *Survey of Current Business* prior to April 1990. In the March 1990 issue, and other earlier issues, a memorandum line giving the ORT balance was included and corresponded to the sum as just described, that is, with line 53 omitted. Then in 1990 the Commerce Department revised its reporting so that now the official settlements balance does not appear at all. This step continued the process of downplaying this balance concept, as mentioned in footnote 6. The official justification given in 1976, when several balances were eliminated or demoted in status, involved the altered nature of responsibilities under floating exchange rates. In addition, there have been suggestions that the unique role of the U.S. dollar as an international reserve currency deprives the U.S. official settlements balance of any meaning that it might have for more typical nations. For some discussion of these issues see Stern et al. (1977) and pp. 18–27 of the June 1976 issue of the *Survey of Current Business*.[9]

A point that needs to be mentioned involves the credit–debit conventions used in official tables and in most discussions of BOP accounting. In Figure 3–1, and especially in Figure 3–2, it will be seen that many items are entered with minus signs attached. Regarding these, the usual discussion of BOP accounting stipulates that "credit items are entered as positive numbers and debit items as negative numbers." It is then necessary to define credit and debit items, and the usual definitions are different for different categories of accounts. See, for example, the headings in the capital-account items of Figure 3–1. Our three-item framework, by contrast, focuses on net exports of three types of items—goods and services, financial claims, and international reserves. Each is entered as a positive number if a positive net export occurs. Accordingly, our procedure implicitly defines each credit item as an export and each debit item as an import, under the stipulation that every item is viewed as an export or import of either (1) goods and services, (2) financial claims, or (3) international

[9] Also, for a more extensive discussion of the U.S. accounts, see Rivera-Batiz and Rivera-Batiz (1994).

Figure 3–2 Balance-of-payments accounts from *Survey of Current Business*, 1994. (Millions of dollars.)

Line	(Credits +; debits –)[1]	1992	1993[r]	Not seasonally adjusted				Seasonally adjusted			
				1993				1993			
				I	II	III[r]	IV[r]	I[r]	II[r]	III[r]	IV[r]
1	Exports of goods, services, and income	730,460	753,898	183,832	189,162	185,740	195,163	183,969	187,679	187,200	195,065
2	Merchandise, adjusted, excluding military[2]	440,138	456,766	112,023	115,811	108,147	120,785	111,480	113,067	111,935	120,234
3	Services[3]	179,710	186,792	45,171	45,628	50,185	45,808	46,476	46,810	46,856	46,654
4	Transfers under U.S. military agency sales contracts[4]	11,015	11,259	3,058	2,950	2,830	2,422	3,058	2,950	2,830	2,422
5	Travel	53,861	56,501	12,384	14,093	16,973	13,051	13,898	14,186	14,285	14,132
6	Passenger fares	17,353	17,849	4,022	4,404	5,360	4,064	4,445	4,530	4,475	4,399
7	Other transportation	22,773	23,508	5,732	5,839	5,856	6,081	5,894	5,894	5,760	5,999
8	Royalties and license fees[5]	20,238	20,414	4,697	5,095	4,952	5,670	4,898	5,223	5,174	5,119
9	Other private services[5]	53,601	56,434	15,115	12,958	14,030	14,331	14,156	13,737	14,148	14,394
10	U.S. Government miscellaneous services	869	827	165	290	184	189	165	290	184	189
11	Income receipts on U.S. assets abroad	110,612	110,339	26,638	27,723	27,408	28,571	26,003	27,802	28,409	28,127
12	Direct investment receipts	49,888	55,815	13,205	14,336	13,535	14,739	12,696	14,339	14,546	14,236
13	Other private receipts	53,687	49,527	12,043	12,297	12,446	12,741	12,043	12,297	12,446	12,741
14	U.S. Government receipts	7,038	4,997	1,390	1,090	1,427	1,090	1,254	1,166	1,417	1,150
15	Imports of goods, services, and income	-763,995	-830,631	-191,037	-207,817	-213,362	-218,415	-198,742	-207,814	-207,700	-216,578
16	Merchandise, adjusted, excluding military[2]	-536,276	-589,244	-136,194	-146,288	-150,099	-156,663	-140,805	-147,465	-147,907	-153,067
17	Services[3]	-123,299	-131,114	-29,399	-33,272	-35,875	-32,569	-31,822	-32,320	-33,001	-33,973
18	Direct defense expenditures	-13,766	-12,286	-3,203	-3,176	-2,958	-2,950	-3,203	-3,176	-2,958	-2,950
19	Travel	-39,872	-42,329	-8,396	-11,387	-13,077	-9,470	-10,446	-10,263	-10,594	-11,026
20	Passenger fares	-10,943	-11,256	-2,404	-2,895	-3,190	-2,767	-2,760	-2,743	-2,790	-2,963
21	Other transportation	-23,454	-24,511	-5,847	-6,092	-6,311	-6,261	-5,930	-6,184	-6,144	-6,254
22	Royalties and license fees[5]	-4,986	-4,748	-1,071	-1,174	-1,252	-1,251	-1,088	-1,201	-1,232	-1,227
23	Other private services[5]	-27,998	-33,595	-7,884	-7,977	-8,453	-9,281	-7,801	-8,182	-8,649	-8,963
24	U.S. Government miscellaneous services	-2,290	-2,388	-594	-571	-634	-590	-594	-571	-634	-590
25	Income payments on foreign assets in the United States	-104,391	-110,273	-25,445	-28,257	-27,389	-29,183	-26,115	-27,829	-26,792	-29,538
26	Direct investment payments	-1,630	-9,837	-795	-3,132	-2,602	-309	-1,465	-2,704	-2,005	-3,664
27	Other private payments	-61,582	-58,545	-14,240	-14,820	-14,201	-15,284	-14,240	-14,820	-14,201	-15,284
28	U.S. Government payments	-41,179	-41,891	-10,410	-10,305	-10,586	-10,590	-10,410	-10,305	-10,586	-10,590
29	Unilateral transfers, net	-32,895	-32,509	-7,471	-7,022	-7,381	-10,636	-7,592	-7,300	-7,591	-10,025
30	U.S. Government grants[4]	-14,688	-14,438	-3,242	-2,730	-3,029	-5,437	-3,242	-2,730	-3,029	-5,437
31	U.S. Government pensions and other transfers	-3,735	-3,946	-679	-954	-728	-1,585	-985	-986	-985	-989
32	Private remittances and other transfers[6]	-14,473	-14,126	-3,550	-3,338	-3,624	-3,614	-3,365	-3,584	-3,577	-3,600
33	U.S. assets abroad, net (increase/capital outflow (–))[7]	-50,961	-143,872	-13,676	-31,201	-44,492	-54,503	-12,715	-29,697	-43,398	-58,062
34	U.S. official reserve assets, net[7]	3,901	-1,379	-983	822	-545	-673	-983	822	-545	-673
35	Gold										

(Figure 3–2 continued)

Line		1	2	3	4	5	6	7	8	9	10
36	Special drawing rights	2,316	-537	-140	-166	-118	-113	-140	-166	-118	-113
37	Reserve position in the International Monetary Fund	-2,692	-4	-228	313	-48	-80	-228	313	-48	-80
38	Foreign currencies	4,277	-797	-615	675	-378	-480	-615	675	-378	-480
39	U.S. Government assets, other than official reserve assets, net	-1,609	-106	535	-275	-181	-186	535	-275	-180	-186
40	U.S. credits and other long-term assets	-7,140	-5,642	-940	-727	-1,536	-2,438	-940	-727	-1,536	-2,438
41	Repayments on U.S. credits and other long-term assets	5,596	5,891	1,807	859	1,924	1,301	1,807	859	1,924	1,301
42	U.S. foreign currency holdings and U.S. short-term assets, net [8]	-65	-355	-332	-407	-568	951	-332	-407	-568	951
43	U.S. private assets, net	-53,253	-142,388	-13,228	-31,749	-43,766	-53,644	-12,267	-30,244	-42,674	-57,203
44	Direct investment	-34,791	-50,244	-9,620	-13,411	-9,441	-17,771	-8,659	-11,906	-8,349	-21,330
45	Foreign securities	-47,961	-125,377	-26,889	-24,098	-45,794	-28,596	-26,889	-24,098	-45,794	-28,596
46	U.S. claims on unaffiliated foreigners reported by U.S. nonbanking concerns	4,551	n.a.	-4,774	443	2,982	n.a.	-4,774	443	2,982	n.a.
47	U.S. claims reported by U.S. banks, not included elsewhere	24,948	34,582	28,055	5,317	8,487	-7,277	28,055	5,317	8,487	-7,277
48	Foreign assets in the United States, net (increase/capital inflow (+))	129,579	226,300	25,218	43,426	72,324	85,412	25,875	42,537	71,637	86,330
49	Foreign official assets in the United States, net	40,684	71,225	10,929	17,699	19,237	23,360	10,929	17,699	19,237	23,360
50	U.S. Government securities [9]	22,403	52,791	1,749	6,750	20,443	23,349	1,749	6,750	20,443	23,349
51	U.S. Treasury securities	18,454	48,700	1,039	5,668	19,098	22,895	1,039	5,668	19,098	22,995
52	Other	3,949	4,091	710	1,082	1,345	954	710	1,082	1,345	954
53	Other U.S. Government liabilities [10]	2,542	1,890	-395	396	1,105	784	-395	396	1,105	784
54	U.S. liabilities reported by U.S. banks, not included elsewhere [11]	16,427	13,959	8,171	9,454	-2,495	-1,171	8,171	9,454	-2,495	-1,171
55	Other foreign official assets [12]	-688	2,585	1,404	1,099	184	-102	1,404	1,099	184	-102
56	Other foreign assets in the United States, net	88,895	155,154	14,289	25,727	53,087	62,052	14,946	24,838	52,400	62,970
57	Direct investment	2,378	31,519	8,101	11,345	3,346	8,728	8,758	10,456	2,659	9,646
58	U.S. Treasury securities	36,893	24,328	13,599	-623	3,474	7,878	13,599	-623	3,474	7,878
59	U.S. securities other than U.S. Treasury securities	30,274	79,612	9,394	15,025	17,257	37,936	9,394	15,025	17,257	37,336
60	U.S. liabilities to unaffiliated foreigners reported by U.S. nonbanking concerns	741	n.a.	2,057	1,361	4,069	n.a.	2,057	1,361	4,069	n.a.
61	U.S. liabilities reported by U.S. banks, not included elsewhere	18,659	12,208	-18,862	-1,381	24,941	7,510	-18,862	-1,381	24,941	7,510
62	Allocations of special drawing rights										
63	Statistical discrepancy (sum of above items with sign reversed)	-12,218	26,735	3,134	13,452	7,171	2,979	9,215	14,395	-148	3,271
63a	Of which seasonal adjustment discrepancy							6,082	943	-7,319	292
	Memoranda:										
64	Balance on merchandise trade (lines 2 and 16)	-96,138	-132,478	-24,171	-30,477	-41,952	-35,878	-29,325	-34,398	-35,972	-32,783
65	Balance on services (lines 3 and 17)	56,411	55,679	15,773	12,356	14,310	13,228	14,654	14,490	13,855	12,581
66	Balance on goods and services (lines 64 and 65)	-39,727	-76,799	-8,398	-18,121	-27,642	-22,640	-14,671	-19,908	-22,117	-20,102
67	Balance on investment income (lines 11 and 25)	6,222	66	1,193	-534	-534	-612	-112	-27	1,617	-1,411
68	Balance on goods, services, and income (lines 1 and 15 or lines 66 and 67) [13]	-33,505	-76,733	-7,205	-18,655	-27,622	-23,252	-14,783	-19,935	-20,500	-21,513
69	Unilateral transfers, net (line 29)	-32,895	-32,509	-7,471	-7,022	-7,381	-10,536	-7,592	-7,300	-7,300	-10,026
70	Balance on current account (lines 1, 15, and 29 or lines 68 and 69) [13]	-66,400	-109,242	-14,676	-25,677	-35,003	-33,888	-22,375	-27,235	-28,091	-31,539

reserves. Adherence to that convention, which can be facilitated by thinking of international reserves as if they were gold, will lead to correct classifications without the need for various definitions of what constitutes credits and debits.

Another point that needs to be mentioned is concerned with terminology pertaining to the capital account. Specifically, it needs to be emphasized that many writers will refer to the foreign purchase of home-country securities (i.e., claims on home-country residents) as involving a "capital import." Thus these writers use the term "import of capital" to refer to the same transaction that our terminology would designate as an "export of financial claims." Presumably the idea is that this transaction tends to give rise to an inflow of money—but, if so, that will show up as an import of reserves (as the balancing item required by double-entry bookkeeping). To the present author, this "capital import" terminology seems conceptually misleading. But it needs to be recognized and understood, so that financial-page analysis as well as scientific analysis can be read without misunderstanding.

3.3 BOP and National Income Accounts

Having explored in an introductory way the topic of BOP accounts, we need now to consider how these accounts are related to concepts of national income accounting. All readers will be familiar from introductory macroeconomics with the division of a nation's gross domestic product (GDP), a measure of its total output, into components reflecting different uses. For a closed economy—one without any foreign trade—we have

$$Y = C + I + G \tag{1}$$

where Y is total production (equivalent to total income), whereas C, I, and G denote the portions devoted to private consumption, investment (i.e., capital formation), and government purchases, respectively. But in an open economy the goods and services available include imports IM as well as Y, whereas the uses include exports EX as well as C, I, and G:

$$Y + \text{IM} = C + I + G + \text{EX}. \tag{2}$$

Letting $X = \text{EX} - \text{IM}$ denote net exports of goods and services, we then have

$$Y = C + I + G + X \tag{3}$$

as the basic national income accounting identity for an open economy. For the United States, these figures can be found in various columns of Figure 3–3, which reproduces the basic national income and product accounts (NIPA) Table B–1 from the 1994 *Economic Report of the President*. In particular, net exports appear as the first column on the right-hand page.

Table 3–3 Comparison of X and Current Account Balance

Year	Net Exports of Goods and Services, BOP accounts	Net Investment Income	Net Unilateral Transfers	Balance on Current Account
1965	4.7	5.3	−4.6	5.4
1970	2.3	6.2	−6.2	2.3
1975	12.4	12.8	−7.1	18.1
1980	−19.4	30.1	−8.3	2.3
1985	−122.1	21.2	−22.9	−123.9
1990	−78.4	20.3	−33.8	−91.9

In Equation (3), X has been defined as net exports of goods and services. In many analytical writings, this sum is treated as approximately equal to the balance on current account. It is recognized that the concepts differ slightly, but presumed that for practical purposes they can be treated as equivalent. Let us accordingly examine the difference. Examination of Figure 3–1 shows that the current-account balance equals the sum of net "unilateral transfers" and "balance on goods, services, and income." The latter in turn equals net exports of goods and services plus net investment income, that is, net receipts of interest, dividends, and so on. Actual figures for some recent years are given in Table 3–3.

In Table 3–3 the first column is obtained by adding columns 3, 4, 5, and 6 of Figure 3–1 (or, equivalently, subtracting column 9 from column 10). From columns 1 and 4 it appears that net exports of goods and services does indeed approximate the current-account balance reasonably well, although the discrepancy can be significant (as it was in 1975 and 1990). Accordingly, we shall occasionally follow this practice of treating the current-account balance and net exports (of goods and services) as it they were the same total.

It will be noted, incidentally, that the figures for net exports of goods and services obtained from the BOP accounts (Figure 3–1) do not agree precisely with those in the national income accounts (Figure 3–3), as illustrated in Table 3–4. Conceptually, however, these items are essentially equivalent. The discrepancy in the published numbers results from a few minor statistical

Table 3–4 Net Exports of Goods and Services ($ bil)

Year	BOP Accounts	NIPA Accounts
1965	4.7	3.9
1970	2.3	1.2
1975	12.4	13.6
1980	−19.4	−14.7
1985	−122.1	−115.6
1990	−78.4	−71.4

56 — *Basic Concepts*

| Year or quarter | Gross domestic product | Personal consumption expenditures | | | | Gross private domestic investment | | | | | | |
		Total	Durable goods	Non-durable goods	Services	Total	Fixed investment Total	Nonresidential Total	Struc-tures	Pro-ducers' durable equip-ment	Resi-dential	Change in busi-ness inven-tories
1959	494.2	318.1	42.8	148.5	126.8	78.8	74.6	46.5	18.1	28.3	28.1	4.2
1960	513.3	332.4	43.5	153.1	135.9	78.7	75.5	49.2	19.6	29.7	26.3	3.2
1961	531.8	343.5	41.9	157.4	144.1	77.9	75.0	48.6	19.7	28.9	26.4	2.9
1962	571.6	364.4	47.0	163.8	153.6	87.9	81.8	52.8	20.8	32.1	29.0	6.1
1963	603.1	384.2	51.8	169.4	163.1	93.4	87.7	55.6	21.2	34.4	32.1	5.7
1964	648.0	412.5	56.8	179.7	175.9	101.7	96.7	62.4	23.7	38.7	34.3	5.0
1965	702.7	444.6	63.5	191.9	189.2	118.0	108.3	74.1	28.3	45.8	34.2	9.7
1966	769.8	481.6	68.5	208.5	204.6	130.4	116.7	84.4	31.3	53.0	32.3	13.8
1967	814.3	509.3	70.6	216.9	221.7	128.0	117.6	85.2	31.5	53.7	32.4	10.5
1968	889.3	559.1	81.0	235.0	243.1	139.9	130.8	92.1	33.6	58.5	38.7	9.1
1969	959.5	603.7	86.2	252.2	265.3	155.2	145.5	102.9	37.7	65.2	42.6	9.7
1970	1,010.7	646.5	85.3	270.4	290.8	150.3	148.1	106.7	40.3	66.4	41.4	2.3
1971	1,097.2	700.3	97.2	283.3	319.8	175.5	167.5	111.7	42.7	69.1	55.8	8.0
1972	1,207.0	767.8	110.7	305.2	351.9	205.6	195.7	126.1	47.2	78.9	69.7	9.9
1973	1,349.6	848.1	124.1	339.6	384.5	243.1	225.4	150.0	55.0	95.1	75.3	17.7
1974	1,458.6	927.7	123.0	380.8	423.9	245.8	231.5	165.6	61.2	104.3	66.0	14.3
1975	1,585.9	1,024.9	134.3	416.0	474.5	226.0	231.7	169.0	61.4	107.6	62.7	−5.7
1976	1,768.4	1,143.1	160.0	451.8	531.2	286.4	269.6	187.2	65.9	121.2	82.5	16.7
1977	1,974.1	1,271.5	182.6	490.4	598.4	358.3	333.5	223.2	74.6	148.7	110.3	24.7
1978	2,232.7	1,421.2	202.3	541.5	677.4	434.0	406.1	274.5	93.9	180.6	131.6	27.9
1979	2,488.6	1,583.7	214.2	613.3	756.2	480.2	467.5	326.4	118.4	208.1	141.0	12.8
1980	2,708.0	1,748.1	212.5	682.9	852.7	467.6	477.1	353.8	137.5	216.4	123.3	−9.5
1981	3,030.6	1,926.2	228.5	744.2	953.5	558.0	532.5	410.0	169.1	240.9	122.5	25.4
1982	3,149.6	2,059.2	236.5	772.3	1,050.4	503.4	519.3	413.7	178.8	234.9	105.7	−15.9
1983	3,405.0	2,257.5	275.0	817.8	1,164.7	546.7	552.2	400.2	153.1	247.1	152.0	−5.5
1984	3,777.2	2,460.3	317.9	873.0	1,269.4	718.9	647.8	468.9	175.6	293.3	178.9	71.1
1985	4,038.7	2,667.4	352.9	919.4	1,395.1	714.5	689.9	504.0	193.4	310.6	185.9	24.6
1986	4,268.6	2,850.6	389.6	952.2	1,508.8	717.6	709.0	492.4	174.0	318.4	216.6	8.6
1987	4,539.9	3,052.2	403.7	1,011.1	1,637.4	749.3	723.0	497.8	171.3	326.5	225.2	26.3
1988	4,900.4	3,296.1	437.1	1,073.8	1,785.2	793.6	777.4	545.4	182.0	363.4	232.0	16.2
1989	5,250.8	3,523.1	459.4	1,149.5	1,914.2	832.3	798.9	568.1	193.3	374.8	230.9	33.3
1990	5,546.1	3,761.2	468.2	1,229.2	2,063.8	808.9	802.0	586.7	201.6	385.1	215.3	6.9
1991	5,722.9	3,906.4	457.8	1,257.9	2,190.7	736.9	745.5	555.9	182.6	373.3	189.6	−8.6
1992	6,038.5	4,139.9	497.3	1,300.9	2,341.6	796.5	789.1	565.5	172.6	392.9	223.6	7.3
1993 ᵖ	6,374.0	4,390.6	537.1	1,350.2	2,502.7	892.0	875.2	622.9	178.6	444.4	252.3	16.8
1982: IV	3,195.1	2,128.7	246.9	787.3	1,094.6	464.2	510.5	397.7	168.9	228.8	112.8	−46.3
1983: IV	3,547.3	2,346.8	297.7	839.8	1,209.3	614.8	594.6	426.9	154.6	272.3	167.7	20.2
1984: IV	3,869.1	2,526.4	328.2	887.8	1,310.4	722.8	671.8	491.5	184.1	307.3	180.4	51.0
1985: IV	4,140.5	2,739.8	354.4	939.5	1,446.0	737.0	704.4	511.3	195.4	315.9	193.1	32.6
1986: IV	4,336.6	2,923.1	406.8	963.7	1,552.6	697.1	715.9	491.7	168.4	323.3	224.2	−18.8
1987: IV	4,683.0	3,124.6	408.8	1,029.4	1,586.4	800.2	740.9	514.3	180.0	334.3	226.5	59.3
1988: IV	5,044.6	3,398.2	452.9	1,105.8	1,839.5	814.8	797.5	560.2	186.8	373.4	237.3	17.3
1989: IV	5,344.8	3,599.1	458.3	1,173.5	1,967.3	825.2	795.0	568.8	198.0	370.8	226.2	30.2
1990: I	5,461.9	3,679.3	479.8	1,201.7	1,997.8	828.9	819.3	586.2	203.6	382.5	233.2	9.6
II	5,540.9	3,727.0	466.0	1,213.6	2,047.5	837.8	804.5	582.1	203.2	378.9	222.4	33.3
III	5,583.8	3,801.7	467.3	1,241.0	2,093.4	812.5	804.1	594.1	203.8	390.3	209.9	8.4
IV	5,597.9	3,836.6	459.5	1,260.7	2,116.4	756.4	780.3	584.4	195.7	388.7	195.8	−23.9
1991: I	5,631.7	3,843.6	448.9	1,252.3	2,142.4	729.1	749.0	566.8	192.2	374.6	182.2	−19.9
II	5,697.7	3,887.8	452.0	1,259.2	2,176.6	721.5	744.5	561.0	188.4	372.6	183.6	−23.0
III	5,758.6	3,929.8	465.1	1,260.0	2,204.8	744.5	745.0	552.6	178.0	374.6	192.4	−.5
IV	5,803.7	3,964.1	465.2	1,260.0	2,239.0	752.4	743.5	543.3	171.7	371.5	200.3	8.9
1992: I	5,908.7	4,046.5	484.0	1,278.2	2,284.4	750.8	755.9	547.0	173.9	373.1	208.9	−5.1
II	5,991.4	4,099.9	487.8	1,288.2	2,323.8	799.7	786.8	566.3	174.5	391.7	220.6	12.9
III	6,059.5	4,157.1	500.9	1,305.7	2,350.5	802.2	792.5	569.2	170.8	398.4	223.3	9.7
IV	6,194.4	4,256.2	516.6	1,331.7	2,407.9	833.3	821.3	579.5	171.1	408.3	241.8	12.0
1993: I	6,261.6	4,296.2	515.3	1,335.3	2,445.5	874.1	839.5	594.7	172.4	422.2	244.9	34.6
II	6,327.6	4,359.9	531.6	1,344.8	2,483.4	874.1	861.0	619.1	177.6	441.6	241.9	13.1
III	6,395.9	4,419.1	541.9	1,352.4	2,524.8	884.0	876.3	624.9	179.1	445.8	251.3	7.7
IV ᵖ	6,510.8	4,487.4	561.9	1,368.4	2,557.2	935.8	924.1	653.0	185.2	467.8	271.1	11.7

See next page for continuation of table.

Figure 3-3 GDP accounts from *Economic Report of the President*, 1994. (Billions of dollars, except as noted; quarterly data at seasonally adjusted annual rates.)

Year or quarter	Net exports of goods and services			Total	Government purchases				Final sales of domestic product	Gross domestic purchases [1]	Addendum: Gross national product [2]	Percent change from preceding period	
	Net exports	Exports	Imports		Total	Federal		State and local				Gross domestic product	Gross domestic purchases [1]
						Total	National defense	Non-defense					
1959	-1.7	20.6	22.3	99.0	57.1	46.4	10.8	41.8	490.0	495.8	497.0	8.7	9.1
1960	2.4	25.3	22.8	99.8	55.3	45.3	10.0	44.5	510.1	510.9	516.6	3.9	3.0
1961	3.4	26.0	22.7	107.0	58.6	47.9	10.6	48.4	528.9	528.4	535.4	3.6	3.4
1962	2.4	27.4	25.0	116.8	65.4	52.1	13.3	51.4	565.5	569.1	575.8	7.5	7.7
1963	3.3	29.4	26.1	122.3	66.4	51.5	14.9	55.8	597.5	599.8	607.7	5.5	5.4
1964	5.5	33.6	28.1	128.3	67.5	50.4	17.0	60.9	643.0	642.5	653.0	7.4	7.1
1965	3.9	35.4	31.5	136.3	69.5	51.0	18.5	66.8	693.0	698.8	708.1	8.4	8.8
1966	1.9	38.9	37.1	155.9	81.3	62.0	19.3	74.6	756.0	767.9	774.9	9.5	9.9
1967	1.4	41.4	39.9	175.6	92.8	73.4	19.4	82.7	803.8	812.9	819.8	5.8	5.9
1968	-1.3	45.3	46.6	191.5	99.2	79.1	20.0	92.3	880.2	890.6	895.5	9.2	9.6
1969	-1.2	49.3	50.5	201.8	100.5	78.9	21.6	101.3	949.8	960.7	955.6	7.9	7.9
1970	1.2	57.0	55.8	212.7	100.1	76.8	23.3	112.6	1,008.4	1,009.5	1,017.1	5.3	5.1
1971	-3.0	59.3	62.3	224.3	100.0	74.1	25.9	124.3	1,089.2	1,100.2	1,104.9	8.6	9.0
1972	-8.0	66.2	74.2	241.5	106.9	77.4	29.4	134.7	1,197.1	1,215.0	1,215.7	10.0	10 4
1973	.6	91.8	91.2	257.7	108.5	77.5	31.1	149.2	1,331.9	1,349.0	1,362.3	11.8	11.0
1974	-3.1	124.3	127.5	288.3	117.6	82.6	35.0	170.7	1,444.4	1,461.8	1,474.3	8.1	8.4
1975	13.6	136.3	122.7	321.4	129.4	89.6	39.8	192.0	1,591.5	1,572.3	1,599.1	8.7	7.6
1976	-2.3	148.9	151.1	341.3	135.8	93.4	42.4	205.5	1,751.7	1,770.7	1,785.5	11.5	12.6
1977	-23.7	158.8	182.4	368.0	147.9	100.9	47.0	220.1	1,949.4	1,997.8	1,994.6	11.6	12.8
1978	-26.1	186.1	212.3	403.6	162.2	108.9	53.3	241.4	2,204.8	2,258.8	2,254.5	13.1	13.1
1979	-23.8	228.9	252.7	448.5	179.3	121.9	57.5	269.2	2,475.9	2,512.5	2,520.8	11.5	11.2
1980	-14.7	279.2	293.9	507.1	209.1	142.7	66.4	298.0	2,717.5	2,722.8	2,742.1	8.8	8.4
1981	-14.7	303.0	317.7	561.1	240.8	167.5	73.3	320.3	3,005.2	3,045.3	3,063.8	11.9	11.8
1982	-20.6	282.6	303.2	607.6	266.6	193.8	72.7	341.1	3,165.5	3,170.2	3,179.8	3.9	4.1
1983	-51.4	276.7	328.1	652.3	292.0	214.4	77.5	360.3	3,410.6	3,456.5	3,434.4	8.1	9.0
1984	-102.7	302.4	405.1	700.8	310.9	233.1	77.8	389.9	3,706.1	3,879.9	3,801.5	10.9	12.2
1985	-115.6	302.1	417.6	772.3	344.3	258.6	85.7	428.1	4,014.1	4,154.3	4,053.6	6.9	7.1
1986	-132.5	319.2	451.7	833.0	367.8	276.7	91.1	465.3	4,260.0	4,401.2	4,277.7	5.7	5.9
1987	-143.1	364.0	507.1	881.5	384.9	292.1	92.9	496.6	4,513.7	4,683.0	4,544.5	6.4	6.4
1988	-108.0	444.2	552.2	918.1	387.0	295.6	91.4	531.7	4,884.2	5,008.4	4,908.2	7.9	6.9
1989	-79.7	508.0	587.7	975.2	401.6	299.9	101.7	573.6	5,217.5	5,330.5	5,266.8	7.2	6 4
1990	-71.4	557.1	628.5	1,047.4	426.5	314.0	112.5	620.9	5,539.3	5,617.5	5,567.8	5.6	5.4
1991	-19.6	601.5	621.1	1,099 3	445.9	322.5	123.4	653.4	5,731.6	5,742.5	5,737.1	3.2	2.2
1992	-29.6	640.5	670.1	1,131.8	448.8	313.8	135.0	683.0	6,031.2	6,068.2	6,045.8	5.5	5.7
1993 ″	-65.7	660.1	725.8	1,157.1	443.4	303 6	139.8	713.7	6,357.2	6,439.7		5.6	6.1
1982: IV	-29.5	265.6	295.1	631.6	281.4	205.5	75.9	350.3	3,241.4	3,224.6	3,222.6		
1983: IV	-71.8	286.2	358.0	657.6	289.7	222.8	66.9	367.9	3,527.1	3,619.1	3,578.4		
1984: IV	-107.1	308.7	415.7	727.0	324.7	242.9	81.9	402.2	3,818.1	3,976.2	3,890.2		
1985: IV	-135.5	304.7	440.2	799.2	356.9	268.6	88.3	442 4	4,107.9	4,276.0	4,156.2		
1986: IV	-133.2	333.9	467.1	849.7	373.1	278.6	94.5	476.6	4,355.4	4,469.8	4,340.5		
1987: IV	-143.2	392.4	535.6	901.4	392.5	295.8	96.7	509.0	4,623.7	4,826.2	4,690.5		
1988: IV	-106.0	467.0	573.1	937.6	392.0	296.8	95.2	545.7	5,027.3	5,150.7	5,054.3		
1989: IV	-73.9	523.8	597.7	994.5	405.1	302.5	102.6	589.3	5,314.6	5,418.7	5,365.0		
1990: I	-73.9	542.0	615.9	1,027.7	422.7	312.1	110.6	605.0	5,452.4	5,535.9	5,482.1	9.1	8.9
II	-61.3	553.5	614.8	1,037.3	423.6	312.5	111.2	613.7	5,507.6	5,602.2	5,559.3	5.9	4.9
III	-78.7	555.3	634.0	1,048.3	423.2	309.1	114.1	625.1	5,575.3	5,662.4	5,599.9	3.1	4.4
IV	-71.6	577.6	649.2	1,076.5	436.5	322.5	114 0	640.0	5,621.8	5,669.5	5,630 0	1.0	.5
1991: I	-34.0	576.5	610.6	1,093.0	450.2	331.4	118.7	642.9	5,651.6	5,665.8	5,656.1	2.4	-.3
II	-11.5	600.7	612.2	1,099.9	449.4	326.3	123.0	650.5	5,720.8	5,709.2	5,710.6	4.8	3.1
III	-19.8	603.0	622.8	1,104.0	446.8	321.2	125.6	657.3	5,759.1	5,778.4	5,766.2	4.3	4.9
IV	-13.0	625.7	638.8	1,100.2	437.4	311.2	126.2	662.8	5,794.8	5,816.7	5,815.5	3.2	2.7
1992: I	-7.0	633.7	640.7	1,118.5	445.5	312.3	133.1	673.0	5,913.9	5,915.8	5,927.6	7.4	7.0
II	-33.9	632.4	666.3	1,125.8	444.6	310.4	134.2	681.2	5,978.6	6,025.3	5,996.3	5.7	7.6
III	-38.8	641.1	679.9	1,139.1	452.8	316.7	136.1	686.2	6,049.9	6,098.3	6,067.3	4.6	4.9
IV	-38.8	654.7	693.5	1,143.8	452.4	315.7	136.7	691.4	6,182.5	6,233.2	6,191.9	9.2	9.1
1993: I	-48.3	651.3	699.6	1,139.7	442.7	304.8	137.9	697.0	6,227.1	6,309.9	6,262.1	4.4	5.0
II	-65.1	660.0	725.0	1,158.6	447.5	307.6	140.0	711.1	6,314.5	6,392.7	6,327.1	4.3	5.4
III	-71.9	653.2	725.1	1,164.8	443.6	301.9	141.7	721.2	6,388.2	6,467.8	6,402.3	4.4	4.8
IV ″	-77.7	675.8	753.5	1,165.3	439.7	300.0	139.7	725.6	6,499.0	6,588.5		7.4	7.7

1 Gross domestic product (GDP) less exports of goods and services plus imports of goods and services.
2 GDP plus net receipts of factor income from rest of the world.

Source: Department of Commerce, Bureau of Economic Analysis.

(Figure 3–3 continued)

discrepancies—different treatments—that are cataloged on page 24 of the June 1992 issue of the *Survey of Current Business.*

Conceptually, the similarity between net exports of goods and services and the current-account balance was even greater for the United States before December 1991. At that time, the official NIPA figures were changed from a GNP to a GDP basis—from emphasis on gross national product (GNP) to emphasis on gross domestic product (GDP). The difference is that GNP is the total output produced by *residents* of a nation over the indicated time period, whereas GDP is output produced within a nation's *geographical boundaries.* If, for example, an American resident owns a plant in France, the contribution to output made by his capital located in France gives rise to profit or interest payments to him. These payments are included in GNP but not in GDP for the United States, because the relevant production is attributable to an American resident but takes place outside of the U.S. boundaries. A similar treatment applies to wages earned by U.S. residentss working abroad (or in reverse to non-residents working in the United States). Since BOP accounts are based on a residency criterion, their tabulation of net exports of goods and services includes payments to U.S. residents earned abroad (with payments to foreign residents earned in the United States netted out)—just as with GNP. The main item of this type for the United States is the net investment income that accounts for part of the difference between net exports in the GDP-based NIPA accounts and the current-account balance (in the BOP accounts). Since that net investment income is included in current production when the national income concept is GNP, it was the case prior to December 1991 that the only important difference between the current-account balance and the "official" national income measure of net exports was that the former included net unilateral transfers.

With these matters disposed of, we can return to our basic accounting identity, Equation (3), with the understanding that net exports X corresponds fairly closely to the BOP balance on goods and services. An important use of Equation (3) concerns the relationship between a nation's net exports (or approximately its current-account balance) and concepts relating to saving and investment. For the private sector of the economy—households and firms— saving is defined as after-tax income minus consumption,

$$S^P = Y - T - C, \tag{4}$$

whereas government saving is

$$S^G = T - G, \tag{5}$$

the negative of the government budget deficit.[10] The sum of these two magnitudes comprises national saving,

$$S^N = Y - C - G, \tag{6}$$

---

[10] Some serious conceptual objections to these definitions have been made by several scholars, including Barro (1993).

which could instead be independently defined as national production minus consumption by private and government sectors. In any event, insertion of Equation (3) yields

$$S^N = C + I + G + X - C - G = I + X, \tag{7}$$

which shows that national saving is used for the purpose of either domestic (I) or foreign (X) investment. The latter magnitude, X, can be justified as measuring net foreign investment since it is approximately equal to the current-account balance which, it should be recalled, is identically equal to the net *import* of reserves or other financial claims on the rest of the world.

Another arrangement of the accounting identities that has received much recent attention uses Equation (4) to obtain $Y = S^P + T + C$, which is inserted into Equation (3) to give

$$S^P + T + C = C + I + G + X. \tag{8}$$

The latter can, however, be rearranged as

$$S^P - I = (G - T) + X. \tag{9}$$

Thus private saving minus domestic investment equals the government budget deficit plus the current-account (BOP) surplus. Consequently, *if $S^P - I$* were determined autonomously, that is, did not respond to fiscal policy actions, then any change in the government budget deficit would be exactly offset by an equal-magnitude change in the current-account BOP deficit. An increase in $G - T$, for example, would give rise to an equal-magnitude fall in X or (equivalently) an equal-magnitude increase in the current-account deficit.[11] This accounting fact has been used by many analysts[12] to argue that the large U.S. current-account deficits recorded each year since 1983 (except 1991) came about because of the Reagan admistration tax cuts of 1981 and 1982, which (with reasonably constant G as a fraction of Y) led to large federal budget deficits in subsequent years.

It is unclear, however, whether this last argument is justifiable, for it rests on the presumption that $S^P - I$ is itself unresponsive to policy changes in $G - T$ (or on a hypothesis to that effect). But there is no clear-cut theoretical basis for such a presumption or hypothesis in mainstream economic theory. Indeed, one well-known line of analysis, due primarily to Robert Barro, provides some fairly persuasive reasons for believing that an autonomous policy change in $G - T$ would tend to induce an offsetting change in $S^P - I$, leaving X virtually unaffected.[13]

In the presentation of this section and the one preceding, virtually nothing has been said of a *normative* nature, that is, about the social desirability or

[11] Actually, in the deficit in the balance on goods, services, and income.

[12] For example, Krugman and Obstfeld (1994, pp. 314–317).

[13] For a textbook explanation, see Barro (1993, Ch. 14).

Year or quarter	Gross domestic product	Personal consumption expenditures				Gross private domestic investment						Change in business inventories
							Fixed investment					
								Nonresidential				
		Total	Durable goods	Non-durable goods	Services	Total	Total	Total	Structures	Producers' durable equipment	Residential	
1959	1,928.8	1,178.9	114.4	518.5	546.0	296.4	282.8	165.2	74.4	90.8	117.6	13.6
1960	1,970.8	1,210.8	115.4	526.9	568.5	290.8	282.7	173.3	80.8	92.5	109.4	8.1
1961	2,023.8	1,238.4	109.4	537.7	591.3	289.4	282.2	172.1	82.3	89.8	110.1	7.2
1962	2,128.1	1,293.3	120.2	553.0	620.0	321.2	305.6	185.0	86.1	98.9	120.6	15.6
1963	2,215.6	1,341.9	130.3	563.6	648.0	343.3	327.3	192.3	86.9	105.4	135.0	16.0
1964	2,340.6	1,417.2	140.7	588.2	688.3	371.8	356.2	214.0	95.9	118.1	142.1	15.7
1965	2,470.5	1,497.0	156.2	616.7	724.1	413.0	387.9	250.6	111.5	139.1	137.3	25.1
1966	2,616.2	1,573.8	166.0	647.6	760.2	438.0	401.3	276.7	119.1	157.6	124.5	36.7
1967	2,685.2	1,622.4	167.2	659.0	796.2	418.6	391.0	270.8	116.0	154.8	120.2	27.6
1968	2,796.9	1,707.5	184.5	686.0	837.0	440.1	416.5	280.1	117.4	162.7	136.4	23.6
1969	2,873.0	1,771.2	190.8	703.2	877.2	461.3	436.5	296.4	123.5	172.9	140.1	24.8
1970	2,873.9	1,813.5	183.7	717.2	912.5	429.7	423.8	292.0	123.3	168.7	131.8	5.9
1971	2,955.9	1,873.7	201.4	725.6	946.7	475.7	454.9	286.8	121.2	165.6	168.1	20.8
1972	3,107.1	1,978.4	225.2	755.8	997.4	532.2	509.6	311.6	124.8	186.8	198.0	22.5
1973	3,268.6	2,066.7	246.6	777.9	1,042.2	591.7	554.0	357.4	134.9	222.4	196.6	37.7
1974	3,248.1	2,053.8	227.2	759.8	1,066.8	543.0	512.0	356.5	132.3	224.2	155.6	30.9
1975	3,221.7	2,097.5	226.8	767.1	1,103.6	437.6	451.5	316.8	118.0	198.8	134.7	−13.9
1976	3,380.8	2,207.3	256.4	801.3	1,149.5	520.6	495.1	328.7	120.5	208.2	166.4	25.5
1977	3,533.3	2,296.6	280.0	819.8	1,196.8	600.4	566.2	364.3	126.1	238.2	201.9	34.3
1978	3,703.5	2,391.8	292.9	844.8	1,254.1	664.6	627.4	412.9	144.1	268.8	214.5	37.2
1979	3,796.8	2,448.4	289.0	862.8	1,296.5	669.7	656.1	448.8	163.3	285.5	207.4	13.6
1980	3,776.3	2,447.1	262.7	860.5	1,323.9	594.4	602.7	437.8	170.2	267.6	164.8	−8.3
1981	3,843.1	2,476.9	264.6	867.9	1,344.4	631.1	606.5	455.0	182.9	272.0	151.6	24.6
1982	3,760.3	2,503.7	262.5	872.2	1,368.9	540.5	558.0	433.9	181.3	252.6	124.1	−17.5
1983	3,906.6	2,619.4	297.7	900.3	1,421.4	599.5	595.1	420.8	160.3	260.5	174.2	4.4
1984	4,148.5	2,746.1	338.5	934.6	1,473.0	757.5	689.6	490.2	182.8	307.4	199.3	67.9
1985	4,279.8	2,865.8	370.1	958.7	1,537.0	745.9	723.8	521.8	197.4	324.4	202.0	22.1
1986	4,404.5	2,969.1	402.0	991.0	1,576.1	735.1	726.5	500.3	176.6	323.7	226.2	8.5
1987	4,539.9	3,052.2	403.7	1,011.1	1,637.4	749.3	723.0	497.8	171.3	326.5	225.2	26.3
1988	4,718.6	3,162.4	428.7	1,035.1	1,698.5	773.4	753.4	530.8	174.0	356.8	222.7	19.9
1989	4,838.0	3,223.3	440.7	1,051.6	1,731.0	784.0	754.2	540.0	177.6	362.5	214.2	29.8
1990	4,897.3	3,272.6	443.1	1,060.7	1,768.8	746.8	741.1	546.5	179.5	367.0	194.5	5.7
1991	4,861.4	3,258.6	426.6	1,048.2	1,783.8	675.7	684.1	514.5	160.2	354.3	169.5	−8.4
1992	4,986.3	3,341.8	456.6	1,062.9	1,822.3	732.9	726.4	529.2	150.6	378.6	197.1	6.5
1993 P	5,132.7	3,452.5	489.7	1,088.1	1,874.7	820.9	805.5	591.3	151.4	439.9	214.2	15.4
1982: IV	3,759.6	2,539.3	272.3	880.7	1,386.2	503.5	548.4	417.2	173.2	244.0	131.2	−44.9
1983: IV	4,012.1	2,678.2	319.1	915.2	1,443.9	669.5	640.2	449.6	162.6	287.0	190.6	29.3
1984: IV	4,194.2	2,784.8	347.7	942.9	1,494.2	756.4	708.4	509.6	189.5	320.1	198.8	47.9
1985: IV	4,333.5	2,895.3	369.6	968.7	1,557.1	763.1	732.9	525.5	198.3	327.2	207.4	30.2
1986: IV	4,427.1	3,012.5	415.7	1,000.9	1,595.8	705.9	725.9	495.5	170.4	325.0	230.5	−20.1
1987: IV	4,625.5	3,074.7	404.7	1,014.6	1,655.5	793.8	733.9	510.6	177.9	332.7	223.3	59.9
1988: IV	4,779.7	3,202.9	439.2	1,046.8	1,716.9	785.0	764.1	538.8	175.7	363.1	225.3	20.9
1989: IV	4,856.7	3,242.0	436.8	1,058.9	1,746.3	769.5	744.6	536.7	179.8	356.9	208.0	24.9
1990: I	4,898.3	3,264.4	454.8	1,059.8	1,749.8	766.5	761.8	550.2	182.9	367.3	211.6	4.7
II	4,917.1	3,271.6	441.8	1,060.6	1,769.2	773.9	745.8	544.5	181.6	363.0	201.2	28.1
III	4,906.5	3,288.4	442.4	1,065.0	1,781.1	751.0	740.1	551.2	180.9	370.3	189.0	10.9
IV	4,867.2	3,265.9	433.2	1,057.5	1,775.2	695.7	716.6	540.2	172.8	367.4	176.3	−20.9
1991: I	4,837.8	3,242.7	420.3	1,048.2	1,774.2	667.8	685.2	521.4	169.0	352.5	163.8	−17.4
II	4,855.6	3,256.9	422.0	1,051.1	1,783.8	659.8	682.1	517.8	165.2	352.6	164.3	−22.3
III	4,872.6	3,267.1	432.6	1,049.3	1,785.2	682.8	683.8	512.8	155.6	357.2	171.0	−.9
IV	4,879.6	3,267.5	431.5	1,044.0	1,792.0	692.3	685.2	506.1	151.0	355.2	179.1	7.1
1992: I	4,922.0	3,302.3	446.6	1,052.0	1,803.7	691.7	696.7	510.5	152.8	357.7	186.2	−5.0
II	4,956.5	3,316.8	447.5	1,055.0	1,814.3	737.0	724.4	528.8	152.9	375.9	195.6	12.6
III	4,998.2	3,350.9	459.0	1,062.9	1,829.0	739.6	730.0	533.8	148.8	385.1	196.2	9.6
IV	5,068.3	3,397.2	473.4	1,081.8	1,842.0	763.0	754.3	543.7	148.0	395.7	210.6	8.7
1993: I	5,078.2	3,403.8	471.9	1,076.0	1,855.9	803.0	773.7	562.3	148.2	414.1	211.4	29.3
II	5,102.1	3,432.7	484.2	1,083.1	1,865.4	803.6	790.6	584.3	151.1	433.2	206.2	13.0
III	5,138.3	3,469.6	493.1	1,093.0	1,883.5	813.4	806.9	594.8	151.2	443.6	212.1	6.5
IV P	5,212.1	3,503.9	509.9	1,100.1	1,893.9	863.6	851.0	623.8	155.1	468.7	227.2	12.7

See next page for continuation of table.

Figure 3–4 Real GDP from *Economic Report of the President*, 1994. (Billions of 1987 dollars, except as noted; quarterly data at seasonally adjusted annual rates.)

Year or quarter	Net exports	Exports	Imports	Total	Federal Total	National defense	Non-defense	State and local	Final sales of domestic product	Gross domestic purchases [1]	Addendum: Gross national product [2]	% chg GDP	% chg Gross domestic purchases [1]
1959	−21.8	73.8	95.6	475.3	265.7			209.6	1,915.2	1,950.6	1,939.6	5.5	5.8
1960	−7.6	88.4	96.1	476.9	259.0			217.9	1,962.7	1,978.5	1,982.8	2.2	1.4
1961	−5.5	89.9	95.3	501.5	270.1			231.4	2,016.6	2,029.3	2,037.1	2.7	2.6
1962	−10.5	95.0	105.5	524.2	287.3			236.9	2,112.5	2,138.6	2,143.3	5.2	5.4
1963	−5.8	101.8	107.7	536.3	285.7			250.6	2,199.6	2,221.4	2,231.8	4.1	3.9
1964	2.5	115.4	112.9	549.1	281.8			267.3	2,324.9	2,338.1	2,358.1	5.6	5.3
1965	−6.4	118.1	124.5	566.9	282.1			284.8	2,445.4	2,476.9	2,488.9	5.5	5.9
1966	−18.0	125.7	143.7	622.4	319.3			303.1	2,579.5	2,634.2	2,633.2	5.9	6.4
1967	−23.7	130.0	153.7	667.9	350.9			317.0	2,657.5	2,708.9	2,702.6	2.6	2.8
1968	−37.5	140.2	177.7	686.8	353.1			333.7	2,773.2	2,834.4	2,815.6	4.2	4.6
1969	−41.5	147.8	189.2	682.0	340.1			341.9	2,848.2	2,914.5	2,890.9	2.7	2.8
1970	−35.2	161.3	196.4	665.8	315.0			350.9	2,868.0	2,909.1	2,891.5	.0	−.2
1971	−45.9	161.9	207.8	652.4	290.8			361.6	2,935.2	3,001.8	2,975.9	2.9	3.2
1972	−56.5	173.7	230.2	653.0	284.4	209.6	74.8	368.6	3,084.5	3,163.6	3,128.8	5.1	5.4
1973	−34.1	210.3	244.4	644.2	265.3	191.3	74.1	378.9	3,230.9	3,302.7	3,298.6	5.2	4.4
1974	−4.1	234.4	238.4	655.4	262.6	185.8	76.8	392.9	3,217.2	3,252.2	3,282.4	−.6	−1.5
1975	23.1	232.9	209.8	663.5	262.7	184.9	77.8	400.8	3,235.6	3,198.6	3,247.6	−.8	−1.6
1976	−6.4	243.4	249.7	659.2	258.2	179.9	78.3	401.1	3,355.3	3,387.1	3,412.2	4.9	5.9
1977	−27.8	246.9	274.7	664.1	263.1	181.6	81.4	401.0	3,499.0	3,561.1	3,569.0	4.5	5.1
1978	−29.9	270.2	300.1	677.0	268.6	182.1	86.5	408.4	3,666.3	3,733.3	3,739.0	4.8	4.8
1979	−10.6	293.5	304.1	689.3	271.7	185.1	86.6	417.6	3,783.2	3,807.4	3,845.3	2.5	2.0
1980	30.7	320.5	289.9	704.2	284.8	194.2	90.6	419.4	3,784.6	3,745.7	3,823.4	−.5	−1.6
1981	22.0	326.1	304.1	713.2	295.8	206.4	89.4	417.4	3,818.6	3,821.2	3,884.4	1.8	2.0
1982	−7.4	296.7	304.1	723.6	306.0	221.4	84.7	417.6	3,777.8	3,767.7	3,796.1	−2.2	−1.4
1983	−56.1	285.9	342.1	743.8	320.8	234.2	86.6	423.0	3,902.2	3,962.8	3,939.6	3.9	5.2
1984	−122.0	305.7	427.7	766.9	331.0	245.8	85.1	436.0	4,080.6	4,270.5	4,174.5	6.2	7.8
1985	−145.3	309.2	454.6	813.4	355.2	265.6	89.5	458.2	4,257.6	4,425.1	4,295.0	3.2	3.6
1986	−155.1	329.6	484.7	855.4	373.0	280.6	92.4	482.4	4,395.9	4,559.6	4,413.5	2.9	3.0
1987	−143.1	364.0	507.1	881.5	384.9	292.1	92.9	496.6	4,513.7	4,683.0	4,544.5	3.1	2.7
1988	−104.0	421.6	525.7	886.8	377.3	287.0	90.2	509.6	4,698.6	4,822.6	4,726.3	3.9	3.0
1989	−73.7	471.8	545.4	904.4	376.1	281.4	94.8	528.3	4,808.3	4,911.7	4,852.7	2.5	1.8
1990	−54.7	510.5	565.1	932.6	384.1	283.6	100.4	548.5	4,891.6	4,951.9	4,916.5	1.2	.8
1991	−19.1	543.4	562.5	946.3	386.5	281.3	105.3	559.7	4,869.8	4,880.5	4,874.5	−.7	−1.4
1992	−33.6	578.0	611.6	945.2	373.0	261.2	111.8	572.2	4,979.8	5,019.9	4,994.0	2.6	2.9
1993 ᵖ	−79.3	596.4	675.7	938.6	355.1	242.7	112.5	583.4	5,117.3	5,211.9		2.9	3.8
1982: IV	−19.0	280.4	299.4	735.9	316.0	229.4	86.6	419.9	3,804.5	3,778.6	3,791.7		
1983: IV	−83.7	291.5	375.1	748.1	322.2	242.9	79.3	425.9	3,982.8	4,095.8	4,046.6		
1984: IV	−131.4	312.8	444.2	784.3	341.7	254.3	87.4	442.6	4,146.2	4,325.5	4,216.4		
1985: IV	−155.4	312.0	467.4	830.5	363.7	272.1	91.6	466.7	4,303.3	4,488.9	4,349.5		
1986: IV	−156.0	342.9	498.9	864.8	377.5	282.2	95.3	487.3	4,447.2	4,583.1	4,430.8		
1987: IV	−136.0	386.1	522.1	893.0	391.6	295.0	96.6	501.4	4,565.6	4,761.5	4,633.0		
1988: IV	−102.7	438.2	540.9	894.5	378.4	285.7	92.7	516.1	4,758.7	4,882.4	4,789.0		
1989: IV	−67.4	487.7	555.0	912.6	376.1	281.5	94.7	536.5	4,831.8	4,924.1	4,875.1		
1990: I	−60.8	501.8	562.6	928.1	385.4	285.3	100.1	542.8	4,893.6	4,959.1	4,916.4	3.5	2.9
II	−58.9	511.1	570.0	930.6	384.7	285.0	99.8	545.9	4,889.0	4,976.0	4,933.4	1.5	1.4
III	−62.2	508.6	570.7	929.2	379.6	278.5	101.1	549.6	4,895.6	4,968.6	4,920.9	−.9	−.6
IV	−36.8	520.4	557.2	942.4	386.5	285.7	100.8	555.8	4,888.0	4,904.0	4,895.4	−3.2	−5.1
1991: I	−21.6	519.4	541.0	948.9	393.8	292.0	101.8	555.1	4,855.2	4,859.4	4,859.3	−2.4	−3.6
II	−13.3	542.9	556.2	952.3	393.6	288.7	104.9	558.7	4,878.0	4,869.0	4,867.5	1.5	.8
III	−25.0	546.9	571.9	947.6	386.6	279.4	107.2	561.0	4,873.5	4,897.6	4,880.3	1.4	2.4
IV	−16.4	564.2	580.7	936.2	372.1	264.9	107.2	564.1	4,872.5	4,896.0	4,890.9	.6	−.1
1992: I	−15.2	571.0	586.2	943.1	372.1	261.2	110.9	571.0	4,926.9	4,937.1	4,939.0	3.5	3.4
II	−38.0	570.2	608.2	940.7	369.2	257.9	111.3	571.5	4,943.8	4,994.5	4,962.2	2.8	4.7
III	−42.5	579.3	621.8	950.2	377.0	264.4	112.5	573.2	4,988.6	5,040.7	5,006.4	3.4	3.8
IV	−38.8	591.6	630.3	946.9	373.7	261.3	112.4	573.2	5,059.6	5,107.1	5,068.4	5.7	5.4
1993: I	−59.9	588.0	647.9	931.3	357.6	246.0	111.5	573.7	5,048.9	5,138.1	5,080.7	.8	2.5
II	−75.2	593.2	668.4	941.1	359.4	246.4	113.0	581.6	5,089.1	5,177.4	5,104.1	1.9	3.1
III	−86.3	591.9	678.2	941.7	353.7	240.1	113.7	588.0	5,131.8	5,224.6	5,145.8	2.9	3.7
IV ᵖ	−95.6	612.5	708.1	940.1	349.8	238.2	111.6	590.4	5,199.4	5,307.7		5.9	6.5

[1] Gross domestic product (GDP) less exports of goods and services plus imports of goods and services.
[2] GDP plus net receipts of factor income from rest of the world.
Source: Department of Commerce, Bureau of Economic Analysis.

(Figure 3-4 continued)

| Year or quarter | Gross domestic product | Personal consumption expenditures | | | | Gross private domestic investment: Fixed investment | | | | |
| | | Total | Durable goods | Non-durable goods | Services | Total | Nonresidential | | | Residential |
							Total	Structures	Producers' durable equipment	
1959	25.6	27.0	37.4	28.6	23.2	26.4	28.1	24.4	31.2	23.9
1960	26.0	27.5	37.7	29.1	23.9	26.7	28.4	24.2	32.1	24.0
1961	26.3	27.7	38.3	29.3	24.4	26.6	28.2	24.0	32.2	24.0
1962	26.9	28.2	39.1	29.6	24.8	26.8	28.6	24.1	32.4	24.0
1963	27.2	28.6	39.7	30.1	25.2	26.8	28.9	24.4	32.6	23.8
1964	27.7	29.1	40.4	30.5	25.6	27.1	29.2	24.7	32.8	24.1
1965	28.4	29.7	40.6	31.1	26.1	27.9	29.6	25.4	32.9	24.9
1966	29.4	30.6	41.3	32.2	26.9	29.1	30.5	26.3	33.6	25.9
1967	30.3	31.4	42.3	32.9	27.8	30.1	31.5	27.2	34.7	26.9
1968	31.8	32.7	43.9	34.3	29.0	31.4	32.9	28.6	36.0	28.4
1969	33.4	34.1	45.2	35.9	30.2	33.3	34.7	30.5	37.7	30.4
1970	35.2	35.6	46.4	37.7	31.9	34.9	36.5	32.7	39.4	31.4
1971	37.1	37.4	48.3	39.0	33.8	36.8	39.0	35.2	41.7	33.2
1972	38.8	38.8	49.2	40.4	35.3	38.4	40.5	37.8	42.2	35.2
1973	41.3	41.0	50.3	43.7	36.9	40.7	42.0	40.7	42.7	38.3
1974	44.9	45.2	54.1	50.1	39.7	45.2	46.4	46.3	46.5	42.4
1975	49.2	48.9	59.2	54.2	43.0	51.3	53.3	52.0	54.1	46.6
1976	52.3	51.8	62.4	56.4	46.2	54.5	56.9	54.7	58.2	49.6
1977	55.9	55.4	65.2	59.8	50.0	58.9	61.3	59.2	62.4	54.6
1978	60.3	59.4	69.1	64.1	54.0	64.7	66.5	65.2	67.2	61.3
1979	65.5	64.7	74.1	71.1	58.3	71.2	72.7	72.5	72.9	68.0
1980	71.7	71.4	80.9	79.4	64.4	79.2	80.8	80.8	80.9	74.8
1981	78.9	77.8	86.4	85.7	70.9	87.8	90.1	92.5	88.5	80.9
1982	83.8	82.2	90.1	88.6	76.7	93.1	95.3	98.6	93.0	85.2
1983	87.2	86.2	92.4	90.8	81.9	92.8	95.1	95.5	94.8	87.3
1984	91.0	89.6	93.9	93.4	86.2	93.9	95.7	96.1	95.4	89.7
1985	94.4	93.1	95.4	95.9	90.8	95.3	96.4	98.0	95.7	92.0
1986	96.9	96.0	96.9	96.1	95.7	97.6	98.4	98.5	98.4	95.8
1987	100.0	100.0	100.0	100.0	100.0	100.0	100.0	100.0	100.0	100.0
1988	103.9	104.2	102.0	103.7	105.1	103.2	102.8	104.6	101.9	104.2
1989	108.5	109.3	104.2	109.3	110.6	105.9	105.2	108.9	103.4	107.8
1990	113.3	114.9	105.7	115.9	116.7	108.2	107.3	112.3	104.9	110.7
1991	117.7	119.9	107.3	120.0	122.8	109.0	108.0	114.0	105.4	111.8
1992	121.1	123.9	108.9	122.4	128.5	108.6	106.9	114.6	103.8	113.4
1993 P	124.2	127.2	109.8	124.1	133.5	108.7	105.3	117.9	101.0	117.8
1982: IV	85.0	83.8	90.6	89.4	79.0	93.1	95.3	97.5	93.8	86.0
1983: IV	88.4	87.6	93.3	91.8	83.7	92.9	95.0	95.1	94.9	88.0
1984: IV	92.3	90.7	94.4	94.2	87.7	94.8	96.4	97.2	96.0	90.7
1985: IV	95.5	94.6	95.9	97.0	92.9	96.1	97.3	98.5	96.5	93.1
1986: IV	98.0	97.0	97.8	96.3	97.3	98.6	99.2	98.8	99.5	97.3
1987: IV	101.2	101.6	101.0	101.5	101.9	101.0	100.7	101.2	100.5	101.5
1988: IV	105.5	106.1	103.1	105.6	107.1	104.4	104.0	106.3	102.8	105.3
1989: IV	110.1	111.0	104.9	110.8	112.7	106.8	106.0	110.1	103.9	108.8
1990: I	111.5	112.7	105.5	113.4	114.2	107.6	106.5	111.3	104.2	110.2
II	112.7	113.9	105.5	114.4	115.7	107.9	106.9	111.9	104.4	110.5
III	113.8	115.6	105.6	116.5	117.5	108.6	107.8	112.7	105.4	111.1
IV	115.0	117.5	106.1	119.2	119.2	108.9	108.2	113.3	105.8	111.1
1991: I	116.4	118.5	106.8	119.5	120.8	109.3	108.7	113.8	106.3	111.3
II	117.3	119.4	107.1	119.8	122.0	109.2	108.3	114.0	105.7	111.7
III	118.2	120.3	107.5	120.1	123.5	109.0	107.8	114.4	104.9	112.5
IV	118.9	121.3	107.8	120.7	124.9	108.5	107.3	113.8	104.6	111.8
1992: I	120.0	122.5	108.4	121.5	126.6	108.5	107.1	113.8	104.3	112.2
II	120.9	123.6	109.0	122.1	128.1	108.6	107.1	114.2	104.2	112.8
III	121.2	124.1	109.1	122.8	128.5	108.6	106.6	114.8	103.5	113.8
IV	122.2	125.3	109.1	123.1	130.7	108.9	106.6	115.7	103.2	114.9
1993: I	123.3	126.2	109.2	124.1	131.8	108.5	105.7	116.3	102.0	115.8
II	124.0	127.0	109.8	124.2	133.1	108.9	106.0	117.5	101.9	117.3
III	124.5	127.4	109.9	123.7	134.0	108.6	105.1	118.5	100.5	118.5
IV P	124.9	128.1	110.2	124.4	135.0	108.6	104.7	119.4	99.8	119.3

See next page for continuation of table.

Figure 3–5 GDP deflators from *Economic Report of the President*, 1994. (Index numbers, 1987 = 100, except as noted; quarterly data seasonally adjusted.)

Year or quarter	Exports and imports of goods and services		Government purchases of goods and services					Final sales of domestic product	Gross domestic purchases [1]	Percent change from preceding period, GDP implicit price deflator [2]
				Federal						
	Exports	Imports	Total	Total	National defense	Non-defense	State and local			
1959	28.0	23.4	20.8	21.5			19.9	25.6	25.4	2.8
1960	28.6	23.8	20.9	21.3			20.4	26.0	25.8	1.6
1961	29.0	23.8	21.3	21.7			20.9	26.2	26.0	1.2
1962	28.9	23.7	22.3	22.8			21.7	26.8	26.6	2.3
1963	28.9	24.3	22.8	23.3			22.3	27.2	27.0	1.1
1964	29.1	24.9	23.4	23.9			22.8	27.7	27.5	1.8
1965	30.0	25.3	24.0	24.6			23.5	28.3	28.2	2.5
1966	31.0	25.8	25.0	25.5			24.6	29.3	29.2	3.5
1967	31.8	26.0	26.3	26.5			26.1	30.2	30.0	3.1
1968	32.3	26.2	27.9	28.1			27.7	31.7	31.4	5.0
1969	33.3	26.7	29.6	29.6			29.6	33.3	33.0	5.0
1970	35.3	28.4	31.9	31.8			32.1	35.2	34.7	5.4
1971	36.6	30.0	34.4	34.4			34.4	37.1	36.7	5.4
1972	38.1	32.2	37.0	37.6	36.9	39.3	36.5	38.8	38.4	4.6
1973	43.6	37.3	40.0	40.9	40.5	41.9	39.4	41.2	40.8	6.4
1974	53.0	53.5	44.0	44.8	44.5	45.5	43.5	44.9	44.9	8.7
1975	58.5	58.5	48.4	49.3	48.5	51.2	47.9	49.2	49.2	9.6
1976	61.2	60.5	51.8	52.6	51.9	54.1	51.2	52.2	52.3	6.3
1977	64.3	66.4	55.4	56.2	55.6	57.7	54.9	55.7	56.1	6.9
1978	68.9	70.7	59.6	60.4	59.8	61.7	59.1	60.1	60.5	7.9
1979	78.0	83.1	65.1	66.0	65.8	66.4	64.5	65.4	66.0	8.6
1980	87.1	101.4	72.0	73.4	73.5	73.3	71.1	71.8	72.7	9.5
1981	92.9	104.5	78.7	81.4	81.1	82.1	76.7	78.7	79.7	10.0
1982	95.2	99.7	84.0	87.1	87.6	85.9	81.7	83.8	84.1	6.2
1983	96.8	95.9	87.7	91.0	91.6	89.5	85.2	87.4	87.2	4.1
1984	98.9	94.7	91.4	93.9	94.8	91.3	89.4	90.8	90.9	4.4
1985	97.7	91.9	95.0	96.9	97.3	95.7	93.4	94.3	93.9	3.7
1986	96.9	93.2	97.4	98.6	98.6	98.6	96.4	96.9	96.5	2.6
1987	100.0	100.0	100.0	100.0	100.0	100.0	100.0	100.0	100.0	3.2
1988	105.3	105.1	103.6	102.6	103.0	101.4	104.3	103.9	103.9	3.9
1989	107.7	107.8	107.8	106.8	106.6	107.3	108.6	108.5	108.5	4.4
1990	109.1	111.2	112.3	111.0	110.7	112.0	113.2	113.2	113.4	4.4
1991	110.7	110.4	116.2	115.4	114.7	117.2	116.7	117.7	117.7	3.9
1992	110.8	109.6	119.7	120.3	120.1	120.8	119.4	121.1	120.9	2.9
1993 ᴾ	110.7	107.4	123.3	124.8	125.1	124.3	122.3	124.2	123.6	2.5
1982: IV	94.7	98.5	85.8	89.0	89.6	87.7	83.4	85.2	85.3	....
1983: IV	98.2	95.4	87.9	89.9	91.7	84.3	86.4	88.6	88.4	....
1984: IV	98.7	93.6	92.7	95.0	95.5	93.7	90.9	92.1	91.9	....
1985: IV	97.7	94.2	96.2	98.1	98.7	96.4	94.8	95.5	95.3	....
1986: IV	97.4	93.6	98.3	98.8	98.7	99.2	97.8	97.9	97.5	....
1987: IV	101.6	102.6	100.9	100.2	100.3	100.1	101.5	101.3	101.4	....
1988: IV	106.6	106.0	104.8	103.6	103.9	102.6	105.7	105.6	105.5	....
1989: IV	107.4	107.7	109.0	107.7	107.5	108.4	109.9	110.0	110.0	....
1990: I	108.0	109.5	110.7	109.7	109.4	110.5	111.5	111.4	111.6	5.2
II	108.3	107.9	111.5	110.1	109.6	111.4	112.4	112.7	112.6	4.4
III	109.2	111.1	112.8	111.5	111.0	112.8	113.7	113.9	114.0	4.0
IV	111.0	116.5	114.2	112.9	112.9	113.1	115.2	115.0	115.6	4.3
1991: I	111.0	112.9	115.2	114.3	113.5	116.7	115.8	116.4	116.6	5.0
II	110.6	110.1	115.5	114.2	113.0	117.3	116.4	117.3	117.3	3.1
III	110.2	108.9	116.5	115.6	114.9	117.2	117.2	118.2	118.0	3.1
IV	110.9	110.0	117.5	117.5	117.5	117.8	117.5	118.9	118.8	2.4
1992: I	111.0	109.3	118.6	119.7	119.6	120.0	117.9	120.0	119.8	3.8
II	110.9	109.6	119.7	120.4	120.3	120.6	119.2	120.9	120.6	3.0
III	110.7	109.3	119.9	120.1	119.8	121.0	119.7	121.3	121.0	1.0
IV	110.7	110.0	120.8	121.1	120.8	121.6	120.6	122.2	122.1	3.3
1993: I	110.8	108.0	122.4	123.8	123.9	123.6	121.5	123.3	122.8	3.6
II	111.3	108.5	123.1	124.5	124.8	123.9	122.3	124.1	123.5	2.3
III	110.4	106.9	123.7	125.4	125.7	124.6	122.7	124.5	123.8	1.5
IV ᴾ	110.3	106.4	123.9	125.7	126.0	125.1	122.9	125.0	124.1	1.4

[1] Gross domestic product (GDP) less exports of goods and services plus imports of goods and services.
[2] Quarterly changes are at annual rates.

Note.—Separate deflators are not calculated for gross private domestic investment, change in business inventories, and net exports of goods and services.

Source: Department of Commerce, Bureau of Economic Analysis.

(*Figure 3–5 continued*)

Year or quarter	Gross saving								Gross investment			Statistical discrepancy
		Gross private saving			Government surplus or deficit (−), national income and product accounts			Capital grants received by the United States (net)[2]		Gross private domestic investment	Net foreign investment[3]	
	Total	Total	Personal saving	Gross business saving[1]	Total	Federal	State and local		Total			
1959	79.4	82.5	22.0	60.5	−3.1	−2.6	−0.5	....	77.6	78.8	−1.2	−1.8
1960	85.1	81.5	20.6	60.9	3.6	3.5	.0	....	82.0	78.7	3.2	−3.1
1961	84.4	87.4	24.9	62.5	−3.0	−2.6	−.4	....	82.2	77.9	4.3	−2.2
1962	92.8	95.8	25.9	69.9	−2.9	−3.4	.5	....	91.8	87.9	3.9	−1.0
1963	100.4	98.8	24.6	74.1	1.6	1.1	.4	....	98.4	93.4	5.0	−2.0
1964	110.0	111.5	31.6	80.0	−1.6	−2.6	1.0	....	109.3	101.7	7.5	−.7
1965	125.0	123.7	34.6	89.2	1.2	1.3	.0	....	124.2	118.0	6.2	−.7
1966	131.5	132.5	36.3	96.1	−1.0	−1.4	.5	....	134.3	130.4	3.9	2.8
1967	130.8	144.5	45.8	98.7	−13.7	−12.7	−1.1	....	131.6	128.0	3.5	.8
1968	141.7	146.4	43.8	102.5	−4.6	−4.7	.1	....	141.7	139.9	1.7	−.1
1969	159.5	149.5	43.3	106.2	10.0	8.5	1.5	....	157.0	155.2	1.8	−2.6
1970	155.2	165.8	57.5	108.2	−11.5	−13.3	1.8	0.9	155.2	150.3	4.9	.0
1971	173.7	192.2	65.4	126.8	−19.2	−21.7	2.5	.7	176.8	175.5	1.3	3.1
1972	201.7	204.9	59.7	145.1	−3.9	−17.3	13.4	.7	202.7	205.6	−2.9	1.1
1973	252.3	245.4	86.1	159.3	6.9	−6.6	13.4	0	251.8	243.1	8.7	−.5
1974	249.5	256.0	93.4	162.6	−4.5	−11.6	7.1	[4]−2.0	250.9	245.8	5.1	1.4
1975	241.4	306.3	100.3	206.0	−64.8	−69.4	4.6	0	247.4	226.0	21.4	6.0
1976	284.8	323.1	93.0	230.0	−38.3	−52.9	14.6	0	295.2	286.4	8.8	10.4
1977	338.2	355.0	87.9	267.1	−16.8	−42.4	25.6	0	349.1	358.3	−9.2	10.9
1978	415.7	412.8	107.8	305.0	2.9	−28.1	31.1	0	423.3	434.0	−10.7	7.6
1979	468.5	457.9	123.3	334.5	9.4	−15.7	25.1	1.1	482.2	480.2	2.0	13.8
1980	465.4	499.6	153.8	345.7	−35.3	−60.1	24.8	1.2	479.1	467.6	11.5	13.6
1981	556.6	585.9	191.8	394.1	−30.3	−58.8	28.5	1.1	567.5	558.0	9.5	10.9
1982	508.4	616.9	199.5	417.5	−108.6	−135.5	26.9	0	500.9	503.4	−2.5	−7.4
1983	501.6	641.3	168.7	472.7	−139.8	−180.1	40.3	0	511.7	546.7	−35.0	10.2
1984	633.9	742.7	222.0	520.7	−108.8	−166.9	58.1	0	624.9	718.9	−94.0	−9.0
1985	610.4	735.7	189.3	546.4	−125.3	−181.4	56.1	0	596.5	714.5	−118.1	−13.9
1986	574.6	721.4	187.5	533.9	−146.8	−201.0	54.3	0	575.9	717.6	−141.7	1.2
1987	619.0	730.7	142.0	588.7	−111.7	−151.8	40.1	0	594.2	749.3	−155.1	−24.8
1988	704.0	802.3	155.7	646.6	−98.3	−136.6	38.4	0	675.6	793.6	−118.0	−28.4
1989	741.8	819.4	152.1	667.3	−77.5	−122.3	44.8	0	742.9	832.3	−89.3	1.1
1990	722.7	861.1	170.0	691.2	−138.4	−163.5	25.1	0	730.4	808.9	−78.5	7.8
1991	733.7	929.9	201.5	728.4	−196.2	−203.4	7.3	0	743.3	736.9	6.4	9.6
1992	717.8	986.9	238.7	748.3	−269.1	−276.3	7.2	0	741.4	796.5	−55.1	23.6
1993 ᵖ				190.3	−223.7	−225.8	2.1	0		892.0		
1982: IV	458.5	615.4	183.8	431.6	−156.9	−183.4	26.5	0	448.4	464.2	−15.8	−10.1
1983: IV	542.4	678.7	176.3	502.4	−136.3	−184.6	48.3	0	556.3	614.8	−58.5	13.8
1984: IV	637.0	764.7	222.6	542.1	−127.8	−186.8	59.0	0	616.5	722.8	−106.3	−20.5
1985: IV	603.8	734.7	179.2	555.5	−130.9	−187.2	56.3	0	597.8	737.0	−139.1	−5.9
1986: IV	550.1	676.3	151.1	525.3	−126.2	−177.5	51.2	0	548.1	697.1	−149.0	−2.0
1987: IV	667.9	783.7	169.8	613.9	−115.8	−152.7	37.0	0	643.0	800.2	−157.1	−24.9
1988: IV	720.1	814.8	156.4	658.3	−94.7	−134.9	40.2	0	694.7	814.8	−120.1	−25.4
1989: IV	728.4	828.6	148.8	679.8	−100.2	−141.5	41.3	0	741.3	825.2	−84.0	12.8
1990: I	735.5	867.4	176.5	690.9	−131.9	−166.4	34.5	0	748.6	828.9	−80.3	13.1
II	765.9	888.5	175.7	712.9	−122.7	−152.0	29.3	0	764.0	837.8	−73.8	−1.8
III	705.5	825.5	151.6	673.9	−119.9	−144.6	24.7	0	720.4	812.5	−92.1	14.9
IV	683.8	863.1	176.2	686.9	−179.3	−191.0	11.7	0	688.7	756.4	−67.7	4.9
1991: I	780.3	919.4	201.5	717.9	−139.1	−145.2	6.1	0	780.5	729.1	51.4	.2
II	734.3	935.0	206.0	728.9	−200.7	−206.2	5.5	0	738.7	721.5	17.2	4.5
III	694.4	906.6	186.8	719.8	−212.2	−217.7	5.5	0	721.8	744.5	−22.8	27.3
IV	726.0	958.7	211.7	746.9	−232.6	−244.7	12.1	0	732.3	752.4	−20.2	6.2
1992: I	709.9	974.1	217.5	756.6	−264.2	−270.2	6.1	0	733.0	750.8	−17.7	23.1
II	715.5	987.7	237.9	749.8	−272.2	−279.9	7.8	0	739.1	799.7	−60.6	23.6
III	727.0	1,016.5	219.6	796.9	−289.5	−290.7	1.2	0	742.7	802.2	−59.4	15.7
IV	718.8	969.4	279.7	689.7	−250.6	−264.2	13.5	0	750.9	833.3	−82.4	32.1
1993: I	762.0	1,024.8	177.9	847.0	−262.8	−263.5	.8	0	796.5	874.1	−77.6	34.4
II	766.7	988.3	208.7	779.6	−221.5	−222.6	1.1	0	778.7	874.1	−95.4	12.0
III	774.3	988.7	179.7	809.0	−214.4	−212.7	−1.7	0	787.6	884.0	−96.4	13.3
IV ᵖ				195.2				0		935.8		

[1] Undistributed corporate profits with inventory valuation and capital consumption adjustments, corporate and noncorporate consumption of fixed capital, and private wage accruals less disbursements.

[2] Consists mainly of allocations of special drawing rights (SDRs).

[3] Net exports of goods and services plus net receipts of factor income from rest of the world less net transfers plus net capital grants received by the United States. See also Table B–21.

[4] Consists of a U.S. payment to India under the Agricultural Trade Development and Assistance Act. This payment is included in capital grants received by the United States, net.

Source: Department of Commerce, Bureau of Economic Analysis.

Figure 3–6 NIPA data on saving and investment from *Economic Report of the President*, 1994. (Billions of dollars; quarterly data at seasonally adjusted annual rates.)

Year or quarter	Receipts from rest of the world				Payments to rest of the world									
	Total [1]	Exports of goods and services			Receipts of factor income [3]	Total	Imports of goods and services			Payments of factor income [4]	Transfer payments (net)				Net foreign investment
		Total	Merchandise [2]	Services [2]			Total	Merchandise [2]	Services [2]		Total	From persons (net)	From government (net)	From business	
1959	25.0	20.6	16.5	4.2	4.3	25.0	22.3	15.3	7.0	1.5	2.4	0.4	1.8	0.1	−1.2
1960	30.2	25.3	20.5	4.8	5.0	30.2	22.8	15.2	7.6	1.8	2.4	.5	1.9	.1	3.2
1961	31.4	26.0	20.9	5.1	5.4	31.4	22.7	15.1	7.6	1.8	2.7	.5	2.1	.1	4.3
1962	33.5	27.4	21.7	5.7	6.1	33.5	25.0	16.9	8.1	1.8	2.8	.5	2.1	.1	3.9
1963	36.1	29.4	23.3	6.1	6.6	36.1	26.1	17.7	8.4	2.1	2.8	.6	2.1	.1	5.0
1964	41.0	33.6	26.7	6.9	7.4	41.0	28.1	19.4	8.7	2.4	3.0	.7	2.1	.2	7.5
1965	43.5	35.4	27.8	7.6	8.1	43.5	31.5	22.2	9.3	2.7	3.0	.8	2.1	.2	6.2
1966	47.2	38.9	30.7	8.2	8.3	47.2	37.1	26.3	10.7	3.1	3.2	.8	2.2	.2	3.9
1967	50.2	41.4	32.2	9.2	8.9	50.2	39.9	27.8	12.2	3.4	3.4	1.0	2.1	.2	3.5
1968	55.6	45.3	35.3	10.0	10.3	55.6	46.6	33.9	12.6	4.1	3.2	1.0	1.9	.3	1.7
1969	61.2	49.3	38.3	11.0	11.9	61.2	50.5	36.8	13.7	5.8	3.2	1.1	1.8	.3	1.8
1970	70.8	57.0	44.5	12.4	13.0	70.8	55.8	40.9	14.9	6.6	3.6	1.2	2.0	.4	4.9
1971	74.2	59.3	45.6	13.8	14.1	74.2	62.3	46.6	15.8	6.4	4.1	1.3	2.4	.4	1.3
1972	83.4	66.2	51.8	14.4	16.4	83.4	74.2	56.9	17.3	7.7	4.3	1.3	2.5	.5	−2.9
1973	115.6	91.8	73.9	17.8	23.8	115.6	91.2	71.8	19.3	11.1	4.6	1.4	2.5	.7	8.7
1974	152.6	124.3	101.0	23.3	30.3	152.6	127.5	104.5	22.9	14.6	5.4	1.2	3.2	1.0	5.1
1975	164.4	136.3	109.6	26.7	28.2	164.4	122.7	99.0	23.7	14.9	5.4	1.2	3.5	.7	21.4
1976	181.6	148.9	117.8	31.1	32.8	181.6	151.1	124.6	26.5	15.7	6.0	1.2	3.7	1.1	8.8
1977	196.5	158.8	123.7	35.1	37.7	196.5	182.4	152.6	29.8	17.2	6.0	1.2	3.4	1.4	−9.2
1978	233.3	186.1	145.4	40.7	47.1	233.3	212.3	177.4	34.8	25.3	6.4	1.3	3.8	1.4	−10.7
1979	299.7	228.9	184.2	44.7	69.7	299.7	252.7	212.8	39.9	37.5	7.5	1.4	4.1	2.0	2.0
1980	360.9	279.2	226.0	53.2	80.6	360.9	293.9	248.6	45.3	46.5	9.0	1.6	5.0	2.4	11.5
1981	398.2	303.0	239.3	63.7	94.1	398.2	317.7	267.7	49.9	60.9	10.0	1.8	5.0	3.2	9.5
1982	379.9	282.6	215.2	67.4	97.3	379.9	303.2	250.6	52.6	67.1	12.1	2.1	6.4	3.6	−2.5
1983	372.5	276.7	207.5	69.2	95.8	372.5	328.1	272.7	55.4	66.5	12.9	1.8	7.3	3.8	−35.0
1984	410.5	302.4	225.8	76.6	108.1	410.5	405.1	336.3	68.8	83.8	15.6	2.3	9.4	3.9	−94.0
1985	399.3	302.1	222.4	79.7	97.3	399.3	417.6	343.3	74.3	82.4	17.4	2.7	11.4	3.2	−118.1
1986	415.2	319.2	226.2	93.0	96.0	415.2	451.7	370.0	81.7	86.9	18.3	2.5	12.3	3.5	−141.7
1987	469.0	364.0	257.7	106.2	105.1	469.0	507.1	414.8	92.3	100.5	16.6	3.0	10.4	3.2	−155.1
1988	572.9	444.2	325.8	118.4	128.7	572.9	552.2	452.1	100.1	120.8	17.8	2.7	10.4	4.8	−118.0
1989	665.5	508.0	371.6	136.4	157.5	665.5	587.7	485.1	102.6	141.5	25.6	8.9	11.3	5.4	−89.3
1990	725.7	557.1	398.7	158.4	168.6	725.7	628.5	509.0	119.5	146.9	28.8	10.1	13.2	5.5	−78.5
1991	747.6	601.5	426.4	175.1	146.1	747.6	621.1	500.7	120.4	131.9	−11.9	10.5	−27.9	5.6	6.4
1992 P	769.7	640.5	448.7	191.7	129.2	769.7	670.1	544.5	125.6	121.9	32.7	10.4	16.3	6.0	−55.1
1993 P		660.1	459.5	200.6			725.8	593.0	132.8		31.4	11.0	14.2	6.1	
1982: IV	357.5	265.6	198.2	67.4	91.9	357.5	295.1	241.6	53.4	64.4	13.8	1.9	8.2	3.7	−15.8
1983: IV	388.3	286.2	218.2	67.9	102.1	388.3	358.0	300.0	58.0	71.0	17.8	2.0	11.0	4.8	−58.5
1984: IV	415.2	308.7	231.4	77.3	106.6	415.2	415.7	344.1	71.6	85.5	20.4	2.5	13.9	4.0	−106.3
1985: IV	402.9	304.7	222.6	82.1	98.1	402.9	440.2	363.0	77.2	82.4	19.4	2.5	13.5	3.4	−139.1
1986: IV	426.7	333.9	235.8	98.1	92.8	426.7	467.1	382.4	84.7	88.9	19.6	2.8	12.8	4.0	−149.0
1987: IV	506.8	392.4	283.3	109.2	114.4	506.8	535.6	437.6	98.0	106.9	21.4	3.1	14.6	3.8	−157.1
1988: IV	606.9	467.0	345.4	121.6	139.9	606.9	573.1	470.1	103.0	130.2	23.8	2.7	15.1	5.9	−120.1
1989: IV	683.1	523.8	380.7	143.1	159.3	683.1	597.7	492.2	105.6	139.1	30.3	9.8	15.1	5.4	−84.0
1990: I	705.9	542.0	391.7	150.2	164.0	705.9	615.9	501.6	114.3	143.8	26.5	9.9	11.6	5.0	−80.3
II	718.9	553.5	399.0	154.6	165.4	718.9	614.8	498.1	116.7	147.0	30.9	10.1	15.3	5.4	−73.8
III	720.5	555.3	395.1	160.1	165.2	720.5	634.0	512.3	121.7	149.0	29.6	10.3	13.4	5.8	−92.1
IV	757.4	577.6	409.0	168.6	179.7	757.4	649.2	523.9	125.4	147.7	28.2	10.2	12.4	5.6	−67.7
1991: I	738.9	576.5	414.3	162.3	162.4	738.9	610.6	489.8	120.8	138.0	−61.1	10.4	−76.9	5.4	51.4
II	747.9	600.7	426.7	174.0	147.2	747.9	612.2	492.3	119.9	134.3	−15.8	10.4	−32.0	5.8	17.2
III	742.1	603.0	424.6	178.3	139.1	742.1	622.8	504.3	118.5	131.5	10.6	10.3	−5.1	5.4	−22.8
IV	761.4	625.7	440.0	185.8	135.7	761.4	638.8	516.3	122.5	123.9	18.9	10.8	2.2	5.9	−20.2
1992: I	768.0	633.7	442.6	191.0	134.4	768.0	640.7	515.4	125.3	115.6	29.6	11.1	12.6	5.9	−17.7
II	765.3	632.4	442.8	189.6	132.9	765.3	666.3	540.6	125.7	127.9	31.6	10.5	15.0	6.1	−60.6
III	768.4	641.1	447.5	193.6	127.3	768.4	679.9	557.3	122.6	119.5	28.5	9.7	12.8	5.9	−59.4
IV	777.0	654.7	462.0	192.8	122.3	777.0	693.5	564.7	128.7	124.8	41.2	10.5	24.6	6.1	−82.4
1993: I	774.1	651.3	453.2	198.0	122.8	774.1	699.6	569.6	130.0	122.4	29.7	11.0	13.1	5.6	−77.6
II	791.8	660.0	458.6	201.3	131.9	791.8	725.0	592.6	132.4	132.3	29.9	11.0	12.9	6.0	−95.4
III	788.3	653.2	452.2	200.9	135.1	788.3	725.1	591.9	133.3	128.7	30.9	10.8	13.7	6.3	−96.4
IV P		675.8	473.7	202.1			753.5	618.1	135.3		35.1	11.4	17.2	6.5	

[1] Includes capital grants received by the United States (net), not shown separately. See Table B–29 for data.
[2] Exports and imports of certain goods, primarily military equipment purchased and sold by the Federal Government, are included in services.
[3] Consists largely of receipts by U.S. residents of interest and dividends and reinvested earnings of foreign affiliates of U.S. corporations.
[4] Consists largely of payments to foreign residents of interest and dividends and reinvested earnings of U.S. affiliates of foreign corporations.

Source: Department of Commerce, Bureau of Economic Analysis.

Figure 3–7 NIPA data on exports and imports from *Economic Report of the President*, 1994. (Billions of dollars; quarterly data at seasonally adjusted annual rates.)

undesirability of BOP deficits of various types. That omission is not accidental, but instead reflects the point of view that it is difficult to make general statements that are not wrong under certain circumstances. A large current-account deficit, for example, may be desirable if it is the result of unusually favorable opportunities for investment in a nation, and these investments are financed partly by foreign rather than domestic savers.[14] But it remains true that a current-account deficit means that the nation's net buildup of claims on foreigners is negative, so that more payments will have to be made to foreigners eventually. Indeed, the most important component of judgments regarding BOP deficit or surplus values on various accounts is simply a clear understanding of precisely what the figure *is*.[15]

3.4 Additional Statistical Material

There are a number of tables that are related in important ways to those that we have utilized in this chapter and the one preceding. For convenience, some of them are included here as Figures 3–4 through 3–7. Specifically, Figure 3–4 gives the GDP accounts from Figure 3–3 in real terms, with the associated price-level deflators appearing in Figure 3–5. Figure 3–6 provides a tabulation of NIPA data on U.S. saving and investment flows, relevant to the discussion in Section 3.3, whereas Figure 3–7 gives more detail on the NIPA version of exports and imports of goods and services.

References

Barro, R. J., *Macroeconomics*, 4th ed. New York: John Wiley, 1993.

Caves, R. E., J. A. Frankel, and R. W. Jones, *World Trade and Payments*, 5th ed. New York: Harper Collins, 1990.

Corden, W. M., "Current Account of the Balances of Payments: Normative Theory," in *The New Palgrave Dictionary of Money and Finance*, P. Newman, M. Milgate, and J. Eatwell, Eds. New York: Stockton Press, 1992.

Council of Economic Advisors, *Economic Report of the President*. Washington, DC: U.S. Government Printing Office, 1992.

Cumby, R., and R. Levich, "Balance of Payments," in *The New Palgrave Dictionary of Money and Finance*, P. Newman, M. Milgate, and J. Eatwell, Eds. New York: Stockton Press, 1992.

Krugman, P. R., and M. Obstfeld, *International Economics: Theory and Policy*, 3rd ed. Glenview, IL: Scott, Foresman, 1994.

[14] Germany just after its 1990 unification may be one example.

[15] For more discussion of this topic, see Corden (1992). One point that should be made is that *bilateral* BOP surplus or deficit magnitudes with any single nation are of virtually no significance from a normative perspective. There is no more reason for the United States to have a balanced current account with Japan (for example) than there is for the reader's family to have zero net purchases from the neighborhood grocery store.

Rivera-Batiz, F. L., and L. A. Rivera-Batiz, *International Finance and Open Economy Macroeconomics*, 2nd ed. New York: Macmillan Publishing, 1994.

Stern et al., *The Presentation of the U.S. Balance of Payments: A Symposium*. Princeton University Eassys in International Finance no. 123, Aug. 1977.

U.S. Department of Commerce, *Survey of Current Business*, published monthly.

Problems

1. Find the balance on current account, capital account, and official reserve transaction account for the United States in 1992.

2. The following figures were reported for Turkey by the OECD:

Balance of Payments	1990	1991	1992	1993
Net trade, $ mil.	−9555	−7340	−8191	−14160
Current balance, $ mil.	−2625	258	−943	−6378
Net capital movements, $ mil.	4037	−2397	3648	8907

On the basis of these figures, estimate Turkey's net increase or decrease in its stock of international reserves for each of the years 1990–1993. Also, roughly estimate Turkey's net exports of services, including investment income, for those years.

3. The tabulation in Figure 3–8 on p. 68, which gives BOP figures for Mexico (in millions of dollars), comes from the IMF's *International Financial Statistics*. Using these figures, determine the Mexican balance on capital account for 1990 and 1991. Also, determine whether Mexican holdings of foreign exchange reserves increased or decreased during 1991.

4. From the tabulations included in the present chapter, estimate the magnitude of taxes collected by U.S. governments (including state and local) for the years 1990, 1991, and 1992.

5. On the basis of the data presented in Problem 3, guess whether Mexico's GDP was larger or smaller than its GNP during 1991. (Why is this answer a guess rather than a strict determination?)

Mexico
273

	1980	1981	1982	1983	1984	1985	1986	1987	1988	1989	1990	1991	
Balance of Payments													
Current Account, nie	-10,750	-16,061	-6,307	5,403	4,194	1,130	-1,673	3,968	-2,443	-3,958	-7,117	-13,283	77a. d
Merchandise: Exports fob	15,511	20,102	21,230	22,312	24,196	21,663	16,031	20,655	20,566	22,765	26,838	27,121	77aa d
Merchandise: Imports fob	-18,896	-23,948	-14,435	-8,550	-11,255	-13,212	-11,432	-12,222	-18,898	-23,410	-31,271	-38,184	77ab d
Trade Balance	-3,385	-3,846	6,795	13,762	12,941	8,451	4,599	8,433	1,668	-645	-4,433	-11,063	77ac d
Services: Credit	5,241	5,893	4,760	4,817	5,847	5,748	5,842	6,955	8,489	10,098	11,512	12,887	77ad d
Services: Debit	-6,221	-8,129	-5,711	-4,213	-4,940	-5,170	-4,875	-5,009	-6,049	-7,689	-9,944	-10,483	77ah d
Income: Credit	1,242	1,642	1,530	1,449	2,335	2,133	1,811	2,289	2,952	3,106	3,237	3,529	77ai d
Income: Debit	-7,911	-11,924	-13,984	-10,714	-12,399	-11,032	-9,514	-9,348	-10,070	-10,903	-10,952	-10,394	77aj d
Private Unrequited Transfers	245	246	232	255	325	327	345	384	397	1,922	2,167	2,055	77ak d
Official Unrequited Trans..nie	39	57	71	47	85	673	119	264	170	153	1,296	186	77af d
Direct Investment, nie	2,156	2,835	1,655	461	390	491	1,160	1,796	635	2,648	2,548	4,742	77ag d
Portfolio Investment, nie	42	1,160	921	-653	-756	-984	-816	-397	-880	438	-5,359	6,937	77bb d
Other Capital, nie	9,374	22,357	-1,113	-8,594	-3,532	-2,578	420	-3,852	-5,625	-2,113	11,257	8,707	77g. d
Resident Official Sector	735	2,052	2,597	7,044	5,910	10,360	8,463	3,835	-3,484	-98	1,801	-869	77ga d
Deposit Money Banks	3,599	11,937	417	681	754	68	220	-707	2,303	-136	8,497	6,536	77gb d
Other Sectors	5,040	8,368	-4,127	-16,319	-10,196	-13,006	-8,263	-6,980	-4,444	-1,879	959	3,040	77gc d
Net Errors and Omissions	-4	-9,016	-6,791	-925	-973	-1,765	458	2,605	-2,840	2,775	890	869	77e. d
Overall Balance	818	1,275	-11,635	-4,308	-677	-3,706	-451	4,120	-11,153	-210	2,219	7,972	78.. d
Reserves and Related Items	-818	-1,275	11,635	4,308	677	3,706	451	-4,120	11,153	210	-2,219	-7,972	79.. d
Reserve Assets	-685	-1,275	3,352	-3,102	-3,391	2,436	451	-5,972	6,721	-543	-3,261	-8,153	79da d
Use of Fund Credit and Loans	-133	—	219	1,069	1,241	295	-624	401	-84	364	958	161	79db d
Liab.Const.Fgn Auth.Reserves	—	—	1,217	-1,217	—	—	712	—	—	—	—	—	79b. d
Exceptional Financing	—	—	6,846	7,558	2,827	975	363	1,450	4,515	389	84	20	79a. d
Memorandum Items													
Total Change in Reserve Assets	-943	-1,333	3,320	-3,222	-3,454	2,363	-858	-6,786	7,147	-407	-3,479	-7,834	79e. d
of which: Revaluations	-258	-58	-32	-120	-63	-73	-234	-815	426	135	-218	320	79f. d

Figure 3–8 Problem 3.

Source: International Finance Statistics Yearbook, 1992. © 1992 International Monetary Fund.

4

Historical Perspective

4.1 Introduction

This chapter amounts to something of a change of pace, its object being to provide the reader with a bit of historical perspective. This perspective relates partly to the behavior of exchange rates, inflation, and other variables, but especially to the evolution of international monetary institutions. Primary emphasis will be given to the postwar (post–World War II) era, with its two distinct subperiods of fixed (1947–1971) and floating (1973–present) exchange rates, but a significant amount of attention will also be devoted to earlier eras and to the prevailing metallic-standard arrangements (e.g., the gold standard) that shaped monetary affairs, both nationally and internationally, prior to 1940.

In thinking about the current international monetary order, it is useful to keep in mind that the period since 1973 marks the first occasion in history in which exchange rates have been free to float with no presumption that this was a temporary arrangement that would be ended in a few years' time by a return to officially sanctioned par values. That can be said since, prior to the 1940s, the world's leading nations generally featured monetary systems based on some *commodity-money* standard or convention. Arrangements with *fiat money*— money that is valuable only because of governmental decree and policy behavior—were intended to be and were thought of as temporary expedients, devices to be resorted to only in wartime or other periods of national emergency. Thus before World War II, the regular, normal state of affairs was generally regarded as one in which the gold standard or some other commodity-money arrangement prevailed.

The emergence of nation states as the predominant form of political and administrative organization is itself a fairly recent phenomenon, of course. Consequently, it is difficult to briefly survey international monetary arrangements prior to, say, 1800 except to point out that all sovereign states specified what forms of money would constitute legal tender within their boundaries, and that most of them minted gold, silver, and/or base-metal (copper, tin, lead) coins for domestic circulation. Regulations concerning international movement of coins and gold or silver bullion varied from place to place and from time to time.

From about 1800 on, however, nation states were of sufficient importance that it is possible to describe in brief terms the international monetary arrangements that prevailed among the nations of Europe and North America, that is, in the industrialized portion of the world. Despite some risk of oversimplification, it may be useful to think of the last 200 years in terms of six distinct periods. These may be dated and characterized as follows:

1. 1797–1821   Disruption due to Napoleonic wars
2. 1821–1875   England on gold standard; other nations on various commodity-money arrangements
3. 1875–1914   Worldwide gold standard[1]
4. 1914–1945   Disruption from two world wars and intervening depression (brief return to gold standard, 1925–1931)
5. 1947–1971   Bretton Woods system of fixed exchange rates
6. 1973–1994   Floating exchange rates among leading nations

This tabular summary needs obviously to be fleshed out with a good bit of elaboration, explanation, and discussion. In that regard, however, the matter probably in greatest need of explanation is the nature and workings of the gold standard and other commodity-money systems. For while such systems were prevalent for centuries, their workings are unfamiliar as a matter of personal experience to anyone born in the past 50 years and are largely neglected in most of today's courses in money and banking or monetary economics. The next section, accordingly, will be devoted to an analytical overview of the workings of the gold standard.

4.2 The Gold Standard

The analytical principles of a commodity-money system are essentially the same whether the economy's standard commodity is silver, gold, zinc, or even a composite-commodity bundle. But because of the historical importance of gold and the mystique that surrounds that metal even today, our discussion will proceed terminologically as if gold were the single monetary commodity and the basis for the monetary standard.

Under a totally pure gold standard, an economy's money—its circulating medium of exchange—would consist of gold coins and bullion. Each nation might have its own coinage system and its own monetary units in terms of which prices are typically expressed (e.g., dollars, florins, lire), but these would actually just be different *names* for specified amounts of gold. If individuals were free to trade gold with residents of other nations, there would be essentially only one integrated monetary system for all the nations in which this pure gold standard prevailed. Furthermore, exchange rates, reflecting prices of one nation's coins in terms of the monetary units of another nation, would be

---

[1] Some analysts would date the beginning of the gold-standard era differently. Bordo (1992), for example, suggests 1880. The reason for using 1875 here is explained in footnote 9.

determined by the specified quantities of gold in the coins and the monetary units of the nations involved. Thus these exchange rates would be firmly and definitely fixed, for as long as each nation maintained its coinage and monetary unit.

In practice, however, gold-standard arrangements were almost always of an "impure" type in which the actual circulating medium consisted largely or even entirely of paper (or other token) claims to units of the monetary commodity, that is, to quantities of gold. This impure type of system tends to arise in practice because it permits a smaller amount of the valuable monetary commodity (gold) to be devoted to monetary use, and therefore frees more of it for use as an ordinary commodity.[2] In addition, the physical management of the medium of exchange can be conducted somewhat more satisfactorily when paper claims, rather than coins or ungraded masses of gold (i.e., bullion), are passed from hand to hand in the course of ordinary transactions.

Let us henceforth base our discussion, accordingly, on a gold-standard system in which the actual circulating medium consists—at least in large part—of paper claims to gold. We will refer to these as currency. The way in which the value of the currency is maintained is by some governmental agency— normally, the central bank—standing ready to exchange currency for gold coins or bullion at the officially stipulated rate, that is, at *par*. Doing so will fix the value of the nation's currency in terms of gold. Consequently, if similar steps are taken in another nation and if the citizens of both are free to trade gold bullion, then the exchange rate between these two national paper currencies will again be fixed.[3] In 1900, for example, the U.S. dollar price of an English pound was about 4.86, since a dollar was equivalent to 0.0484 ounce of gold, whereas the figure was 0.2354 ounce for a pound sterling. This was basically the way in which the system actually worked during the 1875–1914 heyday of the gold standard, although matters were obviously much more complex.[4]

Now the foregoing discussion describes how exchange rates between national currencies are fixed when each individual nation's government supports the currency by making it convertible into gold. But it does not explain how currency prices of goods are determined, or how adjustments take place when some condition of macroeconomic significance changes. As it happens, these important aspects of gold-standard behavior can be most easily and clearly developed in a model that initially ignores the international dimensions of the situation and then reintroduces them later.

Let us consider, then, a model of a closed economy on a gold standard but with a circulating medium consisting entirely of paper currency, one that we

[2] It is also being assumed that the system is one with fractional reserves, that is, with a banking system that holds gold reserves equal in value to only a fraction of the paper claims that circulate as the medium of exchange. If 100 percent reserves were always held, then the system would basically work like a pure one in which gold serves as the circulating medium.

[3] The exchange rates can of course vary within certain limits because of the existence of transaction costs, but these limits will be narrow. For the most part, we will ignore that complication.

[4] For more extensive discussion, the reader might usefully consult Bordo (1981, 1992), Cooper (1982), and Eichengreen (1985).

will call "dollars." The model is based on previous expositions by Barro (1979) and McCallum (1989, ch. 13), but is here simplified significantly. The model is one that makes a sharp distinction between so-called short-run and long-run analysis, with the former pertaining to the *impact* effects at a point in time of some change in conditions and the latter to the *ultimate* effects that come about more slowly as time passes.

To begin with, we need some notation. In particular, let us adopt the symbols P_g and P to denote the (paper) dollar price of a unit of gold and the dollar price of a typical bundle of commodities, respectively. Then P_g is the price that must be kept constant over time for the gold standard to be maintained. It is not a variable in our analysis, but a fixed parameter. Its value is fixed, however, by policy—by the central bank's willingness to buy or sell gold at the per-unit dollar price of P_g (e.g., P_g dollars per ounce). By contrast, P is a crucial variable whose value the model is designed to explain. It is best thought of as the economy's general price level.

From the perspective of impact or short-run analysis, the economy's total stock of gold is viewed as a given or predetermined quantity. It is the amount in existence at the point in time to which the analysis pertains; some passage of time would be required for that amount to be changed. In a short-run supply–demand diagram, with price and quantity on the vertical and horizontal axes, respectively, the point-in-time (or short-run) supply of gold is then a vertical line such as that shown at quantity G^0 in Figure 4–1. In that figure there also appears a downward-sloping demand function for the existing stock of gold. To understand its nature, it is important to keep in mind that this demand curve represents the sum of the quantities demanded for two distinct purposes, monetary and nonmonetary. The latter pertains to gold that is held

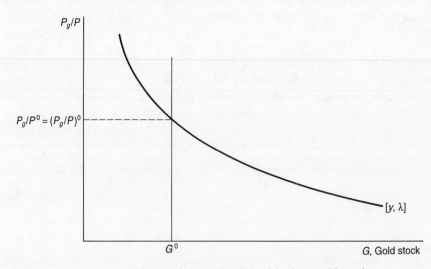

Figure 4–1 Price-level determination with given gold stock.

for use as jewelry, in dental fixtures, or in electronic or other commercial applications. The quantity demanded for such uses is then, as with other commodities, a decreasing function of price. The relevant price is, however, the *relative* price of gold in relation to goods in general. It is therefore the price ratio P_g/P that is relevant, and that appears on the vertical axis in Figure 4–1. The magnitude of the demand for gold for these nonmonetary uses will also depend on the level of income and economic activity in the economy, measured in real terms. Thus the quantity demanded will be greater, at each given value of P_g/P, the greater is national income (in real terms). In symbols, $G_n = f(P_g/P, y)$, with $f_1 < 0$ and $f_2 > 0$. (Here f_i denotes the partial derivative of f with respect to its ith argument.)

The second use of gold is for monetary purposes. To some extent this may involve gold coins, but for the most part monetary gold is held by the central bank (and other banks) in the form of *reserves*. Thus the central bank holds a reserve stock of gold in order to be able to supply it to citizens or banks at the gold-standard price P_g, which it is required to do to maintain the standard. The quantity of gold reserves that needs to be held is of course closely related to the quantity of paper dollars in circulation since these are claims on the central bank's reserves. Indeed, we shall think of the central bank as acting so as to keep the nation's stock of monetary gold proportionate (in value terms) to the quantity of paper dollars in circulation. Thus if G_m is the quantity of monetary gold and M is the volume of dollars outstanding, then we assume that the central bank keeps the *reserve ratio* $\lambda = P_g G_m/M$ constant, except possibly at times of discrete policy change. This implies that the quantity of monetary gold satisfies $G_m = \lambda M/P_g$, with $0 < \lambda \le 1$.

The quantity of monetary gold demanded depends, then, on the quantity of dollars that the public chooses to hold. But from standard money-demand theory, we know that the quantity of paper dollars that individuals and firms wish to hold will be proportional to the price level P multiplied by some function of a variable that measures the volume of transactions being conducted. If we use y, real national income or production, as the measure of transaction volume, we can then express this relationship in symbols as $M = PL(y)$, with $L(\cdot)$ an increasing function.[5] Combining the latter with the equation at the end of the previous paragraph, we obtain $G_m = \lambda PL(y)/P_g$. But this implies that the quantity of gold demanded (indirectly) for monetary purposes is positively related to real national income and negatively related to the relative price P_g/P.

We have concluded, then, that the demands for both monetary and nonmonetary gold depend negatively on P_g/P and positively on y. Consequently, we are justified in drawing the total gold demand function in Figure 4–1 as downward sloping, with a position that is dependent upon y (and also λ). To illustrate analysis with our demand and supply functions for stocks of gold, let us assume that y is determined entirely by the nation's existing productive

[5] Actually, money-demand theory suggests that L will be a function of two variables, $L(y, R)$, with R denoting a nominal interest rate or some other measure of the opportunity cost of holding money and with $L_1 > 0, L_2 < 0$. But here we shall neglect the interest rate effects on money demand in this analysis. (They will be recognized, however, in Chapter 5.)

resources and technical sophistication. That is an approximation that would
be literally correct only if prices were extremely flexible, which is probably
untrue in today's actual economies, but is the assumption typically made in
"classical" macroeconomic analysis. It is highly useful for our purposes, and
may not be too bad as an approximation if we think of it as pertaining to
conditions during the historical gold-standard era.

At a point in time, then, the price ratio P_g/P, the relative price of gold, is
determined as the value at which the stock demand for monetary and
nonmonetary gold intersects the vertical (given) supply. If the supply is G^0 in
Figure 4–1, for example, the relative price of gold will be $(P_g/P)^0$. But since P_g
is specified exogenously—outside our analysis—then it is P that is determined
by the forces of supply and demand for gold. In Figure 4–1, that is, the price
level is determined as $P^0 = P_g/(P_g/P)^0$. It is easy to see, furthermore, that P
would be higher if the existing stock of gold were larger.

But what determines the magnitude of the existing stock of gold? To answer
that question, we must consider processes that add to or subtract from the
existing stock. In most actual open economies, gold flows stemming from
international transactions are crucial, but we are at present discussing a closed
economy. Production of new gold by mining and refining operations is therefore
the only possibility for additions to the economy's stock supply. These
operations are carried out by profit-seeking firms, so flow supply behavior
should be similar to that of other industries. We postulate, then, an upward-
sloping supply relationship, one that makes the quantity produced per unit
time an increasing function of the relative price of gold P_g/P. Such a relationship
is exemplified by the curve labeled $h(P_g/P)$ in Figure 4–2.

Subtractions from the existing stock of gold are also depicted in Figure 4–2,
by means of the downward-sloping curve $\delta f(P_g/P, y)$. This notation is suggestive
of the nature of the process in question, with δ representing a wastage or
depreciation rate—a fractional number such as 0.01 or 0.003—and $f(P_g/P, y)$
continuing to denote the stock of nonmonetary gold. The idea is that gold
employed in nonmonetary uses is unavoidably subject to slow wastage, with
the fraction δ being lost each period. Monetary gold, by contrast, is by
assumption not subject to wastage or depreciation—the central bank keeps its
reserves safely vaulted away.

Figure 4–2 implies, then, that the existing stock of gold will neither grow
nor shrink in size when the prevailing relative price of gold equals $(P_g/P)^*$, for
at that price the rate of new production is just adequate to replace the quantity
lost by depreciation. At higher prices production will exceed depreciation,
however, so the stock of gold will grow, whereas at prices lower than $(P_g/P)^*$
the rate of production will fall short of depreciation and the stock in existence
will shrink as time passes.

The two portions of our model can now be combined, as in Figure 4–3.
Suppose that the various behavioral functions are as illustrated and that the
existing stock of gold is, as a result of conditions in the past, equal to G^0. Then
the prevailing price level will be $P^0 = P_g/(P_g/P)^0$. But at that price for goods in
general, the relative price of gold will be high enough that the flow supply of

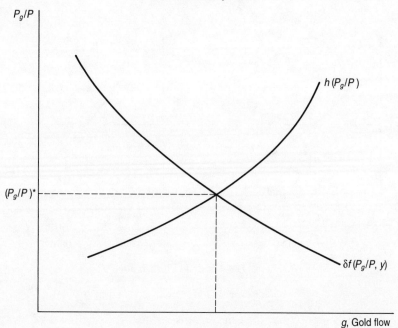

P_g/P

$h(P_g/P)$

$(P_g/P)^*$

$\delta f(P_g/P, y)$

g, Gold flow

Figure 4-2 Flow supply and demand for gold.

newly produced gold will exceed the amount lost by depreciation—$g^1 > g^2$. Consequently, the stock of gold G will grow as time passes; graphically, the vertical stock supply curve will shift to the right. As that happens, the relative price of gold P_g/P will fall—which, with P_g fixed, implies a rising price level. This process continues until the stock in existence reaches G^*, at which time the relative price $(P_g/P)^*$ will call forth a flow supply rate g^* that just offsets depreciation losses. At this position, the system will be in full long-run stock-flow equilibrium.

To analyze the effects of changes in conditions of various types, one can begin with the system in a position of full long-run equilibrium, then shift whichever curve (or curves) is appropriate to represent the relevant change in conditions, and then conduct short-run and long-run analysis using diagrams such as those of Figure 4–3. These will represent the impact and ultimate effects, respectively, as indicated by the model. To illustrate, consider the discovery of a new area fruitful for gold mining. That will shift the flow supply function $h(P_g/P)$ to the right, as depicted in panel b of Figure 4–4, with the other curves remaining unchanged. Beginning with the initial equilibrium position indicated by the price level P^1 and the stock and flow quantities G^1 and g^1, this shift induces additional gold production that moves the stock supply line rightward, lowering P_g/P and thereby increasing the price level P as time passes. The new full equilibrium features $P^2 > P^1$, $G^2 > G^1$, and $g^2 > g^1$.

Another interesting experiment involves a change in the value of λ, the

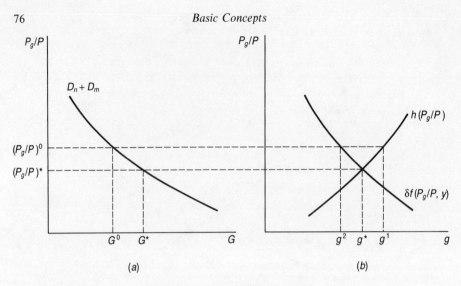

Figure 4–3 Gold standard model.

reserve ratio. Suppose that the central bank reduces λ. Then the stock demand for gold function in panel a of a diagram such as Figure 4–4 would shift downward, since the curve represents the sum of nonmonetary and monetary stock demands and the latter is $G_m = \lambda PL(y)/P_g$. Thus the impact effect of a reduction in λ is a decrease in P_g/P, that is, an increase in the price level. But nothing has changed in the flow supply or depreciation schedules, so at the reduced value of P_g/P depreciation will exceed production and the stock of gold will fall over time. The final equilibrium features the same price level as initially, before the reduction in λ occurred.

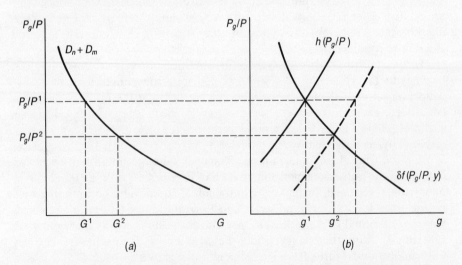

Figure 4–4 Comparative static analysis with gold standard model.

In a sense, however, this last analysis may be somewhat misleading. In particular, the behavior of the monetary authorities with respect to λ is not a matter of indifference, but rather is of great importance to the workings of the system. This is the case, despite the absence of long-run effects of λ on the price level, because the short-run impact effects can be sizable and may be slow to disappear, depending on the slope of $h(P_g/P)$ and the magnitude of δ. Consequently, policy behavior regarding λ can have important effects on price-level behavior over a number of years. Indeed, many scholars attribute the poor functioning of the gold-standard system that prevailed briefly in the 1920s to the behavior of the authorities in attempting to offset the effect on M of international gold flows by variations in λ. It might even be argued that a proper gold-standard system does not exist unless λ is held approximately constant. Also, λ cannot be permitted to become too small or citizens may come to doubt that the gold standard will be maintained, in which case it will break down.

Now we must consider how to modify our model to reflect open-economy and international influences. What is needed, fortunately, is only to replace the flow supply function $h(P_g/P)$, reflecting gold mining and refining operation, with one that represents gold inflows to the economy that result from international trade of goods, services, and securities. Such a modification will still make the gold flow supply relationship an increasing function of P_g/P, that is, a decreasing function of P. Thus an increase in the home economy's price level implies that gold will trade for a smaller quantity of goods and services than previously, relative to other nations. Consequently, gold inflows will decrease. One major difference is that the speed with which large flow changes can take place will be much greater than when limited by mining and refining possibilities; thus the depicted curve will be substantially flatter. Another difference is that the relative level of foreign to domestic income will have a major effect on the position of the curve: higher values of foreign income will enhance domestic commodity exports, thereby tending to increase gold inflows (represented by shifting the curve rightward). Thus we should write the flow supply function as $h(P_g/P, y/y^F)$, where y/y^F is the ratio of home-country to foreign-country real income.

The outstanding feature of price-level behavior under the gold standard is that it is dictated not by policy choices, as in a fiat-money system, but by the forces that determine the relative price of gold in relation to goods in general. These forces include the pace of technical change in the production of goods and gold—that is, supply conditions—and the rate of depreciation of existing gold stocks. Changes in money demand conditions will have short-run but not long-run effects. Consequently, since these real forces can change only gradually and to a limited extent, given the physical nature and historical attractiveness of gold as a metal, one would expect that price-level fluctuations would be fairly limited in magnitude and duration for economies adhering to a gold standard. There would be cyclical movements in P of a few percentage points, but no long-lasting inflationary episodes of major quantitative significance.

4.3 From 1800 to 1914

Armed with our model of price-level behavior for an economy on a gold standard, we are now prepared to briefly consider the first three of the six distinct historical periods listed in Section 4.1. The second and third periods, 1821–1875 and 1875–1914, were both ones during which commodity-money arrangements dominated, so one would expect prices to behave in the fashion predicted by the gold-standard model. One would expect, in other words, that national price levels would fluctuate up and down with the pace of gold (or silver) discoveries and technical progress in the production of goods, but that there would not be any truly rapid or drastic changes in price levels. There would not be, that is, long-lasting periods with inflation rates of even four or five percent per year,[6] much less hyperinflations with prices rising in excess of 50 percent per month. During the years between 1800 and 1921, however, the disruptions of the Napoleonic wars kept England off any metallic standard; during that time the circulating medium of the nation consisted of *unconvertible*[7] paper notes issued by the Bank of England.[8] Consequently, one would not be surprised to learn that the price level rose in England during the wars, and possibly at a fairly rapid rate.

With those considerations in mind it is interesting to examine the actual historical price-level figures reported in Table 4–1. These are wholesale price index numbers assembled by a number of different scholars, with those for years prior to 1900 based on rather scanty information. But they should give a general outline of price-level developments, despite these weaknesses. And, indeed, the Napoleonic war period does show a substantial amount of inflation for the European countries, with price levels being driven back toward prewar levels as commodity-money arrangements were restored (in 1821 for the United Kingdom). Next we also see that over the remainder of the period prior to 1914 there are very few large movements in the price level. The one notable exception shows up in the U.S. data between 1860 and 1870. But that is entirely consistent with our theoretical predictions, for the United States abandoned its metallic standard during the Civil War of 1860–1865 and did not fully return to a metallic basis until 1879 (when it restored gold convertibility at the prewar price).[9] Another notable feature of the numbers is the extent to which prices

---

[6] Note that, say, 25 years of inflation at 5 percent per year will increase the price level by a factor of 3.39, that is, to 3.39 times its initial value.

[7] By unconvertible we here mean that the Bank of England would not redeem the paper currency with gold or silver.

[8] The Bank of England notes were denominated in the traditional British units of pounds, shillings, and pence. They were not declared legal tender by the government, but nevertheless served as the nation's principal medium of exchange until 1821. For a readable account of the period, see Cannan (1925).

[9] The year 1875, rather than 1879, is used in this chapter to mark the beginning of the "worldwide" gold standard because the legislation that mandated the U.S. return to convertibility in 1879 was passed in early 1875. It was almost overturned by Congress but remained in force and induced prices to fall year by year, in preparation for convertibility, throughout the middle and late 1870s.

Table 4-1 Wholesale Price Indexes, 1790–1920.

Year	Belgium	Britain	France	Germany	United States
1790	—	111	—	—	88
1800	—	187	156	135	127
1810	—	189	219	132	128
1820	—	142	132	90	104
1830	—	117	112	78	89
1840	—	127	116	80	93
1850	83	91	96	71	82
1860	94	119	124	94	91
1870	94	116	115	92	132
1880	98	111	103	87	98
1890	86	89	86	86	80
1900	87	86	85	90	80
1910	95	94	93	93	101
1913	100	100	100	100	100
1920	—	316	497	1040	221

Source: U.S. Bureau of the Census (1975) for United States; Mitchell (1975) for all others.

in the different nations tended to move together. Between 1840 and 1850, for example, prices fell significantly in all five nations. That is again what one would expect for a group of nations all adhering to commodity-money systems, even if the standard commodity was silver rather than gold in Germany. This worldwide fall in prices during the 1840s was the result of a "shortage" of gold, which led to a rise in its relative price (and thus, with P_g fixed, to a fall in P). Likewise, after 1900 the supply of gold and silver grew rapidly as the result of mining discoveries and improvements in refining technique, and price levels rose in all nations.

During World I, all of these nations except the United States abandoned their commodity-money standards—that is, they suspended convertibility—and issued paper money in sizable amounts. Prices rose quite generally, as would be expected, as is evidenced by the figures in the final row (pertaining to 1920) of Table 4-1.

In Japan, meanwhile, the yen became the nation's currency unit in 1870, shortly after the Meiji Restoration. Initially the yen was intended to be issued as gold and silver coins and to have an exchange rate of 1.0 with U.S. dollars. Several spells of inconvertibility and devaluation occurred, however, before the gold standard was adopted in 1897. The price of gold was then established at $P_g = 1/0.75 = 1.333$ yen per gram. Since a troy ounce equals 31.103 grams, this resulted in a yen equivalent to $0.75/31.103 = 0.02411$ ounce of gold and therefore implied a yen/dollar exchange rate of $0.0484/0.0241 = 2.01$. Within a short period of time, the Bank of Japan—which was created in 1882—was issuing paper notes convertible into gold, and the yen/dollar rate stayed close to 2.0 until 1931.

4.4 From 1918 to 1945

After World War I it was widely believed in most industrialized nations that a return to the gold standard would provide the best feasible arrangement for the international monetary system. This was the conclusion, in fact, of an international conference held in Genoa in 1922. There was less agreement, however, on the question of the new par value for the various currencies. If the value of P_g, the currency price of gold, were to be returned to its prewar level in a given nation, then its general price level would have to be brought back to the prewar level to be consistent with long-run equilibrium.[10] (That requirement is clearly implied by the model of Section 4.2; see Figure 4–3.) A substantial deflation extending over a period of years would accordingly be required. Nominal wage rates would have to fall, even if productivity increases were tending to raise real wages.

Different nations made different choices in this regard, but Britain chose (against the outspoken advice of John Maynard Keynes, already a leading economist) to return to the prewar par. Thus a substantial deflation, to be induced by monetary stringency, was required. Nominal wages actually fell in Britain during each year from 1926 through 1932. Keynes and a few other economists viewed this period of monetary stringency as largely responsible for the high level of unemployment that persisted in the United Kingdom.[11]

Britain's return to convertibility was effected in 1925, and by 1929 the main industrial nations (other than Germany) were again on the gold standard, with France and Belgium having adopted par values of P_g well above their prewar levels.[12] The downturn in economic activity that developed into the Great Depression was under way in the United States by the end of 1929, however, and as time passed, the depressed conditions in the United States and the United Kingdom spread as those nations' demands for foreign goods declined. There is still much dispute among scholars as to the precise reasons why the industrialized world slipped into the Great Depression, but it did. And as real incomes fell, so did each nation's imports. Consequently, each nation's exports fell. And with many nations on some form of gold standard, exchange rates did not adjust smoothly. So many nations began to adopt *import restrictions*—tariffs and quotas—in attempts to "improve" their current-account balances. The upshot of these restrictions was that there resulted a truly major breakdown in the volume of international trade. This breakdown is documented by the figures in Table 4–2.[13]

---

[10] This statement implicitly assumes that the economy's real technological conditions have not substantially changed.

[11] The British unemployment rate had risen sharply in 1921. It declined somewhat through 1922–1924, but then rose again as the disinflation proceeded. For a few statistics, see McCallum (1989, p. 179).

[12] Germany, Austria, Hungary, Poland, and Russia experienced extreme inflationary episodes, as will be described, following which they adopted new currency units.

[13] For a detailed recent treatment of the period, one that emphasizes somewhat controversially the role of the gold standard, see Eichengreen (1992).

Table 4–2 Decline in International Trade during the Great Depression.

		Ratio of Imports plus Exports to GNP or GDP			
Year	Germany	Italy	Netherlands	United Kingdom	United States
1900	0.321	0.203	2.039	0.427	0.148
1913	0.397	0.239	2.494	0.517	0.133
1925	0.322	0.247	0.744	0.461	0.124
1929	0.338	0.221	0.734	0.414	0.125
1930	0.311	0.204	0.666	0.347	0.109
1933	0.160	0.123	0.420	0.247	0.080
1935	0.117	0.107	0.361	0.252	0.088
1938	0.109	0.131	0.471	0.252	0.087

Source: Mitchell (1975) for Europe; U.S. Bureau of the Census (1975) and Gordon (1986) for the United States.

In the United Kingdom the desire for more expansionary monetary conditions (to increase employment) came in conflict with the requirements of the gold standard, and in 1931 the latter was again abandoned. Other nations followed suit, the United States' response being to increase the dollar price of gold by almost 70 percent in 1933 and to forbid its private citizens to hold gold. In the later 1930s, consequently, international exchange rates were not determined by nations' adherence to commodity-money standards. Rather, they were determined partly as floating rates, but with a substantial amount of intervention on the part of governmental stabilization funds. Indeed, after September 1936 there was in effect a "tripartite agreement" among the United States, the United Kingdom, and France that was also subscribed to by Belgium, the Netherlands, and Switzerland. Under this agreement, those six nations cooperated in utilizing their national stabilization funds to prevent unwanted fluctuations in exchange rates. This system was maintained until the outbreak of World War II. Then as the war progressed, most nations adopted "official" exchange rates, but did not implement them by freely buying and selling gold or foreign currencies at the stipulated par values. Instead, the typical arrangement involved extensive governmental regulations and controls over international transactions of all types.[14] Accordingly, these official exchange rates were not very meaningful in comparison with those determined by multinational adherence to a common commodity-money standard or by a system of freely floating rates.

It needs to be said, incidentally, that the *type* of gold standard that was partially in effect prior to 1933 was crucially different from the version that had prevailed prior to World War I. In particular, the United States did not maintain an approximately constant reserve ratio, comparable to λ in our formal model, but instead acted so as to increase λ when gold flowed in from abroad, as it did in large quantities during the 1920s. We have seen in Section 4.2 that an increase in λ will have no long-term effect on an economy's price

---

[14] Purely domestic economic affairs were also highly regulated during World War II, even to a considerable extent in the United States.

Table 4–3 European Hyperinflationary Episodes of the 1920s.

Country	Dates	Avg. money-growth rate (% month)	Avg. inflation rate (% month)
Austria	Oct. 1921–Aug. 1922	30.9	47.1
Germany	Aug. 1922–Nov. 1923	314.0	322.0
Hungary	Mar. 1923–Feb. 1924	32.7	46.0
Poland	Jan. 1923–Jan. 1924	72.2	81.1
Russia	Dec. 1921–Jan. 1924	49.3	57.0

Source: Cagan (1956).

level. But the short-run effect of an increase in λ is to reduce the price level. In an actual economy, with prices that are not perfectly flexible, such deflationary pressures will tend to manifest themselves partially as reductions in income, which could last for several years. Furthermore, since the United States was a very large participant in the international monetary system, there were even more important effects abroad. In particular, other nations including the United Kingdom were unable to reduce their λ values during the 1920s, because these values were already quite low, while they were losing gold to the United States. Consequently, monetary contractions were generated in these nations. Thus the way in which the gold standard was operated in the United States during the 1920s may well have contributed to the initiation of the Great Depression, for the increase in λ in the United States was substantial. As mentioned above, some critics contend that a system in which λ adjusts in this fashion should not be considered a proper gold standard; Friedman (1963) has used the term "pseudo gold standard."

A striking feature of the interwar period not discussed thus far was the outbreak of *hyperinflation* episodes during the early 1920s in several nations of Europe whose political systems had been severely upset by the outcome of World War I. The basic facts are reported in Table 4–3. It is not clear exactly what political or intellectual forces led the monetary authorities to create money at the enormous rates listed in the first numerical column, but they did so. This was possible, it should be noted, because these nations did not have gold-standard—or other commodity-money—arrangements in place at the time. And prices responded in the manner that standard monetary theory would predict, with monthly inflation rates as indicated in the final column of Table 4–3.[15] The cumulative effect of inflation at these rates over a number of months may be suggested by the following statistic: the German price level at the end of November 1923 was approximately 1.02×10^{10} times its level as of August 1922, only 16 months earlier! The social turmoil created by the episodes was enormous. Many writers have attributed the strongly anti-inflationary posture of the German authorities in recent years to their familiarity with that nation's experience of the 1920s.

[15] For a more formal textbook analysis, see McCallum (1989, pp. 133–144).

4.5 Bretton Woods, 1947–1971

A famous and historic conference held at Bretton Woods, New Hampshire, in July 1944 brought together representatives of 45 nations for the purpose of designing postwar arrangements for an international monetary system. There was a widespread desire to design and implement a rational system that would avoid the perceived disadvantages of both the gold standard and the unsettled conditions of the 1930s, especially the breakdown in trade. The conference led to the adoption of a plan that represented ideas developed mainly by Keynes and by Harry Dexter White, an economist representing the U.S. Treasury.[16] Partly because the United States was at the time much stronger financially— indeed, was subsidizing Britain's war efforts with sizable transfers—the plan adopted was closer to White's original proposals than to those of Keynes.

The Bretton Woods system was one in which exchange rates between nations were to be fixed, but at rates that could be adjusted when necessitated by discrepancies in national growth rates of productivity or other causes that promised to be more or less permanent. The agreement specified the creation of two new organizations, the International Monetary Fund (IMF), whose role was to manage and facilitate operation of the exchange rate system, and the International Bank for Reconstruction and Development (the World Bank), which was to provide loans to needy nations for development projects that promised to enhance the welfare of their citizens. The rules of the IMF called for each nation to specify and support a par value for its currency, expressed in terms of dollars[17]—each nation except for the United States, which was to exchange gold for dollars at the price of \$35 per ounce. Thus the job of other nations was to keep fixed their exchange rates with the United States, and the latter's job was to maintain the value of the dollars (and thus all other currencies) in terms of gold, thereby avoiding major inflationary or deflationary trends. One leading objective of the scheme was for member nations to have convertible currencies, free of the exchange controls that had been so prominent during the war and the depression-ridden 1930s.

A second central objective was to create a mechanism for financing *temporary* balance-of-payments difficulties. Rather than adopting restrictive monetary conditions and thereby tending to induce a recession (as explained in Chapter 7), a nation would obtain the needed international reserves by short-term borrowing from the IMF. The fund from which the IMF would make these loans was provided by each nation's one-time membership or subscription fee, known as its "quota," paid 25 percent in gold or "hard currencies" (i.e., ones that are widely accepted internationally) and 75 percent in its own currency. Short-term borrowings could then be made from the IMF

[16] By this date Keynes had published his *General Theory* and was perhaps the world's most famous economist.

[17] Formally, these rates were expressed in terms of gold or dollars, but it was understood that enforcement of rates relative to the dollar would be the operational mechanism. To some extent, our description applies to the system as it developed in practice rather than the provisions of the 1944 agreement.

in amounts related to the nation's quota. (Quota sizes—and associated voting power—were determined largely by the nation's relative size in world production and trade magnitudes.) Drawings up to 25 percent of the quota could be made at will and up to 50 percent fairly easily, but beyond that point the borrowing nation would have to persuade the IMF that it was adopting policies that would reduce its balance-of-payments difficulties. Since such borrowings were permitted only conditional upon IMF approval of national policies, this practice came to be referred to as IMF *conditionality*.

The IMF came into existence in 1947, but most large members declared par values for their currencies only in later years, Germany waiting until 1953. A conditioning aspect of the early postwar years was the dominant position, in terms of wealth and economic power, of the United States. This strength showed itself in terms of large current-account surpluses in 1946–1948, but a deficit was recorded as early as 1950.[18] That deficit was the result of a large volume of unilateral transfers from the United States to more needy nations; the famous Marshall Plan payments to Europe began in 1947.

Most nations' currencies were not made *convertible* for a number of years; 1958 is usually described as the first year in which convertibility was wide-spread.[19] Thus the Bretton Woods system only began to operate in a whole-hearted manner in that year, and within a very few more years serious difficulties began to manifest themselves. One of these centered around the role of the dollar, which had come to be one of the two main components of international reserves, the other being gold. Trade had been growing rapidly with the "need" for international reserves following in step. But worldwide gold production was much smaller than the growth of desired reserves, so dollars assumed an increasingly important position. And as more and more dollars were held by other central banks, the stock of gold held by the United States became increasingly inadequate as backing for these liabilities. If foreign central banks all decided to convert their dollar holdings into gold, that is, the United States would be unable to fulfill its commitment to sell gold at $35 per ounce. The growth of liquid dollar liabilities in relation to the U.S. gold stock is illustrated in Table 4–4, which shows that the liabilities began to exceed the gold stock in 1960. This tendency naturally led to a declining level of confidence in the soundness of the system. The implied dilemma—the world needed dollar outflows for reserves but each outflow diminished confidence—was emphasized in a notable book by Triffin (1960).

The decrease in confidence in the dollar manifested itself as an increase in the demand for gold, the other main international reserve. In March 1960, the price on the London gold market rose above the $35 per ounce level specified by the Bretton Woods system, reaching $40/oz in October. By October 1961, seven European central banks and the United States had agreed to create a "gold pool" that would cooperate in an attempt to hold the London market

---

[18] The balance on goods, services, and investment income remained in surplus for each year until 1977; see Figure 3–1.

[19] See Schwartz (1983) or Bordo (1992).

Table 4–4 U.S. Monetary Gold Stock and Liquid Liabilities to Foreigners.

End of year	Monetary gold stock ($ bil)	Liquid liabilities to foreigners ($ bil)
1949	24.6	na
1952	23.3	na
1954	21.8	12.4
1955	21.7	13.5
1956	22.1	15.3
1957	22.9	15.8
1958	20.6	16.8
1959	19.5	19.4
1960	17.8	21.0
1961	16.9	22.9
1962	16.1	24.1
1963	15.6	26.3
1964	15.5	29.0
1965	13.8	29.1
1966	13.2	29.8
1967	12.1	33.2
1968	10.9	33.7
1969	11.8	41.8
1970	11.1	43.3
1971	10.2	64.2
1972	10.5	78.7
1973	11.6	87.6

Source: Schwartz (1983); Triffin (1960).

price at $35/oz. Because enough new gold was coming onto the market, this stabilization operation was successful for several years, but then began to break down in 1967. When it became clear in March 1968 that the volume of gold that they would have to supply to the market (to hold the price at $35/oz) would be large, the central banks' agreement was terminated. Soon the free market price of gold rose to about $40/oz.

Between 1968 and 1971, the price of gold fluctuated between $36 and $44, held in check partly by the IMF's introduction of a new type of international reserves, in the form of special drawing rights (SDRs).[20] By 1971, however, the rising volume of U.S. liquid liabilities (resulting from continuing BOP deficits and the partial breakdown of central bank pledges not to purchase U.S. gold) was again putting severe strains on the system. With gold flowing out at a rapid pace and a large payment to France in prospect, the United States finally opted on August 15 to unilaterally suspend its gold sales to foreign central banks, simultaneously adopting a program involving wage and price controls as well as an import tax surcharge. Thus central banks that bought dollars, in the process of pegging their exchange rates, would be unable to redeem them for

[20] Very roughly, SDRs are lines of credit provided by the IMF that enable each member nation to draw on the IMF's pool of currencies. These drawings are in addition to those mentioned previously and are denominated in terms of a bundle of currencies, as with the European Currency Unit (see chapter 11).

gold at \$35/oz as stipulated by the Bretton Woods system. Consequently, these central banks became unwilling to buy dollars with their own currencies when market forces tended to push the exchange value of the dollar below its par. The fixed exchange rate system began to crumble.

In December 1971, a new set of par values was agreed to at a meeting held at the Smithsonian Institution in Washington, D.C., along with a new "official" but operationally irrelevant price of gold of \$38/oz. These new par values reduced the value of the dollar relative to other major currencies by about 8 percent. The extent of this realignment proved inadequate, however, and speculation against the dollar continued, as did upward pressure on the dollar price of gold. A new crisis arose in February 1973, and in March attempts to maintain par values crumbled entirely. To a considerable extent, exchange rates then became free to adjust to market forces. The Bretton Woods system came to an end and the period of floating exchange rates began.

From the foregoing account, sketchy though it is, it should be clear that floating rates were not introduced in 1973 because the world's central banks decided that a floating-rate system would be superior to one with fixed rates. Many economists had been making such an argument, most notably developed by Friedman (1953). But practical men and policymakers had not been persuaded. Instead, floating rates came about simply because central bankers and economic managers of the leading industrial nations found themselves unable to sustain a system of fixed rates. In Schwartz's words, "market forces had triumphed" (1983, p. 350).[21]

4.6 Floating Exchange Rates, 1973–1994

Before reviewing actual experience since 1973, let us pause to consider briefly the nature of a system in which all exchange rates are truly free to float in response to market pressures. In such a system there would be no government intervention in the foreign exchange market; each nation would have its exchange rates free to adjust to whatever values are needed to equate supply and demand for its currency. Accordingly, with no intervention to be conducted, there would be no reason for central banks to hold sizable reserves. Furthermore, with no intervention there would be no flows of reserves to or from official monetary authorities, that is, central banks. Consequently, it will be seen that two strong predictions regarding the operation of a pure floating-rate system are that small volumes of official reserves would be held by central banks and that BOP accounts would show very small deficits or surpluses on official settlements balance. Such predictions were indeed made by proponents of a floating-rate system before 1973 or shortly thereafter, before enough time

---

[21] An interesting account of the breakdown of the Bretton Woods system is provided by Garber (1992). Also see Meltzer (1991).

Table 4–5 Official Settlements Balances since 1973, G-5 Nations ($ bil)

Year	France	Germany	Japan	United Kingdom	United States
1973	−1.9	9.5	−6.3	−2.1	−5.2
1974	−0.3	−6.9	1.2	−7.0	−8.8
1975	3.5	−1.1	−0.6	−2.1	−4.6
1976	−3.0	3.6	3.8	−4.3	−10.5
1977	0.7	2.9	6.5	12.1	−35.0
1978	3.0	9.7	10.0	−2.4	−33.5
1979	1.7	−3.1	−13.1	−18.6	9.9
1980	6.1	−15.6	5.0	−0.7	−9.1
1981	−4.8	1.6	3.6	0.4	−1.2
1982	−3.6	2.9	−4.7	5.1	2.0
1983	4.2	−1.2	1.5	−2.1	−4.0
1984	2.8	−1.1	2.1	−12.3	0.7
1985	2.4	0.9	−0.6	−5.3	5.8
1986	1.4	1.5	14.8	3.4	−33.8
1987	−8.3	20.3	37.9	−6.8	−56.8
1988	−0.0	−18.4	16.5	−1.5	−36.2
1989	−2.3	−10.6	−12.7	−14.4	16.9
1990	11.8	5.5	−6.6	−2.0	−29.8
1991	−5.2	2.1	−6.6	14.4	−22.6
1992	na	43.0	0.6	−1.3	−41.7

* Figures reported are overall balance, sum of current and capital accounts.
Source: IMF, *International Financial Statistics Yearbook* (1993).

had passed for the experience to be evaluated.[22] The extent to which rates would fluctuate, if they were left to float freely, was predicted by proponents to be acceptably small.

Actual experience since 1973 has, of course, resulted in major exchange rate fluctuations—that fact has already been discussed in Chapters 1 and 2. And it was mentioned in Chapter 1 that current-account imbalances have been large in relation to national income for several leading nations, especially in recent years. But the latter observation is not precisely relevant to the position taken by floating-rate proponents, for it is the official settlements balance that should be close to zero with true floating rates, not the current account. Indeed, sizable realized imbalances on official settlements account amount to *prima facie* evidence that exchange rates are *not* being left to float freely. Instead, such imbalances indicate that the monetary authorities are selling or buying foreign exchange, presumably in order to raise or lower the value of the domestic currency on the foreign exchange markets, that is, to influence the exchange rate.

Figure 4–5 and Table 4–5 provide a bit of evidence relating to these two aspects of reserve behavior during the period since 1973. In particular, Figure 4–5 shows that reserve holdings have increased in size as time has passed, and Table 4–5 indicates that the same is true for official settlements imbalances.

[22] The most famous arguments for floating exchange rates were those put forth by Friedman (1953) and Johnson (1969). For an advanced textbook summary written at about the time of the switch to floating rates, see Yeager (1976, pp. 636–643).

Area and country	1952	1962	1972	1982	1990	1991	1992	1993 Oct	1993 Nov
All countries	49,388	62,851	146,658	361,253	670,678	704,672	725,652	760,728	765,608
Industrial countries [1]	39,280	53,502	113,362	214,014	441,946	428,438	424,229	439,197	442,458
United States	24,714	17,220	12,112	29,918	59,958	55,769	52,995	54,747	54,679
Canada	1,944	2,561	5,572	3,428	13,060	11,816	8,662	9,256	8,729
Australia	920	1,168	5,656	6,053	11,710	11,837	8,429	8,318	8,341
Japan	1,101	2,021	16,916	22,001	56,027	51,224	52,937	71,346	.....
New Zealand	183	251	767	577	2,902	2,062	2,239	2,525	.....
Austria	116	1,081	2,505	5,544	7,305	7,924	9,703	10,066	10,381
Belgium	1,133	1,753	3,564	4,757	9,599	9,573	10,914	8,843	9,005
Denmark	150	256	787	2,111	7,502	5,234	8,090	6,448	6,456
Finland	132	237	664	1,420	6,849	5,389	3,862	3,472	3,650
France	686	4,049	9,224	17,850	28,716	24,735	22,522	.....	.....
Germany	960	6,958	21,908	43,909	51,060	47,375	69,489	59,011	60,110
Greece	94	287	950	916	2,517	3,747	3,369	4,476	.....
Iceland	8	32	78	133	308	316	364	321	288
Ireland	318	359	1,038	2,390	3,684	4,026	2,514	4,685	4,693
Italy	722	4,068	5,605	15,108	46,565	36,365	22,438	23,001	23,735
Netherlands	953	1,943	4,407	10,723	13,827	13,980	17,492	24,089	24,072
Norway	164	304	1,220	6,272	10,819	9,292	8,725	14,284	14,448
Portugal	603	680	2,129	1,179	10,736	14,977	14,474	.....	.....
Spain	134	1,045	4,618	7,450	36,555	46,562	33,640	30,142	30,225
Sweden	504	802	1,453	3,397	12,856	13,028	16,667	14,399	.....
Switzerland	1,667	2,919	6,961	16,930	23,456	23,191	27,100	25,186	25,463
United Kingdom	1,956	3,308	5,201	11,904	25,864	29,948	27,300	.....	.....
Developing countries: Total [2]	9,648	9,349	33,295	147,239	228,732	276,234	301,423	321,531	323,149
By area:									
Africa	1,786	2,110	3,962	7,734	12,053	14,587	13,095	13,452	13,230
Asia [2]	3,793	2,772	8,129	44,490	128,826	157,535	164,417	175,191	176,557
Europe	269	381	2,680	5,359	15,535	15,823	15,171	16,321	16,371
Middle East	1,183	1,805	9,436	64,094	37,956	41,777	43,877	45,155	45,296
Western Hemisphere	2,616	2,282	9,089	25,563	34,361	46,512	64,861	71,412	71,696
Memo:									
Oil-exporting countries	1,699	2,030	9,956	67,163	43,875	48,883	45,871	45,534	45,280
Non-oil developing countries [2]	7,949	7,319	23,339	80,076	184,857	227,351	255,552	275,997	277,869

[1] Includes data for Luxembourg.
[2] Includes data for Taiwan Province of China.

Note.—International reserves is comprised of monetary authorities' holdings of gold (at SDR 35 per ounce), special drawing rights (SDRs), reserve positions in the International Monetary Fund, and foreign exchange. Data exclude U.S.S.R., other Eastern European countries, and Cuba (after 1960).

U.S. dollars per SDR (end of period) are: 1952 and 1962—1.00000; 1972—1.08571; 1982—1.10311; 1990—1.42266; 1991—1.43043; 1992—1.37500; October 1993—1.39293; and November 1993—1.38389.

Source: International Monetary Fund, *International Financial Statistics.*

Figure 4–5 Holdings of international reserves, 1952–1993. (Millions of SDRs; end of period.)

However one judges the performance of the post-1973 floating-rate system, therefore, one must recognize that it is not a *pure* floating-rate system that has been in effect.

Turning now to an extremely brief narrative account of pertinent events since 1973, we begin by noting that the U.S. authorities intervened only mildly—according to most accounts—until near the end of the decade. In Europe the situation was somewhat different, however, since most member nations of the European Community had, since April 1972, been keeping their bilateral exchange rates (with each other) within narrower bands than called for by the Smithsonian agreement. After March 1973 they retained these ± 2.25

percent bands, but jointly floated against the dollar in an arrangement known as "the snake." As events transpired, however, several countries left the snake for various periods before the arrangement finally came apart in December 1978. In 1979 a new European scheme came into operation, the European Monetary System (EMS). This system will be discussed rather extensively in Chapter 11. Here we shall pursue the topic no further except to note that the EMS was surprisingly successful until the summer of 1992, since which time several major disruptions have occurred.

Initially the intention of the authorities in most nations was that a new fixed-rate system would be created. Agreement on new par values and operating procedures would have been difficult under the best of circumstances, however, and as the first OPEC oil-price shock came along in late 1973 and 1974, international financial relations were severely disrupted.[23] With the passage of time it became more apparent that agreement would not be possible.

Faced with widespread floating of exchange rates, in violation of its rules, the IMF gradually relaxed its disapproval. After extensive negotiations, the IMF's Articles of Agreement were finallly "amended" so as to permit floating rates, the agreement being reached in 1976 and implemented in April 1978.

Over the years 1971–1979, the value of the U.S. dollar declined considerably (though irregularly) relative to other currencies. The United States was experiencing substantial inflation and continued to run deficits on current account, which caused the supply of dollars on exchange markets to grow faster than the demand. Then in October 1979, Paul Volcker, the new chairman of the Fed's Board of Governors, announced that the Fed would tighten U.S. monetary policy and institute revised monetary control procedures to improve implementation of policy. In terms of domestic conditions the new policy did not become broadly effective until 1981, but nevertheless interest rates rose sharply in October 1979 in quick response. Soon after, the exchange value of the dollar began to rise.

As careful observers of Figure 1–1 will have noted, the value of the dollar continued its rise with only brief interruptions through 1984 and into early 1985. The total change was very large quantitatively, amounting to about 70 percent. There exists some disagreement among economists as to the main cause of this continued climb,[24] but there is no doubt regarding its importance in terms of international economic relations.

Accordingly, in September 1985 the finance ministers of France, Germany, Japan, the United Kingdom, and the United States (the G-5 nations) met and formulated the so-called Plaza Agreement, which called for cooperative action to drive down the value of the dollar (which had already been falling for several months). Official intervention on the foreign exchange markets followed shortly,

---

[23] A useful brief discussion is provided by Kenen (1989, pp. 427–430).

[24] The majority of international economists attribute the dollar's climb, after the initial monetary policy impetus that was released in 1982, to U.S. fiscal deficits and adjustment lags—see Kenen (1989, pp. 439–440). But some scholars have argued that an unusually favorable policy attitude toward business induced foreign firms to wish to invest in the United States, with the resulting demand for dollars serving to bid up their value.

with the central banks supplying dollars for marks and yen. In early 1987 a new agreement, the Louvre Agreement, was reached, in which the G-5 nations announced their belief that prevailing exchange rates were reasonably appropriate and also their intention to cooperatively stabilize these rates at existing levels. A large volume of intervention followed, as market participants apparently disagreed as to the appropriateness of the prevailing rates, and by early 1987 the dollar was again depreciating. Partly for that reason, perhaps, the Fed tightened U.S. monetary policy in 1987, a step that may have contributed to the drastic stock market "correction" of October. In any event, the analytical basis for international cooperative actions, such as those of 1985 and 1987, is of considerable interest and is accordingly the topic of Chapter 12.

A major event in the realm of international finance was the *debt crisis* of many developing nations, which began to attract attention when Mexico announced in August 1982 that it would be unable to make scheduled interest payments on its debt to foreign (mostly U.S.) commercial banks. Similar difficulties soon materialized for other nations, including Argentina, Brazil, Venezuela, Chile, Peru, the Phillipines, and a few African countries. The failure of these nations to make interest payments to their creditor banks led to an unwillingness of anyone to lend to them, thereby worsening the financial situation of the debtor nations. This problem was of great consequence to the United States and other creditor nations because major U.S. banks had enormous loans outstanding to these nations. Indeed, the nine largest U.S. banks had outstanding loans to the Latin American debtors of $51 billion, nearly twice the capital (net worth) of those banks! An outright default by the debtors would then render the largest U.S. banks formally insolvent and threaten a collapse of the entire international financial system.

This frightening situation—which had arisen from a complicated process involving oil-price shocks, U.S. inflation, and world trade cycles as well as some imprudence on the part of borrowers and lenders—immediately attracted the attention and efforts of the IMF and the central banks and other official agencies of creditor nations (including, of course, the United States). Strategies adopted to prevent outright default and financial crisis went through several phases, beginning with debt rescheduling (of payments) and moving on to debt reduction, debt–equity swaps, buybacks, and complex plans devised by James Baker and Nicholas Brady, Secretaries of the Treasury in the United States. These schemes gave rise to a large academic literature that builds upon the fact that sovereign governments cannot be forced to pay international debts, since there is no overriding legal authority, but are likely to lose access to the world's financial markets if they fail to pay. Meanwhile, most of the major Latin American debtor nations have passed through some very difficult times into a period of reasonable economic health and prospects (as of 1994). The international debt problem has not been truly resolved, but conditions have improved and the "crisis" aspect of the problem has receded.[25]

---

[25] For a more extensive (but still brief) account of the debt crisis and a list of references, see Kenen (1992).

Table 4–6 Consumer Price Indexes, 1950–1990.

Year	Belgium	Britain	France	Germany	United States
1950	30.1	13.4	15.5	39.2	29.2
1960	36.5	18.8	26.7	47.2	35.9
1970	49.1	27.7	39.7	61.0	47.1
1980	100.0	100.0	100.0	100.0	100.0
1990	160.2	188.7	183.9	129.4	158.5

Source: IMF, *International Financial Statistics Yearbook* (1984, 1993).

A topic that has been in the news frequently during the early 1990s is the bilateral trade relationship—and the associated bilateral exchange rate—between the United States and Japan. It is a fact that in every year since 1984 the U.S. merchandise trade balance with Japan has involved a deficit in excess of $40 billion. It is also the case that the yen price of a dollar has fallen steadily over that period, from 238 in 1985 to 145 in 1987 to 127 in 1992, 111 in early 1994, and on to values below 100 in the summer of 1994. What to make of these facts is of course the important issue. Regarding the first, most economists would emphasize that even if an overall balance in the current account were an important desideratum—which is far from clear—the same would not be true for the merchandise trade component of the current account, and, more importantly, that *bilateral* balances are inappropriate items of policy concern. There is no reason whatsoever to expect or desire trade between any two nations to balance, just as there is no reason to expect that an ice cream maker's trade with the dairy farm industry should balance. As for the second set of facts, concerning the U.S.–Japanese exchange rate, the reasons for the continued downward movement of the dollar are certainly of great interest in the context of this book's subject matter. Indeed, to develop an understanding of the determinants of exchange rate movements is one of its main objectives. To do so involves some analytical apparatus, the development of which begins in Chapter 5 and occupies the second main part of the book.

To conclude this chapter, it may be of interest to peruse a table of price-level statistics for the postwar era that are comparable to those given in Table 4–1 for the era of the gold standard. Such a tabulation appears in Table 4–6 for the same five nations. The price index used is the CPI rather than the WPI,[26] and the indexes are scaled so as to equal 100 in 1950. The contrast between the gold-standard movements and those of the postwar era could hardly be more striking, as the reader will be asked to spell out in the problems for this chapter.

---

[26] The CPI is usually regarded as slightly more interesting and more reflective of inflation as experienced by typical families. The WPI was used in Table 4–1 because CPI figures for the period prior to World War I are not available. Usually the CPI and the WPI show movements that are reasonably similar.

References

Barro, R. J., "Money and the Price Level under the Gold Standard," *Economic Journal*
     89 (Mar. 1979), 13–34.
Bordo, M. D., "The Classical Gold Standard: Some Lessons for Today," *Federal Reserve
     Bank of St. Louis Monthly Review* (May 1981), 2–17.
———, "Gold Standard: Theory," in *The New Palgrave Dictionary of Money and
     Finance*, P. Newman, M. Milgate, and J. Eatwell, Eds. New York: Stockton Press,
     1992.
———, "The Bretton Woods International Monetary System: An Historical Overview,"
     in *A Retrospective on the Bretton Woods System*, M. D. Bordo and B. Eichengreen,
     Eds. Chicago: University of Chicago Press, 1993.
Cagan, P., "The Monetary Dynamics of Hyperinflation," in *Studies in the Quantity
     Theory of Money*, M. Friedman, Ed. Chicago: University of Chicago Press, 1956.
Cannan, E., Ed., *The Paper Pound of 1979–1821*, 2nd ed. London: P. S. King & Son,
     1925.
Cooper, R. N., "The Gold Standard: Historical Facts and Future Prospects," *Brookings
     Papers on Economic Activity*, no. 1 (1982), 1–45.
Eichengreen, B., Ed., *The Gold Standard in Theory and History*. London: Methuen, 1985.
———, *Golden Fetters*. New York: Oxford University Press, 1992.
Friedman, M., "The Case for Flexible Exchange Rates," in *Essays in Positive Economics*,
     M. Friedman, Ed. Chicago: University of Chicago Press, 1953.
———, "Real and Pseudo Gold Standards," *Journal of Law and Economics* 4 (Oct.
     1963), 66–79.
Garber, P. M., "The Collapse of the Bretton Woods Fixed Exchange Rate System," in
     A Retrospective on the Bretton Woods System, M. D. Bordo and B. Eichengreen,
     Eds. Chicago: University of Chicago Press, 1992.
Gordon, R. J., Ed., The American Business Cycle. Chicago: University of Chicago Press,
     1986.
International Monetary Fund, *International Financial Statistics Yearbook*, various issues.
Johnson, H. G., "The Case for Flexible Exchange Rates, 1969," *Federal Reserve Bank
     of St. Louis Monthly Review* (June 1969), 12–24.
Kenen, P. B., *The International Economy*, 2nd ed. Englewood Cliffs, NJ: Prentice-Hall,
     1989.
———, "Third World Debt," in *The New Palgrave Dictionary of Money and Finance*,
     P. Newman, M. Milgate, and J. Eatwell, Eds. New York: Stockton Press, 1992.
McCallum, B. T., *Monetary Economics: Theory and Policy*. New York: Macmillan, 1989.
Meltzer, A. H., "U.S. Policy in the Bretton Woods Era," *Federal Reserve Bank of St.
     Louis Review* **73** (May/June 1991), 54–83.
Mitchell, B. R., *European Historical Statistics, 1750–1970*. London: Macmillan Press,
     1975.
Schwartz, A. J., "Postwar Institutional Evolution of the International Monetary
     System," in *The International Transmission of Inflation*, M. Darby and J. L.
     Lothian, Eds. Chicago: University of Chicago Press, 1983. Reprinted in Schwartz,
     A. J., *Money in Historical Perspective*. Chicago: University of Chicago Press, 1987.
Triffin, R., *Gold and the Dollar Crisis*. New Haven, CT: Yale University Press, 1960.
U.S. Bureau of the Census, *Historical Statistics of the United States, Colonial Times to
     1970*. Washington, DC: U.S. Government Printing Office, 1975.
Yeager, L. B., *International Monetary Relations: Theory, History, and Policy*, 2nd ed.
     New York: Harper and Row, 1976.

Problems

1. Describe the main differences between the price-level data in Tables 4–1 and 4–6. To what do you attribute these differences?

2. Calculate the (geometric) average inflation rate $\bar{\pi}$ for France over the 40 years of 1950–1990 from the formula $P_{1990} = P_{1950}(1 + \bar{\pi})^{40}$, where P_t denotes the magnitude of the price-level index in period t. Do the same for the 100-year span from 1800 to 1900.

3. Did prices in industrial nations rise more rapidly or less rapidly over the (mostly) floating-rate period of 1970–1990 as compared with the Bretton Woods period, 1950–1970?

4. Using a graphical apparatus such as that of Figure 4–4, analyze the price-level effects in a gold-standard economy of a sharp improvement in the nation's monetary payments technology—such as the introduction of credit cards—that permits a larger volume of transactions to be carried out with any given amount of (real) money holdings. (Assume the initial position is one of full equilibrium.)

5. Conduct analysis such as that of Problem 4 when the initiating change is an increase in the real income of some *other* nations, including some trading partners of the economy under consideration.

II

ANALYTICAL CORE

5

A Basic Model: Building Blocks

5.1 Preliminaries

This chapter is the first of a group, consisting of Chapters 5–9, that form the analytical core of the book. In these five chapters we shall formulate and utilize in several ways a simple but flexible open-economy macroeconomic model that depicts exchange rate determination when policy behavior features floating exchange rates. The model can alternatively be used, moreover, to determine balance-of-payments (BOP) behavior when the regime is one with fixed rates.[1] In most textbooks on international monetary economics, the approach is somewhat different—several alternative models are presented and their properties compared. Our strategy, by contrast, is to develop one fairly general framework, and then consider various special cases that correspond to some of the distinct models of the usual textbook. Each expositional approach has its strengths and weaknesses; the main advantage of ours is that it treats the material in a more unified fashion.

Our analytical framework—our model—will be laid out in the form of three basic behavioral relationships plus two identities, all of which will be discussed in the next few sections. The model includes six endogenous variables— variables determined inside the system—so the five equations will leave us one short. That shortage is then overcome in one of three different ways, depending on the time frame of the analysis to be conducted. For short-run (or impact-effect) analysis, one of the model's endogenous variables is treated as (temporarily) fixed, so that the model's behavioral relations become sufficient in number to solve for the five remaining endogenous variables. Alternatively, one of the variables can reasonably be treated as exogenous—determined outside the system—when long-run (or ultimate-effect) analysis is desired. These two approaches are described in Chapter 6 and used there and in Chapter 7 for floating-rate and fixed-rate systems, respectively.

Neither short-run nor long-run analysis of the comparative static type is fully satisfactory, of course. What would be preferred is true *dynamic* analysis

[1] Similar models have been presented by Flood (1981), Obstfeld (1985), Krugman (1991), McCallum (1989, pp. 271–288), and many others. They are fairly representative of a "mainstream" point of view concerning open-economy macroeconomics.

that traces out the path of all variables as they evolve over time. For this third type of analysis, a sixth behavioral relation is added to the model, one that is itself dynamic in nature. Since dynamic analysis unavoidably involves agents' *expectations* about the future, and these are usually unobservable, this type of analysis is more difficult than either of the two comparative static approaches. Chapter 8 is devoted to an introduction, nevertheless, which should give the reader some understanding of the rudiments of dynamic analysis of exchange rate movements.

The first three of our five basic relationships are closely related to ones studied in courses in intermediate macroeconomics. Consequently, the discussion will proceed fairly rapidly. Readers desiring a review of the closed-economy material could consult one of the standard textbooks in macroeconomics, such as Dornbusch and Fischer (1994), Hall and Taylor (1994), Mankiw (1994), or Barro (1993, ch. 20). The present author's more extended treatment appears in Chapters 5 and 6 of McCallum (1989).

5.2 The Open-Economy IS Relation

One central ingredient in most textbook models of the closed economy is the so-called IS (for "investment" and "saving") function based on the national income identity $Y = C + I + G$. In an open economy the latter becomes, as explained in Chapter 3.

$$Y = C + I + G + X, \tag{1}$$

with X denoting net exports. The variables C, I, and G denote consumption expenditures by households, investment expenditures by firms, and government purchases (of goods and services). The variable Y is a measure of total national product, either GNP or GDP, depending on whether X includes or excludes net factor payments from abroad. Except in special circumstances, we shall henceforth ignore this distinction. All the variables in Equation (1) are expressed in *real*, as opposed to nominal, terms.

To obtain the open-economy counterpart of the IS function, we need to replace the variables C, I, and X in Equation (1) with behavioral relations that determine their values in response to price and income variables relevant to the agents making purchase decisions. The usual assumption is that both consumption C and investment I magnitudes are determined primarily by the prevailing level of national income Y and the real rate of interest, denoted by r. Thus we posit that $C = \tilde{C}(Y, r)$ and $I = \tilde{I}(Y, r)$, where $\tilde{C}$ and $\tilde{I}$ are functions with the properties $\tilde{C}_1 > 0$, $\tilde{C}_2 < 0$, $\tilde{I}_1 > 0$, and $\tilde{I}_2 < 0$. Here $\tilde{C}_1$ is the partial derivative of $\tilde{C}$ with respect to its first argument (Y), $\tilde{C}_2$ is the partial derivative with respect to its second argument, and so on. Thus we assume that both C and I are increasing functions of Y and decreasing functions of r.

Regarding $\tilde{C}$, the idea is that higher levels of income lead to more current consumption spending by households whereas higher rates of interest induce more saving (i.e., nonconsumption) in relation to income. Regarding $\tilde{I}$, the basic idea is that net investment will proceed more rapidly the higher is the marginal product of capital (MPK) in relation to the cost of borrowing r; thus $I = \psi(\text{MPK}/r)$, where $\psi' > 0$ is the derivative of ψ. The MPK refers to a standard production function $Y = F(N, K)$, where N and K are quantities of labor and capital and where the partial derivatives satisfy $F_1 > 0$, $F_2 > 0$, $F_{11} < 0$, $F_{22} < 0$, and $F_{12} = F_{21} > 0$. From the last of these we see that $\text{MPK} = F_2$ will be high when N is high relative to K. Thus $I = \psi(F_2(N, K)/r)$ with $\partial I / \partial N > 0$. But for any given K, N will be high when Y is high. Thus I will be positively related to Y and negatively related to r, as posited above. From this derivation we see that actually K should appear in the investment function, in addition to the Y and r determinants. But the IS function was devised primarily for short-run analysis that treats K as fixed. That is a weakness that will be discussed briefly in Chapter 7.

Turning next to net exports, we assume that $X = \tilde{X}(Q, Y, Y^*)$, where $\tilde{X}$ is a function determining X in response to prevailing values of Y, $Y^* = $ real income abroad, and $Q = $ real exchange rate. For the direction of effect of these determinants, we reason as follows. First, Q is a measure of the price of foreign (import) goods in relation to home (export) goods, so a higher value will tend to inhibit imports and enhance exports.[2] Thus X is positively related to Q; in symbols, $\tilde{X}_1 > 0$. Next, high values of home-country income Y will stimulate the demand for imports and also make it more costly to send export goods abroad, so increases in Y will tend to push X downward ($\tilde{X}_2 < 0$). The effect of income levels abroad is just the opposite, finally, so X responds positively to Y^* ($\tilde{X}_3 > 0$).

The remaining term in Equation (1), government purchases G, is by assumption determined exogenously.[3] We therefore proceed by inserting the three behavioral functions into Equation (1) to obtain

$$Y = \tilde{C}(Y, r) + \tilde{I}(Y, r) + G + \tilde{X}(Q, Y, Y^*). \tag{2}$$

In principle, this equation can be solved for Y in terms of the remaining variables; we suppose the solution is

$$Y = D(r, Q, G, Y^*). \tag{3}$$

[2] This statement glosses over the following issue: even if a higher value of Q inhibits the *volume* of imports, it increases the value in terms of home-country goods of each unit of imports. Thus it is conceivable that the net effect on X *of an increase in* Q would be negative. At this point we simply assume that such an outcome does not occur; some additional discussion is provided in Section 7.6.

[3] We do not mean to suggest that actual governments pay no attention to economic conditions when choosing their levels of government purchases. But here our concern is how the economy works in response to policy choices made by governments, so it is appropriate to proceed as if government purchases were determined from "outside" the macroeconomic system.

Equation (3) is the open-economy counterpart of the IS relation in a closed-economy model. It differs from the latter by recognizing the effects on aggregate demand of two additional variables, the real exchange rate (the relative price of foreign goods in terms of domestic goods) and the level of income abroad. The directions of effect of the arguments of D are as follows: $D_1 < 0$, $D_2 > 0$, $D_3 > 0$, $D_4 > 0$.[4] In words, the total demand for consumption and investment goods plus net exports of the home country depends negatively on the real rate of interest, but positively on the relative price of foreign goods, the rate of (domestic) government spending, and income levels abroad.

For some purposes it will be extremely convenient to have a version of Equation (3) that is *linear* in the relevant variables. This is especially true for *dynamic* analysis, which is inherently quite complicated. Since economic relationships typically come closer to being linear when written in terms of logarithms, for variables except interest rates,[5] let us introduce the notation $y = \log Y$, $q = \log Q$, $g = \log G$, and $y^* = \log Y^*$. Then we write

$$y_t = b_0 + b_1 r_t + b_2 q_t + b_3 g_t + b_4 y_t^*, \tag{4}$$

where the subscripts indicate that the variables are measured as of time period t and are therefore expressed in a manner useful for dynamic analysis—that is, analysis that explicitly recognizes the passage of time from period to period. The values of the parameters $b_0, b_1, \ldots, b_4$ in Equation (4) are related to the more exact original relation (3) as follows: they are chosen so as to make Equation (4) the best possible *approximation* to Equation (3) that is linear in the relevant variables. Since b_2, b_3, and b_4 are elasticities of Y with respect to Q, G, and Y^*, one can also view Equation (4) as an approximation to Equation (3) that is restricted to the class of constant-elasticity functions (for arguments except r). To maintain the appropriate qualitative responses, we specify that $b_1 < 0$ with $b_2 > 0$, $b_3 > 0$, and $b_4 > 0$.

A graphical representation, which will be used extensively in later chapters, is introduced in Figure 5–1. There Equation (4) is plotted on a diagram that places r on the vertical axis and y on the horizontal. Since $b_1 < 0$, the curve[6] representing Equation (4) is downward sloping in the r–y plane. Its position depends on the values of q, g, and y^* that prevail, as is suggested by the symbols in brackets that are shown next to the curve. Different values of any of these variables—q, g, and y^*—would imply a different location for the IS curve. Since b_2, b_3, and b_4 are all positive, a larger value for any one of the

---

[4] The signs of these partial derivatives are not strictly implied by those specified for $\tilde{C}$, $\tilde{I}$, and $\tilde{X}$, but will be guaranteed by a few additional assumptions that are highly plausible.

[5] The reason that interest rates are different is as follows. The purpose of using logarithms is essentially to generate relationships that are linear in *percentage* responses; $\log Y = \alpha + \beta \log X$ implies that a one percent change in X produces a β percent change in Y. (One way of expressing this is to note that β is the constant *elasticity* of Y with respect to X.) But interest rate variables are inherently expressed in percentage form, so taking logarithms is unnecessary (and, arguably, inappropriate).

[6] The curve is drawn as a straight line in this case, to conform with Equation (4), but the graphical representation is also applicable in more general cases.

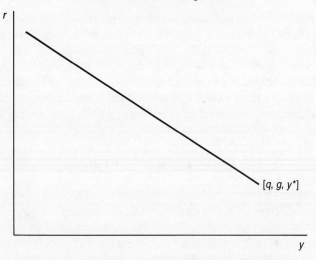

Figure 5–1 Graphic representation of IS relationship.

associated variables would imply a position of the IS curve farther to the right than that shown in Figure 5–1. This aspect of the graphical representation is illustrated in Figure 5–2, where q^2 is a value of q that exceeds q^1.

Some perceptive readers may have noticed that Equations (3) and (4) have been developed in a way that results in the inclusion of government purchases, but not taxes, as an explanatory variable. There is considerable disagreement within the macroeconomics profession over the proper specification, with some scholars arguing that taxes should be included—working in the opposite

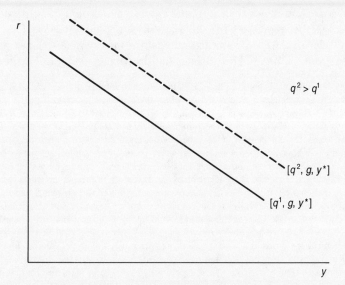

Figure 5–2 Alternative positions of IS curve.

direction from G—and others contending that taxes have no effect. [The latter position, resulting from the "Ricardian equivalence" preposition, is explained and promoted by Barro (1993, Ch. 14).] Here our emphasis will be on G (or g), which both groups agree to be important. Anyone wishing to adopt the non-Ricardian position can nevertheless use our model by interpreting our G variable as $G - T$, with T taxes, or by including T as a separate variable that influences Y negatively via the function $D(r, Q, G, Y^*, T)$, with $D_5 < 0$.

5.3 Open-Economy LM Function

In closed-economy textbook discussions, IS relationships are typically used in conjunction with ones labeled "LM." The latter are relationships that concern the behavior of money demand and supply in the economy in question. Their specification begins with consideration of the nature of money demand, that is, with individual households' choices concerning how much of their wealth to hold in the form of money, rather than in the form of other assets such as bonds, stocks, houses, cars, and so on.[7] The basic choice problem for a household (or other wealth holder) is to balance the expected transactional benefits of holding an additional unit of money—the economy's generally accepted medium of exchange—against the cost of doing so, which is the opportunity cost of extra interest that is lost by not holding bonds or other interest-earning assets.[8]

From simply thinking about the tradeoff in this way, we can easily deduce the main characteristics of the demand for money by an individual household at a point in time. First, since the purpose of holding money is to facilitate planned transactions, more money will be held the greater is the volume of transactions planned. Second, since it is the real quantities of goods and services that people care about, not their nominal values, the relevant quantity of money demanded will be expressed in real (i.e., price-deflated) terms. That is, the behavioral relationship to be studied relates real money balances demanded to real transactions planned. Third, since the drawback to holding money—the

[7] The concept of money being used here, as in almost all economic analysis, is that of a tangible asset that serves as a generally acceptable medium of exchange. In other words, money is a commodity that is routinely accepted in payment by virtually all sellers. Which item serves as the medium of exchange in a society is of less importance than that some item is chosen, for in the absence of any medium of exchange the members of society must devote a great deal of time and effort to conducting transactions by means of barter. Today fiat currencies issued by national governments are the main media of exchange almost everywhere. Empirical money stock measures typically include the quantity of currency held by the nonbank public plus its checking deposits. The latter are included because a checkable deposit is a legal claim to currency, one that can be exercised without delay at the desire of the depositor. In practice it is difficult to decide whether to include some types of deposits that have limited checking privileges and pay interest to their holders.

[8] This statement is worded as if the interest earned on money holdings were literally zero. Such was the case in recent history, but now there are checking accounts that pay interest and can also be used for transactions purposes. Since these accounts pay lower rates of interest than nonchecking accounts, the same type of tradeoff as that described in the statement is still relevant, although the basic nature is somewhat obscured.

cost—is the interest that is sacrificed, the (real) quantity willingly held will be smaller the higher is the rate of interest on alternative assets.

These three properties can be expressed formally in terms of a function relating the quantity of real money demanded by a typical household at time t, M_t/P_t, to its planned spending during period t, Y_t, and the prevailing rate of interest on some relevant asset, R_t. Letting L denote the function, we then assume that the household's money-demand behavior satisfies

$$\frac{M_t}{P_t} = L(Y_t, R_t). \tag{5}$$

Because the variable on the left-hand side is written as it is, this relation satisfies the second property mentioned in the preceding paragraph. The first and third properties concern the direction of response of the left-hand variable to Y_t and R_t, respectively. For them to be satisfied, L must be increasing in Y_t and decreasing in R_t. Let us then complete our specification by assuming that the function L possesses partial derivatives with signs $L_1 > 0$ and $L_2 < 0$. In this formulation we have used Y_t as the symbol to denote the agent's expenditure variable because at the aggregate level, after summing over all individual wealth holders, most expenditure variables are highly correlated with national income. Consequently, we can interpret Equation (5) as an aggregative relationship in which M_t/P_t reflects real money balances held in the economy as a whole, with M_t the nominal money stock and P_t the general price level. Also, Y_t reflects aggregate real GNP or GDP, and R_t is a representative short-term rate of interest.

As before, an approximate version that is linear in the logarithms of the variables (except for R_t) will be very useful. In this case the relation is written as

$$m_t - p_t = c_0 + c_1 y_t + c_2 R_t \tag{6}$$

where m_t and p_t are logarithms of M_t and P_t, respectively, and where $c_1 > 0$ with $c_2 < 0$.

As described, Equations (5) and (6) are alternative representations of money-demand behavior, one of which will be included in the open-economy model that we are in the process of constructing.[9] When using the model, it will typically be assumed that the economy's central bank controls the value of M_t, the domestic money stock, and thus m_t. Other variables in the relation will then have to adjust so that the quantity of money demanded equals the quantity "supplied," that is, the quantity determined by central bank behavior.

For a graphical representation it is most useful to plot Equation (6) on a diagram that places R on the vertical axis and y on the horizontal. Since $c_1 > 0$

---

[9] In each of these equations it would be more appropriate in theory to deflate the nominal money stock by a price index that pertains to all goods appearing on home-country markets, rather than by the price of domestically produced goods [which is one natural interpretation of the price index in Equations (10) and (11)]. But incorporation of that refinement would have only a small effect on the properties of the model. So we neglect it for purposes of analytical simplicity.

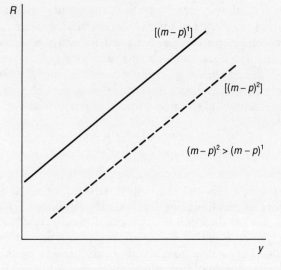

Figure 5–3 Graphic representation of LM relationship.

and $c_2 < 0$, the curve will slope upward and its position will depend on the value of $m - p$ [or M/P if the relevant equation is Equation (5) rather than the linearized Equation (6)]. Since $c_1 > 0$, the curve's position is farther to the right, the larger is $m - p$, as is illustrated in Figure 5–3.

The money-demand relationship summarized in Equation (5) or (6) will depend on various institutional aspects of the economy such as communications and computational technology, credit arrangements, and governmental regulations pertaining to banks and other financial firms. These institutional features change only slowly and gradually over time, so relationships such as Equation (6) will usually remain in place for comparative static experiments. But if there is an abrupt and major change, such as the introduction of new credit networks that affect individual's need to hold money, relations (5) and (6) may shift. The widespread introduction of credit cards in the United States during the 1970s, for example, permitted households to conduct their spending while holding smaller quantities of money than previously.[10] Such a change would be represented algebraically by a reduction in the value of c_0 in Equation (6). Graphically, therefore, it would be represented by a downward (or rightward) shift in the LM curve. Similar reasoning would lead one to expect that LM curves would gradually shift downward as time passes, even without major institutional changes, because of the cumulative effects of improvements in communicational and computational technology.

---

[10] Households need to hold less currency when using credit cards for a substantial fraction of their purchases and can time check payments to the credit card issuers so as to need additional checking account balances for only a few days. Issuing firms have more transactions to make but need to hold extra money less than proportionately, because of economics of scale.

5.4 Two Identities

In the IS and LM functions we have utilized two different interest rate variables, r_t and R_t. The second of these, R_t, represents a rate of interest as normally expressed whereas r_t is the corresponding *real* rate of interest that corrects R_t for the rate of inflation that market participants expect to prevail over the life of the loan. The point, familiar from courses in intermediate macroeconomics, is that the economically relevant rate of interest on any loan specified in monetary terms will depend on the anticipated inflation rate, which measures the loss of purchasing power of money. Thus if R_t is the nominal rate of interest on a 1-year loan, but the lender expects inflation to proceed at the rate π_t over the year, thereby reducing the value of money by π_t in relative terms, the "real" rate of interest to the lender will be

$$r_t = R_t - \pi_t. \tag{7}$$

The same sort of considerations will apply, furthermore, to the borrower.[11] Therefore it is the real rate r_t that is relevant to supply and demand choices in the loan market—hence the presence of r_t in the IS specification of Section 5.2.

Since Equation (5) or (6) represents the demand for real money balances, it might seem that r_t should also appear in that relation, rather than the nominal rate of interest R_t. The latter variable is appropriate, however, for it represents the *difference* between *real* rates of return on money and bonds, these being $0 - \pi_t$ and $R_t - \pi_t$, respectively.[12] Thus R_t is the relevant rate of interest for the LM function and r_t that for the IS function.[13]

In Section 2-2 it was noted that changes in logarithms are approximately equal to percentage changes, expressed in fractional form. Accordingly, we can think of π_t as the expected or anticipated value of $p_{t+1} - p_t$, also denoted by Δp_{t+1}, the value anticipated as of period t. Thus we have $\pi_t = \Delta p_{t+1}^e = p_{t+1}^e - p_t$, where the superscripts e denote expected values. Using this notation, Equation (7) can be expressed as

$$r_t = R_t - (p_{t+1}^e - p_t) \equiv R_t - \Delta p_{t+1}^e. \tag{8}$$

Note that this implies that the interest rate measures r_t and R_t are being expressed in *fractional* rather than percentage units, and in terms of a single period (which might not necessarily be a year). Thus a 10 percent per annum

---

[11] The lender and borrower could conceivably have different expectations about inflation, in which case different values of π would be relevant. But well-informed market participants, such as those active in foreign exchange markets, will typically base their expectations on similar information and will therefore presumably reach roughly similar conclusions regarding prospects for inflation. For our purposes, therefore, it is appropriate to proceed as if lenders and borrowers anticipated the same rate of inflation.

[12] Here it is again being assumed that the rate of interest paid on money is zero.

[13] Actually, it might be more appropriate to have these rates also differing by duration, with a short-term nominal rate appearing in LM and a long-term real rate in IS. We shall not incorporate that elaboration into the model, however, in order to keep it manageable.

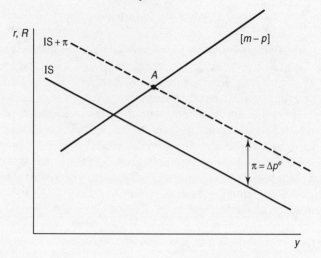

Figure 5–4 IS and LM relations combined graphically.

rate would be expressed, if the time periods represent quarter years, as $0.10/4 = 0.025$.

By making use of the real interest rate's defining equation, Equation (7) or (8), graphical representations of the IS and LM relations can usefully be combined on the same diagram. Thus in Figure 5–4 the curve labeled IS is a plot of r versus y, as implied by a relationship such as Equation (4). Then for the prevailing value of expected inflation Δp^e a second curve, labeled IS $+ \pi$, is drawn that is precisely $\Delta p^e = \pi$ units above IS at each value of y. The latter curve gives the relationship between R and y that is implied by the IS function and the real interest rate definition. The LM relation (6) can then be added by plotting R versus y, and its intersection with IS $+ \pi$ at point A indicates the values of R and y that satisfy all three of the relevant relationships. Frequent use of this diagrammatic device will be made in Chapters 6 and 7.

The second identity to be specified in this section is also a definition, namely, the definition of the real exchange rate as introduced in Section 2.4. There it was expressed as

$$Q_t = \frac{S_t P_t^*}{P_t}, \tag{9}$$

where Q_t and S_t are real and nominal exchange rates (home-currency price of foreign exchange) with P_t and P_t^* denoting home and foreign price indexes. In terms of logarithms, we equivalently have

$$q_t = s_t - (p_t - p_t^*) \tag{10}$$

as in Equation (9) of Chapter 2, but with q_t viewed as a variable.

5.5 Uncovered Interest Parity

Chapter 2 also includes a discussion of the *covered* interest parity relationship, $f_t - s_t = R_t - R_t^*$, where f_t is the log of the one-period forward exchange rate and R_t^* is the foreign nominal interest rate. Brief mention is made there of a related but distinct relationship known as *uncovered* interest parity, which will be adopted now. This relationship is based on the assumption that domestic and foreign securities (bonds, bills, interest-bearing deposits) are close substitutes. We assume in other words, that in the international marketplace lenders (e.g., bond purchasers) are nearly indifferent concerning the nationality of borrowers (e.g., bond sellers) and care only about the yields that they expect to receive. But this indifference does not imply that R_t and R_t^* will be equal, because domestic and foreign securities are denominated in different currencies whose exchange rate (relative value) can change between the time the loan is made and the time at which it is repaid. If, for example, the value of the foreign currency were to increase by 2 percentage points over a one-year loan, the net yield to a home-country resident lending abroad would be $R_t^* + 0.02$, in fractional terms, not R_t^*. Thus if such an appreciation of foreign currency (depreciation in the value of domestic currency) were expected, then a home-country lender would be indifferent between lending abroad at a rate of R_t^* and lending at home at that rate plus 0.02.

Generalizing this line of reasoning, the uncovered interest parity assumption is that the behavior of lenders and borrowers in the international marketplace is such that the following relationship holds:

$$R_t = R_t^* + s_{t+1}^e - s_t. \tag{11}$$

Here $s_{t+1}^e - s_t = \Delta s_{t+1}^e$ is the expected rate of change in the spot exchange rate, the domestic-currency price of foreign currency. If it is expected that the foreign currency will increase in value by Δs_{t+1}^e over the next period, then one-period interest rates in the home economy will tend to equal one-period rates in the foeign economy plus Δs_{t+1}^e, the expected rate of appreciation of foreign currency.[14] If this relation did not hold, the expected yield on domestic and foreign securities would be different. Investors would then shift their funds toward the securities with the higher expected yield, tending thereby to restore the equality.

Equation (11), or its counterpart written in terms of S_t rather than s_t,[15] will then be adopted as the fifth relationship of our basic model of exchange rate behavior. Since expectations can be mistaken, the violation of Equation (11) does not represent an arbitrage possibility, as would the violation of the covered interest parity equation (3) of Chapter 2. Thus it is less certain that Equation (11) holds closely in reality—indeed, some analysts contend that the evidence

[14] As in Section 2.2, it is being assumed that the securities in the two countries are roughly equivalent in terms of risk and other attributes.

[15] The reader should test his or her understanding of Section 2.2 and the present argument by writing out this counterpart equation.

is against it.[16] But no superior relationship has yet been found, and there are good reasons to believe that Equation (11) is a satisfactory approximation.[17]

It will be noted that together Equation (11) and Equation (3) of Chapter 2—that is, both uncovered and covered interest parity—imply that $f_t = s_{t+1}^e$. They imply that the forward exchange rate equals the expected future spot rate. This implication will be considered again in Chapter 9, after more material on expectations and dynamics has been introduced.

5.6 Completion of the Model

At this point we have specified five relationships to be included in our basic model. Each of them can be written either in terms of the raw variables such as Y_t, Q_t, P_t, S_t, or in terms of the logarithmic variables such as y_t, q_t, p_t, s_t. Choosing the latter because of the simplicity of the linear functions implied, the set of Equations (4), (6), (8), (10), and (11) can be brought together as follows:

$$y_t = b_0 + b_1 r_r + b_2 q_t + b_3 g_t + b_4 y_t^* \tag{12a}$$

$$m_t - p_t = c_0 + c_1 y_t + c_2 R_t \tag{12b}$$

$$r_t = R_t - (p_{t+1}^e - p_t) \tag{12c}$$

$$q_t = s_t - (p_t - p_t^*) \tag{12d}$$

$$R_t = R_t^* + s_{t+1}^e - s_t. \tag{12e}$$

In this set there are five variables determined exogenously—g_t, m_t, y_t^*, p_t^*, and R_t^*. But that leaves six to be determined by the model—y_t, r_t, q_t, R_t, p_t, and s_t—even if the expectational variable s_{t+1}^e is not counted.[18] Thus our model is, as it stands, incomplete. To complete it we need to add an additional behavioral relationship that brings in no new endogenous variables, or, more generally, to add a number n of new relationships that together bring in only $n - 1$ new variables.

As mentioned in Section 5.1, there are various alternative strategies used to add relationships that suffice to complete the model. One approach, used in most textbook treatments and also in much of the older research literature, is to limit the model's use to either long-run or short-run comparative static analysis. In the former it is assumed that the purpose of the analysis is to describe the way in which the system behaves (the endogenous variables respond to exogenous changes) *ultimately*, after enough time has passed for all

---

[16] A discussion of the issues will be presented in Chapter 9.

[17] The survey evidence presented by Froot and Frankel (1989, p. 150) is generally supportive, as is the argument developed in McCallum (1994) and summarized in Section 9.4.

[18] The reason why it should not be counted will be explained in Chapter 8.

the indirect and obscure effects of a shock to have taken place.[19] In particular, it is assumed that enough time has passed for price and wage adjustments to be completed, even if these variables are "sticky." Formally, that condition implies that output can be taken as equal to the "capacity" or "full employment" level $\bar{y}_t$, which can reasonably be treated as exogenous.[20] So for long-run analysis we add to Equations (12) the extra condition that $y_t = \bar{y}_t$, and with $\bar{y}_t$ exogenous this completes the model.

In short-run analysis, by contrast, the object is to learn about the immediately occurring impact effects of some change, effects that take place in part because prices and wages are somewhat sticky and so do not fully respond immediately. For such analysis, the formal step is to assume that p_t (or instead a wage rate) is temporarily *fixed* at some historically given level. That reduces the number of endogenous variables by one and therefore renders the model complete. The comparative static responses that will be found with any shock may be very different from those of long-run analysis, of course. Since the short-run effects rely on price or wage stickiness, these effects are best thought of as ones that occur quickly but are transitory or temporary in nature.

The other main approach to completion of the model is to specify precisely how prices and wages respond to shocks through time, period by period. With this approach it is possible to trace out the *dynamic* time response of all variables to any change in conditions. Such an analysis is in principle superior to the use of either short-run or long-run static exercises. But it is also much more difficult to conduct, and it relies on adjustment specifications that may be more uncertain—about which scholars have less knowledge—than other parts of the model. Hence there is a place for each of the three types of analysis—long run, short run, and dynamic—that represent three different ways of completing the basic model specified in the foregoing sections.

In conclusion, explicit mention should be made of the significance of the assumption that y_t^*, p_t^*, and R_t^* are exogenous in the model of this chapter. Formally, that assumption implies that there are no feedback effects from the home-country economy that would significantly alter the values of y_t^*, p_t^*, or R_t^*. Substantively, this implies that the economy under study is one that is "small" in that particular sense—it is insignificant enough in relation to the rest of the world's economy that relevant changes in its national income or price level would not have significant effects on conditions abroad. It therefore requires something of a leap of faith to consider the model to be cleanly applicable to the world's larger economies such as those of the United States, Japan, or Germany. We shall nevertheless frequently utilize the model for analysis of these economies, recognizing that our exogeneity assumptions are

---

[19] In actual economies new shocks will arrive before all effects can be worked out, so no economy is ever observed "in a state of long-run equilibrium." But the tendencies highlighted by long-run analysis are extremely important to understand nevertheless. At every point of time, adjustments of the type identified in long-run analysis are taking place.

[20] Actually, treating $\bar{y}$ as exogenous is reasonable for analysis of some issues but not for others. Our emphasis in this book will be on issues of the first type, but a brief mention of the second type appears in Chapter 7.

not fully appropriate. A bit of analysis designed to relax this "small-economy" assumption is presented in Section 6.6.

References

Barro, J., *Macroeconomics*, 4th ed. New York: John Wiley, 1993.

Dornbusch, R., and S. Fischer, *Macroeconomics*, 6th ed. New York: McGraw-Hill, 1994.

Flood, R. P., "Explanations of Exchange Rate Volatility and Other Empirical Regularities in Some Popular Models of the Foreign Exchange Market," *Carnegie-Rochester Conference Series on Public Policy* **15** (Aug. 1981), 219–249.

Froot, K. A., and J. A. Frankel, "Forward Discount Bias: Is It an Exchange Rate Premium?" *Quarterly Journal of Economics* **104** (Feb. 1989), 139–161.

Hall, R. E., and J. B. Taylor, *Macroeconomics: Theory, Performance, and Policy*, 4th ed. New York: W. W. Norton, 1994.

Krugman, P. R., *Has the Adjustment Process Worked?* Washington, DC: Institute for International Economics, 1991.

Mankiw, N. G., *Macroeconomics*, 2nd ed. New York: Worth, 1994.

McCallum, B. T., *Monetary Economics: Theory and Policy*, New York: Macmillan, 1989.

————, "A Reconsideration of the Uncovered Interest Parity Relationship," *Journal of Monetary Economics* **33** (Feb. 1994), 105–132.

Obstfeld, M., "Floating Exchange Rates: Experience and Prospects," *Brookings Papers on Economic Activity, no.* 2 (1985), 369–450.

Problems

1. Conditional on given, fixed values of p_t, m_t, Δp_{t+1}^e, g_t, q_t, and y_t^*, plot Equations (4) and (6) on a diagram with R_t and y_t on its vertical and horizontal axes, respectively.

2. (Continued from Problem 1.) If the depicted economy's money stock falls, which of the curves shifts? In which direction? Explain.

3. (Continued from Problem 1.) Answer as in Problem 2 for an increase in the real exchange rate and, also, for a fall in incomes abroad.

4. (Continued from Problem 1.) If the expected rate of inflation increases, which curve shifts? In which direction?

6

Long-Run and Short-Run Analysis

6.1 Long-Run Analysis: Stationary States

The objective here is to demonstrate the use, in comparative static analysis of an economy with a floating exchange rate, of the model specified in the previous chapter. We consider first long-run analysis of the simplest type, known as stationary-state analysis. Thus we begin by imagining an economy in a stationary equilibrium, that is, a situation in which all variables are constant through time. Next we specify that some shock occurs, in the form of an altered value for one of the exogenous variables or an altered position for one of the behavioral relations. Then we consider a new stationary equilibrium corresponding to the altered condition and, finally, compare the initial and final values for the endogenous variables of concern. This is the simple procedure, involving a before-and-after comparison, that is the standard fare of introductory and intermediate courses in economics. We shall discuss the procedure initially by means of an algebraic formulation, but will then develop a graphical counterpart that will be used in most of our work.

For convenience let us record again the relations of our model as given in Equations (12) of Chapter 5 plus the long-run equilibrium condition $y_t = \bar{y}_t$:

$$y_t = b_0 + b_1 r_t + b_2 q_t + b_3 g_t + b_4 y_t^* \tag{1a}$$

$$m_t - p_t = c_0 + c_1 y_t + c_2 R_t \tag{1b}$$

$$r_t = R_t - (p_{t+1}^e - p_t) \tag{1c}$$

$$q_t = s_t - (p_t - p_t^*) \tag{1d}$$

$$R_t = R_t^* + s_{t+1}^e - s_t \tag{1e}$$

$$y_t = \bar{y}_t. \tag{1f}$$

Here the parameters satisfy $b_1, c_2 < 0$ and $b_2, b_3, b_4, c_1 > 0$. The endogenous variables are y_t, r_t, R_t, q_t, p_t, and s_t, with the others being exogenous.

For a stationary state, with all values constant through time, these relations can be rewritten as follows:

$$y = b_0 + b_1 r + b_2 q + b_3 g + b_4 y^* \tag{2a}$$

$$m - p = c_0 + c_1 y + c_2 R \tag{2b}$$

$$r = R \tag{2c}$$

$$q = s - p + p^* \tag{2d}$$

$$R = R^* \tag{2e}$$

$$y = \bar{y}. \tag{2f}$$

Note that in Equations (2c) and (2e) some terms disappear. This is because *expectations* of future values are taken to be correct. That is, we have set $p_{t+1}^e = p_{t+1}$ and equated p_{t+1} to p_t (and similarly $s_{t+1}^e = s_{t+1} = s_t$). The rationale for this step is that with values constant through time, expectations are almost bound to be basically correct. From a stationary-state perspective, then, the expected inflation rate $p_{t+1}^e - p_t$ equals zero, so nominal and real rates of interest will coincide. And with zero expected depreciation of the exchange value of domestic money, that is, $s_{t+1}^e - s_t = 0$, these domestic rates of interest are given from abroad by the exogenous foreign interest rate R^*.

From Equations (2), then, we immediately see that the stationary equilibrium values of r and R equal R^* and that $y = \bar{y}$. It remains to solve for the price level p and the real and nominal exchange rates q and s. But the structure of the model makes that task also extremely simple, for with y and r given, q is the only remaining endogenous variable in Equation (2a). So we find that

$$q = \frac{1}{b_2}(y - b_0 - b_1 r - b_3 g - b_4 y^*). \tag{3}$$

Similarly, Equation (2b) implies that

$$p = m - c_0 - c_1 y - c_2 R, \tag{4}$$

and Equation (2d) finally gives

$$s = q + p - p^*$$
$$= \frac{1}{b_2}(y - b_0 - b_1 r - b_3 g - b_4 y^*) + m - c_0 - c_1 y - c_2 R - p^*. \tag{5}$$

This derivation constitutes the first step of the comparative static procedure.

To complete the procedure, one needs to specify precisely what change in conditions is to be considered and then calculate the response of relevant endogenous variables. But these steps also are easy, for the first is just to be specific about what question is being asked whereas the second is made simple by the linear and recursive nature of the present model. To exemplify the process, let us first assume that the change specified is a policy-induced increase in the home country's money stock from the initial value of m^1 to a final value of m^2 with $m^2 > m^1$.[1] Then from the properties of the model as described above, we can quickly determine that there is no change in the equilibrium values of the variables y, r, R, and q; they are all determined by relations in Equations (2) that do not involve m. But Equation (4) indicates that p changes point for point with m, expressed in derivative notation as $dp/dm = 1$, and Equation (5) shows that the same is true for s.[2] So our comparative static responses for this first stationary-state analysis can be summarized as follows: $dy/dm = 0$, $dr/dm = 0$, $dR/dm = 0$, $dq/dm = 0$, $dp/dm = 1$, and $ds/dm = 1$. The model is one that has the important property of long-run monetary *neutrality*.[3]

For a second example, let us next suppose that $\bar{y}$ changes from $\bar{y}^1$ to $\bar{y}^2$. It follows immediately from Equations (2) that $dy/d\bar{y} = 1$, $dr/d\bar{y} = 0$, and $dR/d\bar{y} = 0$. Then from Equation (3) it follows easily that $dq/d\bar{y} = 1/b_2$, and from Equations (4) and (5) that $dp/d\bar{y} = -c_1$ and $ds/d\bar{y} = (1/b_2) - c_1$. Since b_2 and c_1 are both positive parameters, we therefore find qualitatively that q changes in the same direction as $\bar{y}$ and p in the opposite direction. Whether the nominal exchange rate s moves in the same or the opposite direction will depend, finally, on the relative magnitudes of $1/b_2$ and c_1.

A graphical representation of the model is convenient and will be used extensively—indeed, almost exclusively—in what follows. Much of the information can be provided by a single diagram, such as Figure 6–1, that plots interest rates versus output in the IS–LM fashion that is familiar from Chapter 5 or the study of macroeconomics textbooks. In this diagram, Equation $(2f)$ is represented by the vertical line at $y = \bar{y}$ and Equations $(2c)$ and $(2e)$ are together represented by the horizontal line at R^*. For Equations $(2a)$ and $(2b)$ to be satisfied, their plots (labeled IS and LM) must pass through the intersection of the $y = \bar{y}$ and $R = R^*$ lines, as shown.[4] The *position* of the IS line depends on the values of q, g, and y^*, so with y^* and q exogenous the value of q must adjust endogenously to make IS pass through that intersection point. The position of IS is farther to the right for larger values of q, so if IS were to lie to the right of the position shown, the real exchange rate q would have to be lower to attain long-run equilibrium. Similarly, the position of LM depends on the

---

[1] The reader is requested to excuse the loose but convenient usage of language whereby a change from m^1 to m^2 is described as "an increase in the home country's money stock," although m measures the *logarithm* of the money stock rather than its raw value. This usage will occur frequently in this chapter and those that follow.

[2] Thus we see that $p^2 - p^1 = m^2 - m^1$. For very small changes we might record this in "differential" form as $dp = dm$ and use that to justify the conclusion $dp/dm = 1$. More formally, what we are implicitly doing is deriving *reduced-form* equations that express values of the endogenous variables as functions of the exogenous variables alone and then recording values of the (partial) derivatives of these functions.

[3] That is, real variables are "neutral" to monetary changes. For an extensive discussion of the concept, see Patinkin (1987).

[4] Note that in a stationary state $\Delta p = 0$, so $r = R$.

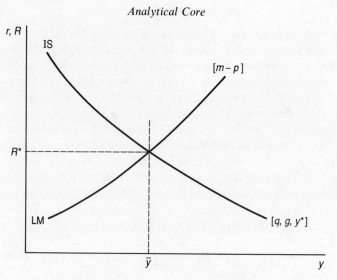

Figure 6-1 Stationary-state diagram.

value of M/P, the magnitude of real money balances, with the position being farther to the right for higher values of M/P (or its log, $m - p$).

Suppose, then, that $\bar{y}$ increases from $\bar{y}^1$ to $\bar{y}^2$, as in Figure 6–2. With foreign values of R^* and y^* unchanged, both IS and LM must shift rightward to pass through the new intersection of $R = R^*$ and $\bar{y} = \bar{y}^2$. That implies that q must rise, that is, that $q^2 > q^1$, and that $m - p$ must rise. With m unchanged, as the exercise assumes, it must therefore be the case that the price level falls—that

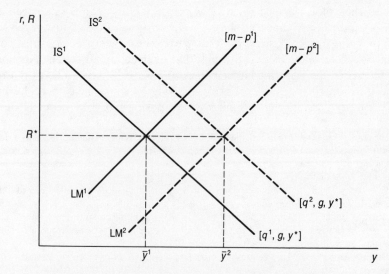

Figure 6-2 Stationary-state analysis of increase in $\bar{y}$.

$p^2 < p^1$. These conclusions are the same as those obtained above by algebraic means. As before, the direction in which s changes is not unambiguously determined.

A different *type* of comparative static analysis postulates changes in private sector behavior patterns or technological conditions, rather than changes in exogenous variables. Households' propensity to save (rather than spend) out of income could increase, for example, which would be represented by a leftward shift in the IS curve. Another possibility might be an improvement in a nation's payments-system technology, reflecting the introduction of credit cards such as VISA or Mastercard, which would be represented by a rightward shift in the LM function. This type of possibility is considered further in Problem 3 at the end of this chapter.

6.2 Long-Run Analysis: Steady States

The restrictive nature of stationary-state analysis, whereby all variables are assumed to be unchanging through time in both initial and final equilibria, seems unrealistic and consequently unsatisfying. A useful generalization that is only slightly more difficult analytically is, fortunately, provided by the concept of a *steady-state* equilibrium. Whereas a stationary state requires that all variables be constant over time, the steady-state requirement is instead that every variable must grow at some *constant rate*, with different rates permitted for different variables. Thus a steady state might in principle have the nominal exchange rate S growing at 5 percent per period, with real income Y growing at 1 percent per period, whereas a stationary state would require that both of these variables grow at zero percent per period. Because s_t and y_t are logarithms of S_t and Y_t, it should be noted that the growth rates just mentioned would be represented numerically by the requirement that $\Delta s_t = 0.05$ and $\Delta y_t = 0.01$ for all t. Thus the steady-state concept offers a considerable degree of generality in comparison with a stationary state.

There are, however, a number of additional restrictions that steady-state growth rates must obey, not because of the definition alone, but because of implications imposed by this definition in combination with the structure of the model in which it is used. In the Appendix to this chapter it is shown that such implications will typically exist and that in the context of the model of Equations (1), the additional restrictions will be as follows:

1. $\bar{Y}$, Y, C, I, G, and X must all grow at the same rate.[5]
2. r, R, and q must remain constant, that is, grow at the rate zero.

Imposing those two restrictions, and again treating expectations as correct

---

[5] The condition would also be satisfied by X remaining constant at the value zero. Since the growth rate of X would not be defined in such a case, this does not actually constitute an exception to statement 1.

(so that $s_{t+1}^e = s_{t+1}$ and $p_{t+1}^e = p_{t+1}$), the model of Equations (1) can then be expressed as follows:

$$\Delta y = b_3 \Delta g + b_4 \Delta y^* \tag{6a}$$

$$\Delta m - \Delta p = c_1 \Delta y \tag{6b}$$

$$r = R - \Delta p \tag{6c}$$

$$0 = \Delta s - \Delta p + \Delta p^* \tag{6d}$$

$$R = R^* + \Delta s \tag{6e}$$

$$\Delta y = \Delta \bar{y}. \tag{6f}$$

From these expressions, some interesting conclusions can be obtained. First, from Equation (6d) we see that steady-state paths of s_t and p_t must satisfy the condition

$$\Delta s_t = \Delta p_t - \Delta p_t^*, \tag{7}$$

which we met with before as Equation (10) of Chapter 2. Thus steady-state behavior of exchange rates will, in the absence of stochastic shocks, conform to the purchasing power parity theory. Second, from Equation (6e) we see that home-country nominal interest rates may differ from those prevailing abroad, the constant difference equaling the expected rate of depreciation of the domestic currency. Third, by eliminating Δs between Equations (6d) and (6e) and then using Equation (6c), we find that

$$r = R^* - \Delta p^*. \tag{8}$$

Therefore, since $R^* - \Delta p^*$ is the foreign real interest rate r^*, we see that steady-state analysis presumes that real interest rates are equalized across countries—that r conforms to the exogenous foreign value r^*. Finally, Equation (6d) indicates that the home country's inflation rate Δp equals $\Delta m - c_1 \Delta y$. Thus if real output is growing at a positive rate, the steady-state inflation rate will be lower than the steady-state rate of growth of the money stock, Δm.[6]

A special case of a steady state is one in which $\Delta \bar{y} = 0$, so that there is no growth in real output. This case may be rendered somewhat more relevant by interpreting the quantity variables in per-capita terms, so that population growth is still permitted, but a more general extension will be developed below. For now, the case with $\Delta y = \Delta g = \Delta y^* = 0$ can be depicted graphically, as illustrated in Figure 6–3. As in Figure 6–1, it is necessary for equilibrium that the IS curve pass through a point defined by the intersection of the vertical line $y = \bar{y}$ and a horizontal line equating domestic and foreign rates of interest. But in this case the latter is represented by condition (8), that $r = r^*$. Indeed, it is

---

[6] The reader may note that we have not discussed the implications of Equation (6a). Since we know that $\Delta y = \Delta \bar{y} = \Delta g$, we can write that equation as $(1 - b_3)\Delta \bar{y} = b_4 \Delta \bar{y}^*$, which becomes another steady-state requirement. If in addition we require $\Delta \bar{y} = \Delta \bar{y}^*$, as suggested by the analysis of the Appendix, then $1 - b_3 = b_4$ is also implied. That condition will be used later.

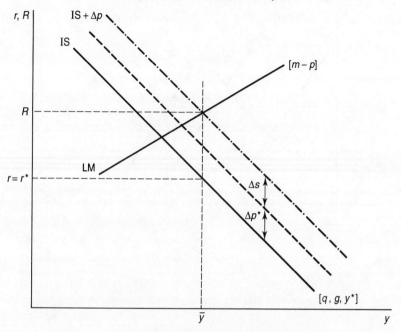

Figure 6-3 Steady-state diagram.

not true that R must equal R^*; we have already seen this in Equation (6e). To determine R, we use Equation (6c) instead and add the inflation rate Δp to $r = r^*$. Graphically it is convenient to do this by plotting a curve labeled IS $+ \Delta p$, which lies above the IS curve by the amount Δp at each point, and then using its intersection with $y = \bar{y}$ to determine R.

That intersection point, furthermore, is also the point of intersection for $y = \bar{y}$ and the LM curve. This can be seen not from Equation (6b) but from Equation (2b), in which $m - p$ is constant when y and R are constant, and implies that M/P is constant (which means that $\Delta p = \Delta m$). Thus LM intersects IS $+ \Delta p$ at the point at which $y = \bar{y}$ and $R = r + \Delta p = r^* + \Delta p$.

Finally, there is the relation (6d), which gives $\Delta s = \Delta p - \Delta p^*$. Figure 6-3 is drawn for an example in which Δp^* is positive but smaller than Δp, giving Δs as the residual distance between the IS and IS $+ \Delta p$ lines. It is of course possible, however, that Δp^* exceeds Δp—in which case Δs would be negative—or that Δp^* is zero or negative.

Analysis of a comparative steady-state experiment in which $\bar{y}$ increases is illustrated in Figure 6-4. Thus we posit a one-time jump of $\bar{y}$ from $\bar{y}^1$ to $\bar{y}^2$, with $\Delta \bar{y} = 0$ in the steady states before and after this jump. Since Δm is the same after the jump, by assumption, so is Δp, so $R^2 = r^* + \Delta p^2$ equals $R^1 = r^* + \Delta p^1$. But the position of the LM curve is farther to the right in the second steady state, so it can be deduced that $(m - p)^2$ exceeds $(m - p)^1$. Assuming that the path of the money stock is continuous at the time of the change, it then follows that the price-level path is lower

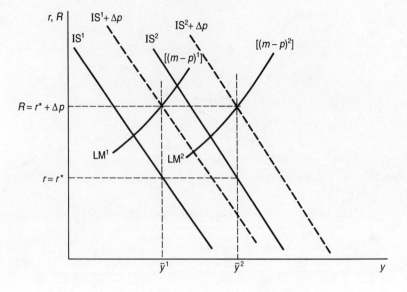

Figure 6–4 Steady-state analysis of increase in $\bar{y}$.

after the increase of $\bar{y}$ to $\bar{y}^2$. The time profile of p_t and m_t is as indicated in Figure 6–5.[7]

A very different experiment is depicted in the two parts of Figure 6–6. This experiment is one in which $\bar{y}$ is the same in before-and-after steady states, but the money stock growth rate increases from Δm^1 to Δm^2. With $\Delta y = 0$, it follows from Equation (6b) that the steady-state inflation rate changes similarly since $\Delta p^1 = \Delta m^1$ and $\Delta p^2 = \Delta m^2$. But the ratio M/P (and therefore the logarithmic difference $m - p$) changes, *falling* from $(M/P)^1$ to $(M/P)^2 < (M/P)^1$! From a steady-state perspective, then, higher growth rates of the nominal money supply lead to lower levels of real money balances. With Δp^* unchanged, by assumption, the steady-state rate of depreciation of the domestic currency increases from Δs^1 to $\Delta s^2 = \Delta p^2 - \Delta p^*$.

The foregoing experiment should not be confused with one in which the money stock is increased discretely at a point in time but with no change in its growth rate. The reader should conduct analysis sufficient to convince himself or herself that in this case all real variables are unaffected, with p_t and s_t jumping up by the same amount as m_t (i.e., with P_t and S_t responding by the same percentage as the change in M_t, so that M_t/P_t and M_t/S_t are unchanged).

Also of much interest from a policy perspective is the response to a change in g, government purchases. Consider an increase in the steady-state value of g. Graphically such an increase would shift the IS function rightward, leaving LM unchanged. But since neither $\bar{y}$ nor r^* is affected by the fiscal policy action, the new steady-state equilibrium must pass through the same $y = \bar{y}$, $r = r^*$

---

[7] For more detail concerning analysis of this type, in a closed-economy context, see McCallum (1989, pp. 109–131).

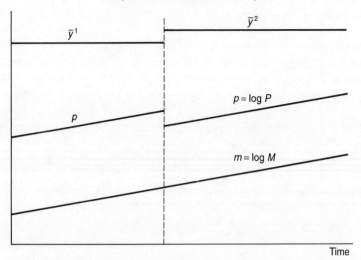

Figure 6–5 Time profile of m and p.

point as before. Thus IS must shift back to its original position. This will happen by means of a reduction in the value of q, a determinant of the position of IS.[8] From a long-run perspective, then, a fiscal policy stimulus has the effect of lowering the real price of foreign goods. With the paths of p_t and p_t^* unchanged, this entails a lowering of the time path of s_t, the nominal exchange rate—an increase in the exchange value of the domestic currency.

Let us now consider an expositional device (i.e., a "trick") that will enable us to utilize diagrams such as Figures 6–3 and 6–4 for steady-state equilibria in which output is *growing*, with $\Delta y = \Delta \bar{y} = \Delta y^* > 0$. The trick is to define a new variable, $\tilde{y}_t$, as the difference between y_t and $\bar{y}_t$, $\tilde{y}_t = y_t - \bar{y}_t$. In a steady state, y_t will equal $\bar{y}_t$, so we will have $\tilde{y}_t = 0$ and $\Delta \tilde{y}_t = \Delta \tilde{y} = 0$. Also, we define $\tilde{g}_t = g_t - \bar{y}_t$ and $\tilde{y}_t^* = y_t^* - \bar{y}_t$. These values will not equal zero but will be constant over time in a steady-state equilibrium. With these definitions (and assuming that $b_3 + b_4 = 1$) we can rewrite the IS function (1a) as

$$\tilde{y}_t = b_0 + b_1 r_t + b_2 q_t + b_3 \tilde{g}_t + (1 - b_3)\tilde{y}_t^*.$$

Then one can plot this curve exactly as we plotted Equation (1a) in Figure 6–3, except that $\tilde{y}$ replaces y (and 0 replaces $\bar{y}$) on the horizontal axis, and that the curve's position is indexed by $[q, \tilde{g}, \tilde{y}^*]$ rather than $[q, g, y^*]$. This position will not change with time, even though $\bar{y}_t$ and y_t are growing.

Similarly, the LM curve can be plotted on this modified diagram by defining $\tilde{m}_t = m_t - c_1 \bar{y}_t$ and making its position depend on $[\tilde{m} - p]$ rather than $[m - p]$. Thus by incorporating these devices, we can obtain a diagram that is exactly like Figure 6–3, except that a few symbols are modified—$\tilde{y}$, 0, $\tilde{g}$, $\tilde{y}^*$, and $\tilde{m}$

---

[8] How do we know that it is q rather than y^* that adjusts to move IS back toward its previous position?

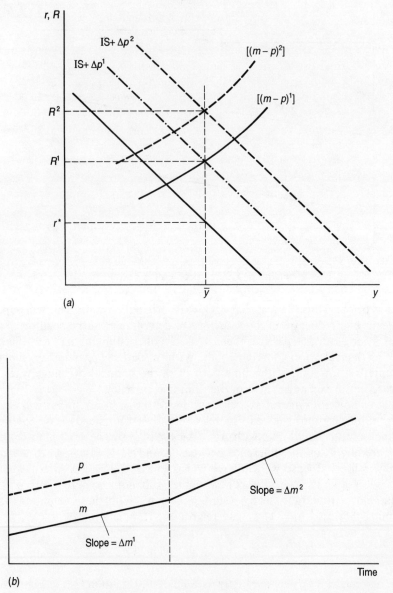

Figure 6–6 Steady-state analysis of change in money-growth rate.

replacing y, $\bar{y}$, g, y^*, and m. Consequently, there is no need to actually draw the new diagram; we can simply reinterpret the one we already have as pertaining to a steady-state equilibrium with growing output. And comparative static analysis, with the steady-state equilibria, can be conducted in the same manner as in the cases already considered with $\Delta y = 0$.

6.3 Short-Run Analysis

We now turn to comparative static analysis of the short-run type, which is designed to provide indications about quickly occurring *impact* effects of various shocks. Since these effects differ from long-run effects primarily because of price and wage rate stickiness, the analytical condition that defines short-run analysis is a (temporarily) fixed price level. Output is permitted to depart from its long-run equilibrium value $\bar{y}_t$, however. Indeed it is assumed that output can exceed $\bar{y}_t$ temporarily when demand conditions are more stimulative than normal.

An important question that arises is what to assume about the expectational variables p_{t+1}^e and s_{t+1}^e. Since we will be considering the immediate impact effects of postulated shocks, it seems fairly reasonable for the analysis to presume that there is no response by these expectational variables. That presumption does not settle the issue, however, because it is unclear whether it is s_{t+1}^e or Δs_{t+1}^e that is by assumption unchanged. (There is no analogous problem with respect to p_{t+1}^e, because p_t is being held fixed, which implies that Δp_{t+1}^e will be unchanged if and only if p_{t+1}^e is unchanged.) Consequently, some analysts have adopted one of these assumptions, with others selecting the other. There are two reasons, however, for assuming that it is Δs_{t+1}^e that is unchanged and, moreover, that its value is zero. One reason is that this is by far the more common assumption in the literature.[9] The second (and better) reason is that exchange rates have been found empirically to behave much like random walk variables, which implies that $\Delta s_{t+1}^e = 0$ is a "rational" expectational condition.[10] It is also common in the literature for $\Delta p_{t+1}^e = 0$ to be assumed. For the most part we shall also adopt that assumption, because it makes exposition of the model especially simple. But it will be shown that this special case is not needed for the analysis—we could just as well proceed with Δp_{t+1}^e assumed to equal any other given value.

With these various short-run assumptions imposed, the model of Chapter 5 can be written as follows:

$$y_t = b_0 + b_1 r_t + b_2 q_t + b_3 g_t + b_4 y_t^* \qquad (9a)$$

$$m_t - p_t = c_0 + c_1 y_t + c_2 R_t \qquad (9b)$$

$$r_t = R_t - \Delta p_{t+1}^e \qquad (9c)$$

$$q_t = s_t - p_t + p_t^* \qquad (9d)$$

$$R_t = R_t^* + 0. \qquad (9e)$$

With $\Delta p_{t+1}^e = 0$, we can substitute the final three equations into the first two and obtain

---

[9] See, for example, Henderson (1979), Kearney (1990, pp. 312–327), and Marston (1985). The minority position is taken by Krugman and Obstfeld (1994, ch. 15).

[10] More discussion of this point will appear in Chapters 8 and 9.

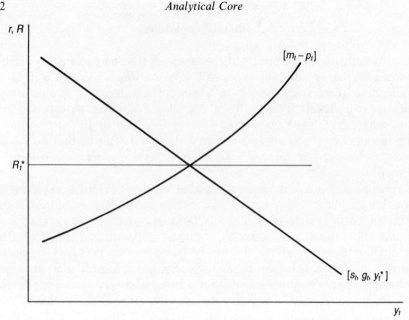

Figure 6–7 Diagram for short-run analysis.

$$y_t = b_0 + b_1 R_t^* + b_2(s_t - p_t + p_t^*) + b_3 g_t + b_4 y_t^* \tag{10}$$

$$m_t - p_t = c_0 + c_1 y_t + c_2 R_t^*. \tag{11}$$

But with R_t^* and m_t exogenous, and p_t held fixed for the purpose of short-run analysis, Equation (11) determines output as $y_t = (1/c_1)(m_t - p_t - c_0 - c_2 R_t^*)$ and then Equation (10) determines s_t in response to that value of y_t.

For a graphical presentation we can again use the R_t versus y_t plot of IS–LM analysis. In Figure 6–7 the equilibrium position is determined by the inter-section of the money-demand function and the $R_t = R_t^*$ line. The exchange rate s_t then adjusts so as to make the IS equation (10) pass through that point. To determine how the endogenous variables s_t and y_t respond to changes in m_t, g_t, R_t^*, or parameter values, one can proceed as in the previous section. One example is provided by a change in g_t. Suppose accordingly that g_t is changed to a value greater than that implicit in Figure 6–7. Then the IS curve would shift to the right if all its determinant variables were unchanged in value. But it must again pass through the indicated LM and $R_t = R_t^*$ intersection for (short-run) equilibrium, so the conclusion is that s_t must fall enough to keep IS in its initial position. Thus we find that an increase in g has no effect on y_t but lowers s_t, raising the value of the home-country currency.

At this point it can quickly be illustrated how the analysis would go if the expected inflation rate Δp_{t+1}^e were equal to some value other than zero. In that case the relevant intersection would be that of the schedules IS $+ \Delta p_{t+1}^e$ and LM, rather than IS and LM. Consequently, Figure 6–7 could be replaced with one in which IS + Δp^e_{t+1} appears where IS is in Figure 6–7, with IS below that schedule by the amount Δp^e_{t+1} (and the vertical scale displaced for r_t). But since Δp^e_{t+1} is a predetermined value, the comparative static analysis would proceed just as before.

Before moving on let us also, for the sake of comparison, consider an increase in the money stock m_t. With p_t fixed and R^*_t given from abroad, there will be a straightforward expansion in output y_t, according to Equation (11). Then s_t also increases, according to Equation (10), and with p_t fixed we see that the real exchange rate q_t rises as well. These responses to a change in m_t are quite different, it will be noted, from those of Section 6.2.

After conducting an analysis of the short-run effects of a given change in policy (or a shift in a behavioral relation), one can continue by letting the price level respond and the system move to its long-run equilibrium. Thus in the just completed short-run analysis of an increase in m_t, the short-run equilibrium features $y > \bar{y}$. But that sort of a situation, with output above its normal or capacity value, would lead to price-level increases as firms tend to exploit the temporary excess of demand over normal productive capacity. As p rises over time, then, $m - p$ will fall, shifting the LM curve to the left. That type of movement will continue, moreover, so long as $y > \bar{y}$. Thus LM will eventually return to its original position with the new value of $m - p$ equal to its original value, $m^2 - p^2 = m^1 - p^1$, implying that $p^2 - p^1 = m^2 - m^1$. Also, as p rises during the transition, $q = s - p + p^*$ will fall, moving IS back toward its original position. In the stationary-state equilibrium, q must equal its original value to make IS pass through the point at which $y = \bar{y}$ and $R = R^*$. Thus s must rise by the same amount as p: $s^2 - s^1 = p^2 - p^1 = m^2 - m^1$. Again we observe the phenomenon of long-run monetary neutrality.

6.4 Discussion

The three variants of the foregoing model are often used by analysts to reach conclusions about macroeconomic policy actions and institutional arrangements. The short-run version,[11] in particular, is frequently used to make comparisons of the relative effectiveness of monetary and fiscal policy actions under fixed and floating exchange rates, a major conclusion being that the effectiveness of monetary policy relative to fiscal policy is greater with flexible than with fixed rates.[12] In fact, we will briefly point to that conclusion in Chapter 7, where analysis with fixed exchange rates is introduced.

---

[11] This version, the one specified in Section 6.3, is typically referred to as the Mundell–Fleming model, as it was specified and utilized in historically notable articles by Robert Mundell (1962, 1963) and Marcus Fleming (1962). The model's use of the IS–LM structure with a fixed price level was typical of the analysis of that time, but the model's introduction of the assumption of capital mobility (via the UIP relation) was a major step forward. This step was taken, moreover, when actual capital mobility was still *much* more restricted than it is today. So the step reflected considerable insight, as well as manipulative skill, by the model's creators.

[12] See Fleming (1962) and Mundell (1963).

It needs to be emphasized, however, that the policy-response predictions of the model are quite different for its different versions. A monetary stimulus leads to an increase in output and the real exchange rate, according to the impact-effect analysis of the short-run version, whereas no ultimate change occurs for either of those variables according to the stationary or steady-state versions.[13] Furthermore, the assumptions pertaining to expectations adopted for the short-run version are rather troublesome—do not expectations respond rather quickly to changed conditions in actual exchange rate markets? Furthermore, the main concerns of policymakers and practitioners probably pertain to behavior over spans of time that are longer than those that can be satisfactorily addressed by short-run analysis yet shorter than can be addressed by long-run analysis of the comparative static type.

For these and other reasons, what an ambitious analyst will naturally strive for is an approach that will permit genuine dynamic analysis, that is, analysis that predicts or explains the period-by-period evolution over time of the system's endogenous variables. Such analysis is quite difficult, of course, partly because it will necessarily involve market participants' *expectations* regarding the future—which are beliefs that cannot be easily or reliably measured. Some headway can be made, nevertheless, by reliance on auxiliary hypotheses regarding expectational behavior. An introduction to such analysis will be the topic of Chapter 8. But before turning to it, two additional topics in comparative static analysis need to be treated briefly, and we need to learn to use our model for economies with fixed exchange rates.

6.5 Representation of Monetary Policy Actions

Throughout the earlier sections of this chapter, monetary policy actions have been described in terms of changes in m, the (log of the) quantity of money. In newspaper or television accounts, by contrast, monetary policy actions are typically described in terms of changes in interest rates. An increase in some key short-term interest rate is, for example, the way in which a tightening of monetary policy is described, with a reduction in that rate interpreted as a loosening of the policy stance.[14] With respect to the effects of such changes on exchange rates, it is usually presumed that a tightening of monetary policy (an increase in R_t) will tend to produce an appreciation of the home nation's exchange rate, that is, a reduction in s_t.

In the context of many policy discussions there is no conflict between the practice of describing a monetary tightening as an increase in R_t and that of describing the same tightening as a decrease in m_t. Indeed, to interpret an

---

[13] The long-run version of our model is related to one that is referred to in the literature as the "monetary" or "monetarist" model of exchange rate analysis. Our version is significantly more general, however, for the monetary model treats the real exchange rate as a fixed constant. As we have seen in Chapter 2, that is often an inaccurate assumption.

[14] In the United States this key rate is the federal funds rate, which is the rate for overnight loans among commercial banks.

increase in R_t and a decrease in m_t as essentially the same thing makes very good sense because they amount to two ways of describing the type of policy action that is typically employed when tighter monetary conditions are desired by a central bank, namely, an open-market sale of securities that it holds. Such a sale directly decreases the amount of base money outstanding[15] and thereby induces a decrease in the money stock. But how does a central bank persuade commercial banks or others to purchase the securities that it offers for sale? The most effective way, of course, is to offer them at a reduced price, and that is *equivalent* to an increased rate of interest on those securities.

In the context of our short-run analysis in Section 6.3, however, it is an important expositional puzzle to reconcile the description of monetary tightening as a reduction in m_t with the popular characterization as an increase in R_t. This is a problem because, according to our short-run analysis, R_t is a variable that is not controllable by the home country's policymakers. That follows from the uncovered interest parity (UIP) equation $R_t = R_t^* + \Delta s_{t+1}^e$, since R_t^* is given exogenously and Δs_{t+1}^e is assumed to be predetermined (perhaps at the value zero). One possible reaction would be to dismiss the popular mode of description as incorrect, on the grounds that changes in the quantity of base money provide the best summary statistic available of the cumulative extent of open-market purchases over any period. But such a reaction would be unproductive and also unreasonable, since the popular mode of description is frequently used by actual policymakers—for example, economists employed by the Fed or the Bundesbank—as well as by media commentators. So a reconciliation is needed.

The best way of providing one is, it seems, to note that a decrease in m_t leads in our model to a decrease in s_t (an appreciation) and other effects that are thought to follow from a policy-driven increase in R_t. Then the other step is to *interpret* the initiating change—the decrease in m_t—as an increase in R_t that is almost immediately erased by a decrease in s_t that is matched by an induced change in s_{t+1}^e. Correspondingly, a loosening of monetary policy, effected by an open-market purchase by the central bank, would be described by the media as a reduction in R_t and would be represented in our model by an increase in m_t that is accompanied by a reduction in R_t that is quickly reversed by an increase in s_t (which is matched by an increase in s_{t+1}^e).

If we were concerned with short-run analysis in a closed-economy version of our model, there would be no puzzle of the type under discussion. Instead, a leftward shift of the LM curve occurring due to a decrease in m_t would simultaneously result in an increase in R_t. Also, in our open-economy context such an increase would occur if the economy were not negligibly small—if it were large enough that its central bank could affect the rate of interest abroad.[16] Alternatively, if international capital mobility was limited—if there were

---

[15] Base money is the sum of banks' reserves and currency held by the nonbank public. The central bank's sale of securities reduces the first or second component, depending on whether the securities are purchased by banks or others. More discussion of this topic appears in Section 7.1.

[16] Such a situation is considered in Section 6.6, but only for long-run analysis, in which case monetary policy has no effect on R_t if stationary-state analysis is conducted.

restricted possibilities for international exchange of financial securities—then the UIP relation (1e) would not hold exactly, so R_t would not be entirely predetermined. It is only for a situation involving extremely high capital mobility and a small open economy that the puzzle even arises, but that combination of conditions is precisely the one that most of our analysis presumes! Accordingly, it is important to recognize that the interpretation of the previous paragraph is available and provides an entirely satisfactory resolution to the expositional puzzle.

In this context it might be noted that the foregoing puzzle would not arise if our short-run expectational assumption were that s_{t+1}^e, rather than Δs_{t+1}^e, is unaffected by the change under consideration in a comparative static experiment. For in this case a decrease in m_t could result in a decrease in s_t together with an increase in R_t and still be consistent with the UIP relation $R_t = R_t^* + s_{t+1}^e - s_t$. Indeed, under this alternative assumption about expectations, and with monetary policy actions expressed as a change in R_t, the UIP relation is evidently the only one needed to determine the reaction of s_t. The single Equation (1e) appears to provide a complete short-run model of exchange rate determination. But despite these attractive features of that alternative assumption concerning exchange rate expectations, we shall not adopt it. Instead, we shall retain our assumption that it is Δs_{t+1}^e that is treated as fixed in short-run analysis. The reason is that it seems implausible that s_{t+1}^e would not change. Why should market participants believe that a policy action, which affects today's exchange rate, would have no effect on tomorrow's (or next month's) exchange rate? Thus it is our contention that it is not legitimate to analyze short-run monetary policy effects on exchange rates by means of the UIP relation alone, with s_{t+1}^e treated as fixed.[17] Treating Δs_{t+1}^e as fixed—in other words; assuming that s_{t+1}^e moves together with s_t—comes much closer to being realistic.

But although the latter assumption is the more attractive of the two considered, it too seems somewhat unrealistic. What would be better would be to utilize some other assumption that is more closely related to the manner in which expectations of s_{t+1} actually adjust when the system is shocked. But any model relating s_{t+1}^e to its determinants will necessarily be dynamic. Thus we conclude again that dynamic expectational analysis is the type that one would like to use for many issues. Such analysis will, as stated before, be introduced in Chapter 8.

6.6 A Two-Country Framework

One significant limitation of the analysis of Sections 6.1 to 6.3 is that the foreign variables y_t^*, p_t^*, and R_t^* are treated as strictly exogenous. That treatment implies that those variables are not influenced by conditions in the economy under

---

[17] This type of analysis, involving only the UIP condition, appears on pp. 352–358 of Krugman and Obstfeld (1994).

study, which makes sense only under the assumption that the home economy is very small in relation to the economy of the rest of the world. It is arguably the case that analysis that treats the home economy as small, in this fashion, is reasonably applicable to most of the nations of the world. But such analysis may be somewhat inaccurate when applied to the United States, and possibly when applied to Japan, Germany, and a few other nations. In any case, an extension of the analysis to remove the small-country assumption is desirable and will be undertaken in this section.

Our strategy will be to develop a two-country model in which it is not assumed that conditions in the "other" country are independent of those in the home economy. In doing so, we will retain Equations (1) for long-run analysis of the home economy, but will add to them the following relations for the foreign economy:

$$y_t^* = b_0 + b_1 r_t^* - b_2 q_t + b_3 g_t^* + b_4 y_t \tag{12a}$$

$$m_t^* - p_t^* = c_0 + c_1 y_t^* + c_2 R_t^* \tag{12b}$$

$$r_t^* = R_t^* - (p_{t+1}^{*e} - p_t^*) \tag{12c}$$

$$y_t^* = \bar{y}_t^*. \tag{12d}$$

Here Equations (12a)–(12c) are analogous to Equations (1a)–(1c) for the home economy, with y_t playing the same role in (12a) as y_t^* does in (1a). The values of the b_j and c_j parameters are for simplicity assumed to be the same as in the home economy, but that restriction is not necessary with our approach, nor is it crucial for the conclusions to be reached. A minus sign appears in front of the coefficient b_2 in Equation (12a) because its associated variable q_t—the price of foreign goods in terms of home goods—has the opposite type of effect from the perspective of foreign economies, in comparison to the home economy.

Together, Equations (1) and (12) provide 10 relationships, which are just sufficient in number to determine values of the 10 endogenous variables, y_t, y_t^*, p_t, p_t^*, r_t, r_t^*, R_t, R_t^*, s_t, and q_t. [Note that no equations are needed as counterparts to Equations (1d) and (1e).] The system's exogenous variables are m_t, m_t^*, g_t, g_t^*, $\bar{y}_t$, and $\bar{y}_t^*$.

We have already seen that from a long-run perspective—either stationary or steady state—the real interest rates r_t and r_t^* will be equal. Accordingly, with the policy variables m_t, m_t^*, g_t, and g_t^* exogenous and with y_t and y_t^* determined by Equations (1f) and (12d), the IS relations, Equations (1a) and (12a), involve only two endogenous variables, $r_t = r_t^*$ and q_t. These two equations may therefore be solved to obtain long-run solution values for r_t and q_t.

From a graphical perspective, this solution could be depicted as the intersection of an upward-sloping r_t versus q_t plot of Equation (1a) and a downward-sloping r_t^* versus q_t plot of Equation (12a). But in terms of our macroeconomic analysis, it will be more enlightening to depict the r_t, q_t determination as in Figure 6–8. There the value of q determined by the model is the only one that would make IS and IS* cut through $\bar{y}$ and $\bar{y}^*$, respectively, at the same value of r. If a higher value of q were to occur, for instance, IS

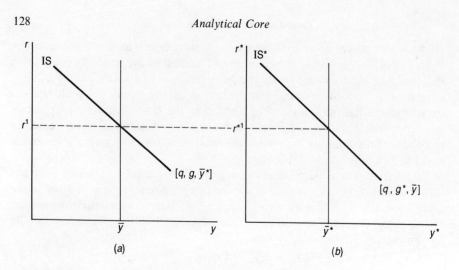

Figure 6–8 Two-country stationary-state determination of *r* and *q*.

would intersect $\bar{y}$ at a higher value of *r* whereas IS* would cut $\bar{y}$* at a lower value of *r**. [The latter is so because an increase in *q* shifts IS* to the *left* as a consequence of the minus sign on b_2 in Equation (12*a*).]

Figure 6–9 shows the stationary-state response in both countries to an increase in *g* in the home country alone. The increase from g^1 to g^2 shifts IS^1 to IS^2, which would require a real interest rate of r^2 to be consistent with long-run equilibrium. But that rate is not consistent with equilibrium in the foreign country, so some adjustment is needed. What happens, from a long-run perspective, is that *q* falls to q^3. As it does so, IS^2 falls back to IS^3 and IS* shifts rightward. The final equilibrium has $r = r^* = r^3 > r^1$ and $q = q^3 < q^1$.

To determine effects on the price-level and nominal exchange rate values in

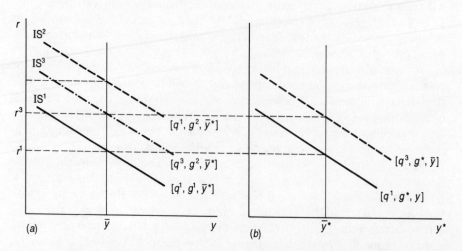

Figure 6–9 Two-country stationary-state effects of increase in *g*.

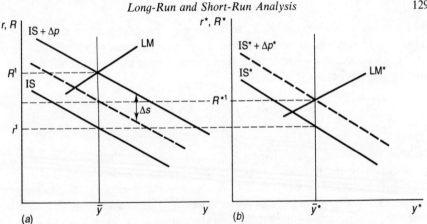

Figure 6–10 Two-country steady-state diagram.

the foregoing experiment, we could add initial and final LM curves for each country. Since the final equilibrium position lies directly above the original position in each country, it would be concluded that the final values of both p and p^* exceed their initial values. Since q falls, the value of $s = q + p - p^*$ will fall if p and p^* rise by the same amount. This will be the case under our assumption that the parameter values are the same in Equations (1a) and (12a), but will not be so in general.

If we were to consider steady-state rather than stationary-state equilibria, the determination of r and q would proceed as before. With floating rates it would be possible for money growth and inflation rates to be different in the home and foreign economies. Figure 6–10 depicts a steady-state equilibrium in which $\Delta p > \Delta p^*$, that is, home-country inflation exceeds that abroad. The steady-state value of Δs, the rate of depreciation of the home country's currency, will then be positive (as shown). Accordingly, R will exceed R^*, as required by UIP.

If one attempts short-run analysis in the two-country framework, it is quickly discovered that interactive effects are important because the position of each country's IS function depends on the current rate of output in the other country. The analysis is, therefore, much more complicated than in the cases considered to this point. We shall consequently delay consideration of this type of analysis, turning to it again in Chapter 12, where we consider alternative exchange rate arrangements from an international perspective.

Appendix

The objective here is to justify the assertion of Section 6.2 that conditions (1) and (2) on p. 115 must hold along any path that is a steady state. To do so it will be useful to begin by demonstrating the validity of a preliminary proposition, which is the following. Let Y, X, and Z be any variables such that $Y = X + Z$. Then for all three to grow at constant rates, it is necessary that all three grow at the *same* rate.[18] To prove that algebraically, note that the growth rate of Y can be written as

$$\frac{Y_t - Y_{t-1}}{Y_{t-1}} = \frac{X_t - X_{t-1}}{Y_{t-1}} + \frac{Z_t - Z_{t-1}}{Y_{t-1}} = \frac{X_{t-1}}{Y_{t-1}}\frac{X_t - X_{t-1}}{X_{t-1}} + \frac{Z_{t-1}}{Y_{t-1}}\frac{Z_t - Z_{t-1}}{Z_{t-1}}$$

so that $G(Y) = (X_{t-1}/Y_{t-1})G(X) + (Z_{t-1}/Y_{t-1})G(Z)$, where $G(\cdot)$ denotes the growth rate of the indicated variable. But this last equation says that $G(Y)$ is a weighted average of $G(X)$ and $G(Z)$. Now suppose $G(X) > G(Z)$. Then the weight X_{t-1}/Y_{t-1} attached to X increases as time passes, causing $G(Y)$ to increase, which violates the steady-growth requirement.

In the exchange rate model of Section 6.2, one of the underlying relationships is the national income indentity $Y = C + I + G + X$. (Here the symbols revert to their meaning in the body of the chapter.) But we can apply the result of the previous paragraph sequentially by first defining $Z = C + I + G$ and concluding that Z and X must grow at the same rate for a steady state (unless $X = 0$ throughout), then applying the result to $Z = (C + I) + G$, and so on. The conclusion is that Y, C, I, G, and X must all grow at the same rate, except that $G(X)$ can equal zero if $X = 0$ in the steady state.

To establish that r, R, and q must grow at the rate zero, let us assume that the consumption function $C = \tilde{C}(Y, r)$ is of the semilog form $c_t = \alpha_0 + \alpha_1 y_t + \alpha_2 r_t$. We know that steady growth requires $\Delta c_t = \Delta y_t$. But then $\Delta r_t = (1/\alpha_2)(\Delta c_t - \alpha_1 \Delta c_t)$ is a constant, and since r_t is *not* a logarithm, constant growth requires $\Delta r_t / r_{t-1}$ to be constant. But with $\Delta r_t =$ constant, the latter will be true only if $\Delta r_t = 0$. And with Δp_t constant, the nominal interest rate $R_t = r_t + \Delta p_t$ will also be constant.

With regard to q, we consider the behavior of X and focus on exports EX and imports IM separately. For the latter, a plausible specification is that the ratio of IM_t to Y_t is negatively related to Q_t (or q_t). But then if IM_t and Y_t are to grow at the same rate, Q_t (and q_t) must remain constant over time. In the case of exports, we assume that the ratio of EX_t to Y_t^* is positively related to Q_t, so a constant Q_t requires that EX_t and Y_t^* grow at the same rate. But $X_t = EX_t - IM_t$ implies that EX_t and IM_t must grow at the same rate, so evidently Y_t^* must grow at the same rate as EX_t, IM_t, and Y_t.

References

Fleming, J. M., "Domestic Financial Policies under Fixed and under Floating Exchange Rates," *International Monetary Fund Staff Papers* **9** (Nov. 1962), 369–379.

Henderson, D. W., "Financial Policies in Open Economies," *American Economic Review* **69** (May 1979), 232–239.

---

[18] The only exception is that X or Z can grow at the rate zero, different from that of the other two variables, if its constant value is zero.

Kearney, C., "Stabilisation Policy with Flexible Exchange Rates," in *Current Issues in International Monetary Economics*, D. Llewellyn and C. Milner, Eds. New York: St. Martin's Press, 1990.

Kenen, P. B., *The International Economy*, 3rd ed. New York: Cambridge University Press, 1994.

Krugman, P. R., and M. Obstfeld, *International Economics: Theory and Policy*, 3rd ed. Glenview, OL: Scott, Foresman, 1994.

Marston, R. C., "Stabilization Policies in Open Economies," in *Handbook of International Economics*, vol. 2, R. W. Jones and P. B. Kenen, Eds. Amsterdam: North-Holland, 1985.

McCallum, B. T., *Monetary Economics: Theory and Policy*. New York: Macmillan, 1989.

Mundell, R., "The Appropriate Use of Monetary and Fiscal Policy for Internal and External Stability," *International Monetary Fund Staff Papers* **9** (Mar. 1962), 70–77.

————, "Capital Mobility and Stabilization Policy under Fixed and Flexible Exchange Rates," *Canadian Journal of Economics and Political Science* **29** (Nov. 1963), 475–485.

Patinkin, D., "Neutrality of Money," in *The New Palgrave: A Dictionary of Economics*, vol. 3, J. Eatwell, M. Milgate, and P. Newman, Eds. New York: Stockton Press, 1987.

Problems

1. Using a graphical analysis, determine the short-run effects on y, p, R, s, and q of an increase in the money stock m. Then continue in order to obtain the stationary-state results as described in the last paragraph of Section 6.3.

2. Suppose that government spending g increases in the economy depicted below in Figure 6–11, with m unchanged. From a long-run (stationary-state)

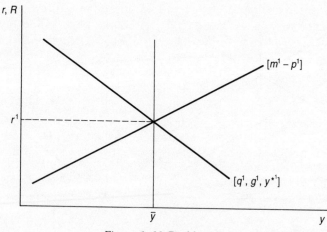

Figure 6–11 Problem 2.

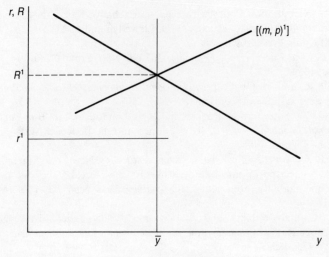

Figure 6–12 Problem 5.

perspective, does the economy's exchange rate appreciate or depreciate? Explain using the diagrammatic apparatus.

3. In a small economy with a floating exchange rate, what will be the short-run and long-run effects on s, q, and y of an improvement in the nation's monetary payments technology, such as the introduction of credit cards? (Recall Problem 4 of Chapter 4.) Assume that the initial position is one of full (long-run and short-run) equilibrium, and describe your graphical analysis of the change.

4. Analyze the short-run and long-run effects of a recession abroad, assuming that there is no policy response in the economy under study.

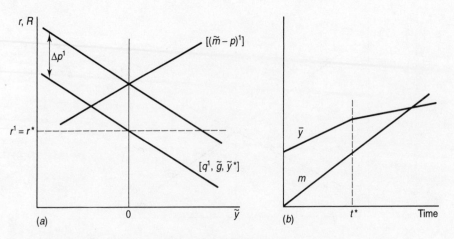

Figure 6–13 Problem 6.

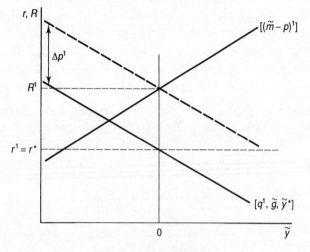

Figure 6–14 Problem 7.

5. The diagram in Figure 6–12 depicts a floating-rate economy in an inflation-ary steady state. Determine diagrammatically the inflation rate Δp^1. Then depict a new steady state with a reduced money growth rate.

6. In the floating-rate economy depicted in Figure 6–13 the rate of growth of capacity output decreases at time t^* from $\Delta \bar{y}^1$ to $\Delta \bar{y}^2$, with no discontinuity in $\bar{y}_t$ and no change in the money stock growth rate or in $\tilde{g}$ or $\tilde{y}^*$. Describe the effects on the economy's steady-state equilibrium values of R, q, and $\tilde{m} - p$.

7. Figure 6–14 depicts an open economy in a steady-state equilibrium with capacity output growing at the rate of 0.02 (i.e., 2 percent per period). The economy's money stock is growing at the rate $\Delta m = 0.10$, foreign inflation is

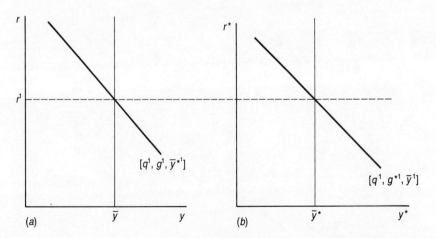

Figure 6–15 Problem 8.

$\Delta p^* = 0.04$, and the money-demand function is $m_t - p_t = 195 + 0.5y_t - 2R_t$. Definitions are $\tilde{y}_t = y_t - \bar{y}_t$, $\tilde{g}_t = g_t - \bar{y}_t$, and $\tilde{m}_t = m_t - c_1\bar{y}_t$.

(a) What is the steady-state inflation rate for this economy?
(b) Is its exchange rate appreciating or depreciating? At what rate?
(c) Why is the LM curve labeled with $[(\tilde{m} - p)^1]$ rather than $[\tilde{m}^1 - p^1]$?

8. The diagrams in Figure 6–15 depict a stationary-state equilibrium in a two-country setting. Suppose that government spending in the foreign country g^* is reduced. Analyze the effects on the new (stationary-state) values of r and q.

7

Analysis with Fixed Exchange Rates

7.1 Loss of Monetary Autonomy

Throughout the analysis of the previous chapter it was assumed that the economy under investigation, the "home economy," was one with floating exchange rates. We presumed, in other words, that the government and monetary authorities of the economy conducted policy so as to leave the nation's exchange rates free to be determined by supply and demand forces at work in the international market for currencies. In the present chapter, by contrast, it will be assumed that policy in the home economy is conducted so as to maintain—permanently or at least for the indefinite future—a fixed value for some weighted average of the bilateral exchange rates involving the nation's currency. Operationally this might involve active intervention to hold fixed only one particular exchange value. That would be the case, for instance, if other nations were also pegging their currency values relative to the same reference asset, such as the U.S. dollar under the Bretton Woods system or gold under earlier arrangements. In terms of a macroeconomic model that includes only one "effective" exchange rate, of course, this distinction does not appear. In our formal model, for example, the fixed exchange rate regime is simply described as one in which the monetary authorities of the home country intervene in the exchange market so as to maintain the value of the spot rate s_t fixed at some specified value s^0.

The most fundamental consequence for a nation of the adoption of a fixed exchange rate regime is that this choice entails a loss of monetary control. More specifically, if monetary policy is assigned the task of keeping s_t equal to the par value of s^0, then it cannot be also directed at the attainment of other objectives. Occasionally the monetary requirements of keeping $s_t = s^0$ might coincide with those implied by some other objective, but in general distinct objectives would call for different settings of monetary policy instruments.

This fundamental point can be illustrated formally in terms of the basic log-linear model utilized in the previous chapters. Consider, for example, a version in which the five equations of Chapter 5 are augmented—the system completed—by the assumption that output equals capacity, that is, $y_t = \bar{y}_t$. For the moment we suppose that price-level flexibility brings about this condition period by period, not that we are conducting long-run analysis. Then the equations of the model can be written as follows:

$$y_t = b_0 + b_1 r_t + b_2 q_t + b_3 g_t + b_4 y_t^* \tag{1a}$$

$$m_t - p_t = c_0 + c_1 y_t + c_2 R_t \tag{1b}$$

$$r_t = R_t - (p_{t+1}^e - p_t) \tag{1c}$$

$$q_t = s_t - p_t + p_t^* \tag{1d}$$

$$R_t = R_t^* + s_{t+1}^e - s_t \tag{1e}$$

$$y_t = \bar{y}_t. \tag{1f}$$

With regard to the issue at hand it should be clear that the foreign variables y_t^*, p_t^*, and R_t^* are exogenous in this system, as are capacity output $\bar{y}_t$ and government purchases g_t. Also, as in the previous chapter, the variables y_t, p_t, r_t, q_t, and R_t are determined endogenously. But now, in contrast to the situation in Chapter 6, s_t is *not* determined endogenously by the system; instead it must be kept constant at the par value s^0. Accordingly, there must be a sixth variable to be determined endogenously by the six Equations (1a)–(1f); otherwise these equations could imply an algebraic and logical inconsistency. But in the system at hand there is only one remaining possibility, so we see that the sixth endogenous variable must be m_t, the (log of the) money stock.[1] In short, the change in the status of s_t from endogenous to exogenous requires an opposite shift in status for m_t, from exogenous to endogenous. And with m_t determined endogenously by the workings of the system, it is clearly not available to be set by choice of the policy authorities.

In response to the contention of the last paragraph it might be asked why some other variable besides m_t could not be reclassified from exogenous to endogenous to make up for the pegging of s_t. But the only other candidates are y_t^*, p_t^*, R_t^*, $\bar{y}_t$, and g_t. The first three of these are determined abroad, so they cannot, since our home country is small, be affected by its policy behavior. Furthermore, current values of the fourth variable, capacity output, are also beyond the influence of policymakers. Consequently only g_t, government purchases, is left to be considered. In fact, g_t could in principle be used to keep s_t close to s^0 on a *temporary* basis. But it cannot serve that function on a permanent basis, as will be demonstrated in the steady-state analysis of Section 7.3. Consequently, since permanent pegging of s_t at the value s^0 is required for a fixed-rate commitment, it is monetary policy that must be devoted to the task.

There is, furthermore, a second and perhaps more interesting way of approaching the issue of monetary endogeneity with fixed exchange rates. Instead of mechanically counting variables in an analytical model, this approach considers the way in which authorities actually behave in economies with fixed exchange rates. We consider, in other words, the process by which authorities act to keep exchange rates equal to—or, more realistically, close to—their

---

[1] Here, as usual, we are not counting expectations as distinct variables.

specified par values. The general nature of that process is already familiar from our discussion in Section 4.2 of the gold standard. Specifically, the way in which the authorities typically maintain the value of their nation's currency in terms of some standard asset is by standing ready to buy or sell that standard asset at the stipulated price that represents the par value of the exchange rate in question. Under the gold standard, for example, the other asset is gold and the monetary authority fixes the exchange rate between gold and the national currency by buying and selling gold at the par or official price (denoted by P_g in Section 4.2). With other types of fixed exchange rate systems, the authority similarly stands ready to buy or sell some reference asset (or assets) at its par value. Doing so clearly fixes the exchange rate between the nation's currency and the reference asset (or assets). Bilateral exchange rates will then be fixed between that nation's currency and all other currencies that are also pegged to the reference asset. Under the Bretton Woods system, for example, all other member nations of the IMF pegged their currencies to the U.S. dollar, so their various bilateral exchange rates were also fixed.

Suppose, then, that the value of some "home" country's currency—called "dollars"—is tending to fall in value relative to those of other nations, the dollar prices of other currencies rising slightly above their par values. Market participants will then bring quantities of dollars to the home country's central bank and use them to buy foreign currencies at the (lower) par values. These market participants will have a great incentive to engage in such activity because it amounts to a guaranteed opportunity to "buy low, sell high." Alternatively, the central bank could take the initiative itself, going into the market place to supply foreign currencies for dollars at a lower price (higher value of dollars) than that prevailing. Either way, the central bank keeps the exchange rate s_t (the dollar price of foreign currency) from rising significantly above s^0 by supplying foreign exchange for dollars at the price s^0. And, conversely, it will when necessary keep s_t from falling below s^0 by buying foreign exchange with dollars.

But the main point is that, in behaving this way, the central bank loses control over the home country's money stock. This is so because each exchange by the central bank of dollars for foreign currency has the effect of changing the home country's stock of "high-powered money" (alternatively referred to as "base money" or the "monetary base"), with purchases of foreign exchange increasing (and sales decreasing) the stock of base money.[2] And, as most readers will know from their study of money and banking, changes in high-powered money tend strongly to induce changes—approximately equal percentage changes—in the stock of money, defined as a medium-of-exchange measure, such as M1 (currency in circulation plus checkable deposits).

---

[2] High-powered money is defined as the sum of currency outside the banking system and bank reserves, with the latter including bank reserves held at the central bank plus vault cash. This sum is clearly equivalent to the sum of currency issued plus reserves at the central bank. The term "base money" is often used to refer to precisely the same concept, but sometimes to a closely related concept that incorporates an adjustment for changes in regulations pertaining to banks' required reserves.

That a purchase (sale) of foreign exchange with (for) dollars leads to an increase (decrease) in the stock of base money can be determined fairly directly from the definition of the latter concept as the sum of currency in circulation (i.e., outside banks) plus bank reserves. To see this, consider four cases: the home-country central bank purchases foreign exchange from (1) home-country banks, (2) home-country nonbank residents, (3) foreign banks, and (4) foreign central banks. In case (1) the purchase will increase the reserves of domestic banks whereas (2) will lead to an increase in currency in circulation. In cases (3) and (4) there will be an immediate increase in the home country's base money stock if payment is made in currency, but not if it is made by increasing a foreign deposit account held with the home country's central bank. But the foreign owner of such a deposit would normally wish to transfer his dollar holdings into some other form that would be more lucrative in items of interest earned, and doing so would usually result in an enhanced stock of base money. Suppose, for example, that the foreign agent purchased a home-country government security from some home-country bank and paid for it by transferring ownership of (part of) its deposit at the home-country central bank to the home-country bank. That would increase bank reserves in the home country and thereby increase the stock of base money.

Thus we see that any exchange by a central bank of home-country for foreign currency will have the effect of changing the stock of high-powered or base money in the home country. Such changes can admittedly be offset by the central bank by means of "open-market" exchanges of domestic money for other domestic assets such as government securities. The effect on the stock of base money of a purchase of foreign currency could be undone, for example, by a sale by the central bank of government bonds. Such an action is termed a *sterilization* of the foreign exchange purchase, which becomes a "sterilized invention." It is the case, then, that central bank interventions in the foreign exchange market may not affect the home-country money stock if they are sterilized. Most research on the issue has indicated, however, that the effects on exchange rates of sterilized market interventions are both weak and short-lived.[3] Thus a central bank can keep its nation's exchange rate fixed only by engaging in nonsterilized interventions.

In visualizing domestic and exchange market purchases or sales by a central bank, it may be useful to have in mind some basic facts concerning the composition of a typical central bank's balance sheet. This is not a difficult task, for the general outline of these balance sheets is extremely simple. Indeed, writers in textbooks and in the international finance literature often proceed as if there were only four significant items, two on each side of central bank balance sheets, as follows:

Assets	*Liabilities*
Foreign reserves	Currency in circulation
Domestic securities	Bank reserves

---

[3] Surveys of this research are provided by Obstfeld (1982) and Henderson and Sampson (1983).

Table 7–1 Central Bank Balance Sheets, End of 1989.

	France (FF bil)	Germany (DM bil)	Japan (¥ bil)	United Kingdom (£ bil)	United States ($ bil)
Foreign assets	404	114.9	8,855	24.3	74.6
Claims on central gov't	57	24.5	13,269	10.6	247.4
Claims on banks	271	175.3	15,684	0.1	—
Other	3	—	—	—	1.1
Total	735	314.7	37,808	35.0	323.1
Liabilities					
Base money	366	234.6	44,568	21.7	298.4
Currency	246	147.9	36,681	16.2	225.5
Foreign liabilities	75	51.6	—	12.6	0.6
Other items (net)	294	28.5	−6,760	0.7	24.1
Total	735	314.7	37,808	35.0	323.1

* Currency outside banks.
Source: IMF, *International Financial Statistics*, 1991.

Furthermore, since the two listed liability items together constitute the monetary base (or stock of high-powered money), these balance sheets are often represented in the form of FR + DS = MB, where the symbols are abbreviations for the listed liability items and the monetary base.

To a practical reader it may be of interest to consider how closely the balance sheets of actual central banks conform to this simplified picture. Consequently, figures pertaining to the end of 1989 are presented in Table 7–1 for the central banks of the G-5 nations: France, Germany, Japan, the United Kingdom, and the United States. Examination of these figures indicates that the other balance sheet items, besides the four key items mentioned, are small in relative magnitude for four of the five central banks considered. Only for France, among the G-5 nations, is there another balance sheet category that is a sizable fraction of total assets. That item, furthermore, is an unusual one termed "capital accounts" in the IMF data source, and it is explained that most of the listed amount has resulted as a counterpart entry necessitated by revaluations of France's sizable gold holdings. These revaluations were made in response to the rise of the market price of gold to levels an order of magnitude higher than the pre-1971 price of $35 per ounce at which France acquired the gold. Consequently, the anomalous figure in the French case represents a "fictitious" accounting entry that does not actually contradict the idea that central bank balance sheets can be satisfactorily approximated by the four-entry simplification listed.

Let us conclude this section by reiterating its central and fundamental message: in order to maintain a fixed exchange rate, a central bank must engage in foreign exchange transactions that prevent it from managing the monetary base so as to achieve other macroeconomic objectives. If monetary policy is dedicated to pegging the exchange rate, it is then unavailable (except on a highly temporary basis) for application to other goals.

7.2 Impact and Stationary-State Analysis

Having seen that adherence to a fixed exchange rate implies lack of monetary policy autonomy when capital mobility is "perfect," as our basic model presumes, let us now utilize this model to conduct comparative static analysis of some important issues concerning fixed exchange rates. In contrast to the practice of Chapter 6, let us begin in each case with impact or short-run analysis, treating the price level p_t as (temporarily) fixed, with output y_t consequently departing from its natural rate or capacity level $\bar{y}$. Thus we replace condition (1*f*) of the previous section with the condition $p = p^1$ for our initial experiment in each case. After that, we revert to condition (1*f*) for long-run stationary-state analysis.

As a first experiment consider an increase—starting from a position of full equilibrium—in foreign real income y^*, assuming no change in the foreign price level p^*. With p and s both fixed, so too is the real exchange rate q. Also, the home country's real interest rate r is given from abroad since $r = R$ with zero expected inflation and $R = R^*$ with zero expected exchange rate depreciation. Thus the IS relation (1*a*) implies an increased value of output or income y. Graphically, the IS schedule shifts rightward, as depicted in Figure 7–1, and

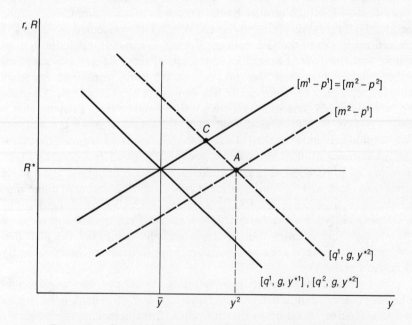

Figure 7–1 Comparative static analysis with fixed exchange rate.

output increases from $\bar{y}$ to y^2. The LM or money demand relation (1*b*) then implies an increased value of *m*, since *p* and *R* are fixed, in response to the higher value of *y*. Graphically, LM shifts rightward with the increased *m*; the new short-run equilibrium is located at point *A* in Figure 7–1.

The foregoing experiment illustrates the monetary authority's loss of monetary control with fixed exchange rates. In response to the rightward shift of the IS schedule, there would be a tendency for the economy to move toward point *C* in Figure 7–1, but the $r = r^*$ (and $R = R^*$) condition—implied by Equations (1*c*) (1*d*) (1*e*) plus (temporary) price-level rigidity—does not permit even a brief interlude at a position such as *C*, where $r > r^*$. Instead, the *tendency* for *r* to exceed r^* brings about a prompt inflow of reserves as foreigners rush to purchase the higher yielding securities available in the home country. But as we have seen in the previous section, this inflow of reserves (a temporary surplus in the official settlements balance) automatically increases the stock of base money in the home country and induces an increase in *m*. Thus the LM curve shifts quickly to the dashed position in Figure 7–1, which intersects IS and $R = R^*$ at point *A*.

But while the latter is a point of short-run equilibrium, it is nevertheless not one at which the economy can settle down. Specifically, with *y* greater than $\bar{y}$ there will be a definite market pressure on the price level *p* to rise. Then as it does so, the LM schedule will shift back to the left if the money stock remains at its new value m^2. Furthermore, the gradual increase in *p* implies a gradual decline in the real exchange rate $q = s - p + p^*$ since *s* is fixed. But we know from Chapter 5 that a decline in *q* entails a leftward shift in the IS schedule, so we conclude that it too will move to the left as time passes. Indeed, since neither $r = r^*$ nor $\bar{y}$ has changed, we see that the leftward movement of the IS and LM schedules will come to a halt only after they have returned to their initial positions. Thus the final effect of the rise in y^* is to increase *m* and *p* equivalently, leaving M/P as before, and to reduce the real exchange rate *q* (which makes foreign goods cheaper in real terms to home-country residents).

The short-run, fixed-price version of our model is especially popular in the textbook and policy-oriented literature as a vehicle for analyzing the effects of monetary and fiscal policy actions.[4] The usual conclusion drawn from such analysis is that fiscal policy is highly effective and monetary policy highly ineffective as tools for domestic stabilization in a setting with fixed exchange rates. Suppose, to illustrate, that the home economy is for some reason at point *A* in Figure 7–2 with output below capacity, $y < \bar{y}$. Then an increase in *g* to g^2 will shift the IS curve to the indicated position and the tendency of *r* to rise above t^* will induce a temporary official settlements surplus that increases *m* to m^2. (Here $g^2 > g^1$ and $m^2 > m^1$.) Output is thereby increased to its capacity rate.

If instead the policy authorities were to try to increase *y* by means of a

---

[4] See, for example, the discusssions in Kenen (1994, pp. 386–393), Krugman and Obstfeld (1994, pp. 474–475, 489–494), and Melvin (1989, pp. 232–236). In some treatments the interest parity relation is relaxed so as to reflect less than perfect capital mobility.

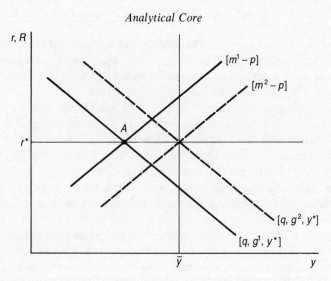

Figure 7–2 Short-run effects of increase in government purchases.

monetary expansion, the short-run effects would be as illustrated in Figure 7–3. The LM curve moves rightward as *m* is increased to m^2, but this movement tends to decrease the domestic interest rate $r = R$ to a value below r^*. That condition quickly leads to an official settlements deficit, a loss of reserves, and downward pressure on the value of domestic currency (upward pressure on *s*), which requires the monetary authority to contract the monetary base. That step induces a reduction in the money stock *m* and shifts the LM curve back

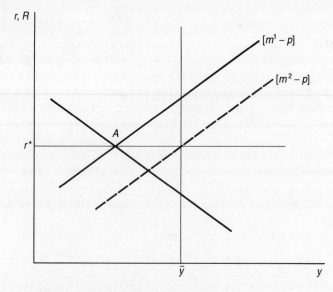

Figure 7–3 Short-run effects of increase in money stock.

toward its initial position. Since neither r^* nor the IS curve has shifted, this process continues until m has fallen back to m^1 and the LM curve has returned to its initial position. Thus an attempt to increase y by monetary means must be unsuccessful when capital is highly mobile and exchange rates are fixed.

This last result is frequently described as indicating that "monetary policy is entirely ineffective" in a fixed exchange rate regime. That way of expressing the result is, however, somewhat misleading. "Ineffectiveness" of monetary policy would seem to refer to the extent of changes in aggregate demand (i.e., horizontal movements in the intersection of the IS and LM curves) brought about by any given change in the money supply m. But this extent depends upon the slopes of the IS and LM curves, which are unaffected by the choice between fixed and flexible exchange rates. What the latter choice impinges upon is, instead, whether changes in m can be made and directed toward domestic objectives (such as an increase in y). And as we have seen, it is not possible to use monetary policy for such purposes when it has already been dedicated to maintenance of a fixed exchange rate. Thus fixed rates actually make monetary policy unavailable, not ineffective, for the pursuit of domestic policy objectives.[5]

Before moving on it should be of interest to consider long-run stationary-state analyses of the situations depicted in Figures 7–2 and 7–3. Consider the latter first. At position A, $y < \bar{y}$, so prices will gradually fall as time passes. The fall in p will then increase both $m - p$ and q, shifting in a rightward direction both the LM and IS schedules. This process will continue until $y = \bar{y}$ with $r = r^*$, the same outcome as that attained more promptly by means of fiscal policy expansion in the case of Figure 7–2. The passage of time would lead to no further changes from the final equilibrium position of Figure 7–2, however, since with $y = \bar{y}$ there is no pressure for continuing adjustment of the price level.

Even in a regime with fixed rates, situations will occasionally arise in which a discrete alteration in par values is deemed necessary or advisable. Let us then consider an experiment in which the home country's exchange rate is altered from s^1 to s^2, with the change believed to be a once and for all permanent adjustment. Let $s^2 > s^1$, so that the change constitutes a currency *devaluation*— that is, a reduction in exchange value—for the home country. With p and p^* fixed, the increase in s implies an increase in the real exchange rate q, which implies a rightward shift in the IS function, as illustrated in Figure 7–4.[6] This shift puts upward pressure on the interest rate and draws in reserves from abroad, so the monetary base and the money stock expand. The LM curve shifts, therefore, to the right. The short-run or fixed-price equilibrium is then at point A in Figure 7–4.

As time passes, however, the price level rises since y exceeds $\bar{y}$ at point A. Thus the LM and IS schedules shift back to the left as $m - p$ and q fall in value.

[5] It should be said that Mundell (1963), in one of the landmark papers describing the result in question, is careful to define monetary policy actions as open-market purchases (or sales) of domestic assets, not changes in the monetary base. Thus his statements about monetary policy ineffectiveness are not subject to the foregoing criticism.

[6] Here we presume that the initial situation is one in which output equals capacity.

Analytical Core

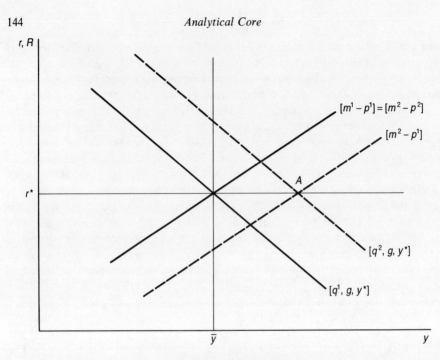

Figure 7–4 Effects of a devaluation.

Indeed, the process continues until y has returned to $\bar{y}$. Since $r = r^*$ and r^* has not changed, it then follows that $m - p$ and q have the same values in the final long-run equilibrium position as in the initial position. Effects of the devaluation on real variables are, therefore, of a temporary nature, given that the initial position is one at which $y = \bar{y}$. If instead the initial position has $y < \bar{y}$, then the long-run effects of a devaluation will include increases in q and y.

7.3 Steady-State Analysis

In order to develop a few significant points, it will be useful also to consider a steady-state version of long-run analysis. For convenience we begin by recording the model's six relations, given previously as Equations (6) of Chapter 6, that serve (with $\Delta s = 0$ exogenously) to determine values of Δy, Δm, Δp, r, R,

---

[7] It will be observed that these equations will actually not determine the value of q, which does not appear in the system as written. Neither, however, does the system determine the level of the p_t series; only Δp appears in the equations. But with an *initial* value given, knowledge of Δp would define the level of p_t for each period, and a similar statement applies to p_t^*. Then knowledge of paths for s, p_t, and p_t^* suffices to determine q_t via a process of cumulation using Equation (2d).

and q.[7] They are as follows:

$$\Delta y = b_3 \Delta g + b_4 \Delta y^* \qquad (2a)$$

$$\Delta m - \Delta p = c_1 \Delta y \qquad (1b)$$

$$r = R - \Delta p \qquad (2c)$$

$$0 = \Delta s - \Delta p + \Delta p^* \qquad (2d)$$

$$R = R^* + \Delta s \qquad (2e)$$

$$\Delta y = \Delta \bar{y}. \qquad (2f)$$

Now, in contrast to the situation of Section 6.2, we have $\Delta s = 0$ given exogenously. Accordingly, Equation (2d) implies that $\Delta p = \Delta p^*$, that is, the home-country inflation rate must equal the rate prevailing abroad. Also, $R = R^*$ is implied by Equation (2e), and Equation (2c) then determines r. Most importantly, with Δy given by Equation (2f), Equation (2b) implies that Δm must conform to the value $\Delta p^* + c_1 \Delta \bar{y}$. This last conclusion confirms, by means of a different approach, the conclusion of Section 7.1, namely, that monetary autonomy is impossible (from a long-run perspective) with a fixed exchange rate; inflation must conform to the rate elsewhere and money must grow at the implied pace. Otherwise it will not be possible to keep s_t fixed.

The steady-state system also shows that it is not possible to free monetary policy for other purposes by devoting fiscal policy to maintenance of the exchange rate. Indeed, for a steady state it is necessary to have Δg equal Δy, as explained in Chapter 6. And even if that were not the case, the value of Δg would be determined by condition (2a). But with Δg so determined, it cannot be used to generate an inflation rate Δp that conforms to Δp^*, as required to satisfy Equation (2d). So fiscal policy cannot be employed to keep an economy's inflation rate consistent with a fixed exchange rate, from a long-term steady-state perspective.

7.4 Imperfect Capital Mobility

The short-run analytical approach of the two previous sections was introduced in the famous papers of Mundell (1962, 1963) and Fleming (1962), which gave rise to the term "Mundell–Fleming model." In two of these papers—those dated 1962—it was, however, assumed that capital mobility among nations is, although substantial, less than complete. (During the postwar period there had in fact been severe governmental restrictions on capital movements—that is, on international security transactions—which were relaxed only gradually, many remaining in place into the 1980s.) Analytically, this condition was represented by assuming that the home country's capital-account balance was positively related to the interest differential $r - r^*$. Consequently, instead of the condition $r = r^*$, which characterizes our model under fixed exchange rates, these models included a relation of the form

$$\Delta FR = PX + \phi(r - r^*), \tag{3}$$

where ΔFR is the change over a period in the country's net holdings of foreign reserves, PX is net exports in nominal terms, and ϕ is an increasing function of its single argument, $r - r^*$. A condition of zero balance on official settlements account would then be written as $0 = PX + \phi(r - r^*)$, and this would imply an upward-sloping curve in r versus y diagrams, such as those of Figures 7–1, 7–2, and 7–3, instead of the horizontal line representing $r = r^*$. Thus the original Mundell–Fleming model had a graphical representation of the form represented in Figure 7–5, where the curve labeled BOP is the locus of r–y combinations that imply zero balance on official settlements account. For points above the BOP curve, prevailing values of r and y would imply a surplus whereas points below the curve would imply a deficit. With such a formulation, m will be increasing as time passes for points above the BOP schedule and decreasing for points below that schedule.

A first impression might be that a generalization of our basic model, to make it incorporate the upward-sloping BOP schedule of Figure 7–5, would be desirable. Unfortunately, however, such a generalization is not analytically justifiable. As Branson (1970) and many subsequent writers have pointed out, portfolio theory would suggest that a given $r - r^*$ interest differential should be systematically related to stocks, not flows, of financial assets. Consequently,

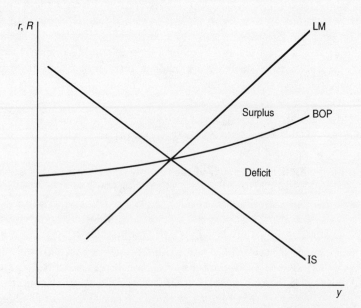

Figure 7–5 Mundell–Fleming diagram with "imperfect capital mobility."

there is no satisfactory way to depict a zero-balance BOP curve on an r versus y diagram of the IS–LM type when capital mobility is substantial but not "perfect." In the perfect-mobility case, however, equality (or, more generally, parity) between home and foreign interest rates can be satisfactorily represented by a horizontal line, as in Figures 7–1 through 7–3. Graphical and algebraic analysis is therefore greatly facilitated by adoption of the perfect-mobility assumption. Such an assumption would not be satisfactory, of course, if it were strongly counterfactual. That capital mobility has actually been very high since the early 1980s is a widely held impression of scholars and practitioners of international finance, however, and empirical studies designed to look for portfolio-theory departures from uncovered interest parity have generally been unsuccessful. Accordingly, there is reason to believe that we are not doing violence to reality by assuming, in our basic model, that uncovered interest parity holds, that is, that perfect capital mobility prevails.[8]

7.5 Current-Account Balance

In the foregoing sections we have referred to BOP deficits and surpluses in passing, but have in general focused very little attention on issues involving payments imbalances. We were able to get by without devoting much attention to possible imbalances for the following reason. In any equilibrium situation in which the money stock m is unchanging, the official settlements account must be in balance. For, as argued in Section 7.1, any imbalance would lead to a gain or loss of foreign reserves that would bring about a rise or fall in the stock of money.[9] Consequently, any equilibrium position in which m is constant will be one with a zero deficit for the official settlements balance.[10]

It must be recognized, however, that the same is not true for the current-account (CA) balance. Since the CA balance is (approximately) equal to net exports, its magnitude is determined in our model by the relation

$$X = \tilde{X}(q, y, y^*), \tag{4}$$

which is embedded in the IS function but not considered explicitly in the foregoing sections of this chapter. In Equation (4), it will be recalled from Chapter 5, the net export function $\tilde{X}$ is increasing in q and y^* but decreasing

[8] Nevertheless, the Appendix to this chapter considers the case in which international capital mobility is entirely absent.

[9] It would be possible for an inflow or outflow of reserves to be sterilized, that is, offset by central bank sales or purchases of domestic assets—so that m would remain constant for some span of time. Such processes could not go on for long, however.

[10] If the economy is growing, then adjustments to this statement must be made using the $\tilde{m}$ construct.

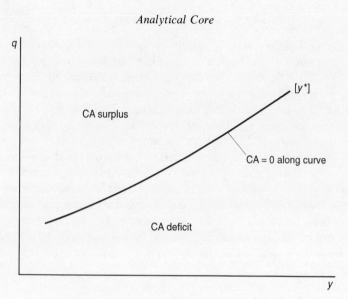

Figure 7–6 Graphic representation of current account.

in y: $\tilde{X}_1 > 0$, $\tilde{X}_2 < 0$, $\tilde{X}_3 > 0$.[11] Therefore we can use relation (4) to keep track of the CA balance in comparative static experiments such as those of Section 7.2.

Our strategy will be to derive a locus of points in a q versus y plot that would result in zero net exports, that is, CA balance. Such a locus is defined algebraically as those values of q and y that satisfy the condition

$$0 = \tilde{X}(q, y, y^*) \tag{5}$$

for the prevailing value of y^*. Since $\tilde{X}_1 > 0$ and $\tilde{X}_2 < 0$, this locus will be an upward-sloping curve in the q versus y diagram, as illustrated in Figure 7–6. The position of the curve will depend on the value of y^* and will lie farther to the right (i.e., lower) for higher values of y^*. Since an increase in q or a reduction in y tends to increase the net export volume, points above the CA = 0 locus imply current-account surplus outcomes and points below imply deficits. The closer a point lies to the locus, the smaller is the magnitude of any surplus or deficit. A diagram such as Figure 7–6 can be used in combination with an IS–LM diagram to determine the effects on the CA balance of policy actions or changes in conditions.

To illustrate this analytical procedure, consider again the effects of an increase in government purchases under a fixed exchange rate, previously depicted in Figure 7–3. Now we utilize Figure 7–7, which includes a plot of the CA balance curve labeled CA = 0, under the assumption of CA balance in

---

[11] In Chapter 5 the net export function is written with Q, Y, and Y^* as its arguments, rather than q, y, and y^*. Consequently the function $\tilde{X}$ here is slightly different than in Chapter 5. But Q and q are positively related, and so on, so it is valid to proceed as this paragraph suggests.

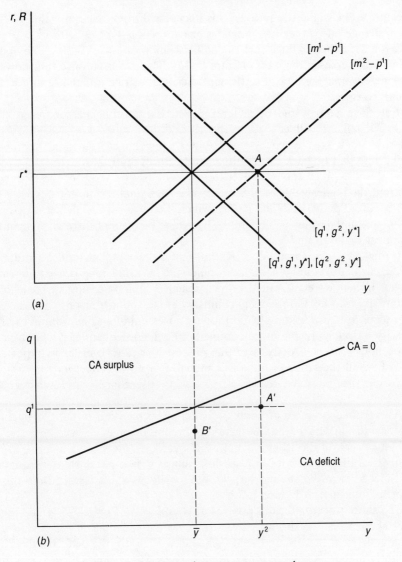

Figure 7-7 Increase in government purchases.

the initial situation.[12] An increase in government purchases from g^1 to g^2, with $g^2 > g^1$, first shifts the IS schedule to the right, as shown in Figure 7-7. The tendency for r to rise causes reserves to flow into the home country, increasing the money stock to $m^2 > m^1$. The short-run equilibrium is therefore at point A

---

[12] If the initial current-account balance were not zero, it would still be possible to conduct short-run analysis by means of a locus of points analogous to CA = 0 but drawn for the initial nonzero value.

in Figure 7–7a, where the price level is unchanged from its initial value p^1. The real exchange rate is then unchanged, since $q = s - p + p^*$, so with $y^2 > y^1 = \bar{y}$ there is a CA deficit in this short-run equilibrium position, as indicated by point A' in the q versus y diagram (Figure 7–7b). There will be offsetting flows of securities so that the official settlements account will be in balance and m can remain constant.

But since $y^2 > \bar{y}$, the price level p will rise as time passes. As it does so, q will fall, as will $m - p$, so the IS and LM schedules in Figure 7–7a will shift back to the left. With $\bar{y}$ and r^* unchanged, the final stationary equilibrium will be back at its initial position in Figure 7–7a with $m^2 - p^2 = m^1 - p^1$ and with q^2 enough lower than q^1 to offset (in terms of the IS curve's position) the higher value of g. Since $q^2 < q^1$, the final position in Figure 7–7b will be at a point such as B', at which there is a CA deficit. Again, a capital-account surplus will be implied, since m is constant through time in the stationary equilibrium.[13]

It might be said, parenthetically, that in a more complete model a situation with a current-account imbalance would not be a full long-run equilibrium. Instead, if there were a CA deficit, the associated capital-account surplus would continually transfer to foreigners claims to home-country income. In terms of our model, this process might be thought of as entailing a continuing fall in capacity output $\bar{y}$. In the more complete model, consequently, $\bar{y}$ would be an endogenous variable. Analysis of this process of wealth transfer is important, but is beyond the scope of our basic model. For an introductory but difficult discussion the interested reader is referred to Blanchard and Fischer (1989, pp. 58–69).

As a second example of analysis including recognition of the CA balance, consider the effects of an increase in foreign income y^* with p^* and r^* unchanged. Again the IS curve shifts rightward, as shown in Figure 7–8, but in this case the CA = 0 locus also shifts since y^* is a parameter of Equation (5). Indeed, it can be shown that the CA = 0 locus shifts farther than the IS curve, as indicated in Figure 7–8.[14]

The short-run equilibrium point is at A and A', in Figures 7–7a and b, the latter showing a CA surplus. Over time p rises, lowering $m - p$ and q and thereby driving the IS and LM schedules back to the left. In the final equilibrium, the CA balance must equal its initial value since $y - A(y, r) - g = \tilde{X}(q, y, y^*)$ with all terms on the left-hand side unchanged from their initial values.[15] Given our assumption or convention that the initial conditions feature CA balance, we conclude that the fall in q from q^1 to q^2 is just enough to restore CA balance.

---

[13] It is assumed that conditions abroad (i.e. p^* and y^* constant) entail a stationary long-run equilibrium.

[14] To prove this, calculate values of the derivative dy/dy^* implied by the two schedules, with r and q treated as constants. For IS we have $dy/dy^*(1 - \partial A/\partial y - \partial \tilde{X}/\partial y) = \partial \tilde{X}/\partial y^*$, and for CA = 0 we have $dy/dy^*(-\partial \tilde{X}/\partial y) = \partial \tilde{X}/\partial y^*$. [Here $A(y, r)$ is an abbreviation for $\tilde{C}(y, r) + \tilde{I}(y, r)$.] Since $\partial \tilde{X}/\partial y < 0$ and $1 - \partial A/\partial y > 0$, it follows that dy/dy^* is larger for the CA = 0 function.

[15] Here, as in footnote 10, $A(y, r)$ equals $\tilde{C}(y, r) + \tilde{I}(y, r)$.

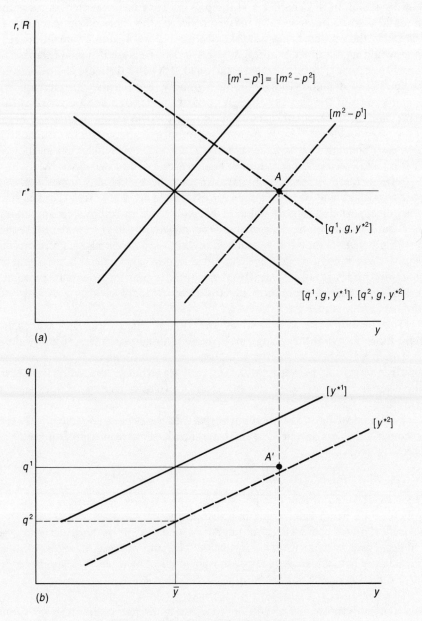

Figure 7–8 Increase in foreign income.

7.6 The J-Curve Effect

The discussion in this chapter and the previous one has neglected an issue that needs now to be discussed. That issue concerns the effect on net exports of a change in the real exchange rate. In Section 5.2 we assumed that an increase in Q would increase net exports, $X = EX - IM$, because it would increase the quantity of export goods demanded abroad (EX) and decrease the quantity of foreign goods demanded in the home economy. But even so, an increase in Q is an increase in the value of foreign goods in terms of domestic goods. In the expression $X = EX - IM$, each term is measured in terms of units of home-country goods; if $IM^\#$ is the volume of imported foreign goods measured in their own units, then $X = EX - IM^\# Q$. Thus it is conceivable that an increase in Q could decrease X even though it increases EX and decreases $IM^\#$.

Indeed, there is considerable reason to believe that the immediate, very short-run effect will be of this "perverse" type. The idea is that it takes some time for export and import volumes EX and $IM^\#$ to respond to any change in Q. But if neither of these magnitudes is changed, it is clear from the expression $X = EX - IM^\# Q$ that X will (temporarily) move in the opposite direction from Q, not in the same direction as is assumed in our basic model. Similarly, if the short-run responses of EX and $IM^\#$ are smaller than the long-run responses, it is possible that the short-run effect of Q on X could be negative even if the long-run effect is positive.

This phenomenon is known as the J-curve effect because of graphical expositions that plot the change in X versus elapsed time—X first jumps down to a reduced level and then gradually rises as time passes. That is a rather unsatisfying reason, perhaps, for the relevant graph does not actually look much like a letter J, but the term has become too well-established to make dissent sensible.

The implication of the phenomenon is that the net export function $\tilde{X}$, used in constructing the IS curve, should perhaps be written in something like the following manner:

$$X_t = \tilde{X}(q_t, q_{t-1}, q_{t-2}, y_t, y_t^*). \tag{6}$$

Here it is recognized that one period's net exports (or CA balance) depend not only on the current value of q_t, but also on the previous values q_{t-1} and q_{t-2}. To reflect the J-curve effect, it might be that $\partial\tilde{X}/\partial q_t$ is negative, but with $\partial\tilde{X}/\partial q_{t-2}$ and possibly $\partial\tilde{X}/\partial q_{t-1}$ positive. The sum of these three terms would presumably be positive, reflecting a long-run effect in which X responds in the same direction as the change in q.

The presence in Equation (6) of q_t, q_{t-1}, and q_{t-2} makes that a *dynamic* relation, and thus calls attention once again to the desirability of proper dynamic analysis, that is, analysis of period-by-period movements through time of the system's variables. As stated before, the next chapter will provide an introduction to that type of analysis. There is one additional point that should be taken up, however, before leaving the subject at hand.

This additional point concerns the possibility that X might be negatively related to Q even from a long-run perspective. To derive a famous condition pertaining to that possibility, let us again write $X = \text{EX} - \text{IM}^{\#}Q$ and let $\partial X/\partial Q$ and $\partial \text{IM}^{\#}/\partial Q$ be the partial derivatives of the relevant behavioral relations governing exports and imports. We could think of these as long-run relations, in which case we would certainly have $\partial \text{EX}/\partial Q > 0$ and $\partial \text{IM}^{\#}/\partial Q < 0$. But nevertheless, the appearance of Q in $X = \text{EX} - \text{IM}^{\#}Q$ makes it possible that the total effect $\partial X/\partial Q$ might be negative.

To see this we write

$$\frac{\partial X}{\partial Q} = \frac{\partial \text{EX}}{\partial Q} - \text{IM}^{\#} - Q\frac{\partial \text{IM}^{\#}}{\partial Q}. \tag{7}$$

Now define the behavioral elasticities $\eta_1 = (Q/\text{EX})\partial \text{EX}/\partial Q$ and

$$\eta_2 = -(Q/\text{IM}^{\#})\partial \text{IM}^{\#}/\partial Q.$$

Using those expressions, Equation (7) can be rewritten as

$$\frac{\partial X}{\partial Q} = \eta_1\frac{\text{EX}}{Q} - \text{IM}^{\#} + \eta_2\text{IM}^{\#}. \tag{8}$$

Now suppose the small change in Q under consideration takes place with a starting condition in which trade is balanced, that is, $\text{EX} - \text{IM}^{\#}Q = 0$. Then Equation (8) can be rewritten again as

$$\frac{\partial X}{\partial Q} = (\eta_1 - 1 + \eta_2)\text{IM}^{\#}. \tag{9}$$

But since $\text{IM}^{\#}$ is an inherently positive number, we see from Equation (9) that $\partial X/\partial Q$ will be positive if and only if $\eta_1 + \eta_2 > 1$. Thus net exports will increase with a depreciation of the real exchange rate, as assumed in Section 5.2, provided that the export and import elasticities (with respect to Q) sum to a total in excess of 1. This is a rather famous condition, known as the Marshall–Lerner condition.[16]

The Marshall–Lerner condition can be considered for elasticities pertaining to short-run or long-run (or other) behavioral relations. As explained above, the elasticities will be small for very short-run behavioral relations, so the condition may not be satisfied for short-run experiments, even though our formal short-run analyses in this chapter assume that it is. For long-run responses, one would expect values of η_2 greater than 1.0 and η_1 around 0.5, so the Marshall–Lerner condition should hold easily. Some evidence supporting that notion is reported by Krugman and Obstfeld (1994, p. 478).

[16] It is named after Alfred Marshall and Abba Lerner, two economists who contributed to its understanding. Note that the elasticities are defined using conventions that make them both positive.

Appendix

The purpose here is to consider short-run analysis under the assumption that capital mobility is entirely absent, in other words, that international borrowing and lending do not take place (or their extent is exogenously controlled by governmental authorities). Let us begin with the case of fixed exchange rates. In the absence of capital mobility, the short-run model becomes

$$y_t = b_0 + b_1 r_t + b_2 q_t + b_3 g_t + b_4 y_t^* \tag{A1}$$

$$m_t - p_t = c_0 + c_1 y_t + c_2 R_t \tag{A2}$$

$$r_t = R_t - \Delta p_{t+1}^e \tag{A3}$$

$$q_t = s_t - p_t + p_t^* \tag{A4}$$

$$\Delta FR = PX. \tag{A5}$$

Here the UIP condition is not included; instead Equation (A5) equates the change in foreign exchange reserves to net exports. In the first four equations, the variables g_t, y_t^*, and p_t^* are exogenous whereas Δp_{t+1}^e, s_t, and p_t are temporarily fixed. That leaves the variables y_t, r_t, q_t, R_t, and m_t. Now from a long-term perspective m_t must be endogenous, as explained in Section 7.1. But with no capital flows it becomes possible for the economy's central bank temporarily to sterilize flows in foreign exchange reserves and keep them from affecting the money stock. Thus we can, for short-run analysis, treat m_t as an exogenously determined policy variable. Then Equations (A1)–(A4) determine short-run equilibrium values of y, r, q, and R.

If we assume that $\Delta p_{t+1}^e = 0$, then $r = R$ and graphical analysis becomes simple. As shown in Figure 7–9, an increase in m from m^1 to m^2, for example, will expand output to y^2 and reduce interest rates to $r^2 = R^2 < R^1 = r^1$. With s and p fixed, q does not change, but the increase in y induces a current-account deficit. This will be financed by an outflow of reserves—so clearly the equilibrium can only be one of the short-run type—which does not require a reduction in m (from m^2) under the assumption that open-market purchases of domestic securities are being made to keep constant the total of foreign reserves plus domestic securities held by the central bank.

If instead government spending were increased, the level of r and R would be raised rather than lowered. Output would be increased again, however, and a current-account deficit created (or enlarged). Again sterilization would therefore be required to prevent m from changing over time—and again the resulting situation could be maintained only temporarily. From a long-run perspective, the initial equilibrium must be restored.

Now let us consider the case with zero capital mobility, but with a floating exchange rate. If the regime is a true float, then there will be no flows of international reserves, so $\Delta FR = 0$. Equation (A5) is replaced, then, with the condition that net exports must equal zero:

$$\tilde{X}(q, y, y^*) = 0. \tag{A6}$$

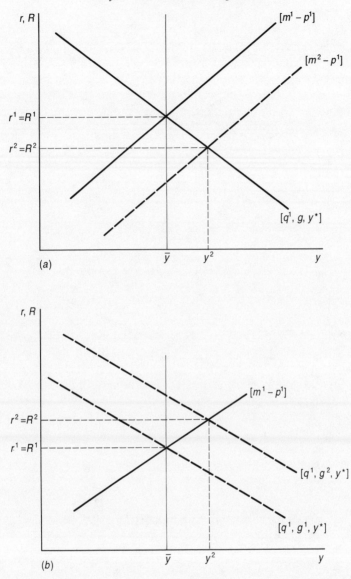

Figure 7–9 Fixed exchange rate with no capital mobility. (*a*) Monetary expansion. (*b*) Fiscal Expansion.

Then Equations (A1)–(A4) and (A6) become sufficient to determine y, r, q, R, and s with m exogenous.

Let us depict graphically the short-run effects, under these conditions, of an increase in the money stock from m^1 to m^2. The LM curve shifts rightward, as shown in Figure 7–10, to intersect the IS function at r^2, y^2. But this cannot be a short-run equilibrium position, because the increased level of output would

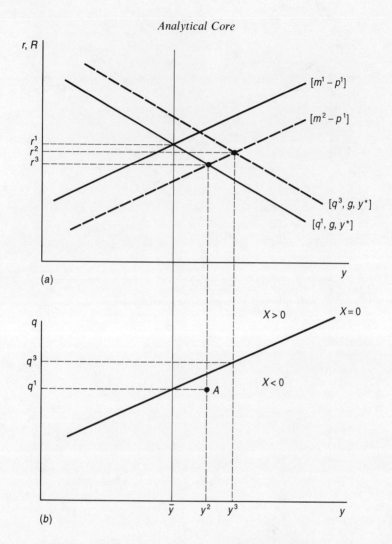

Figure 7–10 Floating exchange rate with no capital mobility. Monetary expansion.

imply a net export deficit with q unchanged at q^1 (as shown at point A in the lower panel) and $X = 0$ is one of the equilibrium conditions. Thus q must exceed q^1, implying that IS is farther to the right than initially. The short-run equilibrium position will then be one such as that shown with values r^3, y^3, and q^3. It cannot be a long-run equilibrium position, of course, because $y^3 > \bar{y}$. As time passes, then, prices will rise, shifting IS and LM back toward their original positions.

References

Blanchard, O. J., and S. Fischer, *Lectures on Macroeconomics*, Cambridge, MA: MIT Press, 1989.

Branson, W. H., "Monetary Policy and the New View of International Capital Movements," *Brookings Papers on Economic Activity*, no. 2 (1970), 235–262.

Fleming, J. M., "Domestic Financial Policies under Fixed and under Flexible Exchange Rates," *International Monetary Fund Staff Papers* **9** (Nov. 1962), 369–379.

Henderson, D. W., and S. Sampson, "Intervention in Foreign Exchange Markets: A Summary of Ten Staff Studies," *Federal Reserve Bulletin* **69** (Nov. 1983), 830–836.

Kenen, P. B., *The International Economy*, 3rd ed. New York: Cambridge University Press, 1994.

Krugman, P. R., and M. Obstfeld, *International Economics: Theory and Policy*, 3rd ed. Glenview, IL: Scott, Foresman, 1994.

Melvin, M., *International Money and Finance*, 2nd ed. New York: Harper Collins, 1989.

Mundell, R., "The Appropriate Use of Monetary and Fiscal Policy for Internal and External Stability," *International Monetary Fund Staff Papers* **9** (Mar. 1962), 70–77.

———, "Capital Mobility and Stabilization Policy under Fixed and Flexible Exchange Rates," *Canadian Journal of Economics and Political Science* **29** (Nov. 1963), 475–485.

Obstfeld, M., "Can We Sterilize? Theory and Evidence," *American Economic Review Papers and Proceedings* **72** (May 1982), 45–50.

Problems

1. Using graphical analysis, analyze the effects on an economy's variables y, p, m, and q of an increase in R^* when the economy has a fixed exchange rate. Consider both short-run and stationary-state effects.

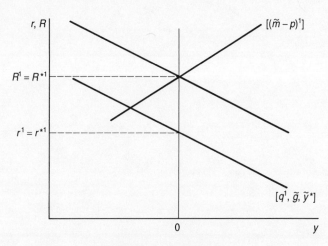

Figure 7–11 Problem 3.

2. Find effects on the current-account balance of the change posited in Problem 1.

3. Figure 7–11 depicts a fixed exchange rate economy in a steady-state equilibrium with positive real growth ($\Delta y = \Delta \bar{y} > 0$) and inflation rate Δp^1. Now suppose that inflation abroad increases from Δp^{*1} to Δp^{*2}, with no change in Δy^* or r^*. Depict the new steady-state equilibrium on a similar diagram. Does it entail larger, smaller, or unchanged values for r, R, $\tilde{m} - p$, and q?

4. What is the relevance of Problem 3 for the situation in Germany (and other European nations) during the years of 1965–1971?

8

Expectations and Dynamic Analysis

8.1 Introduction

As promised, we turn in this chapter to genuine dynamic analysis of exchange rate behavior. Instead of utilizing various types of comparative static analysis—such as short-run impact analysis and longer run steady-state analysis—we now introduce the development of models designed to trace out the time path of exchange rates or other endogenous variables on a period-by-period basis. Analysis of this type is more complete and desirable, but it is also more difficult than the varieties considered previously for three related but distinct reasons. First, there is the inherent difficulty of characterizing period-by-period movements as opposed to unchanging situations. But, second, it is also the case that in considering realistic movements of variables, it is necessary to recognize the presence of random (or "stochastic") disturbances. We must take account, that is, of shocks that impinge on the supply and demand choices of market participants. And third, when situations are changing and random, it will be important for market participants to form expectations of future conditions—expectations that will usually be incorrect to some extent. Adding to the difficulty, moreover, is the fact that expectations are not normally observed or recorded in official statistics, which implies that some special analytical steps must be taken. In particular, some theory must be adopted concerning the manner in which market participants form their expectations.

In response to those additional difficulties engendered by the nature of dynamic analysis, we shall attempt to compensate by adopting a number of simplifying assumptions at various points. In particular, we will ignore fluctuations in some exogenous variables and will assume that others are generated by stochastic processes of a simple type. And we shall begin with a "classical" flexible-price version of our model that will permit us to separate the analysis into *real* and *monetary* portions, which are easier to handle one at a time than simultaneously. Before the end of the chapter, however, we will be compelled by the desire for realism to revert to a sticky-price assumption, which requires the real and monetary portions of the model to be handled simultaneously.

In terms of expectational behavior we shall briefly mention some alternative specifications. Most of our discussion will proceed, however, under the assumption that expectations are formed *rationally*. This, as many readers will be aware, is currently the dominant theory of expectation formation among economic researchers. Techniques for analyzing models with rational expectations will be outlined in Sections 8.4 and 8.5 (plus the chapter's Appendix).

8.2 Preliminary Analysis

We begin by writing once again the equations comprising the basic model that was introduced in Chapter 5 and utilized in Chapters 6 and 7. With one modification they are

$$y_t = b_0 + b_1 r_t + b_2 q_t + b_3 g_t + b_4 y_t^* + v_t \tag{1a}$$

$$m_t - p_t = c_0 + c_1 y_t + c_2 R_t + \varepsilon_t \tag{1b}$$

$$r_t = R_t - (p_{t+1}^e - p_t) \tag{1c}$$

$$q_t = s_t - (p_t - p_t^*) \tag{1d}$$

$$R_t = R_t^* + s_{t+1}^e - s_t. \tag{1e}$$

As before, the variables y_t, p_t, q_t, g_t, m_t, and s_t denote logarithms of real income, the general price level, the real exchange rate, the level of government purchases, the money stock, and the nominal exchange rate, whereas R_t and r_t are nominal and real interest rates. The superscripts e refer to expectations of future values and asterisks indicate foreign variables.

The one modification that appears in Equations $(1a)$–$(1e)$, relative to Chapter 6, is that the first two relations contain additional terms, v_t and ε_t. These terms are included to denote the presence of stochastic shocks affecting the IS and LM relations, thereby representing random shifts (due to taste or technology changes) in saving-investment or money-demand behavior. These stochastic shocks or disturbances v_t and ε_t are viewed as being generated by stochastic processes that are exogenous to the model at hand. The simplest assumption regarding one of these, say v_t, would be that it is generated by a purely random process such that, in each period t, v_t is drawn from an unchanging probability distribution with mean zero and variance σ_v^2. With sequential draws coming from the same distribution, it would then be implied that v_t and v_{t+j} (for any $j \neq 0$) are independent and identically distributed random variables. In such a case, the v_t process is said to be *white noise*. But, as we shall see below, it would probably be more realistic to assume that the v_t and ε_t processes are *random walks*, with the *changes* Δv_t and $\Delta \varepsilon_t$ being white noise. In any event, at present we make no particular assumption about these shock processes.

Equations $(1c)$–$(1e)$ do not, it will be noted, include disturbance terms. For Equations $(1c)$ and $(1d)$ this is the case because these are simply definitions, not behavioral relations. The interest parity equation $(1e)$ is, however, a behavioral relation, so the absence of a disturbance term in this case is just a simplifying assumption. In Chapter 9 it will be argued that a shock term should actually be included in the interest parity relationship.

To the set of Equations $(1a)$–$(1e)$ let us now add the following relation:

$$y_t = \bar{y}_t. \tag{1f}$$

Here the assumption is *not* that we are doing long-run analysis—instead we are embarking on period-by-period analysis—but that the economy under study is one in which prices are fully flexible, so that output y_t conforms to the full employment or market-clearing value $\bar{y}_t$ in each period. The latter, $\bar{y}_t$, is in turn assumed to be generated by an exogenous stochastic process, but for the moment its nature will be left unspecified.

With the model at hand, we now want to engage in some preliminary manipulations that will facilitate the initial analysis. By substituting Equation $(1e)$ into Equation $(1c)$ and rearranging we obtain

$$r_t = R_t - (p_{t+1}^e - p_t) = R_t^* + s_{t+1}^e - s_t - p_{t+1}^e + p_t$$
$$= R_t^* + (s_{t+1}^e - p_{t+1}^e) - (s_t - p_t).$$

But the foreign real rate of interest satisfies $r_t^* = R_t^* - (p_{t+1}^{*e} - p_t^*)$ by definition, so the last expression also equals

$$r_t^* + p_{t+1}^{*e} - p_t^* + (s_{t+1}^e - p_{t+1}^e) - (s_t - p_t)$$
$$= r_t^* + [s_{t+1}^e - (p_{t+1}^e - p_{t+1}^{*e})] - [s_t - (p_t - p_t^*)].$$

Here the bracketed terms can be recognized as equivalent to q_{t+1}^e and q_t, respectively, so our series of equations yields

$$r_t = r_t^* + q_{t+1}^e - q_t. \tag{2}$$

The latter, it will be noted, is of the same form as the interest parity relation $(1e)$, but is expressed in terms of real variables: the difference between home and foreign real rates of interest equals the expected rate of depreciation of the home country's real exchange rate.

Next we use Equation (2) to substitute into the IS function $(1a)$ with Equation $(1f)$ used on the left-hand side. The result is

$$\bar{y}_t = b_0 + b_1(r_t^* + q_{t+1}^e - q_t) + b_2 q_t + b_3 g_t + b_4 y_t^* + v_t. \tag{3}$$

Now notice that this relation involves only q_t and variables that are foreign or policy determined. Also note that all these variables are real, not monetary, in nature. Consequently, the single equation (3) constitutes a complete subsystem for the determination of q_t, in the sense that no other endogenous variables are involved.[1] We will consider the analysis of this subsystem, namely,

---

[1] This is the assumption for the purpose of our analytical discussion. In reality, policy variables such as g_t are partly endogenous.

Equation (3), in a subsequent section, but for now the relevant point is that Equation (3) shows q_t to be exogenous in relation to the economy's monetary variables m_t, p_t, and s_t.

Let us then turn to the monetary portion of the overall system. The first step is to substitute the interest parity relation $(1e)$ into the money-demand equation $(1b)$. Using Equation $(1f)$ for y_t, the result is

$$m_t - p_t = c_0 + c_1 \bar{y}_t + c_2(R_t^* + s_{t+1}^e - s_t) + \varepsilon_t. \tag{4}$$

Then replacement of p_t with $s_t + p_t^* - q_t$ from $(1d)$ yields

$$m_t - (s_t + p_t^* - q_t) = c_0 + c_1 \bar{y}_t + c_2(R_t^* + s_{t+1}^e - s_t) + \varepsilon_t. \tag{5}$$

Suppose now that we collect the exogenous variables together with ε_t and call the result u_t. Formally, we then have

$$u_t = p_t^* - q_t + c_1 \bar{y}_t + c_2 R_t^* + \varepsilon_t, \tag{6}$$

a definition that enables us to express (5) as

$$m_t - s_t = c_0 + c_2(s_{t+1}^e - s_t) + u_t. \tag{7}$$

Now this expression features only the single endogenous variable s_t which is seen to be dependent upon monetary policy (i.e., the generation of m_t), expectations about future values of s_t, and the (composite) shock term u_t. So with generating processes specified for m_t and u_t, Equation (7) can be viewed as a model of the determination of the exchange rate.[2]

As matters stand, the model is incomplete, in part because we have not yet specified monetary policy behavior—that is, how m_t is generated. But even if that step had been taken, we would still have an incomplete model because of the expectational variable s_{t+1}^e. If our aim were to obtain a solution process for s_t, we would obviously have to specify something about the behavior of s_{t+1}^e. Or, alternatively, if our aim were, for example, to estimate the parameters c_0 and c_1 of Equation (7) by regression analysis, again there would be a difficulty—time series data on s_t and m_t could be obtained from standard sources, but the same would not be true for s_{t+1}^e. Indeed, the latter is not directly observable as are s_t and m_t. So in this case as well it would be useful to have some theory or model of expectation formation that related s_{t+1}^e to variables that are observable. To describe such a theory is accordingly the purpose of the next section.

[2] Students of monetary economics may recognize that Equation (7) is of the same form as the famous Cagan demand function for money, but with s_t appearing in place of p_t. For a textbook discussion of the Cagan model, see McCallum (1989, pp. 133–155).

8.3 Expectations

One extremely simple "theory" of expectational behavior would be to assume that agents (i.e., market participants) always expect that the most recently observed value of any variable will continue to prevail in the near future. In the case at hand that theory would be represented algebraically by the equality $s_{t+1}^e = s_t$. For some variables such as the general price level it might be more appropriate to assume that x_{t+1}^e equals x_{t-1}, rather than x_t, because of data collection delays. But for exchange rates information is available almost immediately, so $s_{t+1}^e = s_t$ would be more plausible.

As a general theory of expectational behavior, this so-called static expectations model is not at all attractive. During an inflationary episode, for instance, it would be foolish for agents to expect that the next period's (log) price level p_{t+1} would equal this period's p_t. And this model takes no account of available information regarding other variables that might be useful in forecasting future values of p_t—information on monetary or fiscal policy actions, for example. Accordingly, the static expectations model has never attracted much support among researchers.[3]

Somewhat more attractive would be a related but more general assumption, namely, that x_{t+1}^e is related to current and past values of x_t in a distributed-lag fashion, as in

$$x_{t+1}^e = \lambda_0 x_t + \lambda_1 x_{t-1} + \cdots + \lambda_n x_{t-n}. \tag{8}$$

Here the λ_j coefficients are parameters that are supposed to be constant over time, and which are typically assumed to sum to 1.0. An important special case of Equation (8) is one in which the values of λ_j decrease exponentially in value as j increases without limit, that is, as the attached variables go back in time. In this case, if k is the factor of proportionality we have $\lambda_1 = k\lambda_0, \lambda_2 = k^2\lambda_0, \ldots,$ and for these to sum to 1.0, it is necessary that $k = 1 - \lambda_0$.[4] So we have

$$x_{t+1}^e = \lambda_0 x_t + \lambda_0(1 - \lambda_0)x_{t-1} + \lambda_0(1 - \lambda_0)^2 x_{t-2} + \cdots. \tag{9}$$

For the sake of notational simplicity, let λ_0 be denoted by λ. Then we have

$$x_{t+1}^e = \lambda x_t + \lambda(1 - \lambda)x_{t-1} + \lambda(1 - \lambda)^2 x_{t-2} + \cdots \tag{10}$$

---

[3] Ironically, it is not a bad model for expectations regarding future values of the (log) exchange rate s_t. But the reason is simply that s_t turns out to be close to a random-walk variable, as we shall see later, for which s_t is the rational expectation (from a univariate perspective) of s_{t+1}. Thus the static expectations model works fairly well in this case by chance, not because it is based on a sensible principle.

[4] The sum is $\lambda_0 + k\lambda_0 + k^2\lambda_0 + k^3\lambda_0 + \cdots = \lambda_0(1 + k + k^2 + \cdots)$, which equals $\lambda_0/(1 - k)$ by the familiar formula for the sum of a geometric series. Therefore, the sum will equal 1.0 only if $1 = \lambda_0/(1 - k)$, implying $1 - k = \lambda_0$ or $k = 1 - \lambda_0$.

and the change in expectations between periods t and $t + 1$ becomes

$$
\begin{aligned}
x_{t+1}^e - x_t^e &= \lambda[x_t + (1 - \lambda)x_{t-1} + (1 - \lambda)^2 x_{t-2} + \cdots] \\
&\quad - \lambda[x_{t-1} + (1 - \lambda)x_{t-2} + (1 - \lambda)^2 x_{t-3} + \cdots] \\
&= \lambda[x_t - \lambda x_{t-1} - \lambda(1 - \lambda)x_{t-2} - \lambda(1 - \lambda)^2 x_{t-3} - \cdots] \\
&= \lambda\{x_t - [\lambda x_{t-1} + \lambda(1 - \lambda)x_{t-2} + \lambda(1 - \lambda)^2 x_{t-3} + \cdots]\}. \quad (11)
\end{aligned}
$$

But the term inside square brackets can be recognized as equal to x_t^e, so we end up with the relation

$$
x_{t+1}^e - x_t^e = \lambda(x_t - x_t^e). \tag{12}
$$

The latter implies that the change or adjustment in expectations is proportional to the most recent expectational error, that is, the difference between the anticipated value x_t^e and the realization x_t. This form of "adaptive" adjustment was considered attractive by researchers in the 1950s and 1960s, so the fact that Equations (9) and (12) are equivalent was viewed as a positive feature of the particular distributed-lag formation in (9). The latter became known as the "adaptive expectations" hypothesis, and was arguably the most widely used model of expectational behavior throughout the 1960s.

During the 1970s, however, it became generally recognized that *any* distributed-lag model of expectational behavior is subject to an important criticism, namely, that it can be *consistently* incorrect. Suppose, to illustrate the point, that x_t denotes the inflation rate. Then in a period of accelerating inflation, with $x_t > x_{t-1}$ in every period t, the expected value x_{t+1}^e will be below the outcome x_{t+1} period after period—agents will be continually underestimating the next period's inflation rate. But it seems highly unlikely that market participants would make the same error repeatedly, period after period, because expectational errors are costly to those who are committing them. Indeed, it is a basic premise of standard neoclassical economic analysis that agents do not consistently repeat the same mistakes. Consequently, the adaptive expectations formula in particular, and distributed-lag representations of expectational variables more generally, have fallen out of favor among researchers.

8.4 Rational Expectations

We have argued that because expectational errors are costly to those who make them, purposeful agents will try to form expectations in a manner that eliminates avoidable errors. Furthermore, it is the case that systematic errors—that is, errors that occur predictably under certain conditions—are avoidable; by observing the particular conditions that lead to errors, agents can take action to offset any systematic tendency to err. An attractive hypothesis for economic analysis of expectational behavior, consequently, is that agents are successful in avoiding regular sources of error. Being purposeful, agents manage their affairs in such a way that there is very little systematic component to their expectational error process. Errors are committed, of course, but they occur at random.

But how is the absence of systematic expectational error expressed analytically? Is there some formula, perhaps more complex than that for adaptive expectations, that will yield this condition? In this regard it is important to recognize that the absence of systematic expectational error cannot generally be represented by *any* algebraic formula comparable to the adaptive expectations formula (12). It might be possible to write a formula expressing x_{t+1}^e in terms of x_t, $x_{t-1}, \ldots$ that would avoid errors in the particular case of ever-increasing inflation, but the coefficients in this formula would then be wrong if a different inflationary pattern, say, repeating cycles, was generated by the monetary authority. In fact, *whatever* the coefficients attached to past x_t values in an expression such as Equation (8), there will always be *some* inflation path that will make x_{t+1}^e systematically different from x_{t+1} (i.e., systematically in error).[5]

The message of the foregoing is that to express analytically the hypothesis that agents avoid systematic expectational errors, we want not a formula but instead an analytic *condition* that rules out such errors. To see what the appropriate condition is, let us consider an agent forming an expectation at time t of x_{t+1}—next period's inflation rate, for example—and let us denote that expectation by x_{t+1}^e. Then the expectational error that will occur, when period $t + 1$ comes to pass, is $x_{t+1} - x_{t+1}^e$. And the condition that we adopt is that this error, $x_{t+1} - x_{t+1}^e$, not be systematically related to any information possessed by the agent in period t (when the expectation was formed).

The way to achieve this condition, it turns out, is to assume that expectations subjectively held (i.e., believed) by agents are equal to the mean of the probability distribution of the variable being forecast, given available information. For example, x_{t+1} is from the vantage point of period t a random variable. Its mean from that vantage point is $E(x_{t+1}|\Omega_t)$, the mathematical expectation (i.e., mean) of the probability distribution of x_{t+1}, given the information Ω_t, where this last symbol denotes the set of information available to the agent at time t. Thus the expectational hypothesis that we are seeking can be adopted by assuming that, for any variable x_{t+j} and any period t,

$$x_{t+j}^e = E(x_{t+j}|\Omega_t). \tag{13}$$

In words, this condition requires that the *subjective* expectation (forecast) of x_{t+1} held by agents in t be equal to the *objective* (mathematical) expectation of x_{t+1} conditional on Ω_t (i.e., the mean of the actual conditional probability distribution of x_{t+1} given information available in t).

---

[5] If, for example, the coefficients are λ_0, λ_1, $\lambda_2, \ldots$, then an inflationary path $x_t = \delta + \lambda_0 x_t + \lambda_1 x_{t+1} + \cdots$ will result in x_{t+1} values that will always exceed their forecasts x_{t+1} by the amount δ.

Analytical Core

But where, the reader may well ask, does the *actual* probability distribution of x_{t+1} come from? In a literal sense, it is of course unknown. But any economist who wishes to use this expectational hypothesis in the context of a model, has in the course of constructing that model adopted his (or her) own view of how x_t is actually generated. Thus the only logically coherent way for him to proceed is to use the probability distribution of x_{t+1} *as expressed in his model* as the basis for computing $E(x_{t+1}|\Omega_t)$; his model *is* his view of the actual economy.

To this point we have argued in favor of an expectational hypothesis that rules out systematic errors and have asserted that condition (13) will do so. Let us now prove that this assertion is true. First, we calculate what the average expectational error will be over a large number of periods if Equation (13) is utilized. To do that, we find the mean of the distribution of $x_{t+1} - x_{t+1}^e$ values.[6] That is, we compute

$$E(x_{t+1} - x_{t+1}^e) = E[x_{t+1} - E(x_{t+1}|\Omega_t)] = E(x_{t+1}) - E[E(x_{t+1}|\Omega_t)]$$
$$= E(x_{t+1}) - E(x_{t+1}) = 0 \tag{14}$$

showing that the average error is zero. In this calculation the only tricky step is the next to last one, where the fact that $E[E(x_{t+1}|\Omega_t)]$ equals $E(x_{t+1})$ is used. The validity of that fact, which is a special case of the "law of iterated expectations," is demonstrated in the Appendix to this chapter. This "law" reflects the commonsense idea that the expectation, of an expectation that will be based on more information than is currently available, will simply be the expectation given the lesser information currently available.

Thus we see that the average expectational error under hypothesis (13) will be zero. To complete the demonstration that there will be no systematic relation between $x_{t+1} - x_{t+1}^e$ and any information available in t, let z_t denote *any* variable whose value is known to agents at t. Thus z_t is an element of Ω_t. Then consider the covariance of $x_{t+1} - x_{t+1}^e$ and z_t. Since $E(x_{t+1} - x_{t+1}^e)$ is zero, this covariance will be the mean of the distribution of the product $(x_{t+1} - x_{t+1}^e)z_t$. We evaluate this covariance as follows:

$$E[(x_{t+1} - x_{t+1}^e)z_t] = E[(x_{t+1} - E(x_{t+1}|\Omega_t))z]$$
$$= E(x_{t+1}z_t) - E[E(x_{t+1}|\Omega_t)z_t]. \tag{15}$$

But because z_t is an element of Ω_t, it is true that $z_t E(x_{t+1}|\Omega_t) = E(z_t x_{t+1}|\Omega_t)$. Then using the law of iterated expectations, we see that the final term in Equation (15) equals $E(z_t x_{t+1})$. That shows, then, that the covariance is zero:

$$E[(x_{t+1} - x_{t+1}^e)z_t] = 0. \tag{16}$$

[6] The mean of the distribution of a random variable is, of course, one measure of what the average value of the variable will be when many observations on that variable are taken.

This implies that the expectational error is, in a statistical sense, unrelated to any element of Ω_t (i.e., to any available information).[7] Thus we have shown that the adoption of assumption (13) will, in fact, imply that systematic expectational errors will be absent.

This conclusion accords well, it might be added, with the commonsense idea that the "best" forecast of a value to be realized by a random variable is the mean of the probability distribution of that random variable.[8] The tricky aspect of our current application is that the relevant distribution is a conditional distribution—one that reflects the information available to the agent at the time he or she forms an expectation.

The hypothesis concerning expectations that we have just outlined was first put forth by Muth (1961). Because the type of expectational behavior postulated is purposeful, and the absence of avoidable errors is necessary for optimality on the part of the agents in the modeled economy, Muth chose the term "rational expectations" to describe his hypothesis. As it happens, Muth's ideas were not immediately embraced by the economics profession, in part because his paper was difficult to understand and some aspects were not clearly spelled out. The profession's appreciation of the theory was greatly enhanced in the early 1970s by a number of path-breaking papers by Robert E. Lucas, Jr., in which the rational expectations notion was extended and also applied to important issues in macroeconomics. These papers have been collectively republished in Lucas (1981). Writings by Sargent (1973) and Barro (1977) were also important in developing the widespread support for rational expectations that has existed for the past 10–15 years.

8.5 Analysis with Rational Expectations

At last we are prepared to analyze our first model of exchange rate dynamics. In doing so we shall use the summary relation presented as Equation (7). We begin by rewriting that equation here, but with the expression $E_t s_{t+1}$ inserted in place of s_{t+1}^e, and the symbol α used instead of c_2:

$$m_t - s_t = c_0 + \alpha(E_t s_{t+1} - s_t) + u_t. \tag{17}$$

Here $E_t s_{t+1}$ is used as a shorthand notation for $E(s_{t+1}|\Omega_t)$, so we have in (17) adopted the assumption of rational expectations. This last expression is not fully defined, however, until we specify the content of Ω_t—in other words, until we specify precisely what information is available to agents in period t. It will sometimes be desirable to consider alternative informational specifications, but

---

[7] Actually, our proof shows only that $x_{t+1} - x_{t+1}^e$ is uncorrelated with z_t, not that it is statistically independent (a somewhat stronger condition that is also implied if the variables have normal distributions).

[8] This commonsense criterion breaks down if the model at hand is nonlinear. In general, the discussion of this chapter is fully appropriate only for linear systems. Rational expectations analysis of nonlinear models is extremely difficult and, consequently, is not considered in this book.

for now it will be assumed that Ω_t includes values from period t, and all previous periods, of the model's basic variables m_t and s_t. Thus we assume that in period t agents know $s_t, s_{t-1}, s_{t-2}, \ldots, m_t, m_{t-1}, m_{t-2}, \ldots$. Furthermore, the concept of rationality implies that they understand the workings of the economy; for they need to do so to avoid systematic errors. In the context of the present model this implies that these agents are aware of relationship (17), so they can infer the values of $u_t, u_{t-1}, u_{t-2}, \ldots$. Consequently these, too, are included in Ω_t.

Beginning with Equation (17), and assuming initially that u_t is white noise, we might try to develop a solution for s_t as follows. First we can collect terms and rearrange to give

$$s_t = \frac{m_t - c_0 - \alpha E_t s_{t+1} - u_t}{1 - \alpha}. \tag{18}$$

Clearly, the latter is not a solution, even with m_t exogenous, for it contains the expectational variable $E_t s_{t+1}$. To eliminate the latter, we might proceed by using expression (18) for s_{t+1} and then applying the "operator" E_t, that is, by taking the conditional expectation given Ω_t.[9] Doing so would yield

$$E_t s_{t+1} = \frac{E_t m_{t+1} - c_0 - \alpha E_t s_{t+2}}{1 - \alpha}, \tag{19}$$

in which it is recognized that $E_t u_{t+1} = 0$ (by our assumption that u_t is white noise) and that $E_t(E_{t+1} s_{t+2}) = E_t s_{t+2}$ by the law of iterated expectations. Then substitution of Equation (19) into (18) would get rid of $E_t s_{t+1}$, but would bring in $E_t s_{t+2}$ and $E_t m_{t+1}$. Repeating that same process indefinitely would, with some fairly mild extra assumptions, eliminate all expectations of future s_t values, but would leave us with an expression involving today's (i.e., period t's) expectations of $m_{t+1}, m_{t+2}, m_{t+3}, \ldots$.

This foregoing procedure is not very successful, then, in terms of developing a usable solution for s_t. But it is instructive in that it emphasizes that the value of the exchange rate in period t depends on the values of the money stock that are expected for each period in the entire infinite future. That implies, however, that to solve for s_t the analyst must know something about the future behavior of the monetary authority. The analyst must know, in other words, about the policy *process* generating m_t that is in place.

As an example of a policy process, consider the following specification of money-supply behavior:

$$m_t = \mu_0 + \mu_1 m_{t-1} + e_t. \tag{20}$$

Here the (log of the) money stock in period t depends on its previous value, m_{t-1}, and also on a purely random component e_t. The latter, which is formally a white-noise disturbance, represents the unsystematic component of policy behavior (the systematic part of which is $\mu_0 + \mu_1 m_{t-1}$).

---

[9] Recall that $E_t z_{t+j}$ is defined as $E(z_{t+j}|\Omega_t)$.

Given this specification, it is then possible to determine the expectations at t of future m_t values. For m_{t+1} the expectation is simply $E_t m_{t+1} = \mu_0 + \mu_1 m_t$, which follows because $E_t e_{t+1} = 0$. Next, for m_{t+2} we have

$$E_t m_{t+2} = E_t(\mu_0 + \mu_1 m_{t+1} + e_{t+2})$$
$$= \mu_0 + \mu_1 E_t m_{t+1} = \mu_0 + \mu_1(\mu_0 + \mu_1 m_t). \qquad (21)$$

This type of calculation can in principle be repeated for every future period, ultimately yielding, upon substitution into the equation described at the end of the paragraph containing Equation (19), a proper solution for s_t.

Furthermore, analogous calculations could be carried out if the m_t process were different. But there must be an m_t process specified. With rational expectations, the value of s_t depends on time t expectations of m_{t+j} values into the entire future, and to determine these, some specification of the money-supply process must be made as part of the model.

8.6 Solution Procedure

When a particular policy process for m_t has been specified, however, there is another way of solving the model, which is much simpler than the one just attempted. It works as follows. By combining Equations (17) and (20), the model at hand may be written as

$$c_0 + \alpha E_t s_{t+1} + (1 - \alpha)s_t + u_t = \mu_0 + \mu_1 m_{t-1} + e_t. \qquad (22)$$

This shows s_t to be dependent on the values of m_{t-1}, u_t, e_t, and $E_t s_{t+1}$. But what does the latter depend on? From Equation (19) we know that $E_t s_{t+1}$ depends on $E_t m_{t+1}$ and $E_t s_{t+2}$, since $E_t u_{t+1}$ equals zero. But $E_t m_{t+1}$ is itself determined by m_t, which depends only on m_{t-1} and e_t, so $E_t m_{t+1}$ brings in no additional variables. Also, by extension of the foregoing, $E_t s_{t+2}$ depends on $E_t m_{t+2}$ and $E_t s_{t+3}$, and the former brings in no new variables whereas the latter leads to $E_t s_{t+4}$, and so on.

The upshot of this line of reasoning is that s_t evidently depends only on m_{t+1}, u_t, and e_t; the presence of $E_t s_{t+1}$ does not itself bring in any additional determinants. Consequently, since the model is linear, we conjecture that there is a solution of the form

$$s_t = \phi_0 + \phi_1 m_{t-1} + \phi_2 u_t + \phi_3 e_t, \qquad (23)$$

for some constants $\phi_0, \ldots, \phi_3$, if we can find what they are. But if that conjecture is true, then $s_{t+1} = \phi_0 + \phi_1 m_t + \phi_2 u_{t+1} + \phi_3 e_{t+1}$, and it follows that

$$E_t s_{t+1} = \phi_0 + \phi_1 m_t = \phi_0 + \phi_1(\mu_0 + \mu_1 m_{t-1} + e_t). \qquad (24)$$

Now suppose that Equations (23) and (24) are substituted into Equation (22). The result is, clearly,

$$c_0 + \alpha[\phi_0 + \phi_1(\mu_0 + \mu_1 m_{t-1} + e_t)] +$$

$$(1 - \alpha)(\phi_0 + \phi_1 m_{t-1} + \phi_2 u_t + \phi_3 e_t) + u_t = \mu_0 + \mu_1 m_{t-1} + e_t. \quad (25)$$

But for Equation (23) to be a valid solution, as conjectured, it must hold regardless of the values of u_t and e_t that are generated by chance and whatever m_{t-1} happens to be. Therefore, Equation (25) must also be a legitimate equality *whatever* the values are of m_{t-1}, u_t, and e_t. But that requirement is extremely useful, for it implies that the following conditions must pertain to the ϕ:

$$\alpha\phi_1\mu_1 + (1 - \alpha)\phi_1 = \mu_1 \qquad (26a)$$

$$(1 - \alpha)\phi_2 + 1 = 0 \qquad (26b)$$

$$\alpha\phi_1 + (1 - \alpha)\phi_3 = 1 \qquad (26c)$$

$$c_0 + \alpha\phi_0 + \alpha\phi_1\mu_0 + (1 - \alpha)\phi_0 = \mu_0. \qquad (26d)$$

Now these four conditions—obtained by equating coefficients on both sides of Equation (25) for m_{t-1}, u_t, e_t, and 1—are just what is needed, for they permit us to solve for the four unknown ("undetermined") coefficients, the ϕ. In particular, from Equations (26a) and (26b) we find that

$$\phi_1 = \frac{\mu_1}{1 - \alpha + \alpha\mu_1} \qquad (27)$$

and

$$\phi_2 = \frac{-1}{1 - \alpha}. \qquad (28)$$

Furthermore, using Equation (27) we find from (26c) and (26d) that

$$\phi_3 = \frac{1 - \alpha\phi_1}{1 - \alpha} = \frac{1 - \alpha\mu_1/(1 - \alpha + \alpha\mu_1)}{1 - \alpha} = \frac{1}{1 - \alpha + \alpha\mu_1} \qquad (29)$$

and

$$\phi_0 = \frac{\mu_0(1 - \alpha)}{1 - \alpha + \alpha\mu_1} - c_0. \qquad (30)$$

By putting Equations (27)–(30) into (23), then, we obtain

$$s_t = \frac{\mu_0(1 - \alpha)}{1 - \alpha + \alpha\mu_1} - c_0 + \frac{\mu_1}{1 - \alpha + \alpha\mu_1} m_{t-1} - \frac{1}{1 - \alpha} u_t + \frac{1}{1 - \alpha + \alpha\mu_1} e_t. \qquad (31)$$

The latter is our sought-after *solution* for s_t. That is, it describes the evolution over time of the endogenous variable s_t in terms of the exogenous shocks u_t and e_t and the predetermined variable m_{t-1}. It defines a time path for s_t and is thus a truly dynamic solution.

There are other forms, it should be said, in which this solution can be expressed. A prominent one can be obtained by noting that $\mu_0 + \mu_1 m_{t-1} + e_t$ can be replaced by m_t, giving

$$s_t = \frac{-\alpha\mu_0}{1 - \alpha + \alpha\mu_1} - c_0 + \frac{1}{1 - \alpha + \alpha\mu_1} m_t - \frac{1}{1 - \alpha} u_t. \tag{32}$$

In addition, Equation (20) can be solved for m_t in terms of $e_t, e_{t-1}, \ldots$[10] and put into (32). The result is

$$s_t = \frac{-\alpha\mu_0}{1 - \alpha + \alpha\mu_1} - c_0 - \frac{1}{1 - \alpha} u_t + \frac{\mu_0/(1 - \mu_1) + e_t + \mu_1 e_{t-1} + \cdots}{1 - \alpha + \alpha\mu_1}. \tag{33}$$

But while (32) and (33) are valid solutions, they are just different ways of writing the same solution as (31). That is, for any set of values for $u_t, u_{t-1}, \ldots$ and e_t, $e_{t-1}, \ldots$, each of them implies the same path of s_t values as does (31).

8.7 Properties of the Solution Process

We now wish to examine the dynamic properties of our solution equation for the exchange rate. In doing so, it will be important to keep in mind that $\alpha = c_2 < 0$ and $|\mu_1| \leq 1.0$ so that $1/(1 - \alpha)$ and $1/[1 - \alpha(1 - \mu_1)]$ are both positive. Then inspection of Equation (31) or (33) will show immediately that a positive money-supply disturbance, that is, an e_t value greater than zero, will raise s_t relative to the value that would prevail with $e_t = 0$. A positive value for the composite shock u_t will, however, have the effect of depressing s_t. The economic meaning of these two responses is easy to discern—an increased value of e_t represents an increased supply of domestic money, which tends to lower its foreign exchange value—i.e., to raise the domestic price of foreign exchange. As for the effect of u_t, one needs to refer back to Equation (6) to see how the composite u_t is related to its component variables. For convenience, we reproduce Equation (6) here, using α for c_2:

$$u_t = p_t^* - q_t + c_1 \bar{y}_t + \alpha R_t^* + \varepsilon_t. \tag{6'}$$

Thus we see that u_t is positively related to p_t^*, $\bar{y}_t$, and ε_t and negatively related to q_t and R_t^*. An increase in q_t would then correspond to a decrease in u_t,

---

[10] Repeated elimination of past m_t values, in a manner like that of Section 7.3, indicates that $m_t = \mu_0/(1 - \mu_1) + e_t + \mu_1 e_{t-1} + \cdots$.

for example, which will bring about an increase in s_t according to Equation (31). In words, an increase in the real domestic price of foreign goods will induce an increase in the domestic price of foreign currency (with monetary policy held constant). But an increase in the foreign price level p_t^* would raise u_t and lower s_t, that is, increase the value of domestic currency.[11] A positive value of the money-demand disturbance ε_t would reduce s_t, reflecting the tendency for an increase in the demand for anything to increase its exchange value.

The foregoing responses are similar to ones that would be obtained via comparative static analysis of the short-run (impact) type, as in Chapter 6. But with our present model we can also trace out effects over time. Imagine again, for example, that a money-supply shock $e_t > 0$ is experienced. Then from Equation (33) we see that there will typically be effects extending indefinitely into the future. The effect on s_{t+1} will be $\mu_1 e_t/(1 - \alpha + \alpha\mu_1)$, for example, the effect on s_{t+2} will be $\mu_1^2 e_t/(1 - \alpha + \alpha\mu_1)$, and so on. As time passes, the magnitude of these effects will become smaller, since with $|\mu_1| < 1$ higher powers of μ_1 are smaller in absolute value. In the limit the effect will become negligible, reflecting the fact that the e_t realization is only a temporary shock to m_t, given that $|\mu_1| < 1$.

If $\mu_1 = 1.0$, however, then the m_t process will be a random walk[12] and the effects of an e_t shock will not be reversed as time passes. Each e_t shock will in this case have a permanent effect on m_t and therefore—via our model—on s_t. The magnitude of the e_t effect on s_t will be $\mu_1 e_t/(1 - \alpha + \alpha\mu_1)$ as before, but with $\mu_1 = 1$ this expression will reduce to e_t, so the effect on s_t will be the same magnitude as that on m_t. Since these are logarithmic variables, the implication is that the price of foreign currency changes in the same proportion as the change in the money stock, when the latter is permanent, giving us the same sort of "quantity theory of money" result as was described in Section 6.1. That the effect on s_t is not reversed as time passes can be verified, moreover, by means of the expressions $\mu_1^k e_t/(1 - \alpha + \alpha\mu_1)$ for s_{t+k}.

It is also of interest to consider how v_t shocks or changes in government purchases would affect s_t. In the framework that we have constructed, the effects of these real shocks would be transmitted to s_t by way of the real exchange rate q_t. We need, then, to return our attention to the determination of q_t, which we have put aside for the past several pages. In Section 8.2 we showed that, with flexible prices, q_t would be determined by Equation (3), which can be rearranged as follows:

$$q_t = \frac{-b_1 q_{t+1}^e + (\bar{y}_t - b_0 - b_1 r_t^* - b_3 g_t - b_4 y_t^*) - v_t}{b_2 - b_1}. \tag{34}$$

By treating r_t^* and y_t^* as constants, using $E_t q_{t+1}$ in place of q_{t+1}^e, and

---

[11] It might appear that the same could be said for an increase in $\bar{y}_t$, but in fact such a change would also tend to increase q_t—see Equation (3)—which would have an offsetting effect.

[12] A random walk "with drift," if $\mu_0 \neq 0.0$. The definition of a random walk process appears on p. 160.

defining $\beta_1 = -b_1/(b_2 - b_1)$, $\beta_2 = 1/(b_2 - b_1)$, and so on, we can rewrite the latter as

$$q_t = \beta_0 + \beta_1 E_t q_{t+1} + \beta_2 \bar{y}_t + \beta_3 g_t + \beta_4 v_t. \tag{35}$$

Here $\beta_1 > 0$, $\beta_2 > 0$, $\beta_3 < 0$, and $\beta_4 < 0$. Now with specifications given for the stochastic processes generating $\bar{y}_t$, g_t, and v_t we could obtain a solution for q_t using the same sort of technique as was outlined in Section 8.6. And it can be shown that if $\bar{y}_t$, g_t, and v_t were all generated by white-noise processes, then the same would be true for q_t.[13] But this situation would seem to be rather unlikely in reality, as we shall see shortly. And if q_t is not a white-noise process, then Equation (6') shows us that u_t will not be so either, except possibly under some freakish coincidence. Accordingly, it is time to give some attention to our assumptions regarding exogenous stochastic processes, which have until now been tailored for the purpose of expositional simplicity, rather than realism. We will do so in the next section, in a manner that pays more attention to the actual dynamic properties of several crucial variables. We conclude our present discussion by quickly noting that when all our exogenous processes are white noise, as has been assumed until now, an increase in g_t or the shock v_t—that is, a decrease in the home country's tendency to save—will reduce q_t. By Equation (6'), that will increase u_t, which will decrease s_t. Thus the boost in spending on domestic output tends to appreciate the exchange value of the domestic currency.

8.8 More Realism in Specification

We now wish to alter our dynamic model to be more realistic. In what follows, it will be useful to keep in mind some notable features of the post-1972 data pertaining to exchange rates. Three particularly important regularities are as follows:

1. The purely random component of exchange rate fluctuations is much greater than for national price levels.
2. Real exchange rates exhibit a great deal of persistence in their fluctuations.
3. Exchange rates respond more promptly than national price levels to most shocks.

For the first two of these features it is reasonably easy to document their existence in the U.S. data. In the case of regularity 1, second-order autoregressions of the quarterly first differences over 1972–1991 yield residual standard error values of roughly 0.04 and 0.004, respectively, for s_t and p_t.[14] Thus the residual variance is about 100 times as large for Δs_t as for Δp_t. As for

[13] This proposition is the subject of Problem 3 at the end of the chapter.
[14] The series used are logs of the Fed's effective exchange rate (mentioned in Chapter 2) and the GNP deflator.

regularity 2, we have seen in Chapter 2 that real exchange rates move very closely with nominal rates (Figures 2–5) and also that swings in nominal rates are quite long lasting. We will also see in Chapter 9 that, at the level of monthly data, nominal exchange rates behave in a manner that is very close to a random walk. And in random walk processes there is no tendency for fluctuations to be reversed—shocks are in a sense "completely" persistent.

In the case of regularity 3, documentation is much more difficult to develop and so will not be presented here. Many researchers—including Dornbusch (1976) in a famous theoretical study devoted to the topic—take the validity of fact 3 to be sufficiently obvious as to require no documentation. Careful (though nonconclusive) arguments have been presented by Mussa (1986) and Meese (1984).

The relevant point, in any event, is that the solution presented above—for the model (17) and (20) with white-noise shocks—possesses none of the features 1–3. That is obvious for property 2, since q_t is white noise by assumption in that model, and it is also apparent that both s_t and p_t will respond promptly to all shocks, in contrast to property 3. Furthermore, derivation of a solution expression for p_t indicates that its residual variance is about the same as for s_t.[15] Consequently, some modification of the model is needed.

In line with regularity 2, we would like for our model to yield a solution process for q_t that is close to a random walk. Accordingly, we now assume that the exogenous variables $\bar{y}_t$, r_t^*, g_t, y_t^*, and v_t are generated by random-walk processes. Under such conditions, the q_t process will itself be a random walk—as can be verified by the solution procedure of Section 8.6.[16] For the income variables $\bar{y}_t$ and $\bar{y}_t^*$ this random-walk assumption is in fact highly consistent with the data, as many studies have shown, and the same is true for r_t^*. The actual process for the government spending variable g_t is somewhat less close to a random walk, but the discrepancy is not severe. And one would expect the v_t disturbance to be much like a random walk since the kind of behavioral shifts that are implied would presumably have a large permanent component.

Next, in modifying the system we shall alter the money-supply specification so as to be a first-order autoregression in money growth rates, like Δm_t, rather than in log levels. In other words, we now assume that m_t is generated by the process

$$\Delta m_t = \mu_0 + \mu_1 \Delta m_{t-1} + e_t \tag{36}$$

with e_t white noise and $|\mu_1| \leq 1.0$. This will give us a much more realistic specification for the United States than Equation (20); estimation of (36)

---

[15] That can be shown as follows. From the definition of q_t we have $p_t = s_t + p_t^* - q_t$, and using Equation (6') then gives $p_t = s_t + u_t - (c_1\bar{y}_t + \alpha R_t^* + \varepsilon_t)$. But the unpredictable component of the term in parentheses is small in variability in comparison with u_t, as will be shown in the next to last paragraph of this section, and u_t also dominates in the variability of s_t. So to an approximation the comparison will be between $[1/(1-\alpha)]^2\sigma_u^2$ for s_t and $[-\alpha/(1-\alpha)]^2\sigma_u^2$ for p_t. These will be equal if $\alpha = -1$, and the latter will be larger if $|\alpha| > 1$, which is highly plausible.

[16] See Problem 4.

with quarterly data over 1954–1990 gives an indication of a rather good fit, as follows[17]:

$$\Delta m_t = 0.005 + 0.62\Delta m_{t-1} + \hat{e}_t$$
$$(0.001) \quad (0.064)$$

$$R^2 = 0.39 \qquad SE = 0.0076 \qquad DW = 2.16$$

(Readers unfamiliar with any of these symbols should consult fn. 2 of Chapter 9.) Thus μ_1 is estimated at approximately 0.6 and the estimated standard error of the e_t disturbance process is 0.0076.

Finally to be consistent with our shift in specification toward one that pertains to growth rates, we assume that the u_t disturbance in Equation (17) is generated by a random-walk process rather than as white noise. That assumption is consistent with our assumptions regarding q_t and also reflects the idea that shifts in money-demand behavior (represented by ε_t) are due primarily to technological changes in the payments system, which are changes of a type that will be mostly permanent. With u_t in Equation (17) thus satisfying $\Delta u_t = \xi_t$, where ξ_t is white noise, we can then take first differences of the variables in (17), rearrange, and express the resulting relation as follows:

$$\Delta m_t - \Delta s_t = \alpha(E_t \Delta s_{t+1} - E_{t-1}\Delta s_t) + \xi_t. \tag{37}$$

In sum, our new model consists of Equations (36) and (37). Since the disturbances e_t and ξ_t are white noises, the system is of almost the same form as (17) and (20), but with growth rates Δm_t and Δs_t appearing in place of the log levels m_t and s_t. It is necessary to include the word "almost" in the preceding statement, however, because of the presence of the E_{t-1} operator attached to Δs_t on the right-hand side of Equation (37). Since the systems are not quite of the same form, we will not be able to reuse the solution expressions (31)–(33) with Δs_t in place of s_t, but will instead have to obtain a new solution. It should be mentioned that since Δq_t is a component of $\xi_t = \Delta u_t$, the variance of the disturbance ξ_t in the system is much larger than for e_t.[18]

To solve Equations (36) and (37) for Δs_t we proceed much as before. For reasons analogous to those discussed in Section 8.6 we conjecture that the solution for Δs_t will be of the form

$$\Delta s_t = \phi_0 + \phi_1 \Delta m_{t-1} + \phi_2 \xi_t + \phi_3 e_t. \tag{38}$$

Then to evaluate the unknown coefficients $\phi_0, \ldots, \phi_3$ we begin by determining that $E_t \Delta s_{t+1}$ satisfies

$$E_t \Delta s_{t+1} = \phi_0 + \phi_1 E_t \Delta m_t + \phi_2 E_t \xi_{t+1} + \phi_3 E_t e_{t+1}$$
$$= \phi_0 + \phi_1(\mu_0 + \mu_1 \Delta m_{t-1} + e_t) \tag{39}$$

---

[17] Here M1 is used as the money-supply measure, with m_t its logarithm.

[18] The standard deviation of quarterly changes in the Fed's q_t series is about 0.042, whereas that for the residuals of estimated money-demand functions is around 0.005.

and accordingly that

$$E_{t-1}\Delta s_t = \phi_0 + \phi_1 E_{t-1}\Delta m_{t-1} = \phi_0 + \phi_1 \Delta m_{t-1}. \tag{40}$$

Substituting Equations (36), (38), (39), and (40) into Equation (37) then yields

$$\mu_0 + \mu_1 \Delta m_{t-1} + e_t - (\phi_0 + \phi_1 \Delta m_{t-1} + \phi_2 \xi_t + \phi_3 e_t)$$
$$= \alpha[\phi_0 + \phi_1(\mu_0 + \mu_1 \Delta m_{t-1} + e_t)] - \alpha(\phi_0 + \phi_1 \Delta m_{t-1}) + \xi_t. \tag{41}$$

But for the latter to hold as an equality for all possible values of $\Delta\mu_{t-1}$, e_t, and ξ_t it must be true that the following conditions hold:

$$\mu_1 - \phi_1 = \alpha\phi_1\mu_1 - \alpha\phi_1 \tag{42a}$$

$$-\phi_2 = 1 \tag{42b}$$

$$1 - \phi_3 = \alpha\phi_1 \tag{42c}$$

$$\mu_0 - \phi_0 = \alpha\phi_0 + \alpha\phi_1\mu_0 - \alpha\phi_0. \tag{42d}$$

Solving these as before we find that

$$\phi_1 = \frac{\mu_1}{1 - \alpha + \alpha\mu_1} \tag{43}$$

$$\phi_2 = -1 \tag{44}$$

$$\phi_3 = \frac{1 - \alpha}{1 - \alpha + \alpha\mu_1} \tag{45}$$

$$\phi_0 = \frac{\mu_0(1 - \alpha)}{1 - \alpha + \alpha\mu_1}. \tag{46}$$

Here it will be noted that the implied values of ϕ_0 and ϕ_1 are the same as in our previous model, but those for ϕ_2 and ϕ_3 are different. That difference results because of the presence of the E_{t-1} operator on the right-hand side of Equation (37).

Our solution for Δs_t can then be written out explicitly as

$$\Delta s_t = \frac{\mu_0(1 - \alpha)}{1 - \alpha + \alpha\mu_1} + \frac{\mu_1}{1 - \alpha + \alpha\mu_1}\Delta m_{t-1} - \xi_t + \frac{1 - \alpha}{1 - \alpha + \alpha\mu_1}e_t. \tag{47}$$

And by using Equation (36), this can be alternatively written as

$$\Delta s_t = \frac{-(\alpha + e_t)}{1 - \alpha + \alpha\mu_1} + \frac{1}{1 - \alpha + \alpha\mu_1}\Delta m_t - \xi_t. \tag{48}$$

The latter expression will be particularly useful in what follows.

We wish now to determine whether the solution processes in this modified model match the three important empirical regularities mentioned at the start of this section. We already know that regularity 2, the persistence of movements in real exchange rates, is implied by the system because our disturbance assumptions were chosen so as to make q_t behave as a random walk. But how about regularities 1 and 3? The former asserts that the purely random component of exchange rate movements is much larger than for national price levels. In our model the purely random component of Δs_t is $-\xi_t + e_t(1 - \alpha)/[1 - \alpha(1 - \mu_1)]$, as inspection of Equation (47) reveals immediately. But to obtain a similar expression for Δp_t requires a bit of work. First, we have that $\Delta p_t = \Delta s_t + \Delta p_t^* - \Delta q_t$ from the definition (1*d*). But furthermore Equation (6) implies that $\Delta q_t = \Delta p_t^* - c_1 \Delta \bar{y}_t - c_2 \Delta R_t^* - \Delta \varepsilon_t + \Delta u_t$. So these together give

$$\Delta p_t = \Delta s_t - c_1 \Delta \bar{y}_t - c_2 \Delta R_t^* - \Delta \varepsilon_t + \Delta u_t.$$

Inserting our solution expression (47) for Δs_t then yields

$$\Delta p_t = \frac{\mu_0(1 - \alpha)}{1 - \alpha + \alpha\mu_1} + \frac{\mu_1}{1 - \alpha + \alpha\mu_1} \Delta m_{t-1} + \frac{1 - \alpha}{1 - \alpha(1 - \mu_1)} e_t$$
$$- c_1 \Delta \bar{y}_t - c_2 \Delta R_t^* - \Delta \varepsilon_t \tag{49}$$

where the terms $-\xi_t$ and Δu_t cancel out. Consequently we see that the purely random (unpredictable) component of Δp_t consists only of terms involving e_t and $\Delta \varepsilon_t$, plus the unpredictable component of $c_1 \Delta \bar{y}_t + c_2 \Delta R_t^*$. But any realistic specification of the exogenous processes for these variables will imply variances that are quite small in comparison with the variance of Δq_t.[19] What that means in terms of the model in Equations (1) is that the variability of the IS disturbance v_t (and perhaps the random parts of g_t and y_t^*) is large in relation to that of $\Delta \varepsilon_t$ (plus the random parts of $c_1 \Delta \bar{y}_t$ and $c_2 \Delta R_t^*$). The disturbance v_t affects Δq_t and as a consequence Δs_t, but has no effect (in the model at hand) on Δp_t. In sum, with the assumptions that v_t is important and that the shocks are close to random walks—assumptions suggested by Stockman (1987)—our model becomes one that is consistent with the empirical regularities 1 and 2 of the actual floating-rate data.

It is the case, however, that in the model p_t still responds to monetary shocks just as promptly as does s_t. This can be seen in Equation (49), which shows Δp_t to be dependent upon current values of e_t and $\Delta \varepsilon_t$. So, in order to match item 3 of our list of important regularities, it will be necessary to alter the model more radically. Indeed, it will be necessary to adopt some form of a "sticky-price" assumption. That task will require a separate section.

---

[19] For $\bar{y}_t$, we note that its variability will be less than that of y_t itself, and the standard deviation of the residuals from a second-order regression based on the log of actual real GNP for the United States is about 0.009. The comparable statistic for the U.S. Treasury bill rate is about 0.0025.

8.9 Model with Sticky Prices

To construct a version of our model that incorporates sticky prices, it will be necessary to revert to the complete specification given in Equations (1), rather than the streamlined version provided by Equations (7) and (6) with q_t exogenous. This reversion is necessary because when prices are not entirely flexible, the model does not dichotomize into real and monetary portions. Instead, real variables including y_t and q_t are determined jointly with monetary variables.

To specify a stricky price system, the first step is to eliminate equation (1f), replacing it with a model of noninstantaneous price-level adjustments plus an assumption that in each period output y_t is determined by the quantity demanded, that is, the quantity implied by Equations (1a)–(1e) and the prevailing price level.[20] Unfortunately, there is very little professional agreement as to the appropriate way in which to specify the price-level adjustments themselves.[21] We will be required, accordingly, to select one of the many existing theories of p_t adjustment for inclusion in our macroeconomic model of exchange rate determination.

For reasons outlined in McCallum (1989, ch. 10), our strategy will be to adopt a specification in which each period's price level is specified before the period begins at a value that is rationally *expected* to be the market clearing value. When shocks impinge on supply or demand conditions, making those conditions different than expected, the preset price will prevail despite its discrepancy from the value that would be needed to clear the market. The shocks occurring in period t will then be taken account of in the setting of p_{t+1}, which is based on expectations concerning period $t + 1$.

Symbolically, the assumption is that

$$p_t = E_{t-1}\bar{p}_t, \tag{50}$$

in other words, that p_t is set at the value that is expected in period $t - 1$ to equal $\bar{p}_t$, the value that would equate aggregate demand to $\bar{y}_t$, the "capacity" level of output, in the absence of price stickiness. The value of $\bar{p}_t$ is then the value of p_t that would make y_t in Equations (1a) and (1b) equal to $\bar{y}_t$ if it were to prevail, given the existing values of other variables. An advantage of this particular specification is that it incorporates temporary rigidity of the price level in a relatively simple way, yet permits full adjustment of prices in later periods so that long-run properties of the system are not distorted. It is, moreover, a special case of a gradual price adjustment specification that has many attractive theoretical properties.[22]

[20] Some analysts might not make this assumption, but most would.

[21] For a textbook survey of alternative theories, see McCallum (1989, ch. 9).

[22] See Mussa (1982) and McCallum (1983). The more general scheme is $p_t - p_{t-1} = \theta(\bar{p}_{t-1} - p_{t-1}) + E_{t-1}(\bar{p}_t - \bar{p}_{t-1})$, with θ $(0 < \theta \leq 1)$ reflecting the pace of gradual adjustments. The special case of Equation (50) has been used by Flood (1981) in an investigation that is fairly similar to the one being conducted in the present section and the one preceeding.

The other change that we shall make relative to the model of Section 8.8 is that μ_1 will be set equal to zero so that $\Delta m_t = \mu_0 + e_t$—that is, so that m_t is a random walk with drift. The IS and LM shocks v_t and ε_t will again be assumed to be random walks. The other simplifying step that we shall take is to assume that $\bar{y}_t$, R_t^*, p_t^*, y_t^*, and g_t are all constants. That eliminates the possibility of examining the response of s_t to changes in these variables, but our main interest at this point is in responses to the shocks e_t and v_t. And the expressions involved will still be rather complex, as will be seen. Finally, we shall assume that units of measurement are chosen so that the (constant) values of p_t^* and y_t^* are zero. And we shall also set R_t^* and g_t at zero.

With these simplifications, Equations $(1c)$–$(1e)$ can be substituted into Equations $(1a)$ and $(1b)$, with the following expressions resulting:

$$y_t = b_0 + b_1(E_t s_{t+1} - s_t - E_t p_{t+1} + p_t) + b_2(s_t - p_t) + v_t \tag{51}$$

$$m_t - p_t = c_0 + c_1 y_t + c_2(E_t s_{t+1} - s_t) + \varepsilon_t. \tag{52}$$

Also we have

$$\Delta m_t = \mu_0 + e_t \tag{53}$$

$$v_t = v_{t-1} + \xi_t \tag{54}$$

$$\varepsilon_t = \varepsilon_{t-1} + \zeta_t \tag{55}$$

where e_t, ξ_t, and ζ_t are white noises. With m_t determined by (53), Equations (50), (51), and (52) are designed to determine time paths for s_t, p_t, and y_t. But for that to be possible, we need one additional relation to determine $\bar{p}_t$.

As mentioned previously, $\bar{p}_t$ represents the value that p_t would assume in this model if prices were not sticky. To determine an expression for $\bar{p}_t$, then, we can replace Equations (50) with $y_t = \bar{y}$ and solve the model as in the previous section. The resulting solution for p_t will then be an expression that we can use for $\bar{p}_t$. Carrying out these steps,[23] we then find that

$$\bar{p}_t = \mu_0(1 - c_2) - c_0 - c_1\bar{y} + m_t - \varepsilon_t. \tag{56}$$

Then, since $E_{t-1}m_t = \mu_0 + m_{t-1}$ and $E_{t-1}\varepsilon_t = \varepsilon_{t-1}$, we have from Equations (56) and (50) that

$$p_t = -m_0 c_2 - c_0 - c_1\bar{y} + m_{t-1} - \varepsilon_{t-1}. \tag{57}$$

In this model, then, p_t does not respond to monetary shocks until one period after they occur, when the response is one for one. This statement is true for both money-supply and money-demand shocks e_t and ε_t, with the response

[23] See Problem 5.

being negative to demand shocks. There is no response of p_t to saving-investment shocks.

Armed with Equation (57) for p_t, we can now turn our attention to Equations (51) and (52), which jointly determine s_t and y_t. Because m_t and ε_t enter the model in an offsetting fashion, let us simplify the exposition by subsuming ε_t into m_t, so that m_t is interpreted as money supply net of the shock to money demand and ε_t, ε_{t-1}, and ζ_t do not explicitly appear. Then since our main interest is in exchange rate behavior, we substitute Equation (51) into Equation (52), eliminating y_t and obtaining

$$m_t - p_t = c_0 + c_1 b_0 + c_1 b_1 (E_t s_{t+1} - s_t - E_t p_{t+1} + p_t) + c_1 b_2 (s_t - p_t)$$
$$+ c_1 v_t + c_2 (E_t s_{t+1} - s_t) \tag{58}$$

From Equation (57) with ε_t subsumed we find that $E_t p_{t+1} - p_t = E_t(m_t - m_{t-1}) = \mu_0 + e_t$. Using that as well as Equations (53) and (57), we rewrite Equation (58) as follows:

$$\mu_0 + m_{t-1} + e_t + c_2 + c_0 + c_1 \bar{y} - m_{t-1}$$
$$= c_0 + c_1 b_0 + c_1 b_1 (E_t s_{t+1} - s_t - \mu_0 - e_t)$$
$$+ c_1 b_2 (s_t + c_2 + c_0 + c_1 \bar{y} - m_{t-1}) + c_1 v_t + c_2 (E_t s_{t+1} - s_t). \tag{59}$$

Inspection indicates that the relevant state variables are m_{t-1}, e_t, and v_t, so we conjecture that the solution for s_t is of the form

$$s_t = \phi_0 + \phi_1 m_{t-1} + \phi_2 e_t + \phi_3 v_t. \tag{60}$$

Then

$$E_t s_{t+1} = \phi_0 + \phi_1 (\mu_0 + m_{t-1} + e_t) + \phi_3 v_t \tag{61}$$

since v_t is a random walk.

Putting Equations (60) and (61) into (59) yields

$$\mu_0 + e_t + c_2 + c_1 \bar{y} = c_1 b_0 + c_1 b_1 [\phi_1 \mu_0 + (\phi_1 - \phi_2)e_t - \mu_0 - e_t]$$
$$+ c_1 b_2 (\phi_0 + \phi_1 m_{t-1} + \phi_2 e_t + \phi_3 v_t + c_2 + c_0$$
$$+ c_1 \bar{y} - m_{t-1}) + c_1 v_t + c_2 [\phi_1 \mu_0 + (\phi_1 - \phi_2)e_t]. \tag{62}$$

Equating coefficients, we find the implied identities to be

$$0 = c_1 b_2 \phi_1 - c_1 b_2 \tag{63a}$$

$$1 = c_1 b_1 (\phi_1 - \phi_2) - c_1 b_1 + c_1 b_2 \phi_2 + c_2 (\phi_1 - \phi_2) \tag{63b}$$

$$0 = c_1 b_2 \phi_3 + c_1 \tag{63c}$$

$$\mu_0 + c_2 + c_1 \bar{y} = c_1 b_0 - c_1 b_1 \mu_0 + c_1 b_1 \phi_1 \mu_0 + c_1 b_2 (\phi_0 + c_2 + c_0) + c_2 \phi_1 \mu_0. \tag{63d}$$

From the first of these we see that $\phi_1 = 1$. Then the second implies $\phi_2 = (1 - c_2)/[c_1(b_2 - b_1) - c_2]$, and the third gives $\phi_3 = -1/b_2$. (We will not write out the expression for the constant term, ϕ_0.) Our solution for the exchange rate is then

$$s_t = \phi_0 + m_{t-1} + \frac{1 - c_2}{c_1(b_2 - b_1) - c_2} e_t - \frac{1}{b_2} v_t. \tag{64}$$

Now consider the dynamic properties of the response of s_t to the shocks e_t and v_t. In doing this it will be useful to have in mind the approximate quantitative magnitude of the term $c_1(b_2 - b_1)$ that appears in the denominator of the composite coefficient on e_t in Equation (64). The signs of the individual coefficients are $c_1 > 0$, $b_1 < 0$, and $b_2 > 0$, so that $c_1(b_2 - b_1)$ is definitely a positive term. But it will be important to determine whether its magnitude is larger or smaller than 1.0. Estimates provided by various researchers indicate that c_1 is somewhat smaller than 1.0—say, about 0.7—whereas the sum $b_2 - b_1$ is about 0.5 or perhaps smaller.[24] The product, then, is clearly much smaller than 1.0.

That conclusion is of importance because with $c_2 < 0$ it implies that the composite parameter on the money-supply shock e_t in Equation (63) is larger than 1.0. Since the s_t and m_t variables are logarithms, this means that the contemporaneous response of the exchange rate to a money-supply shock is more than proportionate—a one percent positive shock to M_t increases S_t by more than one percent. But the steady-state effect is proportionate—the money-supply terms in Equation (64) can be written as

$$m_{t-1} + \frac{1 - c_2}{c_1(b_2 - b_1) - c_2} (m_t - m_{t-1} - \mu_0)$$

where the sum of the coefficients is 1.0. So the model at hand is one that features exchange rate "overshooting"—the impact effect of a money-supply shock on s_t is greater than the long-term effect, the former being partly reversed as time passes. Since we have subsumed money-demand shocks, initially denoted by ε_t, into m_t, the same pattern applies, but with movements in the opposite direction. In addition, we see that, with $b_2 > 0$, v_t has a negative effect on s_t. A positive spending shock, that is, tends to appreciate the exchange value of the nation's currency.

We have shown, then, that the present model with sticky prices matches all three of the important regularities listed at the start of Section 8.8. It is also of interest to see how y_t responds to monetary shocks in the model. To do so, we can use Equation (64) to find that

$$E_t s_{t+1} - s_t = (m_t - m_{t-1}) - \phi_2 e_t$$

$$= \mu_0 + e_t - \frac{1 - c_2}{c_1(b_2 - b_1) - c_2} e_t. \tag{65}$$

---

[24] Ghosh and Masson (1991) estimate the values to be about $0.11 + 0.15 = 0.26$ for the United States and $0.17 + 0.38 = 0.55$ for the world's other industrial nations combined.

Then from Equation (52), with $m_t = \mu_0 + m_{t-1} + e_t$, we see that the per-unit response of y_t to e_t is

$$\frac{1}{c_1}\left[1 - c_2\left(1 - \frac{1 - c_2}{c_1(b_2 - b_1) - c_2}\right)\right]. \qquad (66)$$

The term inside square brackets can be written as

$$1 - \frac{c_2[c_1(b_2 - b_1) - 1]}{c_1(b_2 - b_1) - c_2} = \frac{c_1(b_2 - b_1) - c_2 c_1(b_2 - b_1)}{c_1(b_2 - b_1) - c_2}. \qquad (67)$$

But the numerator of the latter equals $(1 - c_2)c_1(b_2 - b_1)$, which is un-ambiguously positive. Thus since the denominator is positive and so is c_1, the same is true for expression (66). Thus output responds positively to money supply shocks in our model, just as most economists believe that it does in reality. The response to ε_t would be of the same magnitude but in the opposite direction.

8.10 Conclusion

The last two sections of this chapter have been rather technical, with a large amount of algebraic manipulation tending to obscure the point of the discussion in terms of exchange rate behavior. But although the derivations are admittedly tedious, they involve no difficult mathematics and they have yielded some major results. In particular, they demonstrate that our modified model with sticky prices features exchange rate behavior that conforms rather well to patterns observed in the actual data. That is one major accomplishment of the chapter. The other is that we have developed a method for dynamic analysis of models with rational expectations that can be used in a wide variety of contexts—in macroeconomics and microeconomics more generally, not just in the modeling of exchange rate behavior.

Appendix: Two Properties of Mathematical Expectations

The purpose of this appendix is to demonstrate two facts regarding mathematical expectations that are used in Chapter 8. The presentation presumes that the reader is familiar with some notions of probability theory, including the concepts of discrete and continuous random variables, density functions, and means and variances of univariate and bivariate distributions. A brief review is provided by McCallum (1989, pp. 160–171).

We begin by defining the concept of the *mathematical expectation* of a random variable. From one perspective the mathematical expectation is simply the mean of the distribution of a random variable; if X is a continuous random variable with mean μ_x and variance σ_x^2, then its mathematical expectation $E(X)$ equals $\int xf(x)\,dx = \mu_x$. But there is a reason for introducing the additional term, for it permits a generalization that is extremely useful. Suppose X is a discrete *or* continuous random variable with density $f(x)$. Then let $\phi(X)$ be a function that pertains to the various possible outcomes x. This function defines a new (related) random variable $\phi(X)$. It would be possible to determine its density function and from it the mean of $\phi(X)$. But we can short-cut that process by utilizing the following definition: the mathematical expectation of $\phi(X)$ is denoted by $E[\phi(X)]$ and is given by[25]

$$E[\phi(X)] = \int \phi(x)f(x)\,dx \qquad (A1)$$

in the continuous case and by

$$E[\phi(X)] = \sum \phi(x)f(x) \qquad (A2)$$

in the discrete case.[26] Thus the mathematical expectation of $\phi(X)$ is simply the probabilistic average of $\phi(X)$ computed relative to the density function for X. It is identical to the mean of the distribution of the implied random variable $\phi(X)$, but can be determined without ever explicitly deriving the density function for that random variable itself.

The usefulness of the concept of mathematical expectation as defined in Equations (A1) and (A2) stems from the flexibility and generality provided by the function $\phi(X)$, and also from a fact of considerable notational convenience: many formulas expressed in terms of the expectation operator $E(\cdot)$ are precisely the same for discrete *and* continuous random variables. Whenever using such formulas, consequently, there is no need to specify which type is involved. For example, consider two special cases in which $\phi(X) = X$ and $\phi(X) = (X - \mu_x)^2$, respectively. Then it is almost immediately apparent from Equations (A1) and (A2) that we have $E(X) = \mu_x$ and $E[(X - \mu_x)^2] = \sigma_x^2$, whether X is discrete or continuous. The first of these special cases shows clearly that the mathematical expectation or *expected value* of X is the same entity as the mean of the distribution of X.

There are a few relationships involving expected values that are so useful and simple that commitment to memory is recommended. Three of these are as follows. Let X be any random variable with mean $E(X)$, let c_0 and c_1 be arbitrary constants, and let $\phi_1(X)$ and $\phi_2(X)$ be functions with means $E[\phi_1(X)]$ and $E[\phi_2(X)]$. Then

$$E(c_0) = c_0, \qquad (A3)$$

$$E(c_0 + c_1 X) = c_0 + c_1 E(X), \qquad (A4)$$

$$E[c_1\phi_1(X) + c_2\phi_2(X)] = c_1 E[\phi_1(X)] + c_2 E[\phi_2(X)]. \qquad (A5)$$

[25] It is assumed throughout this appendix that all integrals and summations are absolutely convergent.

[26] Here integration and summation is over all values of x.

These relationships are straightforward implications of the linearity properties of summation and integration operations. Thus a proof of (A5) for the continuous case is as follows:

$$E[c_1\phi_1(X) + c_2\phi_2(X)] = \int [c_1\phi_1(x) + c_2\phi_2(x)]f(x)\,dx$$

$$= c_1 \int \phi_1(x)f(x)\,dx + c_2 \int \phi_2(x)f(x)\,dx$$

$$= c_1 E[\phi_1(X)] + c_2 E[\phi_2(X)].$$

For the discrete case, the steps would be similar but with summations used instead of integrals. Note that Equations (A3) and (A4) are simply special cases of (A5) and so do not require separate proofs.

Equation (A5) is the first of the two "facts" to be explained here. The second is the *law of literated expectations*, which is used in Section 8.4. In expositing it, we shall for simplicity assume that only two random variables are involved, but in fact the basic logic is applicable in more general cases.

Let the two variables at hand be denoted by X and Y and suppose that they are continuous random variables with a bivariate probability density function $f(x, y)$. Suppose also that the conditional density of Y given X is denoted by $f(y|x)$ and that the marginal (univariate) densities for Y and X are $f(y)$ and $f(x)$. Relationships between bivariate and univariate distributions imply that $f(y|x) = f(x, y)/f(x)$, that $f(y) = \int f(x, y)\,dx$, and that $f(x) = \int f(x, y)\,dy$.

In this context the law of iterated expectations asserts that the (unconditional) mean of the conditional mean of Y given X, which is random in any context in which X is random, equals the (unconditional) mean of Y itself. In symbols, the mean of $E(Y|X)$, which is $E[E(Y|X)]$, is equal to $E(Y)$. To prove this, we first note that $E(Y|X) = \int yf(y|x)\,dy$.

Then the mean of *that* is

$$E\left[\int yf(y|x)\,dy \right] = \iint \left[\int yf(y|x)\,dy \right] f(x, y)\,dy\,dx.$$

But $\int yf(y|x)\,dy$ is not a function of y, so the preceding expression can be written as

$$\int \left\{ \left[\int yf(y|x)\,dy \right] \int f(x, y)\,dy \right\} dx.$$

Then, since $\int f(x, y)\,dy = f(x)$, we have

$$\int \left[\int yf(y|x)\,dy \right] f(x)\,dx = \iint y \frac{f(x, y)}{f(x)}\,dy f(x)\,dx = \iint yf(x, y)\,dy\,dx$$

$$= \int y \left[\int f(x, y)\,dx \right] dy = \int yf(y)\,dy.$$

But the final expression *is* the mean of the unconditional distribution of Y. Thus we have shown that

$$E[E(Y|X)] = E(Y).$$

If X and Y had a discrete, rather than continuous, bivariate distribution, all of the foregoing could be redone by interpreting the density functions as discrete probability (mass) functions and using summations rather than integrals.

References

Barro, R. J., "Unanticipated Money Growth and Unemplyment in the United States," *American Economic Review* **67** (Mar. 1977), 101–115.

Dornbusch, R., "Expectations and Exchange Rate Dynamics," *Journal of Political Economy* **84** (Dec. 1976), 1161–1176.

Flood, R. P., "Explanations of Exchange Rate Volatility and Other Empirical Regularities in Some Popular Models of the Foreign Exchange Market," *Carnegie–Rochester Conference Series on Public Policy* **15** (Autumn 1981), 219–249.

Ghosh, A. R., and P. R. Masson, "Model Uncertainty, Learning, and the Gains from Coordination," *American Economic Review* **81** (June 1991), 465–479.

Lucas, R. E., Jr., *Studies in Business-Cycle Theory*. Cambridge, MA: MIT Press, 1981.

McCallum, B. T., "The Liquidity Trap and the Pigou Effect: A Dynamic Analysis with Rational Expectations," *Economica* **50** (Nov. 1983), 395–405.

————, *Monetary Economics: Theory and Policy*. New York: Macmillan, 1989.

Meese, R. A., "Is the Sticky Price Assumption Reasonable for Exchange Rate Models?" *Journal of International Money and Finance* **3** (Aug. 1984), 131–139.

Mussa, M., "A Model of Exchange Rate Dynamics," *Journal of Political Economy* **90** (Feb. 1982), 74–104.

————, "Nominal Exchange Rate Regimes and the Behavior of Real Exchange Rates," *Carnegie–Rochester Conference Series on Public Policy* **25** (Autumn 1986), 117–214.

Muth, J. F., "Rational Expectations and the Theory of Price Movements," *Econometrica* **29** (June 1961), 315–335.

Sargent, T. J., "Rational Expectations, the Real Rate of Interest, and the Natural Rate of Unemployment," *Brookings Papers on Economic Activity* (no. 2, 1973), 429–471.

Stockman, A. C., "The Equilibrium Approach to Exchange Rates," *Federal Reserve Bank of Richmond Economic Review* **73** (Mar.–Apr. 1987), 12–30.

Problems

1. Consider a market for some unspecified commodity in which supply depends on the current price,

$$q_t = b_0 + b_1 p_t + u_t, \qquad b_1 > 0$$

whereas demand depends on the current price and also the value rationally expected to prevail in the near future,

$$q_t = a_0 + a_1 p_t + a_2 E_t p_{t+1} + v_t.$$

Here $a_1 < 0$ and $a_2 > 0$, whereas v_t and u_t are white-noise disturbances. Assuming that Ω_t includes $q_t, q_{t-1}, \ldots, p_t, p_{t-1}, \ldots$ and that $E_t p_{t+1} = E(p_{t+1} | \Omega_t)$, find the rational expectations solution for p_t.

2. In many cases disturbances will be neither white noise nor random walks. Repeat Problem 1 under the assumption that $u_t = \rho u_{t-1} + \varepsilon_t$, where ε_t is white noise and $|\rho| < 1.0$. Then repeat again, assuming $u_t = \varepsilon_t + \theta \varepsilon_{t-1}$.

3. Show that if $\bar{y}_t, g_t, r_t^*, y_t^*,$ and v_t are all generated by white-noise processes, then the solution for q_t in the model of Equation (34) is also white noise.

4. Show that if the processes of the previous problem are random walks, rather than white noises, then the same will be true for q_t.

5. Consider the model of Equations (51) and (52), with exogenous processes as in Equations (53)–(55). Find the solution for p_t that would prevail if price flexibility led to $y_t = \bar{y}$ in each period.

9

Empirical Evidence

9.1 Introduction

In this chapter the objective is to present empirical evidence concerning the validity of the various components of the model of exchange rate behavior that has been developed and utilized in the preceding four chapters. Much of our space will be devoted to the uncovered interest parity (UIP) relation because a number of researchers have suggested that existing evidence shows it to be empirically invalid. But we shall begin in Section 9.2 with the two relationships that pertain to money demand and saving-investment behavior. Then, after an extensive discussion of UIP in Sections 9.3 and 9.4 and a bit of evidence on price-level stickiness in Section 9.5, we shall conclude (in Section 9.6) with evidence concerning the long-run validity of the purchasing power parity (PPP) relationship between exchange rates and relative inflation levels. Throughout, the evidence presented will be a mixture of results developed by various researchers and tables or graphs assembled by the author especially for this chapter.

9.2 Money Demand and Saving-Investment Relations

It will be recalled from the previous chapters that our basic model consists of five equations, of which two are identities and therefore not appropriate for empirical study. Equations (1a), (1b), and (1e) of Chapters 6 and 8 are, however, postulated behavioral relationships that may or may not be consistent with empirical evidence taken from actual economies. The first two of these pertain to open-economy versions of aggregative relationships that appear in standard macroeconomic models, so readers may be familiar with other discussions of their empirical validity. Our treatment will therefore be brief.

Equation (1a) of Chapter 6 is the so-called IS function, which summarizes the behavior of households and firms with respect to saving and investment decisions. In an open-economy context, we have seen (in Section 5.2) that the magnitude of the real exchange rate and the level of real income in other nations are relevant explanatory variables, in addition to the real interest rate and government spending variables that appear in closed-economy versions. This is because behavior regarding imports and exports is also incorporated. The left-hand side variable in the equation as usually presented is the level of real output in the economy under study—the "home" economy in our context. In the log-linear representation that we have been using, this relationship is written as

$$y_t = b_0 + b_1 r_t + b_2 q_t + b_3 g_t + b_4 y_t^* + u_t, \tag{1}$$

where $b_1 < 0$, $b_2 > 0$, $b_3 > 0$, $b_4 > 0$, and u_t is a stochastic disturbance term. The variables are denoted, as in previous chapters, as follows: $y_t = $ log of real output, $r_t = $ real rate of interest, $q_t = $ log of real exchange rate, $g_t = $ log of real government spending, and $y^* = $ log of output (income) abroad.

As it happens, a relationship of almost exactly this form[1] has been estimated for the United States, using annual data for 1966 through 1986, by Ghosh and Masson (1991). For the foreign or "rest of the world" variables, these analysts used an aggregate of the other Western industrial nations as included in MULTIMOD, the IMF's econometric model of the world economy. The results obtained by Ghosh and Masson are as follows, where the values in parentheses are estimated standard errors[2]:

$$y_t = \;\; 5.196 \; - \; 0.152 r_t \; + \; 0.114 q_t \; + \; 0.300 g_t \; + \; 0.054 y_t^* \; + \; 0.020 t \tag{2}$$
$$\quad\;\; (2.30) \quad\;\; (0.34) \quad\;\; (0.05) \quad\;\; (0.166) \quad\;\; (0.209) \quad\;\; (0.009)$$

$$\bar{R}^2 = 0.988 \qquad SE = 0.021 \qquad DW = 1.78.$$

The last term in Equation (2) is a time trend, which it is reasonable to include although our theoretical discussion did not mention one. The point estimates in Equation (2) are in other respects quite consistent with our theoretical specification, but the precision with which the values are estimated is rather low and, as a consequence, the coefficients attached to r_t and y_t^* are not significantly different from zero, in a formal statistical sense. The equation's degree of explanatory power is reasonably high—this is better judged by the SE statistic than by $\bar{R}^2$—and the DW statistic indicates that residual auto-correlation is not severe.

Also reported in Ghosh and Masson's paper is an analogous equation pertaining to an aggregate of "other industrial" countries, with the United States treated as the foreign economy. In this case the results are fairly similar, except that the responsiveness of y_t to r_t, g_t, and y_t^* is noticeably greater and there is more of a problem of residual autocorrelation.

[1] Exactly the same except that, as mentioned below, the Ghosh and Masson (1991) version includes a linear trend variable.

[2] In Equation (2), and in others to follow, the parenthesized figures below coefficient estimates are associated standard errors, whereas SE denotes the estimated standard deviation of the disturbance term and DW is the Durbin–Watson statistic. The R^2 statistic is adjusted for degrees of freedom if an overbar appears above the R. In Equation (2) the estimation procedure was instrumental variables, rather than ordinary least squares (OLS), with the instruments including "money stocks, government spending, time, and lagged prices and output" (Ghosh and Masson, 1991, p. 468).

Ghosh and Masson (1991) also present estimates of money-demand functions fairly similar in form to Equation (1*b*) in Chapter 6, namely,

$$m_t - p_t = c_0 + c_1 y_t + c_2 R_t + \varepsilon_t, \tag{3}$$

where m_t and p_t are logs of the money supply and price level, respectively, R_t is the nominal interest rate, and ε_t is a disturbance. There are two major specificational differences, however, one of which is that they include another term in the equation, namely, the lagged value of the dependent variable. The usual rationale for this common practice is that portfolio adjustments occur slowly; for a textbook discussion see McCallum (1989, ch. 3). The second specificational change is that the price level used in Equation (3) is the (log) deflator for domestic absorption rather than for domestic output, a conceptional improvement on our formulation that was mentioned but not adopted in Chapter 5. With those two changes incorporated, the estimates for the United States are as follows:

$$m_t - p_t = \underset{(0.86)}{0.302} + \underset{(0.051)}{0.184 y_t} - \underset{(0.32)}{1.387 R_t} + \underset{(0.160)}{0.680(m_{t-1} - p_{t-1})} \tag{4}$$

$$\bar{R}^2 = 0.691 \qquad \text{SE} = 0.029 \qquad \text{DW} = 1.63.$$

Very similar estimates are obtained for the "rest of the world." Here the "long-run" slope coefficients comparable to c_1 and c_2 in Equation (3) are $0.184/(1 - 0.68) = 0.575$ and $-1.387/(1 - 0.68) = -4.33$; these are entirely consistent with theoretical preconceptions. One questionable aspect of the results is that no trend term is included in Equation (4); many analysts would expect to find a trend to represent the effects of ongoing improvements in payments technology in the industrialized world.[3]

All in all, the results of Ghosh and Masson (1991) are highly supportive of the specification of these two relations in our basic model. There are many more relevant studies that could be described but, for the reasons mentioned, it seems best to turn at this point to interest parity relationships, which will require a lengthy consideration.

9.3 Interest Parity

In this section we shall review the evidence pertaining to the covered (CIP) and uncovered (UIP) interest parity relationships, the latter being a behavioral component of our basic model. It will be recalled from the discussion in Chapter 2 that significant deviations from CIP would seem to be especially unlikely to occur, since they would imply the existence of riskless arbitrage possibilities. Quite a few empirical studies have been conducted nevertheless by a number of scholars using various techniques. One approach begins with the collection

[3] See McCallum (1989, p. 46).

of published market data on the variables s_t = log of spot exchange rate, f_t = log of forward exchange rate, R_t = domestic interest rate, and R_t^* = foreign interest rate. It proceeds via determination of whether $f_t - s_t = R_t - R_t^*$ holds in this data set by estimating the regression equation

$$f_t - s_t = \alpha + \beta(R_t - R_t^*) + \varepsilon_t \tag{5}$$

and observing whether the estimated parameter values are approximately equal to $\alpha = 0.0$ and $\beta = 1.0$. One such study has been conducted by Fratianni and Wakeman (1982). Results based on monthly observations for the floating-rate period of 1975.01–1980.09 are shown in Table 9–1 for one-month forward rates and one-month eurocurrency interest rates.

The standard errors associated with the estimators of α and β are roughly 0.0001 and 0.03, except in the case of Belgium, so most of the point estimates differ from the hypothesized values (of $\alpha = 0$ and $\beta = 1$) by enough to be statistically significant at the 0.05 level. But in terms of economic significance the estimates are quite close to the CIP values. A macroeconomic model in which $\alpha = -0.0003$ and $\beta = 1.05$ would function very much like one with $\alpha = 0.0$ and $\beta = 1.0$. Qualitatively similar findings were reported by Fratianni and Wakeman (1982) for 3-month and 6-month forward rates as well, and also by Cosiander and Lang (1981), who used 3-month rates over 1962–1978 together with on-shore money-market (as well as eurocurrency) interest rates.

A different approach has been taken by investigators whose main concern is the possibility of profitable arbitrage operations. From that perspective it is crucial that the various interest and exchange rates appearing in the CIP formula refer to market rates that pertain at a single point in time and are available to a single market participant. In particular, the observations need to be synchronized quite exactly—to within a very few minutes. Consequently, published market data are not satisfactory for a study of this type. Satisfactory data based on rates quoted by foreign exchange and money-market brokers in London have been collected and utilized, however, by Taylor (1987, 1989), who examined several thousand potential arbitrage possibilities to see whether opportunities for profit existed, with account being taken of bid–ask spreads and transaction costs. While a few profit opportunities were found around dates

Table 9–1 CIP Estimates

U.S. relative to	Est. of α	Est. of β	R^2	DW
Germany	−0.00035	1.078	0.98	2.07
France	−0.00031	1.097	0.97	1.70
Italy	−0.00073	1.111	0.95	1.99
Netherlands	−0.00033	1.053	0.93	2.71
Belgium	−0.00080	1.194	0.76	1.56
United Kingdom	−0.00029	1.036	0.97	1.88

Source: Fratianni and Wakeman (1982).

of events that generated market turbulence, Taylor's evidence is predominantly supportive of the hypothesis that the CIP condition is not violated.[4] Since our main concern involves a macroeconomic perspective, which is less demanding, it then seems clear that we can proceed under the presumption that CIP is empirically valid.

This last conclusion is useful in the context of studying the UIP relationship,

$$s_{t+1}^e - s_t = R_t - R_t^*, \tag{6}$$

since it implies that we can replace $R_t - R_t^*$ in the latter with $f_t - s_t$. Thus we can express the UIP condition as the hypothesis that $\alpha = 0.0$ and $\beta = 1.0$ in the following equation:

$$s_{t+1}^e - s_t = \alpha + \beta(f_t - s_t). \tag{7}$$

We do not have observations on s_{t+1}^e, of course, but under the assumption of rational expectations ($s_{t+1}^e = E_t s_{t+1}$) we know that the expectational error $\varepsilon_{t+1} \equiv s_{t+1} - E_t s_{t+1}$ will be uncorrelated with all information known in period t at the time of expectation formation.[5] Consequently, we can replace s_{t+1}^e in Equation (7) with $s_{t+1} - \varepsilon_{t+1}$ and shift ε_{t+1} to the right-hand side. That leaves us with the relation

$$s_{t+1} - s_t = \alpha + \beta(f_t - s_t) + \varepsilon_{t+1}, \tag{8}$$

in which the disturbance ε_{t+1} is uncorrelated with the right-hand variable $f_t - s_t$. So the parameters of Equation (8) can be consistently estimated by means of ordinary least-squares regression.[6]

The results of estimating Equation (8) using monthly data, 1978.01–1990.07, for the \$/DM, \$/£, and \$/yen exchange rates are given in Table 9–2.[7] There the results are spectacularly negative—that is, apparently inconsistent with the UIP hypothesis. For the slope estimates not only fail to be close to the hypothesized value of 1.0, but in fact are negative—and significantly so. Thus it seems to be suggested by the data that the UIP condition fails drastically. Since UIP is one of the principal constituents of our basic model of exchange rate behavior, that suggestion is rather alarming. But UIP is also a constituent of virtually all contemporary exchange rate models, from small-scale theoretical systems (such as ours) to large-scale econometric systems constructed and tended by teams of researchers employed by organizations such as the IMF. Indeed, the apparent failure of UIP to hold even approximately

---

[4] The recent reporting change by the *Financial Times*, which *presumes* that CIP holds from the perspective of actual market participants, also provides strong supportive evidence.

[5] Recall the discussion of Section 8.6.

[6] This statement is correct, but ignores the fact that the OLS standard errors may be inconsistent estimators of parameter–estimator standard deviations if the disturbance term features heteroschedasticity.

[7] These values are taken from McCallum (1994). Similar results have been reported in dozens of other studies.

Table 9–2 UIP Estimates

United States relative to	Estimates (std. errors)		Statistics		
	Constant	Slope	R^2	SE	DW
Germany	−0.0156 (0.006)	−4.201 (1.70)	0.040	0.0351	2.20
Japan	0.0153 (0.0052)	−3.326 (1.17)	0.051	0.0364	2.02
United Kingdom	−0.0078 (0.0032)	−4.740 (1.09)	0.111	0.0332	2.21

Source: McCallum (1994).

as an empirical matter is such a serious problem, from the perspective of exchange rate analysis, that it will be appropriate to devote an entire section to its discussion and resolution.[8]

Before turning to that task, it will be useful to document the failure of β to equal 1.0 in Equation (8) in another fashion. If in fact β equaled 1.0 and α equaled 0.0, then Equations (7) and (8) would collapse to $s_{t+1}^e = f_t$ and $s_{t+1} = f_t + \varepsilon_t$, respectively. Thus the forward rate would equal the value expected for s_{t+1}, and s_{t+1} would differ from f_t only randomly (assuming that expectations are rational). Now in fact, values of f_t and s_{t+1} move together quite closely over the cycle, as Figure 9–1 demonstrates for the \$/yen rate over 1978.01–1990.06. But the association depicted in this figure is misleading in an important sense. First, the plot of f_t and s_t coincides even more closely—it is not shown because the two series are virtually indistinguishable. Second, it can be seen in Figure 9–1 that movements of f_t typically *follow* movements of s_{t+1}, which is the opposite of the pattern that would prevail if f_t were a good predictor of s_{t+1}. Finally, if the time series for $s_{t+1} - s_t$ and $f_t - s_t$ are plotted, the result is as shown in Figure 9–2. Thus practically none of the movement from month to month in $s_{t+1} - s_t$ is explained by $f_t - s_t$. That finding is the graphical representation of the numerical results for regression estimates of Equation (8) listed in Table 9–2.

9.4 Apparent Failure of UIP

We now turn to the task of making sense of the foregoing results. Let us begin by noting that Equation (6), the condition representing UIP, was written as an

---

[8] It should be recognized that estimates quite close to $\alpha = 0$, $\beta = 1$ are obtained when the equation estimated is not Equation (8) but instead $s_{t+1} = \alpha + \beta f_t + \varepsilon_{t+1}$, which is equivalent under the null hypothesis that $\beta = 1$. It is widely agreed by researchers, however, that Equation (8) is preferable to this other formulation. The reason is that with f_t and s_t both close to random-walk variables, the estimated slope coefficient in $s_t = \alpha + \beta f_{t-1} + \varepsilon_t$ will be spuriously close to 1.0 if the long-run relationship is one to one, even if the within-period response is entirely different. For more discussion, see McCallum (1994) and Meese (1989).

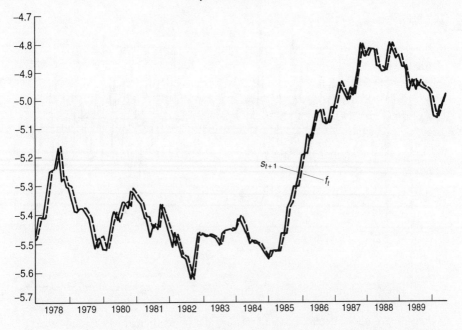

Figure 9–1 \$/¥ exchange rates, January 1978.01–June 1990. s_t—log of spot rate, last day of month t; f_t—log of 30-day forward rate, last day of month t. *Source*: BIS.

exact relationship, that is, without any random disturbance term. As a direct consequence, the disturbance term in Equation (8), the empirically implemented relationship, consists entirely of expectational error. Therefore, if expectations are rational, then the disturbance term ε_{t+1} will be uncorrelated with the regressor $f_t - s_t$, and OLS estimates of α and β will be consistent. But if Equation (6) had itself included an error term, then this error would be part of the disturbance in Equation (8) and the latter would not necessarily be uncorrelated with $f_t - s_t$. In that case, OLS estimates could be systematically biased.

In fact, it seems extremely likely that a nontrivial error term should be included in Equation (6). In justification of that assertion, notice first that (6) is of interest and macroeconomic relevance at the level of market aggregates, not individual traders. And published market data have been used to obtain the estimates reported here (and in many other studies yielding similar results). But we have seen that nontrivial error terms are found empirically even in studies of *covered* interest parity when market data are utilized. Furthermore, since the absence of UIP does not imply riskless arbitrage possibilities, it is reasonable to believe that deviations would exist and fluctuate from week to week even at the level of individual traders, just as they do in most behavioral relationships. Accordingly, let us modify Equation (6) to become

$$s_{t+1}^e - s_t = R_t - R_t^* + \xi_t, \qquad (6')$$

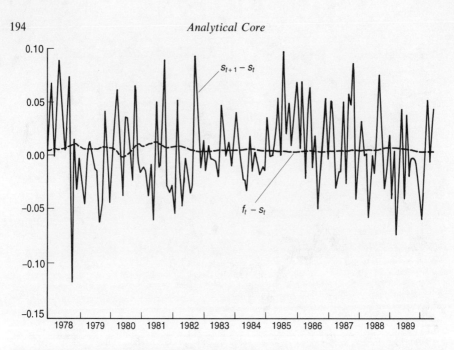

Figure 9–2 $/¥ spot rate changes and forward discounts, January 1978–June 1990.
Source: Bank for International Settlements.

where ξ_t is a random disturbance. Then, with $\varepsilon_{t+1} = s_{t+1} - s_{t+1}^e$, the counterpart of Equation (8) would become

$$s_{t+1} - s_t = \alpha + \beta(f_t - s_t) + \varepsilon_{t+1} + \xi_t. \tag{8'}$$

As before, the UIP hypothesis would be represented by $\beta = 1.0$,[9] but now the composite disturbance term includes ξ_t as well as ε_{t+1}, and the reasoning no longer applies that led to our previous conclusion that the disturbance and regressor would be uncorrelated.

In fact, there is a rather strong reason for believing that the regressor $f_t - s_t$ *will* be systematically correlated with the ξ_t component of the disturbance. To understand the reason, recall that $f_t - s_t$ is being used as an empirical stand-in or proxy for $R_t - R_t^*$, the home–foreign interest rate differential. Now, in practically oriented analysis, this interest differential is viewed as reflecting monetary policy choices by the home country's and foreign countries' central banks.[10] But the fact that variables are policy controlled does not make

---

[9] We have expressed it previously as $\beta = 1.0$ and $\alpha = 0.0$, but there are good reasons for not including the latter condition. For an explanation, see Meese (1989).

[10] In our theoretically oriented discussions in Chapters 5–8 we have usually viewed the central bank as choosing money stock magnitudes rather than interest rates, because that is an analytically clearer way of conceiving monetary policy. In Section 6.5, however, it was explained that most actual central banks, even those that use money stock targets as a guide to policy, put their policy choices into effect by means of operating procedures that are designed around manipulation of short-term interest rates (e.g., the Federal Funds rate in the United States). For the purposes of the present argument, it will simplify matters considerably to conceive of policy merely in terms of interest rate settings, and this will not involve any analytical error.

them empirically unresponsive to the system's endogenous variables. It is often analytically convenient to conduct thought experiments that involve "exogenous" changes in policy variables, but in actual practice most central bankers set their interest rate variables partially in response to current conditions in the economy. In particular, central bankers often choose interest rate settings partially in response to recent or ongoing movements in exchange rates.

The particular hypothesis that our argument will rely upon is that interest rates are often set so as to moderate (or slow down) exchange rate fluctuations that are currently under way, while at the same time acting so as to "smooth" interest rates (i.e., keep them from changing too rapidly). Behavior reflecting these two objectives can be expressed analytically as follows:

$$R_t - R_t^* = \lambda \Delta s_t + \gamma(R_{t-1} - R_{t-1}^*) + e_t. \tag{9}$$

Here the parameters λ and γ are intended to represent the type of policy behavior just described. The first, λ, will be positive to reflect the notion that when the exchange rate s_t is increasing (i.e., $\Delta s_t > 0$) then R_t will be raised relative to R_t^* to partially offset that tendency. But for economies that are not on fixed exchange rates, the magnitude of λ will not be large when R_t, R_t^*, and Δs_t are expressed in comparable units (e.g., percentage points or fractions on an annual or monthly basis). By contrast, the policy parameter γ will be positive, but close to 1.0 in value, to reflect the notion that central banks wish for interest rates to move slowly, that is, usually to remain close to their level of the previous period.[11] The stochastic disturbance e_t, finally, reflects other influences on policy choices.

Now consider a system in which Equations (6') and (9) describe market and policy behavior, respectively, with s_t and R_t the endogenous variables, R_t^* being treated as exogenous. And suppose that a positive ξ_t disturbance occurs. Then for given values of s_{t+1}^e and $R_t - R_t^*$, the positive ξ_t tends to push s_t downward according to (6'). But the value of $\tilde{R}_t \equiv R_t - R_t^*$ is not "given," according to (9).[12] Indeed, the latter implies that $\tilde{R}_t$ will also respond in a downward direction since $\lambda > 0$. Thus since $\tilde{R}_t$ is represented empirically by $f_t - s_t$, it will not be true that $f_t - s_t$ is uncorrelated with ξ_t in (8'). Instead, there will be a systematic negative correlation. So statistical estimation procedures predicted on the assumption that $f_t - s_t$ is independent of the equation's disturbance term will yield systematically biased estimates of β.

The exact way in which this bias will work out depends on the way in which expectations are formed and the time series properties of the processes that

[11] Actually, central bankers are presumably concerned with smoothing their own domestic interest rates—R_t for the home country—rather than the differential $R_t - R_t^*$. But by assuming that $R_t - R_t^*$ is the interest variable that appears on both sides of Equation (9), as well as in Equation (6), our system is simplified considerably without much effect on the results. These would be much the same if we instead assumed that the foreign rate R_t^* is constant—a familiar device in international analysis—or even merely that it is exogenous.

[12] Here we define $\tilde{R}_t$ as the interest differential $R_t - R_t^*$ in order to simplify notation in the expressions that follow.

generate ξ_t and e_t. To get a general idea about the likely effect (on estimates of β) of our assumptions, however, let us suppose that expectations are rational, that e_t is white noise, and that ξ_t is a random walk: $\xi_t = \xi_{t-1} + \zeta_t$, with ζ_t being white noise. Then we can develop a rational expectations solution, using tools developed in Chapter 8, as follows. We use $s^e_{t+1} = E_t s_{t+1}$ in Equation (6') and rewrite it as

$$E_t s_{t+1} - s_t = \tilde{R}_t + \xi_t. \tag{10}$$

Then write $E_t s_{t+1} - s_t = E_t \Delta s_{t+1}$ and also substitute (9) into (10):

$$E_t \Delta s_{t+1} = \lambda \Delta s_t + \gamma \tilde{R}_{t-1} + e_t + \xi_t. \tag{11}$$

Based on Equation (11), we will seek a solution for Δs_t and will conjecture, as suggested by the procedure of Chapter 8, that it is of the form

$$\Delta s_t = \phi_1 \tilde{R}_{t-1} + \phi_2 e_t + \phi_3 \xi_t. \tag{12}$$

But if that is so, then

$$E_t \Delta s_{t+1} = \phi_1 \tilde{R}_t + \phi_3 \xi_t \tag{13}$$

since $E_t e_{t+1} = 0$ and $E_t \xi_{t+1} = \xi_t$.

Putting Equation (9) into (13) and then substituting the resultant, $E_t \Delta s_{t+1} = \phi_1(\lambda \Delta s_t + \gamma \tilde{R}_{t-1} + e_t) + \phi_3 \xi_t$, into (11) and also using (12) in the latter, we obtain

$$\phi_1[\lambda(\phi_1 \tilde{R}_{t-1} + \phi_2 e_t + \phi_3 \xi_t) + \gamma \tilde{R}_{t-1} + e_t] + \phi_3 \xi_t$$
$$= \lambda(\phi_1 \tilde{R}_{t-1} + \phi_2 e_t + \phi_3 \xi_t) + \gamma \tilde{R}_{t-1} + e_t + \xi_t. \tag{14}$$

But for Equation (14) to hold as an equality for all possible values of $\tilde{R}_{t-1}$, e_t, and ξ_t it must be true that the following three conditions prevail:

$$\phi_1^2 \lambda + \phi_1 \gamma = \lambda \phi_1 + \gamma \tag{15a}$$

$$\phi_1 \lambda \phi_2 + \phi_1 = \lambda \phi_2 + 1 \tag{15b}$$

$$\phi_1 \lambda \phi_3 = \lambda \phi_3 + 1 - \phi_3. \tag{15c}$$

The first of these can be solved for ϕ_1. Since Equation (15a) is a quadratic equation, there are two solutions:

$$\phi_2^{(1)} = \frac{(\lambda - \gamma) + \sqrt{(\gamma - \lambda)^2 + 4\lambda\gamma}}{2\lambda}$$

$$\phi_1^{(2)} = \frac{(\lambda - \gamma) - \sqrt{(\gamma - \lambda)^2 + 4\lambda\gamma}}{2\lambda}. \tag{16}$$

Simplifying these expressions, we find that $\phi_1^{(1)} = 1$ and $\phi_1^{(2)} = -\gamma/\lambda$. Technical considerations that are beyond the scope of this book[13] indicate that $\phi_1^{(2)} = -\gamma/\lambda$ is the proper value for ϕ_1, and from Equations (15b) and (15c) it then follows that $\phi_2 = -1/\lambda$ and $\phi_3 = -1/(\lambda + \gamma - 1)$. So the model's solution can finally be written as

$$\Delta s_t = -\frac{\gamma}{\lambda} \tilde{R}_{t-1} - \frac{1}{\lambda} e_t - \frac{1}{\lambda + \gamma - 1} \xi_t. \tag{17}$$

Let us now consider what the latter demonstrates. It is the solution to a model that consists of Equations (9) and (10), where the former represents a plausible form of policy behavior and the latter reflects market behavior with rational expectations and conforming to UIP, as expressed in Equation (6')—or in (7)—with $\alpha = 0.0$ and $\beta = 1.0$. But the coefficient on $\tilde{R}_{t-1} = R_{t-1} - R_{t-1}^* = f_{t-1} - s_{t-1}$ in (17) is unambiguously negative, since γ and λ are both positive constants. Furthermore, since λ is presumably small and γ close to 1.0, the absolute value of this negative coefficient will most likely be large. And that means that even though $\beta = 1.0$ in Equation (7), a regression of Δs_t on $R_{t-1} - R_{t-1}^*$ will yield a negative slope in this system. Since such a regression is, given CIP, exactly the same as a regression of Δs_{t+1} on $f_t - s_t$, we see that the evidence relating to (8) in the previous section actually does not constitute evidence against UIP.

The model just developed not only reconciles UIP with the findings reported in Section 9.3, but in addition can be modified so as to match properties of the actual time series data on s_t and f_t in other significant ways. With the modification, for example, the model implies that s_t and f_t are close to random walks, as is approximately true in actuality, and that both of these series are much more variable than the differential $f_t - s_t = R_t - R_t^*$. The modification that is required replaces the assumption that the ξ_t disturbance process is a random walk (as before) with the assumption that it is an autoregressive process of the form $\xi_t = \rho \xi_{t-1} + \zeta_t$, with ρ being less than but fairly close to 1.0. For details, the interested reader is referred to McCallum (1994).

It should be mentioned that there are other theories that serve to reconcile the UIP condition with the empirical problem outlined in Section 9.3. Froot and Frankel (1989), for example, have argued that Equation (6') holds but that expectations are not rational—in which case ε_{t+1} in (8') could be correlated with $f_t - s_t$, making estimates of β biased and inconsistent. Other writers, including Evans and Lewis (1992) and Kaminsky (1993), have suggested that the empirical anomalies arise because it takes time for market participants— even reasonably rational ones—to learn about monetary policy processes after governments change their behavior, as they unquestionably do from time to time.

The upshot of this discussion, then, is that while the evidence of Section 9.3 is awkward for the UIP hypothesis, it does not necessarily show UIP to be invalid. And from a theoretical perspective UIP is extremely attractive, at least

---

[13] For a bit of textbook-level discussion, see McCallum (1989, pp. 157–160).

as an approximation. Consequently, it would seem that the hypothesis should continue to be maintained, and included as a component of exchange rate models, at least until some attractive alternative has been developed. To date, none has.

9.5 Price-Level Stickiness

It will be recalled that Section 8.9 was devoted to the introduction of price-level stickiness into our open-economy macroeconomic model. Even though a particularly simple form of sticky-price adjustments was adopted, the analytical difficulties were fairly severe. Accordingly, it is appropriate that we consider additional evidence (besides the bit mentioned in Chapter 8) concerning the need to recognize price-level stickiness as a crucial ingredient of realistic macroeconomic models. Here we will briefly review two types of evidence.

The first of these is applicable to closed-economy analysis, as well as in models including exchange rates and international trade. A particularly tidy presentation was provided by Rotemberg (1987) in the form of impulse response patterns in a vector-autoregression (VAR) system. A VAR system is simply a set of dynamic regression equations, one explaining each of the important variables of the system—here the macroeconomy—all of which are viewed as endogenous. In Rotemberg's setup, for example, the recognized variables are real GNP, the GNP deflator (price level), the (M1) money stock, the rate of interest on U.S. Treasury bills, and real military spending by the government—all in logarithmic form. In each equation the dependent variable is explained by lagged values (four in Rotemberg's study) of each of the system's variables. The residuals in each equation are viewed as the originating sources of all variation, and the residual in the money stock equation is interpreted as reflecting the irregular component of monetary policy actions. The system of equations can be solved to determine the sequence of responses of any variable to any of the disturbances. Of relevance for our present discussion is the time pattern of responses of the price level and real GNP to money-supply shocks. In Rotemberg's (1987) system,[14] estimated with quarterly U.S. data for 1953–1986, the responses are as shown in Table 9–3.

From the last column in Table 9–3 it is seen that the response of the price level to a monetary shock is spread over five quarters—only a small percentage response occurs in the quarter that the shock appears, some additional response takes place in the next quarter, and so on. Correspondingly, the figures in column 2 indicate that there is a positive response of real output to a monetary shock, a response that grows for two quarters and then begins to be reversed. Thus the figures are qualitatively suggestive of an economy in which monetary policy actions have important but temporary effects on real aggregates because prices are "sticky" and thus respond slowly to the policy shocks. There are

---

[14] These values pertain to this system estimated with first differences of each variable. The responses are much the same for another version in which detrended (log) levels are used.

Table 9–3 Percent Response of GNP and
Price Level to 1 Percent Money Shock.

Lag in (quarters)	Real GNP	Price level
0	0.48	0.21
1	0.63	0.38
2	1.13	0.60
3	1.00	0.86
4	0.74	1.09

Source: Rotemberg (1987).

many questions that could be raised concerning details of Rotemberg's system, but this kind of finding has appeared in many studies. Probably the most dubious part of the argument is the interpretation of money stock equation residuals as monetary policy shocks, but recent work by Christiano and Eichenbaum (1992) goes a long way toward elimination of this weakness.

The second type of evidence to be mentioned here pertains to the effects of monetary "surprises," that is, unexpected changes in money stock growth rates. In the sticky-price model presented in Section 8.9, real output responds positively to the shock term e_t of the money-supply rule, as was shown with Equation (67) of Chapter 8. That result can be generalized to a setting in which money growth rates are autocorrelated (rather than white noise) and in which lagged shocks, as well as current shocks, affect current output.[15] In models with completely flexible prices, by contrast, money stock changes typically have no effect on real output—not even the unanticipated or surprise component of these changes.

To see what the empirical evidence has to say in the context of these contrasting implications of sticky and flexible price models, consider some evidence based on quarterly U.S. data for the period of 1954.3–1991.3. In Equation (18) we report OLS estimates for a regression of y_t (log of real GNP) on a time trend and two lagged values of itself, together with current and two lagged values of e_t, with the latter estimated as the residual series from an autoregression for Δm_t. (Here m_t is the log of the M1 aggregate.)[16]

$$y_t = 0.299 + 0.00026t + 1.268y_{t-1} - 0.309y_{t-2} + 0.209e_t + 0.220e_{t-1} + 0.315e_{t-2}$$
$$(0.14) \quad (0.00014) \quad (0.076) \quad \quad (0.077) \quad \quad (0.10) \quad \quad (0.10) \quad \quad (0.10)$$

$$R^2 = 0.999 \quad \quad SE = 0.0089 \quad \quad DW = 2.10. \tag{18}$$

Here it will be seen that e_t, e_{t-1}, and e_{t-2} all enter as significant explanatory

[15] For a textbook demonstration, see McCallum (1989), pp. 211–212.
[16] The autoregression for 1954.3–1991.3 is similar to the one reported in Chapter 8. The estimated values are $\Delta m_t = 0.0049 + 0.622\Delta m_{t-1}$, with $R^2 = 0.391$, SE = 0.0075, DW = 2.16, and a standard error for the slope coefficient of 0.064.

variables with positive coefficients.[17] Thus there is indirect evidence from this direction that U.S. markets are characterized by a significant amount of price stickiness.[18]

9.6 Long-Run Purchasing Power Parity

Since q_t is an endogenous variable, not a constant, our model does not include purchasing power parity (PPP) as a maintained assumption. Indeed, fluctuations in q_t have been viewed in Chapter 8 as one of the sources of variation in the nominal exchange rate s_t. But a sympathetic reading of the literature on PPP suggests that this doctrine should not be interpreted as a claim that q_t is literally constant or, equivalently, that

$$\Delta s_t = \Delta p_t - \Delta p_t^* \tag{19}$$

holds period by period. Instead, PPP doctrine should be understood as promoting the two following hypotheses. First, changes in monetary conditions—policy changes—will have no long-run effects on real exchange rates. In particular, a one-time increase in the money stock M_t will raise P_t and S_t equiproportionally,[19] leaving $s_t - p_t$ and therefore $q_t = s_t - p_t + p_t^*$ unchanged, as in our comparative static experiment in Section 6.1. Second, under conditions in which monetary policies are markedly different in the nations or monetary regions under consideration, nominal exchange rate movements will be similar to relative price-level movements, as in Equation (19). Over long spans of time, then, Equation (19) will provide a good approximation to the data—changes in s_t will tend to mimic changes in $p_t - p_t^*$. The same will also be true over periods of only a few years *if* the prevailing conditions are such that drastically different inflationary records are experienced. (An example is provided by major wars; indeed, Cassell's (1928) original development of the PPP theory was stimulated by the experiences of World War I.[20]) Thus with Δs_t definitionally equal to $\Delta p_t - \Delta p_t^* + \Delta q_t$, the values of Δs_t will be well approximated in reality whenever $\Delta p_t - \Delta p_t^*$ values are large even though Δq_t is not zero, because values

---

[17] If the equation is estimated in first differences, the slope coefficients on the e_t variables are slightly smaller and the standard errors somewhat larger so that only e_{t-1} is formally significant. But the implied response pattern is qualitatively similar.

[18] It might be noted that this result features no identifying assumptions designed to assure that the e_t measures represent surprise components, that is, nothing has been done to overcome the "observational equivalence" problem described by Sargent (1976). But in the context of our demonstration that output responds to monetary policy actions, that problem is not actually relevant.

[19] The discussion of this section assumes either that exchange rates are floating, or that observations are taken over a long enough span of time that devaluations will have been numerous enough to bring about the necessary exchange rate adjustments.

[20] An extensive review of the PPP literature is provided by Officer (1976).

Table 9–4 Data Relating to PPP.

Nation	Exchange value of currency in 1975 re 1913	Ratio of foreign to domestic prices in 1975 re 1913	$s_{1975} - s_{1913}$	$p_{1975} - p_{1975}^* - p_{1913} + p_{1913}^*$
Austria	0.414	0.608	0.882	0.497
Canada	1.220	1.181	−0.199	−0.166
Denmark	0.731	0.515	0.313	0.664
France	0.0300	0.0256	3.506	3.665
Germany	5.023	3.882	−1.614	−1.356
Italy	0.0078	0.0097	4.854	4.636
Japan	0.0088	0.0052	4.733	5.259
Netherlands	0.821	0.666	0.197	0.406
Norway	0.821	0.854	0.197	0.158
Spain	0.108	0.131	2.226	2.032
Sweden	1.032	0.984	−0.031	0.016
Switzerland	4.364	2.431	−1.473	−0.888
United Kingdom	0.381	0.447	0.965	0.805
United States	5.469	7.495	−1.699	−2.014

Source: Officer (1980).

of Δq_t will almost always be reasonably small and will have some tendency to offset one another over a span of years.[21]

Some impressive evidence in favor of this second version of the PPP doctrine has been collected by Officer (1980). In particular, his study assembles values of s_t, p_t, and p_t^* on a weighted-average or "effective" basis for 14 countries, with the time span including years before World War I and continuing into the 1970s. The data that Officer presents for the time span from 1913 to 1975 are listed in Table 9–4.[22]

In terms of our usual symbols, the first numerical column is the ratio of $1/S_{1975}$ to $1/S_{1913}$ whereas the second is the ratio of $(P^*/P)_{1975}$ to $(P^*/P)_{1913}$. Therefore, the reciprocal of the first column is S_{1975}/S_{1913} and the logarithm of that value is $s_{1975} - s_{1913}$. Similarly, the log of the reciprocal of the second column is $(p_{1975} - p_{1975}^*) - (p_{1913} - p_{1913}^*)$. Those values, tabulated in the last two columns of Table 9–4, are plotted in Figure 9–3. Since $s_{1975} - s_{1913}$ is the counterpart of Δs_t in Equation (19), and the column 4 magnitude is the counterpart of $\Delta p_t - \Delta p_t^*$, the cross-country implication of PPP is that the points in Figure 9–3 should cluster around a line with slope 1.0 that passes through the (0.0) origin. As can readily be verified, that condition is met with an unusually high degree of conformity. Officer's data, then, provide a

[21] This statement should not be interpreted as contradicting the discussion in Section 2.6, which mentions forces that will cause Δq_t to remain positive or negative for a number of years. The *magnitude* of these Δq_t values will not be large, and the originating forces are unlikely to continue for long.

[22] For Canada and France the initial dates are 1910 and 1905–1913 (average), respectively, because statistics for 1913 itself were not available.

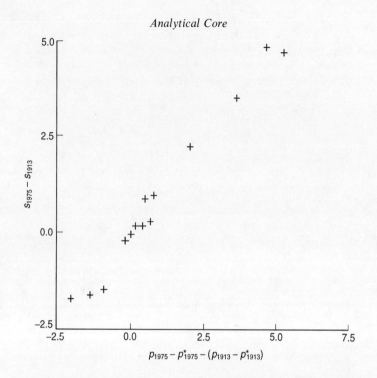

Figure 9–3 Officer's evidence on long-run PPP. *Source*: Officer (1980).

substantial amount of support for our second version of the PPP doctrine. Another batch of data referring to a long span of time, but tabulated on a bilateral basis for only seven nations, has been presented by Gailliot (1970). This data set is similarly supportive of PPP as a long-run proposition.

References

Cassell, G., *Post-War Monetary Stabilization*. New York: Columbia University Press, 1928.

Christiano, L. J., and M. Eichenbaum, "Identification and the Liquidity Effects of a Monetary Shock," in *Business Cycles, Growth, and Political Economy*, A. Cukierman, L. Z. Hercowitz, and L. Leiderman, Eds. Cambridge, MA: MIT Press, 1992.

Cosiander, P. A., and B. R. Lang, "Interest Rate Parity Tests: Switzerland and Some Major Western Countries," *Journal of Banking and Finance* 5 (1981), 187–200.

Evans, M. D. D., and K. K. Lewis, "Trends in Expected Returns in Currency and Bond Markets," NBER Working Paper no. 4116 (July 1992).

Fratianni, M., and L. M. Wakeman, "The Law of One Price in the Eurocurrency Market," *Journal of International Money and Finance* 1 (1982), 307–323.

Froot, K. A., and J. A. Frankel, "Forward Discount Bias: Is It An Exchange Rate Premium?" *Quarterly Journal of Economics* 104 (Feb. 1989), 139–161.

Gailliot, H. J., "Purchasing Power Parity as an Explanation of Long-Term Changes in Exchange Rates," *Journal of Money, Credit, and Banking* 2 (Nov. 1970), 348–357.

Ghosh, A. R., and P. R. Masson, "Model Uncertainty, Learning, and the Gains from Coordination," *American Economic Review* **81** (June 1991), 465–479.

Kaminsky, G., "Is There a Peso Problem? The Dollar/Pound Exchange Rate, 1976–1987," *American Economic Review* **83** (June 1993). 450–472.

McCallum, B. T., *Monetary Economics: Theory and Policy.* New York: Macmillan, 1989.

———, "A Reconsideration of the Uncovered Interest Parity Relationship," *Journal of Monetary Economics* **33** (Feb. 1994), 105–132.

Meese, R., "Empirical Assessment of Foreign Currency Risk Premiums," in *Financial Risk: Theory, Evidence, and Implications*, C. C. Stone, Ed. Boston: Kluwer Academic Publ., 1989.

Officer, L. H., "The Purchasing-Power-Parity Theory of Exchange Rates: A Review Article," *IMF Staff Papers* **23** (1976), 1–60.

———, "Effective Exchange Rates and Price Ratios Over the Long Run: A Test of the Purchasing-Power-Parity Theory," *Canadian Journal of Economics* **8** (May 1980), 206–230.

Rotemberg, J., "The New Keynesian Microfoundations," *NBER Macroeconomics Annual 1987*, S. Fischer, Ed. Cambridge, MA: MIT Press, 1987.

Sargent, T. J., "The Observational Equivalence of Natural and Unnatural Rate Theories of Macroeconomics," *Journal of Political Economy* **84** (June 1976), 631–640.

Taylor, M. P., "Covered Interest Parity: A High-Frequency, High-Quality Data Study," *Economica* **54** (Nov. 1987), 429–438.

———, "Covered Interest Aribtrage and Market Turbulence," *Economic Journal* **99** (June 1989), 376–391.

Problems

1. What is the meaning of the R^2 and DW statistics reported in Equations (2) and (4)?

2. What is the meaning of the standard errors attached to regression coefficients in Equations (2) and (4)? How are they related to the overall standard error denoted by SE?

3. How does one evaluate "statistical significance" of regression coefficients in estimated relations such as Equations (2) and (4)?

4. Why does the present chapter devote so much space and effort to the uncovered interest parity relationship?

5. Summarize briefly and in simple language the argument of Section 9.4.

6. Why was no attention paid in Chapter 9 to Equations ($1c$) and ($1d$) of Chapters 6 and 8?

III

APPLICATIONS

10

Fixed Versus Floating Exchange Rates

10.1 Introduction

In this chapter we turn to one of the most dramatic and fundamental topics in international monetary economics, namely, whether an economy would be better off with floating, market-determined exchange rates or with a rate pegged by central bank intervention.[1] Actually, the relevant topic can be viewed as broader in scope, in the sense that there are more than two options. Besides (1) floating freely and (2) pegging a particular bilateral rate, it would instead be possible for a nation to (3) peg to a bundle of currencies, (4) float in a "managed" fashion, or (5) maintain a dual or multiple set of exchange rates for different categories of transactions.[2] The main analytical points are brought out most clearly, however, by consideration of the basic choice between a simple fixed rate and a freely floating rate. We shall, accordingly, focus most of our attention on that choice. Throughout the chapter, moreover, we shall maintain the perspective of a single nation making this choice, reserving the multicountry perspective for Chapters 11 and 12.

In considering the merits of fixed versus floating exchange rates, an essential step is to avoid two frequently committed fallacies. The first, often put forth by proponents of fixed rates, is to associate floating rates with periods of great disruption and turbulence, and consequently to suggest that floating rates are responsible.[3] But it is clearly possible that periods of unusual turbulence are merely those in which the random shocks hitting the system happen to be unusually large. These shocks—stemming from wars or other forms of political instability, major inventions, extreme weather conditions, and so on—are then likely to be the cause of unusual turbulence, which in turn leads to the adoption of floating rates. These rates are set free to float precisely because it has become difficult to keep them fixed, in the face of the initiating turbulences. While this pattern of causation is not the only logical possibility, it would appear to be the one that has been most important historically. Certainly the turbulence of the 1930s was, as discussed in Chapter 4, the cause rather than the result of

---

[1] Here the word "intervention" should be understood as referring principally to nonsterilized intervention.

[2] This list of possibilities is fairly similar to that of Flood and Marion (1992).

[3] A famous and influential study that makes this argument is Nurkse (1944).

the floating-rate episodes of that decade. In sum, it is usually a fallacy to blame floating rates for troubled economic conditions. It is more fruitful to determine the identity of the originating shocks and then to carefully consider whether conditions would have been even worse if rates had been kept fixed.

The second major fallacy is one occasionally committed by supporters of floating rates. It stems from inappropriate application of the basically correct idea that free and unregulated markets work better than markets with price controls, rationing, or other governmental impediments. The fallacy is to suggest that there is an exact analogy between fixed exchange rates and price controls in markets for typical commodities.[4] But such is not the case; money is not a typical commodity. If the money prices of all goods were perfectly flexible, then all markets would clear under fixed as well as floating rates, doing so in the fixed-rate case by an automatic adjustment of the money supply (an adjustment that does not require the use of productive resources in a fiat-money world).[5] In actuality, of course, the prices of many goods are not perfectly flexible—the consequences of which will be considered shortly—but that does not imply that fixed exchange rates themselves prevent the occurrence of market clearing.

One way of seeing that the usual case for free markets is not directly applicable in this context is to consider the question: if it is desirable to have an adjustable rate of exchange between the moneys of two nations, then why not for two states (of the United States) or two cities (such as Pittsburgh and Philadelphia), or even neighborhoods? Why not have different moneys with a floating exchange rate for two different neighborhoods of a single city? More realistically, it is in fact true that the dollar bills issued in different Federal Reserve districts of the United States are physically distinguishable.[6] So why not have floating rates between Federal Reserve districts?[7] But the common-sense and correct reaction is that this would produce confusion and be inefficient, which suggests that the usual case for free markets is not applicable.

One reason for the invalidity of the analogy between floating exchange rates and free markets is that exchange rates are prices of moneys; but *money* is an inherently communal phenomenon,[8] so its provision is likely to have

---

[4] Niehans (1984, p. 286) mentions Johnson (1969) as guilty of this fallacy. Note that there *is* a valid analogy between import controls (tariffs or quotas) and ordinary price controls.

[5] Maintaining a bureau for the design and production of high-quality paper bills and coins does, of course, involve some productive resources. But their quantity is small, in relation to a nation's national income, and the extent to which this usage of resources varies with the volume of money in circulation is smaller still. So, to a good approximation, it is legitimate to neglect resource usage for the provision of fiat money.

[6] On each bill, the name of the issuing Federal Reserve Bank is inscribed. Its identifying number also appears and the corresponding letter is part of the bill's serial number.

[7] There are, as many readers will know from the study of money and banking, 12 districts, each with its own Federal Reserve Bank. These are located in Atlanta, Boston, Chicago, Cleveland, Dallas, Kansas City, Minneapolis, New York, Philadelphia, Richmond, San Francisco, and St. Louis.

[8] Money is, by definition, a *generally acceptable* medium of exchange, with the identity of those items that are generally acceptable being chosen by the community. For additional discussion see McCallum (1989, ch. 2) or any textbook of money and banking.

"externality" or "public good" aspects. In such cases, as is emphasized in the study of public finance, the usual presumption in favor of free markets does not automatically prevail.[9]

Having discussed these two fallacies, let us now turn more constructively to an analysis of the comparative advantages of fixed and floating rates for a small open economy of the type analyzed in Chapters 5–8. There are three distinct categories of effects that need to be considered, as follows:

1. Microeconomic effects involving the efficiency of resource allocation
2. Macroeconomic effects involving short-run stabilization policy
3. Policy discipline, concerning the long-run avoidance of inflation.

The three types of effects will be discussed in Sections 10.2, 10.3, and 10.5, respectively, with Section 10.4 devoted to the development of some useful analytical distinctions. Subsequently, Section 10.6 will consider intermediate cases between the purely fixed and floating extremes, and finally Section 10.7 will bring together different lines of argument and attempt to reach some overall conclusions.

10.2 Microeconomic Efficiency

The first type of effect concerns the usefulness of money as a medium of exchange (MOE) and medium of account (MOA). In most societies there is some particular commodity that is generally accepted in exchange, even by sellers with no desire to consume that commodity (who will merely pass it on to others). This is so because the existence of a commonly accepted medium dramatically reduces the time and other resources that must be expended in conducting exchanges. In other words, almost all societies use money—that is, the MOE—as an intermediary in most transactions because doing so reduces transaction costs and is therefore much more efficient than conducting exchanges by means of barter.[10] In addition, exchange is facilitated by the existence of a common MOA, some quantity of which serves as a "unit of account" in pricing. Then with all prices quoted in terms of the same unit, it becomes unnecessary for sellers to state their offered exchange prices in terms of all conceivable commodities—the single unit-of-account price conveys all the needed information to potential buyers. As a result of these two transaction-facilitating properties of money, economies in which money circulates can be enormously more productive than ones in which barter prevails.

What the foregoing discussion has to do with exchange rates is that basically the same points continue to apply if one considers an economic area that includes more than one national economy. Indeed, if the members of several economies engage in trade with each other, the presence of national boundaries

[9] For elaboration, see any textbook in public finance.
[10] For additional discussion and references, see McCallum (1989, pp. 16–18).

does not negate the transactional cost savings that could in principle be gained by use of a single money (MOE and MOA) across the entire area. Having fixed exchange rates is not the same thing as having a single money, of course, but it provides a large step in that direction. If the exchange rate between two economies was truly fixed, permanently, and free trade prevailed, then the situation would be almost the same as if the two economies shared the same money.[11] The only difference would be that different names would be used for the same amount of money in the two nations and that conversion charges would be made on international transactions. But then households and firms would gradually learn to think in terms of either unit of account, if they had a substantial volume of international business, after which the effect would differ from that of a single money only because of conversion costs.[12]

Actual "fixed" exchange rates in today's world are not fixed *permanently*, of course, as the possibility of relignments—that is, official par-value changes— in the foreseeable future is usually present. But analytical clarity may be gained by first considering the pure case of truly fixed rates, and then later developing the modifications to the argument that must be made to accommodate cases in which rates are fixed but are subject to possible change.

In many discussions of the present topic it is taken for granted that the main advantage of a fixed-rate arrangement is that it reduces uncertainty over exchange rates. With floating rates, firms engaging in foreign trade or investment must be concerned not only with the profitability of their basic business activities as measured in local currency, but also with the possibility that exchange rate changes will wipe out (or perhaps enlarge!) the net rewards measured in their own country's currency. Such uncertainty is often presumed to have an inhibiting effect on international trade. Now, of course, it is true that for ventures whose time horizon is short—a year or less—it is possible to avoid exchange rate risk by means of the appropriate currency purchase or sale in the forward maket. But many ventures have a more distant horizon for which forward contracts are not available. Furthermore, such contracts are not free. So it is certainly the case that exchange rate risk or uncertainty is an undesirable feature of floating-rate arrangements.

It needs to be emphasized, however, that although fixed-rate arrangements

---

[11] The argument of this paragraph and the one before has been succinctly presented by Laidler (1988) as follows. "A single unit of account economizes on record keeping and communications costs associated with trade; a single means of exchange economizes on the search costs that would, in its absence, be incurred in finding willing partners with whom to engage in barter; and further cost savings may be realized by using the means of exchange as a unit of account, hence reducing by half the number of relative prices in the economy. Furthermore, a "nation" is a political entity with no self-evident significance for economics. As far as pure economic theory is concerned, trade is trade and that which happens to take place across political boundaries is no different from any other kind. Computational and transactions costs are smaller the smaller is the number of separate currencies involved in mediating trade, regardless of whether it is domestic, international, or a mixture of the two. It follows, then, ... that, from the point of view of [micro]economic efficiency, the best monetary arrangement for a world-wide economy is a single currency."

[12] The importance of such conversion costs, and the difference between fixed rates and a common currency, will be emphasized in Section 11.3.

eliminate (or reduce) uncertainty regarding rate changes themselves, they do not eliminate the underlying sources of risk and uncertainty. The possibility of political instability, major inventions, extreme weather, and so on, cannot be avoided by *any* scheme of international monetary arrangements. The actual difference is that the effects of such uncertainties manifest themselves differently with different arrangements. That point should become clearer in the next section.

Even more important to recognize is the point that reduced exchange rate uncertainty is not an *additional* advantage for fixed rates, on top of those provided by having a single money (or a close approximation) throughout an international area. It is, instead, just one aspect of the advantages of having a single money. For if the same currency prevails as the MOE in two areas, then there is no variable exchange rate between those areas whose value is subject to uncertainty.

Indeed, it can more generally be argued that all of the major microeconomic advantages of fixed over floating exchange rates can be viewed as particular aspects of the benefits of having a single money. This point warrants emphasis because there is a clear analytical advantage of adopting this unified viewpoint, rather than listing each of the special aspects. The advantage is that the unified view makes it possible for certain general conclusions to be drawn. In particular, it leads rather naturally to the conclusion that the advantages of fixed rates to a country are relatively more important, the larger is the share of that country's transactions that involve international trade (of goods, services, or financial claims). The more *open* is an economy, in other words, the more likely it is that fixed exchange rates will be advantageous for it. This point will be utilized in the following sections.

10.3 Macroeconomic Flexibility

Now we turn our attention to the relative macroeconomic effects of fixed and floating exchange rate regimes. In this regard, the balance of advantages goes the other way. The fact[13] that goods prices are sticky—slow to adjust—implies that short-run effects of shocks will frequently include induced departures of output y_t from its market-clearing value $\bar{y}_t$, departures that are socially undesirable.[14] Suppose, for example, that an economy's IS function is shocked to the left by altered conditions abroad—say, a reduction in y^*. Then if the (log) exchange rate s is fixed, the short-run equilibrium will be as at point A in Figure 10–1, where $y^2 < \bar{y}$. But if the exchange rate floats, with monetary

[13] Discussed in Section 9.5.

[14] It is undesirable for y_t to fall short of $\bar{y}_t$ because less output (and employment) are forthcoming than are warranted by prevailing tastes, technology, and productive resources. But it is also undesirable for y_t to exceed $\bar{y}_t$ because such situations require excessive wear and tear of productive capital, insufficient leisure hours relative to workers' preferences (temporarily overridden according to most labor contracts), and sometimes mistaken views about real wages. In some analytical setups, the creation of inflationary conditions is also regarded as a cost of $y_t > \bar{y}_t$.

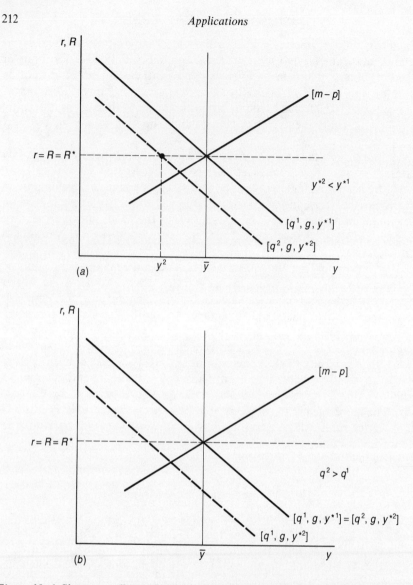

Figure 10–1 Short-run effects of shock to income abroad (*a*) Fixed exchange rate. (*b*) Floating exchange rate.

policy keeping m (log of money stock) fixed,[15] then the short-run equilibrium (depicted in Figure 10–1*b*) will not involve a departure of y from $\bar{y}$. Instead, an induced increase in s will generate a real exchange rate value q^2 greater than q^1, such that the short-run equilibrium involves no change in either y or p.

But what about other kinds of shocks—shifts in the LM or $\bar{y}$ schedules, for

---

[15] This is a metaphor for keeping m_t on its specified course, which could be given by a policy rule with various types possible.

example, or changes in R^*? For these entail a preferable short-run position for y in the fixed-rate case when LM shifts, and equally undesirable positions with fixed and floating rates when $\bar{y}$ and R^* are shocked.[16] But for these cases it is crucial to recognize that it is not necessary *in actuality* for m to be held fixed when the shock occurs with a floating exchange rate.[17] Instead, m could in principle be contracted or expanded so as to yield a short-run equilibrium with $y = \bar{y}$.

Indeed, it is more generally true that short-run stabilization policy could always be effected, in principle, when the exchange rate is floating. Thus the greater flexibility of monetary policy with a floating rate implies that macroeconomic considerations work in the direction of favoring regimes with floating rates.

A variant of this argument is developed by Milton Friedman in a 1953 paper, "The Case for Flexible Exchange Rates," which has probably been the most famous and influential single pience of writing on exchange rate arrangements. The heart of Friedman's argument is that adjustments in *real* exchange rates are often necessary, in response to various shocks, for the restoration of balance-of-payments equilibrium.[18] But if s cannot change, because of exchange rate fixity, then p must do so (since $q = s - p + p^*$). But the adjustment of price levels is usually a slow, disruptive, and painful process. If p needs to fall to raise q, for instance, a recession is typically required to bring about this reduction. So why not let s do the adjusting? That is one way of expressing Friedman's argument. In addition, he emphasizes that since recessions are highly unpopular, governments will often attempt to avoid them by adoption of quantitative controls and barriers to trade—two courses of action that are extremely harmful to the longer term efficiency of the economy. Again there is the possibility of avoiding both types of restriction by having the exchange rate free to do the adjusting in response to the initiating shock.

It needs to be explicitly recognized that the reactions to shocks by y_t and other endogenous real variables are different under fixed and floating rates only from a short-run perspective. The long-run (stationary state) analysis of a shock to IS or LM, or $\bar{y}$, would find the same ultimate equilibrium values whether rates are fixed or flexible. That fact is illustrated in Figures 10–2 and 10–3, which show that the long-run responses to changes in g or $\bar{y}$ are the same (except for p and m) whether s is fixed or floating. In Figure 10–2 the long-run equilibrium is where $R = R^*$ and $y = \bar{y}$ in both panels, whereas in Figure 10–3 it is where $R = R^*$ and $y = \bar{y}^2$. It could also be recognized that these long-run

---

[16] These results can be established by short-run analysis of the type introduced in Chapters 6 and 7. The reader should construct diagrams analogous to Figure 10–1 to be certain that his or her analysis agrees with our statement.

[17] In our comparative static exercises, m is held fixed (when some other variable is shocked) for analytical convenience, so as to focus on one thing at a time. But actual policy makers will be apt to respond to shocks.

[18] Thus the focus is an imbalance of payments, rather than $y \neq \bar{y}$, as the main criterion of disequilibrium. That difference in emphasis, relative to the foregoing discussion, is not of major significance.

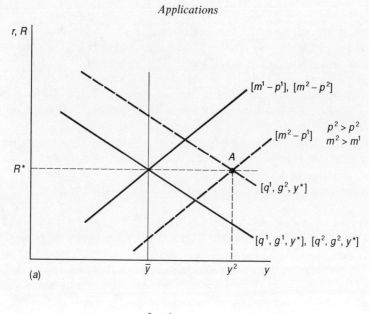

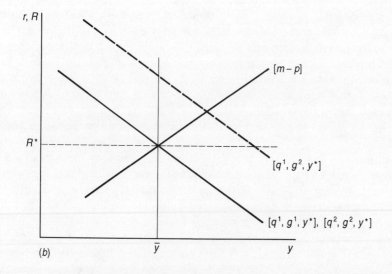

Figure 10-2 Comparative effects of change in government spending. (*a*) Fixed exchange rate. (*b*) Floating exchange rate.

responses would be obtained promptly if goods prices were highly flexible. The similarity of the outcomes with fixed and floating rates in this case illustrates the point argued on p. 251, namely, that "all markets would clear under fixed as well as floating rates, doing so in the fixed-rate case by an automatic adjustment of the money supply."

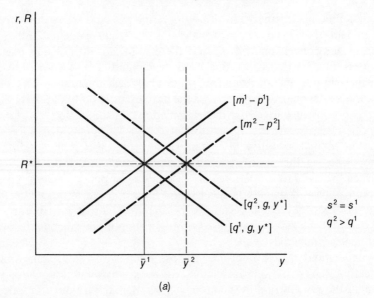

(a)

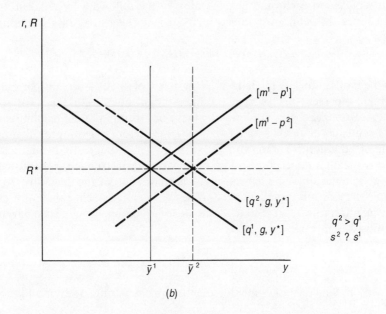

(b)

Figure 10–3 Comparative effects of change in $\bar{y}$. (*a*) Fixed exchange rate. (*b*) Floating exchange rates.

10.4 Rules versus Discretion in Monetary Policy

In the two previous sections we have seen that truly fixed exchange rates are superior in terms of microeconomic efficiency, whereas flexible rates permit monetary policy responses to shocks that can in principle yield superior macroeconomic performance. In this section and the next we wish to evaluate the argument that fixed rates provide more *discipline* against inflationary pressures. Our conclusion will be that there is in fact little if any reason to prefer fixed rates on that basis. But a full understanding and evaluation of the argument is important and requires some analytical apparatus. The present section will be devoted, accordingly, to the development of that apparatus, with its application to exchange rate issues spelled out in the section that follows.

Our first step involves explanation of the "rules versus discretion" controversy in monetary policy. As its name suggests, this long-standing controversy concerns the relative merits of conducting policy on the basis of established "rules" rather than at the "discretion" of policy makers. Although the topic has been discussed frequently for several decades, the nature of the dispute has been altered in recent years. In particular, it has recently been recognized that the rules versus discretion issue is not the same as the issue of activist versus nonactivist policy.

To understand this distinction, suppose temporarily (and somewhat unrealistically) that a nation's monetary authority manipulates as its policy instrument the growth rate of the money stock, denoted by Δm_t. Suppose also that it sets Δm_t in each quarter according to the following formula, in which UN_t denotes the economy's unemployment rate (measured as a fraction) for quarter t:

$$\Delta m_t = 0.01 + 0.5(UN_{t-1} - 0.05). \tag{1}$$

Thus the money stock is made to grow at a rate of about 1 percent per quarter (or about 4 percent per year) if the unemployment rate for the most recent quarter is 0.05 (i.e., 5 percent), and at a more or less rapid rate if unemployment has been greater or smaller than 0.05. Now, for present purposes the significant feature of Equation (1) is that it represents monetary policy that is activist, by which is meant that each period's setting of the instrument depends in an "active" manner on some aspect of the current state of the economy. In this example the relevant aspect is taken to be the unemployment rate, but it could be the inflation rate or an exchange rate or some combination of such variables. By contrast, a formula such as

$$\Delta m_t = 0.01, \tag{2}$$

which specifies a constant value for the instrument setting, or even one such as

$$\Delta m_t = 0.01 + 0.0002t, \tag{3}$$

which makes the setting increase over time, is nonactivist. That is the case since neither Equation (2) nor Equation (3) incorporates any policy response to the state of the economy.

Now let us ask whether the activist policy behavior of Equation (1) reflects an example of rules or discretion. Unfortunately, this question is a bit harder to answer. If Equation (1) represents a formula that is implemented each period by the monetary authority, then it consists of a policy rule. But it is conceivable that (1) could instead be a representation of the *outcomes* of policy making by discretion. Thus if no more is known about (1) than that it accurately describes the values of Δm_t that are generated by the policy authority in periods 1, 2, . . . , then one cannot tell from the formula alone which type of policy making is being followed. This difficulty exists because the rules versus discretion distinction centers on the *process* by which the Δm_t (or other instrument) values are determined, not what those values turn out to be.

Let us then consider different policy processes. Presumably the monetary authority will, whichever way it proceeds, be attempting to optimize relative to some consistent objective function and some perception of how the economy operates. But the attempt at optimization enters the policy process at different stages under the two different types of policy making. Specifically, discretionary policy prevails when the monetary authority selects each period's value of Δm_t on the basis of a fresh optimization calculation.[19] Thus policy is discretionary when it is conducted on a period-by-period basis, with no necessary connection between the choices of different periods. By contrast, policy making according to a rule exists when the policy maker merely *implements* in each period a rule or formula [such as Equation (1)] that has been chosen to be applicable for a large number of periods, not just the one currently at hand. In the case of a rule, the authority's optimization efforts are exerted in the *design* of the formula to be utilized, not in the choice of any single period's action. So if the formula in Equation (1) is one that was designed to be applicable for periods $t = 1, 2, . . .$, that it constitutes a rule even though it reflects activist policy. The same type of reasoning indicates, moreover, that one cannot be certain that the Δm_t outcomes specified in Equation (2) result from a policy rule, even though these outcomes are the same in each period.[20]

In summary, rule-type policy making involves implementation in each period (or in each case) of a formula designed to apply to periods (or cases) in general, whereas discretionary policy making involves freshly made decisions in each period (or case). This subtle but important distinction was first clearly developed in a famous paper by Kydland and Prescott (1977). With respect to monetary policy, that paper's discussion was based in large part on an important example, one that was later refined and extended by Barro and Gordon (1983). It will be useful for us now to consider a version of the Kydland–Prescott example.

To explain the relevant model, let us first suppose that the monetary authority's policy objectives focus on the avoidance of inflation and unemployment. Specifically, the monetary authority (MA) wishes to keep the

---

[19] It is not necessary for this definition that calculation be conducted in a formal manner on the basis of an explicit model. Instead, the policy maker can be relying on an informal model, that is, a nonexplicit but coherent view (or perception) of the way in which the economy works. Similarly, his or her objective function may be one that is not spelled out explicitly. In the analysis of policy makers, as well as households and firms, the agents' optimization problems are properly thought of in an "as if" fashion, not as a literal description of agents' thought processes.

[20] This point is substantiated by the example given below.

inflation rate close to zero and the unemployment rate low.[21] In addition, let us also suppose that the MA believes that inflation rates are largely determined by money growth rates and that unemployment in any period is negatively related to that period's rate of *unexpected* money growth. The first of these beliefs is widely shared by analysts, whereas the second reflects the model of aggregate supply sketched in Section 8.9. Under these suppositions we can represent the MA's objectives in terms of the variables Δm_t and $\Delta m_t - \Delta m_t^e$, where the latter is the unexpected or "surprise" component of money growth. For concreteness, let us then adopt a specific functional form and assume that the MA's objective for period t is to minimize the value of

$$z_t = \frac{a}{2} \Delta m_t^2 - b(\Delta m_t - \Delta m_t^e) \tag{4}$$

where $a > 0$ and $b > 0$. Finally, let us assume that expectations are formed rationally, so that (in the notation of Chapter 8) $\Delta m_t^e = E_{t-1} \Delta m_t$.

Our object now is to determine what Δm_t values would be chosen by the MA, with the objective function (4), under rules and under discretion. Since the parameters a and b are constants, there is no reason for the chosen Δm_t values to differ from period to period in the highly simplified setup at hand. Consequently, let us determine what constant value for Δm_t would be chosen if the MA were choosing a single value to prevail over a large number of periods.[22] In making a choice of this type, the MA will take into account the fact that on average rational agents will neither overpredict nor underpredict Δm_t.[23] Consequently, the second term of expression (4) will equal zero and the problem will reduce to finding the value of Δm_t that minimizes $(a/2)\Delta m_t^2$. But obviously, since $a > 0$ and squared values are nonnegative, that minimum will be obtained with the choice $\Delta m_t = 0$. Thus the rule chosen by the MA in this setting is $\Delta m_t = 0$ for all t.

Next we contrast that choice with those that would be made under discretion, that is, with choices made on a period-by-period basis. In this case we imagine the MA to be making a choice of Δm_t at some specific point in time, say, $t = 4$. For example, the object might be to choose Δm_4 to minimize the value of

$$z_4 = \frac{a}{2} \Delta m_4^2 - b(\Delta m_4 - \Delta m_4^e). \tag{5}$$

The difference that characterizes this case is that Δm_4^e, the value of Δm_4 that private agents expect or anticipate, has already been determined (at the end of

---

[21] There is a variant of the model in which the aim regarding unemployment is to keep UN_t close to its natural-rate or market-clearing value. Also, the inflation-rate objective could be some number other than zero.

[22] This is a special case of a rule, one that is not activist.

[23] This is a fact under our assumption of rational expectations. But note that the condition necessary for the following argument is simply that $\Delta m_t^e = \Delta m_t$ on average, which is a less demanding condition than full rational expectations.

period 3). From the perspective of the MA's choice problem Δm_4^e is therefore a fixed number. Consequently, the second term of Equation (5) does not necessarily equal zero in the minimization calculation. Instead, the value of Δm_4 that minimizes (5) is found by calculating the derivative

$$\frac{\partial z_4}{\partial \Delta m_4} = a\Delta m_4 - b \tag{6}$$

and setting it equal to zero. Solving the resulting equation, we find that $\Delta m_4 = b/a$ is the optimal value. Under discretion, this value as calculated pertains only to period 4. However, when period 5 comes around, the situation will be the same in the sense that the objective $z_5 = (a/2)\Delta m_5^2 - b(\Delta m_5 - \Delta m_5^e)$ has the same form as Equation (5). In addition, Δm_5^e will already have been determined and will be a fixed number from the MA's perspective. Consequently, the "optimal" value chosen for Δm_5 will be the same as for Δm_4, namely, b/a. Furthermore, it is clear that this same choice will be made in periods 6, 7, 8, and so on. Thus the sequence of Δm_t values chosen by the MA when conducting policy on the period-by-period basis is, in this example, $\Delta m_t = b/a$ for all t.

We have seen, then, that in the economy considered, policy conducted according to a rule (chosen to pertain to a large number of periods) would lead to a money growth rate of zero: $\Delta m_t = 0$ for all t. In the same economy and with the same policy objectives, by contrast, policy choices made in a discretionary period-by-period fashion would lead to $\Delta m_t = b/a$ for all t.

10.5 Rules, Discretion, Discipline, and Exchange Rates

Having seen that rules and discretion lead to different money growth rates in our example, we can now evaluate the desirability of these two alternatives and then consider the relevance for exchange rate rarrangements. In doing so, our criterion will be the value of z_t that results on average, that is, over a large number of periods. The first step in our evaluation is to recognize that while Δm_t can be chosen in any single period to differ from Δm_t^e, on average Δm_t^e and Δm_t will be equal under both types of policy making. This follows from the assumption that private agents' expectations are rational.[24] So whichever type of policy making is adopted, the average performance will involve $\Delta m_t - \Delta m_t^e = 0$. Thus the difference in outcome arises only because $\Delta m_t = 0$ with a rule and $\Delta m_t = b/a$ under discretion. But with the objective function as specified in Equation (4), this result clearly favors the rule. Specifically, the average value of z_t, which the MA wishes to minimize, is zero when $\Delta m_t = 0$ and is $(a/2)(b/a)^2 = b^2/2a$ when $\Delta m_t = b/a$. Since $a > 0$, it is the case that $b^2/2a > 0$ and the value of z_t is higher than under the rule.

In terms of the inflation and unemployment goal variables used to

---

[24] Or from the weaker assumption mentioned in footnote 23.

rationalize the specification of z_t, the foregoing result can be interpreted as follows. With either type of policy making, rational private agents will form their expectations of money growth and inflation in a manner that yields an average expectational error of zero; the average value of $\Delta m_t - \Delta m_t^e$ will be (approximately) zero over any large number of periods. Thus the average effect of monetary policy on unemployment will be zero and the difference in the two policy approaches will consist of different amounts of inflation. But rule-type policy making leads to zero inflation, whereas discretionary policy making leads to positive inflation. Given the assumption that zero inflation is desirable, then, policy conducted according to a rule is superior.

The *reason* that discretionary policy making is inferior in the foregoing example can be understood in the following way. In a typical period t it is true that Δm_t^e is given and unalterable by policy action, so the monetary authority is correct to believe that $\Delta m_t - \Delta m_t^e$ will be higher (and unemployment lower) the greater is the value chosen for Δm_t. Consequently, there is, *from the perspective of the period at hand*, a tradeoff between the reduced-unemployment benefits of faster monetary growth and the increased-inflation costs of faster growth. So the equating of marginal costs and benefits leads to a value of Δm_t that is a compromise between the zero-inflation value of $\Delta m_t = 0$ and higher values of Δm_t that would make $\Delta m_t - \Delta m_t^e$ even larger. But the discretionary emphasis on this particular outcome for the single period at hand fails to recognize the longer run effects of the policy *process*. In particular, it fails to recognize that the value at which Δm_t^e is "given" is itself determined by the character of the ongoing policy process. The values of Δm_t that are chosen each period under discretion (i.e., $\Delta m_t = b/a$ for all t) themselves lead agents to believe that Δm_t values will equal b/a, and to form the expectation $\Delta m_t^e = b/a$. This effect of policy on expectations is not taken into account in period-by-period decision making. For that reason, the MA gives too much consideration under discretion to a variable—$\Delta m_t - \Delta m_t^e$ or unemployment—that it cannot affect on average. The advantage of decision making by rules is that it views the problem not as a sequence of unrelated decisions, but as the choice of an ongoing process.

The foregoing result has been developed as an example, generated in a particular model. But it can be shown that the same type of result prevails when the setup is generalized in several important ways.[25] Thus the basic point is in fact one that applies quite generally, and can sensibly be regarded as well established for the consideration of policy alternatives.

But what, it may be asked, does all of this have to do with the fixed versus floating exchange rate issue? The answer is that a fixed exchange rate regime is one in which monetary policy is conducted according to a rule. Consequently, some analysts might be inclined to suggest that the desirability of monetary policy rules, relative to discretion, implies that fixed exchange rates are superior—at least in terms of this one criterion—to policy regimes with floating

---

[25] See McCallum (1989, ch. 12), on which the foregoing presentation is based.

rates. Fixed rates might thus be said to have the advantage of providing the discipline needed to avoid inflation.[26]

Clearly, however, this conclusion does not follow—it is simply a non sequitur. For there are many other monetary policy regimes, requiring floating rates, that constitute rules that would (if maintained) prevent ongoing inflation. Indeed, as alert readers will have already noted, our example as here developed was expressed in terms of money-supply behavior, not exchange rates, with $\Delta m_t = 0$ representing policy conforming to a rule. And in our example, that rule would generate zero inflation on average.

The specific features of this particular example should not, however, be permitted to create the impression that constant-money-growth rules are the only interesting alternatives to discretion and fixed exchange rates. There are, on the contrary, many monetary policy rules that do not involve fixed exchange rates *or* fixed money growth rates. And these may well be activist, in the sense explained in the previous section. Indeed, a monetary policy rule involving activist manipulating of a monetary base instrument, designed so as to keep nominal GNP growth rates close to a steady noninflationary growth path, has been promoted by the present writer in a number of publications.[27]

Recently some sophisticated analysts, who certainly understand all the points expressed here, have nevertheless argued in favor of fixed exchange rates as a practical means of avoiding inflation.[28] The arguments presented in these writings deserve careful consideration, but it is essential to recognize that they do not establish the *economic* superiority of fixed exchange rates over other rules with floating rates. Instead, they argue that there are certain *political* advantages to fixed rates. It is often suggested, for example, that membership in the European Monetary System, with its fixed-rate commitments, has been helpful to the Bank of Italy in attempting to maintain monetary discipline. Thus the existence of an international commitment regarding lira exchange rates can be used by the Bank of Italy, when under political pressure to adopt a more expansionary monetary stance, to resist such pressure.[29] In the opinion

[26] Actually, most writers who have emphasized the disciplinary feature of fixed exchange rates have not explicitly utilized the rules versus discretion distinction described. Some of these, such as Einzig (1970) and Yeager (1976, pp. 639–643), wrote before the formal distinction had been developed, whereas more recent contributions have often been expressed in the context of practical debates involving the European Monetary System. (Many such discussions appeared during the years of 1990–1992 in *The Economist*.) The point to be developed here, in the next two paragraphs, retains its validity, however, whether or not the rules versus discretion distinction is the basis for the contention that fixed rates provide more discipline than regimes with floating rates.

[27] See McCallum (1989, ch. 16) for an exposition of one version and some references.

[28] Actually, these arguments have called not for literally fixed exchange rates, but for monetary policy to be directed at exchange rate targets that grow over time in a predetermined fashion—see, for example, Helpman and Liederman (1988) or Drazen and Helpman (1987). That variation on the usual type of (constant) exchange rate peg does not affect the argument of the present paragraph.

[29] It is true that Italian inflationary experience was better during the 13 year span 1979–1992, between the creation of the European Monetary System (EMS) and Italy's withdrawal from the exchange rate mechanism, than during the eight years between the breakdown of the Bretton Woods system and the formation of the EMS. For more discussion of this organization, see Chapter 11.

of the present author, there may be something to such arguments in certain cases, but they are of dubious validity when the economy in question is an advanced one in a country with a mature and responsible political system. And, in any event, these arguments are—to repeat—political rather than economic in nature.

Nevertheless, it is necessary to recognize that such political arguments are applicable in certain cases. For nations with immature or poorly developed institutions, fixed exchange rates may provide the best of the feasible arrangements for generating monetary discipline, which in turn tends to promote fiscal discipline.[30] In such cases it is of course important for the nation to actually maintain the fixed rate, rather than announcing that it has one but then repeatedly devaluing. One mechanism for promoting maintenance of a fixed rate is the adoption of a *currency board*. Under such an arrangement, a nation not only fixes its exchange rate firmly to that of another currency, but also issues its own currency only in exchange for this designated foreign "reserve" currency and holds 100 percent reserves in liquid assets denominated in that reserve currency. Furthermore, some constitutional safeguards are needed to assure that the arrangement will be reasonably long lasting. When in place, however, a currency board provides rather solid assurance that the adopting nation's exchange rate will remain fixed to that of the reserve country, and thus that there will be approximately the same inflation rate in both countries. Historically, such arrangements were common in the British empire, especially in African colonies, during the first half of the present century. Also, several French and Italian colonies had currency board systems, as did the Philippines (with the U.S. dollar as its reserve currency). In recent years, Hong Kong and Singapore have utilized arrangements with some (incomplete) currency board features and in 1991 Argentina established a currency board link with the U.S. dollar. Even more recently, there has been considerable interest in developing such arrangements in republics that were members of the USSR. In particular, experiments have begun in Estonia and Latvia. Whatever the outcome may be, these cases provide some insight into the types of situations in which fixed exchange rates can be useful for disciplinary reasons.[31]

Laidler (1988) has emphasized the point that floating exchange rates, which permit a nation to choose its average long-term inflation rate, may enable it to finance government expenditures more efficiently since money creation provides "inflation tax" revenues to the government. For nations with a poorly developed tax structure that argument has some merit. But for nations with a well-developed tax system it would appear that an efficient mix of taxes would not include the inflation tax. For the revenue raised by the inflation tax is quite small in relation to the allocational distortion created, in comparison to other

---

[30] If the monetary authority of a nation follows a rule that governs the amount of base money that it issues, either directly or indirectly via an exchange rate rule, then it is constrained from financing government deficits (beyond those sanctioned by the rule). Then the government is required to balance its budget or obtain financing of additional deficits from willing lenders, which is possible only when the deficit amounts are moderate.

[31] For a discussion of currency board history and prospects, see Schwartz (1993).

taxes, such as an income tax, a consumption tax, or a value-added tax. Some analysis pertaining to these marginal costs and benefits of inflation is presented in McCallum (1989, ch. 6). It is useful, nevertheless, to keep in mind that flexible exchange rates permit a nation to choose its own preferred inflation rate, which could be higher or lower than those of its neighboring economies.

10.6 Intermediate Arrangements

Next we turn to consideration of alternative exchange rate arrangements, conforming to neither of the extreme cases of a pure float or a perfectly and forever fixed rate. An obviously relevant intermediate case is that of rates that are fixed but susceptible to occasional adjustments in the "par value" at which the peg is maintained. Interestingly, Friedman devoted considerable attention to this possibility in his 1953 paper. Basically, his argument was that this intermediate option would be not only worse than floating, but also even worse than permanent fixity. (Recall that his paper presented "the case *for* flexible rates.") The main reason is that it creates a self-destructive inducement for speculative transactions. In Friedman's words (1953, p. 164),

> Because the exchange rate is changed infrequently and only to meet substantial difficulties, a change tends to come well after the onset of difficulty, to be postponed as long as possible, and to be made only after substantial pressure on the exchange rate has accumulated. In consequence, there is seldom any doubt about the direction in which an exchange rate will be changed, if it is changed. In the interim between the suspicion of a possible change in the rate and its actual change, there is every incentive to sell the country's currency if a devaluation is expected... or buy it if an appreciation is expected.

But if market participants act to sell the currency, that tends to force its value downward and thus to *add* pressure for a devaluation (and correspondingly when an upward revaluation is expected). So the system features built-in incentives that induce speculation and thereby undermine its own stability. Furthermore, as Friedman says, "partly for this reason, partly because of their innate discontinuity, each exchange rate change tends to become the occasion for a crisis" (1953, p. 163). "In short, the system of occasional changes in temporarily rigid exchange rates seems... the worst of two worlds" (p. 164). It possesses, that is, features that are more undesirable than those of either purely floating or purely fixed rates. The basic correctness of Friedman's agument has recently been illustrated, in rather dramatic fashion, by the crises and breakdowns during 1992 and 1993 of the European exchange rate mechanism (discussed in Chapter 11).

A different type of compromise system, based on the writings of Williamson (1985), has recently been promoted by the *Economist*. Under this system, the bands within which fluctuations of the exchange rate around its par value are permitted are quite wide—say, ± 10 percent—and even these are not required to be strictly enforced. Furthermore, in an even greater departure from the usual fixed-rate arrangement, the par value is fixed in *real* terms. Thus any inflation difference between the country in question and others will cause the nominal par value to be adjusted. (If $q_t = s_t - p_t + p_t^*$ is fixed, then changes in $p_t - p_t^*$ require offsetting changes in s_t.)

The disadvantages of this proposal are fairly obvious. First, the adoption of wide bands around par does not overcome the self-induced speculative problem. When the exchange rate approaches its minimum or maximum value, the one-sided nature of realignment prospects still tends to reinforce speculative pressures. These would be reduced somewhat by the provision that the band limits would not be rigidly enforced, but in that case the advantages of fixed rates are also being surrendered. And the feature of fixing the par value in real terms completely erases the anti-inflationary discipline effects that traditional fixed rates share with some other monetary rules. If p_t rises more rapidly than p_t^*, then the target value of s_t rises in step. There will then be no signal from the foreign exchange market that monetary policy is too expansionary and needs to be tightened.

10.7 Conclusions

In the foregoing sections of this chapter we have seen that a fixed (nominal) exchange rate has the advantage of enhancing microeconomic efficiency by extending the benefits of a monetary economy, that is, the transactional cost savings that arise from the use of a common medium of exchange and medium of account. A fixed rate keeps monetary policy from being available to combat short-run cyclical fluctuations, however, which is possible with a floating rate. The latter permits better macroeconomic performance to be achieved, therefore, although this potential advantage may not be realized in practice. Neither type of arrangement is necessarily superior from the inflation-preventing (disciplinary) point of view; monetary rules that would eliminate inflation are available for nations with floating exchange rates. In addition, we have seen that "compromise" arrangements—with rates fixed but subject to occasional adjustment—encourage speculative attacks that would bring about the downfall of the supposedly fixed rate. They have, that is, self-destructive features.

In any specific case, then, it is in principle necessary to evaluate the quantitative magnitudes of the costs and benefits of the fixed-rate and floating-rate alternatives. Unfortunately, the nature of these costs and benefits makes such quantitative measurements extremely difficult. Nevertheless, it is possible to discern one general (but conditional) qualitative conclusion, as follows. The medium-of-exchange advantages of a fixed rate are relatively large—as we mentioned in Section 10.2—for a nation whose transactions include a large fraction that are international in scope. The disadvantages of a fixed rate, by contrast, arise when macroeconomic conditions in a country are frequently different from those in nations with which its rate is fixed.[32] But the smaller

---

[32] This sort of tradeoff, or balancing of advantages, also figures prominently in the literature on "optimal currency areas." Since it takes a global (rather than single-country) perspective, it will be discussed in Chapter 12.

two (neighboring) nations are, the more likely it is that a given macroeconomic shock will affect them both. Consequently, we see that fixed rates will be relatively more attractive for small, open economies that engage in a large volume of international trade (relative to their size). Floating rates, correspondingly, are more suitable for large and relatively self-sufficient economies. Thus it is not surprising, according to this conclusion, that we find that the rate between the United States and Japan is basically a floating rate, whereas that between Belgium and Luxembourg is rigidly fixed (and has been since 1922). Relatively speaking, these arrangements seem to be sensibly chosen to enhance the welfare of the nations' citizens.

References

Barro, R. J., and D. B. Gordon, "A Positive Theory of Monetary Policy in a Natural-Rate Model," *Journal of Political Economy* **91** (Aug. 1983), 589–610.

Drazen, A., and E. Helpman, "Stabilization with Exchange Rate Management," *Quarterly Journal of Economics* **102** (Nov. 1987), 835–855.

Einzig, P., *The Case against Floating Exchanges*. New York: St. Martin's Press, 1970.

Friedman, M., "The Case for Flexible Exchange Rates," in *Essays in Positive Economics*, M. Friedman, Ed. Chicago: University of Chicago Press, 1953.

Helpman, E., and L. Liederman, "Stabilization in High-Inflation Countries: Analytical Foundations and Recent Experience," *Carnegie-Rochester Conference Series on Public Policy* **28** (Spring 1988), 9–84.

Flood, R. P., and N. P. Marion, "Exchange Rate Regime Choice," in *The New Palgrave Dictionary of Money and Finance*, P. Newman, J. Eatwell, and M. Milgate, Eds. New York: Stockton Press, 1992.

Johnson, H. G., "The Case for Flexible Exchange Rates, 1969," *Federal Reserve Bank of St. Louis Review* (June 1969), 12–24.

Kydland, F. E., and E. C. Prescott, "Rules Rather than Discretion: The Inconsistency of Optimal Plans," *Journal of Political Economy* **85** (June 1977), 473–491.

Laidler, D. P., "What Remains of the Case for Flexible Exchange Rates?" *Pakistan Development Review* **27** (Winter 1988), 425–445.

McCallum, B. T., *Monetary Economics: Theory and Policy*. New York: Macmillan, 1989.

Niehans, J., *International Monetary Economics*. Baltimore, MD: Johns Hopkins University Press, 1984.

Nurkse, R., *International Currency Experience: Lessons of the Inter-War Period*. League of Nations, 1944.

Schwartz, A. J., "Currency Boards: Their Past, Present, and Possible Future Role," *Carnegie-Rochester Conference Series on Public Policy* **39** (Autumn 1993), 147–187.

Williamson, J., *The Exchange Rate System*, rev. ed. Washington, DC: Institute for International Economics, 1985.

Yeager, L. B., *International Monetary Relations: Theory, History, and Policy*, 2nd ed. New York: Harper and Row, 1976.

Problems

1. Section 10.2 argues that "although fixed-rate arrangements eliminate (or reduce) uncertainty regarding [exchange] rate changes themselves, they do not eliminate the underlying sources of risk and uncertainty.... The actual difference is that the effects of such uncertainties manifest themselves differently with different arrangements" (pp. 210–11). How do the effects of shocks to real income abroad manifest themselves to an economy with fixed exchange rates?

2. Describe an important communal choice relevant to automotive traffic.

3. Explain the reason for the proviso made in footnote 1.

4. Suppose that the monetary authority discussed in Section 10.4 has as its objection function $z_t = (a/2)(\Delta m_t - \overline{\Delta m})^2 - b(\Delta m_t - \Delta m_t^e)$, instead of Equation (4). (Here $\overline{\Delta m}$ represents an inflation rate target that may be different from zero.) Determine the choice of Δm_t that would be made for each t under rules and under discretion. How does the comparison of Δm_t values in this case relate to the one discussed for objective function (4)?

5. Would it be more advantageous for Portugal or France to have fixed exchange rates with Spain? Explain.

11

The European Monetary System

11.1 Background

The present European Monetary System (EMS) has been in operation since 1979, but monetary cooperation among European nations began earlier. Indeed, a noteworthy example of unusually successful international cooperation is provided by the European Payments Union (EPU). This postwar organization came into existence in 1950 in order to facilitate multilateral clearing of payments imbalances among its members, which included most of the nations of western Europe. At the end of World War II, many nations had large accumulated demands for imports of various goods, but were unusually low on the international reserves needed for payments. Although exchange rates were nominally fixed, most currencies were not yet "convertible," that is, private individuals and firms were not permitted to buy and sell foreign exchange freely. Indeed, foreign transactions of all types were highly regulated. In this setting, there was a strong tendency for national governments to negotiate *bilateral* trade agreements. Such agreements were helpful under the prevailing conditions, but they hampered the process of returning to a free-market system with institutions appropriate for the efficient multilateral exchange of goods, services, and securities.

Realizing the ultimate undesirability of bilateral arrangements, the member nations of the Organization for European Economic Co-operation signed an agreement on September 1, 1950, to create the EPU in order to facilitate multilateral clearing, which was effected monthly through the auspices of the preexisting, Basel-based Bank for International Settlements (BIS). Since each member was required to settle only its *net* position with the union, using credits with some nations to offset deficits with others, aggregate holdings of international reserves could be significantly reduced. Furthermore, various undesirable incentives were eliminated or reduced by the arrangement.[1] As it turned out, the workings of the EPU were highly successful. Import demands normalized and member nations built up reserves to the point that all were able, by the end of 1958, to make their currencies convertible, at least to a

---

[1] For an extensive description of the EPU and its activities, see Yeager (1976, pp. 407–430).

substantial extent.[2] With the need for the EPU thereby reduced, its member nations actually agreed to disband the organization as of December 1958, with the BIS returning the EPU's assets to its creditor members!

The end of the EPU did not, however, bring an end to European monetary cooperation. Instead, the EPU was succeeded by a European Monetary Agreement, designed in advance, which facilitated member central banks in making settlements in gold or dollars. There was also a fund to which members might apply for loans, but credit extensions were not automatic (as they had been with the EPU) and as it turned out were rarely used. The European Monetary Agreement came to an end in December 1972, but by that time new modes of cooperation had begun, as we shall see.

It will be recalled from Chapter 4 that the worldwide Bretton Woods system of fixed exchange rates, managed by the IMF, began distintegrating when the United States ceased to supply gold for dollars (at the Bretton Woods price of $35 per ounce) in August 1971, and other currencies began to float aginst the dollar. Then the Smithsonian Agreement of December 1971 called for a new set of par values at the center of widened bands (of ± 2.25 percent) within which rates were to be kept. But the provisions of this agreement were very short-lived; by March 1973 the system had broken down and many major currencies were again floating against the dollar.

During 1972, however, the member nations of the European Community had agreed to keep their rates with each other within bands around par that were considerably narrower than those implied by the bands via-à-vis the dollar as specified by the Smithsonian Agreement. This arrangement was colorfully nicknamed "the snake within the tunnel," so when the tunnel (i.e., the Smithsonian limits) disappeared in March 1973, the European scheme became simply "the snake." Initially, in April 1972, participating nations included all members of the European Community except Denmark, Ireland, and the United Kingdom. These joined the snake in May 1972, but quickly withdrew. Denmark and Ireland rejoined, but the latter withdrew again, as did Italy in late 1972 and France in 1974 and 1976. Norway and Sweden also participated for a spell, but at the time of its demise and replacement by the EMS (in 1978–1979), the snake included only Denmark, Germany, the Netherlands, and Belgium-Luxembourg[3] (Tew, 1988, p. 158). The lack of success of the snake, manifest in the limited participation by large nations other than Germany, led many observers to predict that the EMS would be ineffective or short-lived. Instead, however, its exchange rate mechanism attracted increasing participation with the passage of time, and adjustments of par values became increasingly rare. As of late 1991, most analysts would have described the existing EMS as remarkably successful and as giving every promise of leading, within a matter

---

[2] Most of the nations kept restrictions in place on their own citizens, but permitted free exchange of their currencies by foreigners when acquired by way of current-account transactions (but not capital-account transactions). Again see Yeager (1976, pp. 419–423).

[3] Belgium and Luxembourg agreed in 1921 to form a monetary union, with Belgian francs serving as legal tender in both nations. Luxembourg also issues franc notes and coins, but keeps these interchangeable with their Belgian counterparts.

of a very few years, into a genuine monetary *union*—one with, most probably, a single currency. Indeed, in December 1991 the governmental leaders of all EMS nations agreed to the Maastricht Treaty, which specified the formation of a monetary union (as well as other ambitious steps in the direction of a more unified Europe). Since that time, however, several major setbacks have occurred, leaving the future highly uncertain. In order to devote attention to both the promise and problems of the EMS, we shall proceed by first describing the EMS as it existed in December 1991 and then turning to subsequent developments.

11.2 The EMS as of December 1991

The central institution of the EMS has from its beginning been the Exchange Rate Mechanism (ERM), a system of fixed but possibly adjustable exchange rates. Each member currency has a par value termed its "central rate," expressed in terms of the European Currency Unit, or ECU.[4] These values imply, moreover, central-rate par values for bilateral rates pertaining to each pair of currencies. The value of each nation's currency is then required to be maintained within a specified percentage of its central value relative to the ECU and to every other currency by means of market interventions conducted by central banks and supported by necessary adjustments in monetary policy. From 1979 through 1992, the specified limits for permissible exchange rate fluctuations were ± 2.25 percent, implying a set of rates pegged within rather narrow bands.[5] Occasional changes in central values were permitted by the rules of the EMS, but only when agreed to by all participating nations. Several adjustments were needed during the system's early years, since toleration of (or addiction to) inflation had differed significantly across member nations, but these adjustments became increasingly rare during the late 1980s. A tabulation of all official changes in central values, from the inception of the ERM in March 1979 through December 1991, is presented as Table 11–1.[6]

When the EMS began operation, its members included Belgium–Luxembourg, Denmark, France, Germany, Italy, Ireland, the Netherlands, and the United Kingdom. The latter, however, did not participate in the ERM until October 1990. Greece, Spain, and Portugal joined the system subsequently, but Greece had not entered the ERM in December 1991.

Although the ERM has been the heart of the EMS, the latter is more than an arrangement for maintaining fixed (but adjustable) exchange rates. In the

---

[4] The term "ecu" is an acronym for European currency unit, but it is also the name of some ancient French coins. In 1337, for example, the *Ecu à la chaise* was minted as a gold coin of 4.53 grams, whereas the *Ecu au soleil* minted in 1475 comprised only 3.50 grams of gold (Grierson, 1975). At various times these had different values in the system of accounts based on livre, sous, and denier (analogous to the British pounds, shillings, and pence).

[5] Exceptions, permitting fluctuations of up to ± 6.0 percent, had been made for Italy, Spain, and the United Kingdom, with these still in force for the latter two nations as of December 1991.

[6] The changes and withdrawals that erupted in 1992 and 1993 will be mentioned later.

230   *Applications*

Table 11–1 EMS Realignments prior to 1992—Changes in Central Rates* (percent).

Date	Belgian franc	Danish krone	German mark	French franc	Italian lira	Irish pound	Netherlands guilder
Sept. 24, 1979		−2.9	+2.0				
Nov. 30, 1979		−4.8					
Mar. 23, 1981					−6.0		
Oct. 05, 1981			+5.5	−3.0	−3.0		+5.5
Feb. 22, 1982	−8.5	−3.0					
June 14, 1982			+4.25	−5.75	−2.75		+4.25
Mar. 21, 1983	+1.5	+2.5	+5.5	−2.5	−2.5	−3.5	+3.5
July 22, 1985	+2.0	+2.0	+2.0	+2.0	−6.0	+2.0	+2.0
Apr. 07, 1986	+1.0	+1.0	+3.0	−3.0			+3.0
Aug. 04, 1986						−8.0	
Jan. 12, 1987	+2.0		+3.0				+2.0
Jan. 08, 1990					−3.7		

* Reported as percentage change in relation to currencies whose bilateral parities remained unchanged, except for realignments of March 21, 1983, and July 22, 1985. In these two cases, the percentages are as shown in the official communiqué.
Source: Ungerer et al. (1990).

words of Ungerer et al. (1983, p. 2), the EMS "has a political dimension that makes adherence to the system not just a question of economic expediency. Features such as the ECU, the procedures to decide in common about exchange rate changes, and the general emphasis on the convergence of economic policies and developments underline the community aspect of the EMS and the mutual dependence and responsibility of its members." And since those words were written, over a decade ago, the extension of the "political dimension" has been dramatic, as will be stressed in Section 11.3.

It was mentioned that central values of exchange rates are expressed in relation to the ECU, the official unit of account of the EMS. This unit plays other roles as well. In particular, it serves as the official accounting unit for use in transactions not only for all EMS-related institutions, including the European Monetary Cooperation Fund and various credit facilities, but also for all financial activities of the European Community itself—its budget, agricultural regulations, development fund, and so on.[7] The ECU was intended to serve, in addition, as a major reserve and settlement asset for the central banks of the EMS member nations. Some discussion of the nature of the ECU is, accordingly, of importance for the understanding of the EMS.

Basically, the ECU is a unit of account defined as a "bundle" or "basket" of currencies of member nations. In principle, that is, the ECU consists of a specified number of Belgian francs, plus a specified number of Danish kroner, plus a specified number of French francs, and so on, with the exact number of

[7] The European Community was, in December 1991, the name of the organization that began in 1958 as the European Economic Community. Currently its title is the European Union.

Table 11–2 Composition of the ECU.

Currency	Number of currency units in official basket		
	Mar. 13, 1979 to Sept. 14, 1984	Sept. 17, 1984 to Sept. 18, 1989	Since Sept. 21, 1989
Belgian franc	3.66	3.71	3.30
Danish krone	0.217	0.219	0.1976
French franc	1.15	1.31	1.332
German mark	0.828	0.719	0.6242
Irish pound	0.00759	0.00871	0.008552
Italian lira	109.00	140.00	151.8
Luxembourg franc	0.14	0.14	0.131
Netherlands guilder	0.286	0.256	0.2198
British pound	0.0885	0.0878	0.08784
Greek drachma	—	1.15	1.44
Spanish peseta	—	—	6.885
Portuguese escudo	—	—	1.393

Source: Financial Times, various issues.

each of the constituent currencies being as indicated in the final column of Table 11–2. (Columns one and two of Table 11–2 indicate the composition of the ECU in earlier periods between 1979 and 1989; EMS regulations originally called for redefinitions designed to keep the relative weights of the various currencies approximately constant and to bring into the bundle currencies of new members.) With the composition of the ECU thus fixed, its value relative to constituent currencies will vary somewhat from day to day as the bilateral exchange rates vary within their specified limits—and will change discretely at the time of any central-rate realignments. In the absence of revisions in the ECU's definition, its value would tend to be progressively more dependent upon those currencies that rise in relative value at the time of realignments, such as the DM and the Dutch guilder, and less dependent on those currencies that depreciate, such as the Italian lira.[8]

Since different currencies have different values, the numbers of currency units given in Table 11–2 do not indicate the relative importance of the various components—i.e., individual currencies—in determining the value of an ECU. Such magnitudes can, however, readily be determined by using current exchange rates to value each component, in terms of whatever reference currency is chosen, and then adding these 12 values together. A sample calculation pertaining to December 3, 1991, is provided in Table 11–3, with the U.S. dollar used as the reference currency. After summing the component values, it is a very simple matter to determine the fraction of the ECU's total value that is contributed by each component currency. Such fractions, termed "weights," are reported in the final column of Table 11–3. These weights will vary slightly

---

[8] This is one reason for the periodic redefinitions mentioned. These have been halted by the Maastricht Treaty.

Table 11–3 ECU Component Weights.

Currency	Units per ECU	Dollar price per* unit, Dec. 3, 1991	Value of component	Fraction or weight
Belgian franc	3.30	0.0301	0.0993	0.0786
Danish krone	0.1976	0.1594	0.0315	0.0249
French franc	1.332	0.1814	0.2416	0.1913
German mark	0.6242	0.6197	0.3868	0.3064
Irish pound	0.00855	1.650	0.0141	0.0112
Italian lira	151.8	0.000822	0.1248	0.0988
Luxembourg franc	0.131	0.0301	0.0039	0.0031
Netherlands guilder	0.2198	0.5499	0.1209	0.0957
British pound	0.08784	1.7715	0.1556	0.1232
Greek drachma	1.44	0.00544	0.0078	0.0062
Spanish peseta	6.885	0.00971	0.0668	0.0529
Portuguese escudo	1.393	0.00699	0.0097	0.0077
			1.2628	1.0000

Source: New York Times.

from day to day as bilateral rates change, and will change to a greater extent whenever central-value realignments occur. On any given day, the weights should be independent of the reference currency used in their determination.

As an asset, the ECU's role is limited by the fact that it is not an actual currency—tangible ECU coins and banknotes do not exist. Instead, ECU assets are *claims* (expressed in ECU units) of EMS central banks on each other or on agencies of the European Community. Thus the various national central banks will hold ECU-denominated deposit accounts with each other that can be credited or debited to make payments. Only a few specially designated private banks hold central bank ECU deposits, however, or have ECU deposits with central banks. Consequently, the official ECU is as an asset transferable only among central banks, with minor exceptions. Private individuals or businesses cannot, therefore, use the official ECU as an asset for making transactions with each other. They can, however, denominate private loans in terms of the ECU unit of account. Indeed, such practices have become quite important. They lie entirely outside the sphere of the official ECU as an asset, however, and so will be discussed separately in Section 11.5.[9]

Other features of the EMS include rules concerning mutual lines of credit among central banks, designed to facilitate exchange market intervention needed to keep rates within their specified bands, and also slightly longer term credit facilities for nations experiencing temporary balance-of-payments

[9] Another intangible basket currency is the SDR, mentioned in Sections 3.2 and 4.5, which was introduced by the IMF in 1969 as an additional form of international reserves. As of July 1994, the composition of an SDR was 0.452 U.S. dollars, 0.527 German marks, 33.4 Japanese yen, 1.01 French francs, and 0.0893 British pounds.

difficulties at prevailing exchange rates. For additional discussion of EMS arrangements, and also a useful chronology, the reader is referred to Ungerer et al. (1990).

In judging how well the EMS functioned over the dozen years prior to 1992, one should not consider only that the organization had stayed together and reduced the extent of fluctuations in members' exchange rates. In principle, it is desirable also to look at the macroeconomic performance of the member nations, since keeping an exchange rate fixed amounts to one way of conducting monetary policy. In this regard it is somewhat impressive to note that the inflation rates of member countries had tended to converge toward a common value, as required for full long-run equilibria under fixed rates (recall Chapter 6). Some relevant figures are reported in Table 11–4. Performance in terms of unemployment rates had not been so good, however, as Table 11–5 documents all too clearly. In fact, long-lasting unemployment at levels unimagined during the 1950s and 1960s was the major European economic problem of the 1980s. It seems unlikely, however, that this problem can be attributed to the exchange rate regime. Long-run output–employment behavior is, according to orthodox neoclassical analysis as well as our model of Chapters 5–8, independent of the choice of exchange rate systems—flexible or fixed.

Finally, some attention should be given to the growth of trade between member nations of the EMS. In Table 11–6 growth in the volume of intra-ERM international trade is compared with values for previous years and for countries not in the ERM. The figures do not suggest that the exchange rate stability within the ERM stimulated any increased volume of trade among its member nations.

Table 11–4 CPI Inflation Rates under EMS

Nation or Region	Annual Averages for Years Indicated			
	1975–1978	1979–1982	1983–1986	1987–1990
Belgium	8.4	6.9	5.0	2.3
Denmark	9.9	10.9	5.4	4.0
France	10.0	12.3	6.3	3.2
Germany	4.2	5.3	1.9	1.8
Ireland	14.2	17.3	7.1	3.2
Italy	16.1	18.0	9.7	5.7
Netherlands	7.5	5.8	2.1	0.9
Portugal	22.1	20.7	21.3	11.25
Spain	19.0	15.1	10.3	5.9
United Kingdom	17.8	13.0	4.8	6.6
Non-ERM Europe*	11.0	9.8	5.2	5.2
Other industrial[†]	9.2	8.9	4.5	4.6

* Average for Austria, Norway, Spain, Sweden, Switzerland, and United Kingdom.

[†] Average for Australia, Canada, Japan, and United States.

Source: Ungerer et al. (1990); IMF, *International Financial Statistics*.

Table 11–5 Unemployment Experience under EMS.

	Averages for Years Indicated				
Nation	1971–1974	1975–1978	1979–1982	1983–1986	1987–1990
Belgium	3.5	8.9	13.4	17.6	13.9
Denmark	1.8	6.8	8.0	9.6	9.0
France	2.8	4.8	7.1	9.8	7.2
Germany	1.5	4.5	5.2	9.1	8.2
Ireland	NA	8.7	9.4	16.8	18.1
Italy	5.9	6.8	8.2	10.3	11.9
Netherlands	2.7	5.1	8.2	16.2	13.9*

* Value for 1987, 1988 only. Statistical procedures revised, leading to discontinuity in series. New series gives value of 5.3 for 1989–1990 (and 6.4 for 1987).

Source: OECD, *Main Economic Indicators: Historical Statistics.*

Table 11–6 Trade Experience under EMS.

	Annual percentage growth in real exports plus imports			
	With ERM Nations		With Non-ERM Nations	
Nation	1973–1978	1979–1986	1973–1978	1979–1986
Belgium	7.7	2.2	12.5	4.5
Denmark	12.8	3.8	5.2	3.2
France	6.8	2.9	8.5	5.7
Germany	7.0	2.9	7.6	6.8
Ireland	20.0	9.4	8.2	4.8
Italy	4.6	8.1	5.4	10.1
Netherlands	6.2	2.4	10.5	5.3
Canada	4.4	6.5	4.2	7.2
Japan	11.6	9.5	7.2	10.0
Sweden	6.0	4.6	3.8	4.9
Switzerland	8.0	4.5	6.8	3.8
United Kingdom	11.4	5.4	5.1	4.2
United States	4.4	7.3	4.2	8.5

Source: Belongia (1988).

11.3 The Maastricht Treaty

As of the end of 1991 it seemed almost certain—as a result of the December 9–10 European summit meeting in Maastricht—that the EMS would within a decade be converted into a full-fledged *currency union* of several nations with a single currency and a unified monetary policy. The purpose of this section is to summarize plans as expressed in the Maastricht Treaty and to outline the process that led, rapidly and dramatically, to their development over the years of 1989–1991.

An important prior development in terms of European economic unification was Project 1992, a program designed to remove remaining impediments (within the European Community) to trade and movement across borders of goods and services, capital, and labor. This program, which was set in motion by the Single Europe Act of 1985, preceded and stimulated action regarding monetary union. That action began in earnest with the so-called Delors Report of April 1989. This was the report of a committee chaired by Jacques Delors, President of the European Commission,[10] that recommended monetary unification to be carried out in a series of three stages.[11] Plans for the first stage were accepted by the European Council[12] in June 1989 (Madrid summit) and put into effect in July 1990. The contents of the Delors Report may be best summarized by listing the steps toward monetary union that were specified to be taken at each stage. These were as follows.

Stage One was specified as bringing about "full participation" in the ERM by all members of the EMS, by which was meant successful adoption of the regular ± 2.25 percent bands for their exchange rates. There was also supposed to be greater cooperation among the central banks of member nations and considerable convergence[13] of macroeconomic policies and conditions.

In Stage Two, then, the exchange rate bands would be tightened further— according to the Delors Report— and central-rate realignments would become a "last resort" means of adjustment. Also, this stage was to see the creation of a European System of Central Banks (ESCB), an organization including all member central banks that would have some very limited powers of monetary management.

Finally, in Stage Three there would be "irrevocable" fixing of exchange rates and a unified monetary policy—including external exchange rate policy—that would be taken over by the newly created Council of the ESCB. This Council would be composed of the governors of the national central banks plus the members of an ESCB Board, who would be appointed by the European Council. The ESCB Council members would be independent, that is, not open to instructions from national governments or authorities of the European Community. Furthermore, the ESCB "would be committed to the objective of

[10] The European Commission is an appointed agency of the European Union (EU) that has 17 members. These members are in principle civil servants of the EU, not national representatives. The European Commission functions as something of an executive body for the EU.

[11] The Delors Report was also concerned with various nonmonetary matters regarding Project 1992. Indeed, the report was officially designated "Report on Economic and Monetary Union in the European Community."

[12] The European Council is not a collection of individuals, but a forum in which relevant ministers from all nations of the European Union meet to consider and act upon proposed legislation. A meeting concerning agricultural issues might, for example, bring together the ministers of agriculture from each member nation. For matters of great scope or importance, the nations' representatives will be their prime ministers (or the president in the case of France), in which event the meeting will be a "summit."

[13] Here convergence means "coming together"; thus convergence of inflation rates, for example, means that these rates in different countries should become nearly equal in value.

price stability." The creation of a common currency was mentioned as a "natural outcome" of monetary union, but was not expressly specified by the Delors Report.

As events transpired, Stage One did begin in July 1990. Subsequent to that time, the United Kingdom entered the ERM—on October 8, 1990, with ±6.0 percent bands—and Italy reduced its bandwidth to the regular ±2.25 percent. During most of the calendar year 1991 an intergovernmental conference worked on details concerning Stages Two and Three, producing a document that was submitted for consideration at Maastricht. The agreement that was finally reached at the Maastricht summit included several changes and additions relative to the Delors Report. Some of these stemmed from desires of the German officials to end up with a system that would be as reliable a safeguard against inflation as the Bundesbank, which would be required in Stage Three to surrender its policy-making power.

Some of the more important provisions of the Maastricht Treaty[14] were that Stage Two would begin on January 1, 1994, with the new organization of central banks to be known as the European Monetary Institute (EMI), rather than the ESCB. This terminological change was designed to emphasize that the organization's task will be mainly to prepare the way for Stage Three, not to take over policy from the Bundesbank and other national central banks. Then in Stage Three the EMI would become the European Central Bank (ECB). According to the treaty, that stage would begin on January 1, 1997, if a majority of the members of the EMS have achieved certain specified convergence criteria—pertaining to exchange rates,[15] inflation,[16] interest rates, and fiscal behavior—and if a qualified majority voted to begin.[17] Otherwise Stage Three would begin in 1999, with the participation of only those nations that had achieved the convergence goals, others joining in later after achieving convergence.[18] Thus it seemed almost certain in early 1992 that at least a few nations would form a single-currency monetary union by 1999 at the latest.

One notable feature of the Maastricht Treaty was that the United Kingdom was given the special privilege of deciding later, by a vote of Parliament, whether to participate in the single-currency union. Also, Denmark was to be permitted to ratify its decision to join by means of a national referendum. For all other

[14] It should be mentioned that the Maastricht summit and treaty were concerned with provisions for political union as well as monetary unification. For a careful discussion of the latter, see Kenen (1992).

[15] The requirement is that "... the Member State has respected the normal fluctuation margins ... without severe tensions for at least the last two years.... In particular, the Member State shall not have devalued its currency's bilateral central rate against any other Member State's currency on its own initiative for the same period."

[16] The inflation-rate criterion, for example, is that over the previous year the rate for the nation in question should be within 1.5 percentage points (on an annual basis) of the third lowest rate recorded by any member.

[17] A "qualified majority" is a majority on a ballot that counts the votes of different nations differently, a large nation in effect getting more votes than a small nation.

[18] At least in the case of the fiscal goals, the treaty provides for some flexibility in deciding whether adequate convergence has been achieved.

nations, by contrast, the treaty constituted an agreement to enter the monetary union as soon as all the specified conditions were met. Ratification of the treaty by the separate national governments was thought to be a foregone conclusion, with the process requiring a public referendum only in Denmark.

Clearly, this agreement of sovereign nations to give up their national currencies, and their control over monetary policy, constituted a dramatic and historic step. It should be considered, therefore, whether there is a strong or clear economic justification for the additional step—beyond that of "irrevocably fixing" their exchange rates—of adopting a common currency. In this regard, the critical observation is that policy autonomy is surrendered by a move to either truly fixed exchange rates or a common currency, but the full gains in terms of increased transactional efficiency come only from the latter. A system with fixed rates eliminates uncertainty concerning rates within the system, but still requires currency exchanges that are costly to participants. It would seem, therefore, that there is a prima facie case for moving on to a single currency, if it is determined that fixed exchange rates will be adopted.

It is worth considering, nevertheless, the *magnitude* of the transaction-cost savings that promise to be reaped by the final step of eliminating separate currencies. Are these costs large quantitatively or trivially small? In response to that question, it is necessary to admit that the magnitudes are difficult to estimate and that, as a consequence, very little research has been devoted to the topic. One set of estimates has been produced, however, by a study group of the European Community. Let us then briefly consider the magnitudes obtained by that study.[19]

The most straightforward type of transaction cost that would be avoided by adoption of a single currency is measured—under the presumption that charges reflect resource costs incurred by banks or other organizations providing the service—by explicit fees charged for conversions from one currency to another. In the case of tourists and very small businesses, these charges are made for conversion of banknotes, traveler's checks, Eurocheques,[20] and credit cards. Given their recent volume, the EC study estimates savings on the order of 1.8–2.5 billion ECU per year for such transactions. Much larger sums are involved, however, in the "wholesale" interbank market in foreign exchange—the market for large deposit transfers whose exchange rates are reported daily in the *Financial Times*, the *Wall Street Journal*, and elsewhere. Although transaction charges are much smaller[21] as a fraction of the sums exchanged, those sums are so much larger that the resulting magnitude of their transaction charges is substantially greater. The EC study's estimate, to be specific, is in the range of 6.4–10.6 billion ECU per year. Together, then, these two types of explicit transaction charges that could be avoided by the adoption of a single currency come to about 8.2–13.1 billion ECU per year.

[19] Results are reported in a document published by the Commission of the European Community entitled *European Economy No. 44, One Market, One Money* (Oct. 1990).

[20] Eurocheques are checks that can be expressed in various European currencies and cleared via a network of participating banks. There is an upper limit of roughly $200 on the payment guarantee.

[21] At least one order of magnitude, that is, a factor of 10. See Chown and Wood (1991, p. 44).

In addition, substantial resource savings should be possible within large multinational firms, that is, savings in terms of accounting and managerial activities that are needed only because of complexities brought about by their dealings in numerous European currencies. Estimating the magnitude of these costs is perhaps even more difficult and fraught with uncertainty than in the case of explicit (external) transaction charges, but the EC study made an attempt. Their range of values obtained was 3.6–4.8 billion ECU per year, an estimated magnitude between those pertaining to explicit charges in the "retail" and "wholesale" markets.

Finally, the EC study also lists charges for making *cross-border* payments per se, with an estimated saving of 1.3 billion ECU per year from the adoption of a single currency.[22] Adding together all four categories yields, then, a range of potential savings that extends from 13.1 to 19.2 billion ECU per year. Such numbers are not trivial, of course, but neither are they large in relation to the combined national incomes of the EMS nations. With a combined 1990 GDP of about 4600 billion, that is, the cost savings from moving to a single currency would be just about 0.4 percent of total income. One is inclined to suspect, therefore, that the enthusiasm of the European Community for the single-currency development has been motivated largely by a belief or feeling that the existence of a single currency would bind the nations together more closely and thereby be of great political importance.

It should of course be asked if there are only benefits—cost savings—to be had from movement to a single currency; are there no costs? In response it must be admitted that there would be *some* costs incurred, even if relatively small. These costs are of a one-time nature, however, rather than of the type that are repeated year after year. The most obvious is the resource cost of printing and coining the new currency; its neglect represents a typical practice by monetary economists (who almost invariably neglect the resource costs of a fiat-money system). Somewhat less obvious, but arguably much larger in magnitude, is the cost of businesses and especially individuals throughout Europe having to learn to work with the new and unfamiliar monetary units. In principle, these one-time costs should be compared with the present value of the future benefits discussed above.

In the discussion prior to the Maastricht meeting, one issue that was much debated is whether monetary unification with a single currency requires that the member nations coordinate their *fiscal* policies. They would all have the same monetary policy, with a single currency in use, but would that require a common fiscal stance? Evidently a common fiscal policy would not be strictly required; the existence of different fiscal traditions in the states of the United States demonstrates that point conclusively. But what was feared by proponents of fiscal coordination (e.g., German representatives) was that some nations would run large government deficits and borrow to an excessive extent. This would force up interest rates and thereby put pressure on the ECB to finance

---

[22] It is unclear to this writer why such charges could not be eliminated under a fixed-rate scheme with multiple currencies, in which case they should not actually be included in the current reckoning.

the deficit spending by money creation—which would have inflationary potential for the entire monetary union. But a rather convincing response is that if the ECB makes price-level stability its overriding goal and refuses to finance deficits from any nation, then the problem would be avoided. Then if, say, Italy were to borrow excessively, European lenders would come to require higher interest rates on loans to the Italian government than to others. And if the ECB avoids validation of the borrowing, then Italy would be the sufferer, not the whole community.

11.4 Post-Maastricht Developments

After the signing of the Maastricht Treaty, rapid progress toward monetary unification appeared virtually certain. But each nation had some internal steps that were necessary for ratification of the treaty. In Denmark, a national referendum was constitutionally required and, to the surprise of most observers, the nation's voters failed to ratify the treaty on June 3, 1992. The margin of rejection was very narrow, but nevertheless this vote suggested that the treaty's plans for European integration were much less popular with the people of Europe than with their political leaders. The very next day, President Mitterand scheduled a September 20 referendum for France, even though such a step was not needed for ratification.[23] Soon thereafter market pressures began pushing down the exchange values of the currencies of Britain, Italy, Finland, and Sweden.[24] The opinion pools from France gave signs that the outcome of the September 20 referendum was in doubt. Since another negative vote would seriously jeopardize the existing plans for monetary (and political) union,[25] thereby undermining the existence of the EMS and ERM, these poll results led to much speculative activity against the lira and the pound. The lira was devalued on September 12, but as September 20 approached, the speculative pressures intensified and finally overwhelmed the efforts of the EMS central banks to maintain exchange rates within their ERM limits. Finally on September 17, the Spanish peseta was devalued while Italy and Britain suspended their participation in the ERM, leaving their currencies to float.

Speculators, who had been betting that the peseta, lira, and pound could not be kept within their ERM bands, made enormous profits on these events and turned their attention next to the French franc, Irish pound, Portuguese escudo, Danish krone, and the Scandinavian currencies. Major interventions by the Bundesbank and the other affected central banks were needed to keep

[23] Apparently he believed that the French public would give strong support to the treaty and thereby positively influence citizens of other nations.

[24] Although Finland and Sweden were not members of the EMS, they (and Norway) were pegging their exchange rates with the ECU. In part, this was to prepare for possible admission to the European Community and the EMS.

[25] In this regard it should be mentioned that, as a formal matter, the Maastricht Treaty was being treated as a set of amendments to the Treaty of Rome, which established the European Economic Community in 1958. This fact is important because such amendments require unanimous approval of all nations to be adopted.

these currencies within their bands—and even so there were devaluations of the peseta and the escudo in November. Both Finland and Sweden were forced to let their currencies float, despite overnight lending rates by the Swedish Riksbank as high as 500 percent (per annum)!

Was there any logical basis for the speculative attacks on these different currencies? In some cases there was reason to believe that their real exchange values were too high, relative to the German mark, because of recent inflation or current fiscal imbalances. But in all cases it was true that monetary policy was being forced to be tighter than current domestic conditions warranted in order to prevent depreciation against the German mark, German monetary policy being rather tight in an effort to combat perceived inflationary pressures stemming from the German reunification of July 1, 1990, and some associated fiscal laxity. And it is possible that to some extent speculators decided that speculative attacks, which would be enormously profitable if successful, could not be defeated by central banks since the speculators could overwhelm the limited resources of central banks.[26]

Market conditions remained relatively peaceful during the first half of 1993, although there were three more devaluations—of the Irish pound in February and the peseta and the escudo in May. During this period, there appeared many complaints in the media (some stemming from central banks) that the German Bundesbank was following an overly stringent policy geared excessively to domestic conditions (and perhaps unwisely so, at that). Then in mid-July another major outbreak of speculation began against the French franc, Belgian franc, Danish krone, and the peseta and the escudo. When the Bundesbank failed, in its meeting of July 29, to lower the discount rate as anticipated— it did reduce the Lombard rate slightly[27]—the markets reacted strongly and the French, Belgian, and Danish exchange rates fell below their ERM limits.

Over the weekend of July 31–August 1, the EMS finance ministers and central bank governors held an emergency meeting to decide how to handle this crisis situation. The action taken, effective immediately, was to widen the allowable EMS exchange rate bands from ±2.25 to ±15.0 percent. Doing so obviously gave each nation much greater latitude to implement a monetary policy more nearly appropriate to its domestic cyclical conditions. From one perspective this step might be viewed as the end of the ERM, since it would

---

[26] On typical days, roughly $1000 billion worth of foreign exchange is traded. So if net sales of a currency, say French francs, were one percent of that sum on a given day, the amount would be $10 billion. Indeed, during September 1992 there were reportedly some days in which net private sales of francs amounted to $7–9 billion. To support the franc by buying these excess supplies, the Bank of France must sell off its reserves of foreign exchange. But the Bank of France's total foreign exchange reserves amounted to only about $29 billion as of August 1992. For more detail and an extensive discussion of the September 1992 ERM crisis, see Goldstein et al. (1993).

[27] The Bundesbank's discount rate is the interest rate charged banks for loans that normally constitute a significant fraction of the monetary base. It is a subsidy rate, usually below current market clearing rates, so the quantity of discount rate loans is strictly rationed. The Lombard rate is a higher rate at which the Bundesbank will make day-to-day loans to banks with an exceptional and temporary need for base money. The usual quantity of Lombard loans is very small.

no longer be keeping exchange rates approximately fixed. But the EMS officials expressed a reaffirmation of the existing central parities and an intention to continue, more or less as planned, the steps toward monetary union. In fact, there was apparently an intention to regard those nations with currencies remaining within the new ± 15.0 percent bands as satisfying the Maastricht Treaty's convergence requirement that a nation's exchange rate must have "respected the normal fluctuation margins ... for at least the last two years." (Whether that interpretation of the treaty will hold up remains to be seen.) In addition, the officially announced position included the intention of returning to an arrangement with narrower bands as soon as circumstances would permit.

During the first year following this "modification" or "breakdown" of the ERM, depending on one's point of view, the experiences were reasonably favorable.[28] No currency in the ERM—Britain and Italy remained out—violated the ± 15.0 percent bands, or even came close to doing so. Macroeconomic conditions improved in several nations, partly in response to loosened monetary conditions.[29] As of July 31, 1994, however, it is extremely difficult to be confident about the future course of the EMS's drive toward monetary unification. Possibly the most likely outcome is the creation of a monetary union including only Germany and the Benelux countries—Belgium, Luxembourg, and the Netherlands. If France were to join this group, then a major historic step would have been taken, paving the way for additional members at later dates. But without some large nation besides Germany, the organization would risk being viewed as a GMU rather than an EMU. Yet France is perhaps reluctant to join without Italy, which would provide a counterweight to German influence—after all, a major motivation in France for the EMU is to replace Bundesbank monetary leadership with that of a European entity not under German dominance. Apparently Italy would like to be a member nation from the outset, but the consistent German position has been that only countries with good anti-inflationary records and encouraging fiscal prospects may be admitted—partly because the German public is unenthusiastic—to put it mildly—about the prospect of ECUs replacing German marks as their medium of exchange. In the presence of these conflicting pressures, it is not easy to be optimistic about early prospects for European monetary unification. The attempt remains one of enormous interest, nevertheless, and will be closely watched by all students of monetary economics and international affairs.[30]

[28] Ironically, the Maastricht Treaty was ratified by the U.K. Parliament on September 5, 1993, just a few weeks after the July 31–August 1 ERM debacle. Shortly thereafter the treaty passed its last legal hurdle in Germany, thereby attaining ratification in all 12 member nations. The treaty was formally adopted at the end of October and took effect officially on November 1, 1993.

[29] For a more detailed chronology of the ERM developments from June 1992 to September 1993, see International Monetary Fund (1993).

[30] For a useful alternative discussion of events since December 1991, see Whitt (1994). Also, an alternative version of many of this chapter's topics is provided by Bean (1992).

11.5 Alternative Forms of ECU

The main purpose of this section is to discuss other forms of the European currency unit besides the official ECU unit of account. It will be useful to begin, however, by briefly reviewing the position on monetary unification taken by the United Kingdom, which over the years has expressed opposition to the Delors Report and other plans for a unified currency. This opposition has been based in part on the loss of monetary autonomy that is implied by a single currency—or by truly fixed exchange rates. That the United Kingdom has taken such a position has been viewed as ironic by several commentators, since its inflationary experience has been distinctly worse than that of Germany and, indeed, most of the nations that have been members of the ERM since 1979. Be that as it may, the U.K. representatives put forth several counter proposals and arguments concerning European monetary union, especially the move to a single currency, that are of some interest despite all the events that have taken place subsequently.

The first of the British counterproposals (November 1989) suggested that the economic case for adoption of a single currency was not fully established by the Delors Report, and argued that it would be better to take an "evolutionary, market-driven" approach to monetary union. The idea was to eliminate restrictions in each nation on the use of other nations' currencies in conducting domestic transactions. Then there would be a tendency, according to the British argument, for the currencies of stable noninflationary nations to be used more widely and those of high-inflation nations to be used less widely. Since it is in a nation's interest to have its currency used widely,[31] there would then be a tendency for less inflation to be generated by the nations of the EMS. If one currency became dominant through this process of "currency competition," that fact would constitute evidence that its adoption was desirable—and if it did not, movement to a single currency would not be economically justifiable and should not be "imposed."

The foregoing proposal met with general disapproval by the other nations of the EMS, which viewed it as entirely nonconstructive. A second British proposal, put forth by the U.K. Treasury in June 1990, was more constructive. It generated substantially more interest and was for a few months considered to be a serious rival to the Delors proposals. This proposal for a "hard ECU" did not win out in the process culminating at Maastricht, as we have seen, but remains of interest nevertheless. The proposal was to create a new European currency, termed the hard ECU, that could facilitate a gradual move toward a full monetary union. Whereas the existing ECU is little more than a unit of account, the proposed hard ECU would be an actual tangible currency with some special features. In particular, it would be "hard" in the sense that it would never fall in value (except within intervention limits) against any of the EMS national currencies—its central value would never fall relative to any

---

[31] When agents in one nation hold currency issued by another nation, the effect is that of an interest-free loan from the first nation to the second.

EMS currency. This property would make the hard ECU attractive to money holders. One can imagine that it could become widely used throughout the EU, with individuals and businesses holding stocks of hard ECUs as well as their national currencies. This tendency would be enhanced if it were agreed to make the hard ECU legal tender in all member countries, although that was not part of the British proposal. Such an impetus might be needed since merchants would be resistant to the hard ECU's introduction, which would complicate their cash-handling facilities.[32]

In any event, the British proposal was that a new organization, dubbed the European Monetary Fund (EMF), would issue hard ECU notes and deposits in exchange for national currencies of member nations. The EMF would hold 100 percent reserves, so there would be no direct effect on the total money supply of the European Community. The "hard" feature—never being devalued—would imply that any time an exchange rate realignment took place, the EMF would suffer a capital loss on its holdings of the devaluated currencies. Accordingly, the EMF would be given the right to sell national currencies back to member central banks at rates prevailing before the realignment. An alternative possibility would be to permit the EMF to impose financial penalties on devaluing nations.

The U.K. Treasury argued that the presence of the hard ECU would tend to induce member central banks to avoid inflation to a greater extent than otherwise. This position is somewhat dubious, but the proposal was designed in a way that should at least keep it from being inflationary. More generally the basic idea of the proposal seems rather sensible—the hard ECU would have been attractive to travelers and others with international transactions to conduct, and could have conceivably evolved into the European Community's single currency. But the proposal did not win support, in part, perhaps, because it came along at too late a date.

To this point we have discussed the official ECU of the EMS and the British Treasury's hard ECU proposal. The latter has not been adopted, however, so hard ECU assets do not exist. And official ECU claims are only available to EMS central banks and a few other institutions. Neither of these ECU instruments is, therefore, traded in actual financial markets of Europe. *Privately issued* ECU deposits and securities are traded, however, and indeed have been of quantitative significance: as of March 1991, bank liabilities denominated in terms of ECUs totaled almost $200 billion whereas ECU bonds outstanding came to about $80 billion.[33] It is of importance, therefore, to consider briefly the nature of these private Ecu—or, henceforth, simply Ecu—instruments.[34]

The main question to be considered may be put as follows: Precisely what

[32] That an ECU currency would be attractive to individuals, even if it were not "hard" as in the U.K. proposal, has been argued by Chown and Wood (1991).

[33] These sums are on the order of 5 percent of the totals for all currency denominations on international markets.

[34] The parenthetical phrase indicates that we will henceforth use the term Ecu to refer to private Ecus, reserving the uppercase designation ECU to refer to the official basket.

does it mean to say that a bank deposit or a security is "denominated in Ecu"? One might think that this phrase would imply that the owner of an Ecu deposit could redeem it for an equal number of ECU baskets—that the holder of a 100 Ecu deposit could obtain from his bank 62.42 DM plus 133.2 French francs; plus ... . Or, since transactions with such baskets of currencies would be inconvenient, that he could obtain a quantity of his nation's currency equal to 100 times the current exchange value of an ECU basket, calculated as in Table 11–3. If this were the case, then an Ecu would have the same value as an ECU basket.

In fact, the latter option was available from the early 1980s through most of 1987. Up until October 1987, that is, an Ecu deposit could be redeemed for the value equivalent of an ECU. This was possible because a few major European banks were intervening in the market so as to peg at 1.0 the exchange value of Ecu deposits in terms of ECU baskets. All but one of these banks halted their Ecu pegging activities in October 1987, however, and the remaining bank did so in November 1988.[35] Since that time, consequently, the value of the Ecu relative to the ECU has fluctuated around 1.0, and with departures that are not trivial in magnitude or duration. Prior to 1992 the Ecu/ECU exchange rate departed from 1.0 by as much as 40 basis points (i.e., 40/100 of one percent) several times and once by 90 basis points. Then in September 1992, during the time of the ERM crisis, the Ecu/ECU rate exceeded 1.0 by more than 50 basis points for a few weeks, with a discrepancy of over 200 basis points occurring on September 18 and again on September 24. Daily observations from December 4, 1991, through February 18, 1993, are plotted in Figure 11–1 (where gaps represent weekends or other days on which the Brussels foreign exchange market was closed). During this 443-day span the Ecu was less valuable than an ECU basket most of the time, but the opposite has been true during other periods. In particular, the Ecu/ECU rate stayed below 1.0 throughout the second half of 1990 and the first two months of 1991.

Essentially the same situation holds, furthermore, for Ecu bonds and other Ecu securities, because these are basically claims to ECU deposits. Thus to value Ecu securities in terms of ECU—or national currencies—the crucial step is to determine the ECU value of Ecu deposits.

Our discussion has emphasized that the Ecu rate currently varies against the ECU since many observers—and even some market participants—seem to believe incorrectly that an Ecu is a claim to (the value equivalent of) one ECU basket. But such is simply not the case under current institutional arrangements (as of July 1994). It is quite possible that these arrangements could change in the future,[36] but as of December 1991 there is no necessary one-to-one connection between the value of an Ecu and that of an ECU basket. It is consequently a dubious practice to say that Ecu deposits are "deposits

---

[35] The final bank was Kredietbank N.V. of Belgium. For more details, see Folkerts-Landau and Garber (1992) and Steinherr et al. (1991).

[36] Some analysts seem to think it likely that the ECB, or the central banks of the EMS, will begin to peg the value of the Ecu at 1.0 ECU at some time in the future. To this writer that possibility seems unlikely.

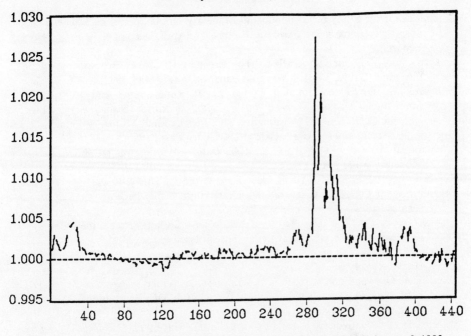

Figure 11–1 Exchange rate, Ecu per ECU basket, December 4, 1991–February 8, 1993. *Source*: Kredietbank N.V.

denominated in ECU," and it is entirely uninformative to say that "Ecu deposits are deposits denominated in Ecu." It is also misleading to suggest that "the ECU or Ecu will become the single currency of Europe." The ECU cannot become the single currency because it is not a currency at all; it is merely a unit of account. And it is unlikely that the EMS would provide official status for the Ecu, as that would entail a large financial obligation. What actually does seem likely (if monetary unification occurs) is that the EMS will develop a new currency named "ECU" based on the ECU basket; a new currency that would initially consist of claims to ECU baskets (or to the equivalent value in other currencies) and would then turn into the single EMS currency by a process that would entail the discontinuation of marks, francs, pounds, and so on.

References

Bean, C. R., "Economic and Monetary Union in Europe," *Journal of Economic Perspectives* **6** (Fall 1992), 31–52.

Belongia, M. T., "Prospects for International Policy Coordination: Some Lessons from the EMS," *Federal Reserve Bank of St. Louis Review* **70** (July/Aug. 1988), 19–29.

Chown, J., and G. Wood, *The Road to Monetary Union*. London: Institute of Directors, 1991.

Commission of the European Communities, European Economy no. 44, *One Market, One Money* (Oct. 1990).

Committee for the Study of Economic and Monetary Union. *Report on Economic and Monetary Union in the European Community* (Apr. 1989). [This is the "Delors Report."]

Folkerts-Landau, D., and P. Garber, "The Private ECU: A Currency Floating on Gossamer Wings," NBER Working Paper no. 4017 (Mar. 1992).

Goldstein, M., D. Folkerts-Landau, P. Garber, L. Rojas-Suárez, and M. Spencer, *International Capital Markets: Part I, Exchange Rate Management and International Capital Flows.* Washington, DC: International Monetary Fund, 1993.

Grierson, P., *Numismatics.* Oxford: Oxford University Press, 1975.

International Monetary Fund, *World Economic Outlook* Washington, DC: International Monetary Fund (Oct. 1993).

Kenen, P. B., *ECU after Maastricht.* New York: Group of Thirty, 1992.

Organization for Economic Cooperation and Development, *Main Economic Indicators*, various issues.

Steinherr, A., et al., "The Ecu—To Be or Not to Be a Basket—That is the Question," *Ecu Banking Association Newsletter*, Special Issue 6, June 1991.

Tew, B., *The Evolution of the International Monetary System, 1945–1988.* London: Hutchinson, 1988.

Ungerer, H., O. Evans, and P. Nyberg, *The European Monetary System: The Experience, 1979–1982.* Occasional Paper no. 19. Washington, DC: International Monetary Fund, 1983.

Ungerer, H., J. J. Hauvonen, A. Lopez-Claros, and T. Mayer, *The European Monetary System: Developments and Perspectives.* Occasional Paper no. 73. Washington, DC: International Monetary Fund, 1990.

Whitt, J. A., Jr., "Monetary Union in Europe," *Federal Reserve Bank of Atlanta Economic Review* **79** (Jan./Feb. 1994), 11–27.

Yeager, L. B., *International Monetary Relations: Theory, History, and Policy*, 2nd ed. New York: Harper and Row, 1976.

Problems

1. Suppose the British pound were to appreciate from 1.50$/£ to 1.56 $/£, with other EMS currencies unchanged via-à-vis the dollar. What would be the change, in dollars, in the value of an ECU?

2. Under the circumstances of Problem 1, what would be the initial weight of the pound in the ECU if the $/ECU exchange rate at the time was 1.25?

3. Using data for July 27, 1994 (see Chapter 2), determine ECU component weights.

4. On what types of transaction would the largest resource cost savings be anticipated, if the EMS were to adopt a single currency?

5. In the British proposal of 1990 for a "hard Ecu," what is the meaning of the term "hard?"

6. Using the graphical apparatus of Chapter 7, show how an upward shift in spending relative to saving in Germany could induce a short-run contraction in other member nations of the ERM.

7. In discussions of the creation of a European monetary union, with a single currency or at least a set of exchange rates that are irrevocably fixed, it has been argued that it is important for the "correct" values to be chosen for these exchange rates (or for initial conversion rates of national currencies into ECU). Similarly, it has been argued that when the United Kingdom entered the ERM in October 1990, it did so at an overvalued exchange rate that led to difficulties in 1992. To analyze such issues using the graphical technique of Chapter 7, depict an economy in full equilibrium and then consider the effects of a one-time but permanent decrease in s (i.e., an exchange rate appreciation) that makes the exchange rate differ from its full equilibrium value. What conclusions can be drawn? Are the conclusions different from short-run and long-run perspectives?

12

International Policy Cooperation

12.1 Introduction

In this concluding chapter, the objective is to briefly sketch some analytical results concerning international policy cooperation and then consider that topic from the practical perspective. Before beginning, we need to introduce a pair of conceptual and terminological distinctions that will be important in the discussion. The first of these involves the distinction between cooperation involving macroeconomic policy and that involving international institutions. The former type of cooperation has to do with the settings of monetary and fiscal policy instrument variables (e.g., money-growth or interest rates, tax rates, or levels of government spending) that are chosen each period, either by a rule or in a discretionary fashion. By contrast, the second type of cooperation involves the establishment and maintenance of a monetary system of fixed or flexible exchange rates and also a prevailing set of rules and regulations to govern trade in goods, services, and securities. The institutions relevant for this latter type of cooperation will be changed only infrequently and will therefore be viewed as semiexogenously "given" by the policy makers who choose monetary and fiscal instrument settings several times each year. It is clear that the establishment of international institutions—such as, for example, the IMF, the EMS, and GATT[1]—is inherently a multinational undertaking and will therefore inevitably involve international cooperation. But in the case of macroeconomic policy settings it is not *necessary* that nations cooperate, so the issue of whether cooperation is mutually desirable is an interesting and nontrivial one.

A second distinction of some importance has to do with the difference implied by the terms "cooperation" and "coordination." In the economics literature, the former term has recently been given a comparatively broad meaning, whereas the latter is more specific: coordination is a certain specified type of cooperation. In particular, macroeconomic coordination exists when nations choose their instrument settings in a manner that could make their values differ from those that would be chosen if no account were taken of the

---

[1] Here reference is to the International Monetary Fund, the European Monetary System, and the General Agreement on Tariffs and Trade. In early 1995 the latter evolved into the World Trade Organization.

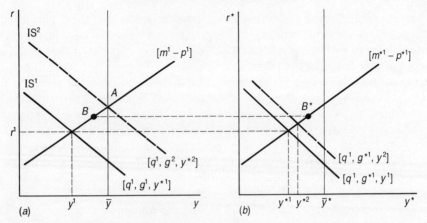

Figure 12–1 Interdependence of large economies. (*a*) Home country. (*b*) Other country.

macroeconomic consequences for other nations.[2] Coordination entails, therefore, some sacrifice of national sovereignty whereas cooperation (without coordination) does not. The latter may involve nothing more drastic, for example, than the exchange of information—an exchange that could, nevertheless, be quite valuable.

12.2 The Case for Coordination

The major analytical result featured in most discussions of international policy cooperation involves a theoretical demonstration that macroeconomic policy coordination can be mutually beneficial in certain circumstances. Any such analysis will, of course, involve two or more economies that are *not* small, that is, that are large enough to affect economic conditions abroad. The main point can be explained most clearly in the context of a two-economy example, similar to the one utilized in Section 6–6. Consider, then, a short-run equilibrium situation with output below capacity (i.e., with above-normal unemployment) in both economies. Assume, moreover, that the situation is one in which trade between these two economies is balanced—net exports equal zero in both economies. Such a situation is depicted by $y = y' < \bar{y}$, $y^* = y^{*1} < \bar{y}^*$, and $r^1 = r^2 = R^1 = R^2$ in Figure 12–1, in which the two countries are labeled "home" and "other."

Now suppose that the home country's government attempted to eliminate the gap between y and $\bar{y}$ by increasing government spending to g^2, which would shift the IS function to position IS^2. Clearly, point A would not represent a

---

[2] A definition proposed by Wallich (1984) is often encountered. It is that coordination "implies a significant modification of national policies in recognition of international economic interdependence."

situation of short-run equilibrium. One reason might be that the expansion of y would shift the other nation's IS curve rightward, which would increase y^* and thereby move the home country's IS function even farther to the right. But suppose that that effect is taken into account in drawing IS^2, as its attached array of symbols $[q^1, g^2, y^{*2}]$ suggests. Still it is not the case that point A can reflect a short-run equilibrium, for interest rates must be equal in the two economies, given our usual assumption that they were equal in the initial equilibrium. So the IS curve of the home country must be to the left of position IS^2, and the IS curve for the other country must be to the right of the dashed one shown. This adjustment will be brought about, as explained in Section 6–6, by a decrease in q. So the short-run equilibrium will be at a position such as that indicated by points B and B^*, where y exceeds y^1 but falls short of $\bar{y}$ and where $y^* > y^{*1}$. Also, the equilibrium value of q will be smaller than q^1.

Now it is true that the home country could continue to increase g until y was increased to $\bar{y}$, but this would decrease q even more. So if its government is concerned about the nation's net export balance $X(q, y, y^*)$, it will probably be unwilling to increase g enough to bring y all the way up to $\bar{y}$ because of the effect of q on X. We will return to that issue in a moment.

There are two main points to be drawn from the foregoing example. The first is simply that when an economy is large, its macroeconomic policy actions will affect macroeconomic variables in other nations, and will affect its own real exchange rate. This conclusion is not surprising, but is important nevertheless.

Second, the problem mentioned in the next to last paragraph can in principle be overcome by coordination constituting joint fiscal expansion in both countries. If government spending is increased to g^2 and g^{*2}, where account is taken of the effects of income levels abroad, then there is no necessary adjustment in the real exchange rate. Starting from a position of net export balance, then, no problems pertaining to that balance are created by the joint fiscal expansion. The short-run outcomes at $r^2 = r^{*2}$ in Figure 12–2 are more satisfactory for both countries as a consequence of the coordinated fiscal policy action.

12.3 Macroeconomic Coordination, Continued

The following question arises naturally, however: why is coordination needed? Why would not the outcome in Figure 12–2 be generated by each government simply acting in the best interest of its own economy? After all, it makes no sense for the other economy to remain at the short-run equilibrium depicted in Figure 12–1 since its government could apparently improve matters by expanding its own spending.

For an answer to this question, we have to adopt some additional assumptions. These are somewhat dubious, but let us make them nevertheless in order to develop an understanding of the case for coordination. Afterward

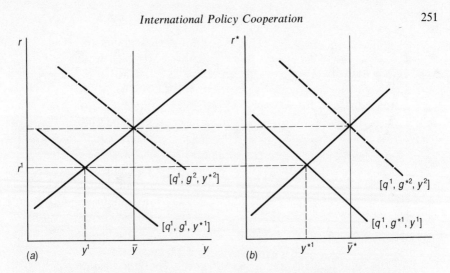

Figure 12-2 Coordinated fiscal actions. (*a*) Home country. (*b*) Other country.

we can consider whether that case is convincing, in light of these assumptions and other considerations. Accordingly, let us now assume that the policy maker's objectives in each country pertain to their own deviations of output from capacity ($y - \bar{y}$ for the home country) and of q from the value that would be needed for net export balance (say, $q - q^0$). But each of these magnitudes is influenced by the fiscal policy variables of *both* countries, as the discussion of the previous section has shown. So the short-run equilibrium "welfare" levels in the two countries, W and W^*, are both functions of both g and g^*:

$$W = \tilde{W}(g, g^*), \qquad\qquad W^* = \tilde{W}^*(g, g^*). \qquad\qquad (1)$$

For a graphical analysis, then, it is natural to develop systems of welfare indifference curves on diagrams with g and g^* on their axes. But these indifference curves will not be shaped as they are in the analysis of a consumer choice problem, in which quantities of different goods are plotted on the axes. Instead, since too much g is as undesirable as too little (and the same is true for g^*), the indifference curves for the home country will be shaped roughly as shown in Figure 12–3a. There the iso-welfare curves closest to the optimal point, marked as point A, reflect the highest attainable level of welfare for the home country, given the short-run situation at hand. The iso-welfare curves are shaped as shown—elliptically elongated in the vertical direction—because changes in g will affect the home country's welfare more (for a given magnitude) than will changes in g^*. Correspondingly, the iso-welfare curves for the other country are elongated in the horizontal direction.

Now consider the choice of g by the government of the home country. Under the assumption that it has no influence over the level of g^* chosen by the

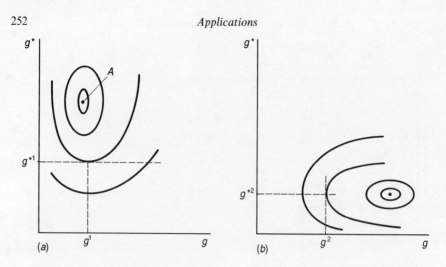

Figure 12-3 Welfare indifference curves. (*a*) Home country. (*b*) Other country.

other country, its best choice of g is that value implied by the point of tangency of an iso-welfare curve with the horizontal line reflecting the given quantity of g^*. Thus if g^{*1} is given, as in Figure 12-3, the chosen value for g will be g^1. Analogously, the other country will choose g^{*2} if g^2 is the prevailing value of g as indicated in Figure 12-3*b*.

To illustrate the potential benefits of coordination, it is useful to plot the welfare indifference curves for both nations on the same axes, as in Figure 12-4. There it will be seen that the g, g^* outcome, given that the two nations choose their fiscal policy variables independently (although recognizing the effects of the other nation's choice), will be at point A. That is so because A is the only point at which the indifference curve for the home country is horizontal whereas that for the other country is vertical.[3] It thus represents the only point at which each nation's government will be acting optimally, taking the fiscal choice of the other nation as given.

But since indifference curve II reflects a higher level of welfare for the home country than does curve I, and analogously curve IV is preferred to III by the foreign country, point B would reflect a choice of g, g^* values that would be better than A for *both* nations. Indeed, any point within the lens-shaped area enclosed by curves I and III, between points A and C, would be better than A for both countries. So there is clearly scope for fiscal policy coordination, in this example. If the home country agrees to set g equal to some value between g^A and g^C, the other country will have available a range of values for g^* that will make both nations better off than if they acted independently.

That conclusion presumes, of course, that the agreement is kept. But there will be an incentive for each nation to renege, for once the other country sets

---

[3] For each country, only one indifference curve passes through any given point, of course, by construction.

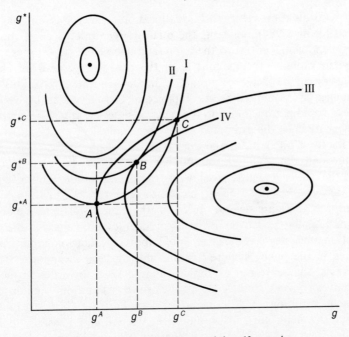

Figure 12–4 Analysis of potential welfare gains.

g^* (say, at g^{*B}), then the home country will be tempted to reduce its value of g. Similarly, the other country will be tempted to reduce g^* from the agreed level, once it believes that g is fixed at g^B. There is a tendency, in other words, for the outcome to gravitate to the so-called Nash equilibrium point A (i.e., the outcome in which the two countries do not coordinate but instead optimize while taking the other's policy choice as given). That destructive tendency may be overcome to some extent, however, by each country's recognition that the fiscal policy choices are not made just once, but have to be made over and over again, year after year. In the face of that recognition, the incentive to honor agreements—to uphold agreements to choose g^B and g^{*B}, for example—is greatly enhanced.[4]

12.4 Qualifications

The analysis of the previous two sections draws on a long line of research, to which a few of the leading contributions were made by Hamada (1976), Canzoneri and Gray (1985), Oudiz and Sachs (1984), and Canzoneri and Henderson (1991). There are several important qualifications that must be considered, however, in any sensible evaluation of the case for international

[4] It has long been recognized, by economists working in the area of game theory, that cooperative outcomes are much more likely to prevail with indefinitely *repeated* plays of a game than if it is played only once. For an early discussion, see Lave (1962).

economic coordination. One such qualification, which was emphasized by Oudiz and Sachs (1984), concerns the quantitative importance of the policy-spillover phenomena central to the analysis. In the cited paper, these authors attempted to estimate the magnitude of the potential gains from coordination by using quantitative econometric models of the interactions among the economies of the United States, Japan, and Germany. On the basis of the model's estimated parameters, and the types of shocks that occurred over some period prior to 1984, the estimated gains were equivalent to about 0.5 percent of GNP for the United states and Germany, and about 0.7 percent for Japan. These figures are not negligible, but neither are they very large. And since they represent the *maximum* gains possible, as estimated, these quantitative results must be viewed as mostly unfavorable for the case for coordination.[5]

In addition, there are several objections that can be made to the argument of Sections 12.2 and 12.3, even at the theoretical level. One is that the case for coordination presumes that the number of important macroeconomic objectives represented in the policy welfare function must exceed the number of policy instruments available. In our example of Figure 12–4, for instance, there were two objectives (income close to $\bar{y}$ and q close to q^0) and only one instrument (government spending g). If monetary policy had also been treated as an available instrument, then it would have been found possible to achieve point B in Figure 12–4 without coordination. Now monetary policy *is* in fact an available policy instrument, when exchange rates are floating, so the case for coordination requires that there be at least three macroeconomic objectives of considerable importance. In considering that requirement, one's first reaction is to recall that the governments of actual nations seem to have *many* macroeconomic goals, according to their pronouncements. But then upon reflection one realizes that this first reaction is a superficial one; that what matters is the analyst's own list of truly significant and distinct macroeconomic goals. And from that perspective, the matter is not so clear. Perhaps low inflation and y close to $\bar{y}$ are the only two goals that should be of analytical concern. The net export balance (or q close to q^0) is another plausible contender, however, which would leave us with three goals and two instruments. So this requirement is not crippling to the case for coordination.

A particularly important issue concerns the time horizon over which coordination is supposed to apply. The analysis of Sections 12.2 and 12.3 is strictly short run in nature, suggesting that a group of nations would have to experience and recognize the situation needing remedy, develop national governmental position, then work toward and reach international agreement on steps to be taken, obtain parliamentary or congressional approval, imple-

---

[5] The range of magnitudes estimated by Oudiz and Sachs is reasonably consistent with values subsequently found by other researchers, such as Canzoneri and Minford (1988). Admittedly, some researchers have found significantly larger gains—see, for example, Holtham and Hughes-Hallett (1987)—but this outcome seems to arise in postulated situations in which the governments are (by assumption) pursuing objectives that are mutually incompatible. International cooperation involving information interchange, and not requiring coordination, would seem to be sufficient to avoid such conflicts.

ment the policy actions, and wait for private market responses to develop—all before the short-run situation changes and calls for a different set of actions. The other possibility for short-run effectiveness is for the nations involved to adopt a set of policy rules that explicitly taken account of conditions in other nations, something that is rather difficult to imagine—at least for the governments of the United States, Japan, and Germany or other nations large enough for the analysis to be applicable.

Alternatively, is there a possibility of coordination applicable to long-run equilibrium situations? From that perspective there is no scope for actions to remedy departures of y from $\bar{y}$, for $y = \bar{y}$ in long-run equilibria. But what about departures of q from the value that creates net export balance? Our analytical model has not been specified in a fashion that is satisfactory for consideration of that possibility, but it seems clear from recent U.S. experience that balance of payments problems can last for many years. We need more important macroeconomic goals than instruments, however, for coordination to be profitable relative to optimal independent policies. And from a long-run perspective, it seems reasonable to posit two goals—low inflation and net-export balance—and two instruments (money-growth rates and fiscal policy). It is unclear, then, that there is much scope for fruitful coordination directed at long-run situations.

Indeed, Rogoff (1985) has argued that international coordination tends to promote more expansionary macro policies and thereby tends to undermine the protection that rule-based policy making gives a nation against the inflationary bias of discretionary policy (as discussed in Section 10.3). This conclusion may not be generally applicable; the collection of analytical possibilities considered by Rogoff is quite complex, so it is not easy to see whether minor changes in the model would result in altered conclusions. Actually, the same could be said, however, for most of the results in the entire area of discussion (i.e., international macroeconomic coordination).

On the basis of the various results and qualifications mentioned above,[6] analysts could justifiably reach different conclusions regarding the scope for fruitful macroeconomic policy coordination. But in light of the numerous objections that can be raised to the basic argument, plus the empirical results indicating quantitatively small payoffs in any event, the present writer finds it difficult to believe that there is in fact much scope for coordination. The writer would, instead, tend to agree with the view "that there would be little need for coordination if each country were taking good care of its own domestic policies."[7]

---

[6] Plus many others that have not been mentioned. One interesting and important line of research concerns the situation that occurs when the governments of different nations, which are inclined to coordinate, believe that different models of each economy are accurate. Notable papers in this branch of the literature have been contributed by Frankel and Rockett (1988), Ghosh and Masson (1988), and others.

[7] The quote is from Fischer (1988, p. 36), which provides an unusually sensible discussion of many aspects of the issue at hand.

12.5 Attempts at Coordination, 1973–1993

At this point it will be useful to turn to a brief discussion of some actual attempts at international macroeconomic coordination that transpired during the first two decades of the current floating-rate regime, namely, between 1973 and 1993. During that period there were numerous meetings of high-level officials from the principal economic powers, with regular summit meetings of the G-7 nations (United States, Japan, Germany, France, Italy, United Kingdom, and Canada) taking place annually since 1975[8] and gatherings at the finance-minister level occasionally. Three of these occasions have been especially notable because they resulted in fairly specific and substantive agreements that implied macro-economic coordination—that is, they involved modifications of national policies designed to be favorable internationally. The first of these notable agreements was reached at the so-called Bonn summit of July 1978. At the time GNP was expanding more rapidly (relative to capacity growth) in the United States than in other leading economics, so the U.S. net export balance was deteriorating and the dollar exchange rate was tending to depreciate. The U.S. government wanted to counter these last two tendencies, but was reluctant to slow demand growth. Accordingly, it sought more rapid demand growth in Germany and Japan, that is, more stimulative monetary and fiscal policy actions. The other nations, in turn, wanted the United States to decontrol domestic oil prices, letting them rise toward levels prevailing elsewhere. In fact, an agreement involving these steps—plus some additional understandings regarding future tariff reductions—was successfully concluded and implemented. In terms of economic effects, however, the agreement was only partially successful. Oil price decontrol was itself beneficial for the United Sates, but the U.S. balance of payments did not show the desired improvement and by October 1979 the U.S. inflation rate had become so serious that the Federal Reserve announced major policy changes designed to bring it under control.[9] The Germans, mean-while, were experiencing a small but unwelcome increase in inflation and were beginning to reconsider the wisdom of the Bonn Agreement, a process that eventually resulted in the view that their demand expansion had been unwise.

A second notable example of macroeconomic coordination was the so-called Plaza Accord, adopted by the G-5 nations at the Plaza Hotel in New York during September 1985. The focus of attention in this case was the exchange value of the U.S. dollar, which had risen spectacularly from 1980 through the end of 1984.[10] During those years the U.S. government had resisted calls for intervention, but (partly because of the explosion in the U.S. current-account

---

[8] The first several such meetings—those prior to 1986—actually involved only the G-5 group, which does not include Canada or Italy.

[9] The Fed's October 6, 1979, change in operating procedures was dramatic and reflected a genuine determination to pursue a more restrictive policy. Money-growth rates did not drop sharply until 1981, however, in part because of an ill-fated credit-control scheme adopted (and quickly abandoned) by the Carter administration in mid-1980.

[10] This rise, which was mentioned in Chapter 1, shows up clearly in Figures 1–1 and 2–7 through 2–12.

deficit) this position was reversed in 1985. Thus the Plaza Accord embodied an agreement that the G-5 governments would jointly intervene to reduce the exchange value of the dollar. Its value did decline sharply, as we have seen in Chapters 1 and 2, through 1985 and 1986. The downward movement had begun in February 1985, however, so a number of observers would not attribute it to the coordination intervention of the G-5 finance ministries and central banks.

Despite the dollar's fall over 1985–1986, the U.S. net export balance remained deeply in deficit. The U.S. government again wanted Germany and Japan to pursue more expansionary policies, but Bonn summit experience had made these nations wary of such actions. Nevertheless, in October 1986, Japan acceded to a bilateral agreement whereby the Bank of Japan would be more expansionary in return for which the U.S. government would "continue to fight protectionism" (Fischer, 1988, p. 33) and would agree that the current dollar–yen exchange rate (of 154 yen per dollar) was appropriate—in other words, that the dollar did not need to fall further.[11] A more general agreement to that effect (regarding the U.S. exchange rate) was adopted by the G-7 governments in February 1987 at a Paris meeting; this agreement is often termed the Louvre Accord. In addition, Germany and Japan agreed to small fiscal stimuli while the United States would attempt to reduce its federal budget deficit. Some observers have suggested that the expansionary stance promised by Japan was a significant contributing factor in the famous Japanese asset price "bubble" of 1987–1989, during which land and stock market prices soared to extraordinary heights.[12] As a result, in 1990 the Bank of Japan was forced to take deflationary measures, after which Japan entered its most serious recession of the postwar era.

The outcome of these three particularly notable coordination experiences have not, then, been uniformly satisfactory. Furthermore, there have not been a lot of *major* agreements to discuss. Critics of the process would suggest that neither of these conclusions should come as a surprise, for it seems unlikely that the governments of major economies would let their policy actions be influenced strongly by considerations as dubious as those involved—which do not promise enormous gains even if successful. Indeed, some critics are generally inclined to view most efforts toward international coordination as thinly disguised attempts by national governments—chiefly the United States, thus far—to get other nations to take actions that might rescue them from the consequences of their own unwise but politically advantageous domestic policies.

[11] The phrase quoted by Fischer (1988, p. 33) was that the exchange rate was "broadly consistent with the present underlying fundamentals."

[12] From the end of 1985 to the end of 1989, for example, the value of stock market shares increased from 196 trillion yen to 630 trillion. Meanwhile, the aggregate value of property assets—that is, residential and commercial land—grew from 1004 trillion yen at the end of 1985 to 2389 trillion at the end of 1990.

12.6 Optimal Currency Areas

One extreme form of monetary cooperation among a group of nations is to maintain fixed exchange rates with each other or, in the limit, to create a currency union with a single common money. We have considered some of the pros and cons of such arrangements in our Chapter 10 discussion of fixed versus floating exchange rates and in our Chapter 11 review of the European Monetary System. In neither place, though, did we explicitly consider the theory of optimal currency areas. A brief discussion is therefore appropriate at this point.

The theory of optimal currency areas, introduced by Mundell (1961), is concerned with the same general sort of tradeoff between microeconomic efficiency and macroeconomic flexibility as that described in Sections 10.2 and 10.3—an extension of the area over which a single currency prevails enhances efficiency but reduces the possibility of monetary policy responses to shocks that affect various subareas differently. The difference relative to Chapter 10 is that here our perspective is *global*, involving the desirability from the point of view of all nations together, rather than from the viewpoint of a single nation. The question is, how many distinct currency areas (each with its own money) should there be for joint welfare maximization? At one extreme, the entire world could in principle use the same single money. But instead each nation could use its own national money and let its exchange rates with all others float.[13] It seems likely that the global optimum would lie somewhere between these two possibilities, but what are the relevant factors that determine where the lines should be drawn?[14]

In his original paper Mundell (1961) emphasized labor mobility as a crucial consideration. Suppose several nations or regions that share a common currency are hit by shocks that affect them differently, causing aggregate demand to be too large in some places and too small in others. Thus, with sticky wages and prices, there will be excessive employment (leading to future inflation) in some areas and unemployment in others—for monetary policy cannot be used to offset the shocks. But if labor were highly mobile, workers could leave the depressed regions and move to the ones with excess demand, thereby reducing the demand–supply imbalance in both places.[15] Thus the greater the mobility of labor between two areas, the more likely it becomes that they could beneficially be combined in a single currency union.[16]

A second consideration is the extent of trade among different regions. As

[13] Still more extreme in this direction, as we recognized in Chapter 10, is the possibility of multiple moneys within a single nation.

[14] It will be noted that we are not considering areas with fixed exchange rates among different currencies. The reason will be discussed shortly.

[15] This sort of movement is clearly most relevant for shocks of fairly long duration.

[16] Similar reasoning applies in principle to other factors of production, such as land, physical capital, and intermediate materials. But land cannot move and much physical—as opposed to financial—capital is installed in such a way that its movement is extremely expensive. Intermediate goods can move, of course, but we are presuming that they (like other goods) are very highly mobile. So labor is the main factor that is relevant in the present context.

was mentioned in our discussion in Chapter 10, a greater volume of commodity trade between areas tends to enhance the benefits of a single currency and therefore to increase the likelihood that a monetary union would be desirable. In addition, McKinnon (1963) put forth a second argument suggesting that exchange rate flexibility is less valuable for a nation, the greater is its volume (in relative terms) of foreign trade. The point seems to be that if a nation's domestic price level is viewed as a weighted average of home-produced and foreign goods,[17] then the larger the share of foreign goods, the more price-level instability will be induced by fluctuations in exchange rates needed to maintain trade balance. This is not a particularly telling point, however, and stronger claims have been refuted by Niehans (1984, pp. 292–294). Nevertheless, the first argument remains valid.

In conducting the present discussion, we have been considering only matters relevant for determining the optimal composition of single-currency monetary unions with floating exchange rates among these unions. We have not, in other words, considered arrangements with blocks of countries, each maintaining fixed exchange rates but distinct national currencies. We have proceeded in that fashion for reasons mentioned in Chapters 10 and 11. First, fixed but not "immutably" fixed exchange rates are subject to destabilizing speculation, as emphasized in Section 10.6. Second, an arrangement with fixed rates surrenders the benefits of macroeconomic flexibility provided by floating rates, yet does not capture all of the efficiency gains provided by a single currency—recall the EMS magnitudes mentioned in Section 11.3. Consequently, it seems best to focus on the two "pure" cases, since the intermediate fixed-rate possibility appears to be dominated by them.

It will perhaps be clear, from the vagueness of the foregoing discussion, that the theory of optimal currency areas has not yet been developed to an extent that would enable one to apply it quantitatively or operationally to actual economies.[18] Indeed, some critics would suggest that the ideas involved do not actually amount to a *theory*, but merely an enumeration of the various tradeoffs involved. That judgment is probably warranted, but it should not be permitted to obscure the value of this enumeration. Simply from recognizing the nature of the tradeoffs, one is driven away from the view that an optimal arrangement would feature either a single worldwide currency or a set of floating exchange rates among all pairs of national currencies. Some intermediate arrangement—involving a few currency areas, each with a single money, linked by floating exchange rates—would probably be preferable, and the theory of optimal currency areas helps to clarify that point.

---

[17] In our formal model of Chapter 5–8, no distinction was made between the price level and the price of home-produced goods. This convenient simplification was adopted because it is approximately correct for economies with a small trade share and is not seriously misleading in other cases.

[18] For a recent summary and review, see Kawai (1992).

12.7 Concluding Remarks

There are additional modes of international cooperation that are of great practical importance. Leading examples are provided by the activities of international organizations, including the IMF and the World Bank. The IMF's original mission, as the overseer of the Bretton Woods fixed exchange rate system, disappeared during the 1970s along with that system. The IMF has continued to play a significant international role, nevertheless, in various ways. The basis for the IMF's clout is its status as a substantial lender of hard currency, on a fairly short-term basis, to nations that satisfy its "conditionality" requirements.[19] Since these conditions must be met to earn an IMF loan, it can have considerable influence over economic policies adopted by nations that are potential borrowers. Specifically, the main conditions often include monetary and financial policies designed to keep the nation in question from encountering serious BOP or inflationary difficulties. In order to be prepared for possible loan applications, the IMF conducts annual investigations of economic conditions in all member nations, even those that have no intention of asking for loans in the near future. Consequently, the IMF's annual reports on its 160+ member nations provide a valuable source of information about most of the world's significant national economies. These reports, then, constitute one form of international cooperation managed by the IMF.

Because of its status as a potential lender to national economies, the IMF was able to play a special role in negotiations involving the debt crisis faced during 1982–1992 by many Latin American economies.[20] In particular, American and Japanese banks viewed the IMF's willingness to lend to specific nations as an indication that those nations had improved their circumstances sufficiently to again become plausible credit risks. The IMF preferred not to approve its own lending until after consortia of private banks had agreed to also lead, since the banks together had much greater resources. But their special position gave the IMF a role as principal coordinator of the developed world's efforts. And it also served—as it does at other times—as a "scapegoat," an external force that governments can blame for politically unpopular actions needed to restore creditworthiness and financial stability.

The World Bank also played some role in the debt crisis, but one that was smaller than the IMF's because the World Bank's fundamental mission is to make long-term project loans—that is, loans designed to finance specific

---

[19] These requirements serve a double purpose—not only do they push the borrowing nations to follow responsible financial and monetary policies, but they also make it more likely that the IMF will be able to collect its interest and repayments on schedule. The latter is crucial, since the IMF's financial viability depends on its own commercial success as a lender. While the IMF's capital exists as the result of past subscription (i.e., gifts) from its member governments, these have become difficult to obtain and the organization has (of course) no taxing power.

[20] As mentioned in Chapter 4, the crisis began in August 1982, when the government of Mexico would be unable to make scheduled payments on its debt to foreign banks. By the end of 1986, over 40 other nations—mostly in Latin America and Africa—had announced similar difficulties. For more discussion of the topic, see Krugman and Obstfeld (1994, ch. 23).

investment projects such as the construction of a major dam or transportation link—rather than loans for helping the recipient over a period of macroeconomic difficulty.

Recently, both the IMF and the World Bank have become heavily involved in Eastern Europe. As the member nations and satellites of the former Union of Socialist Soviet Republics have turned away from Moscow-dominated central planning toward a more market-based economic structure, there has been a need for loans to assist this wrenching process of change. The IMF's policy of making loans conditional upon actions designed to assure macroeconomic stability has led to a flood of IMF missions to Eastern Europe for the purpose of investigation and advice giving.[21]

All of the foregoing activities amount to forms of international cooperation and are clearly of major importance. Even more important, however, is cooperation among nations to encourage the removal and prevention of barriers to international trade. Because the effects of trade barriers (such as tariffs and quotas) are such that their benefits are narrowly focused and their costs widely dispersed across national populations, political pressures tend to favor such barriers, although they are in most cases harmful to the average citizen of all affected nations. The influence of U.S. automakers, for example, has led to restrictions on the ability of American consumers to purchase Japanese cars—even though the costs to potential buyers outweigh the gains to U.S. auto producers. Such issues of free versus restricted (or "managed") trade fall outside the scope of this book, as was explained in Chapter 1, so analysis will not be undertaken here. It should be mentioned, nevertheless, that major advances in the direction of free trade have been negotiated since 1947 by the nations subscribing to GATT—the General Agreement on Tariffs and Trade, a system of trade rules administered from Geneva. Specifically, major multilateral reductions in tariffs were agreed to in 1967 (the Kennedy Round), 1979 (the Tokyo Round), and 1993 (the Uruguay Round). It would be difficult to overemphasize the importance of this particular form of international policy cooperation.

References

Canzoneri, M. B., and J. A. Gray, "Monetary Policy Games and the Consequences of Non-Cooperative Behavior," *International Economic Review* **26** (Oct. 1985), 547–564.

Canzoneri, M. B. and P. Minford, "When International Policy Coordination Matters: An Empirical Analysis," *Applied Economics* **20** (1988), 1137–1154.

Canzoneri, M. B., and D. W. Henderson, *Monetary Policy Coordination in Interdependent Economies: A Game Theoretic Approach*. Cambridge, MA: MIT Press, 1991.

Fischer, S. "Macroeconomic Policy," in *International Economic Cooperation*, M. Feldstein, Ed. Chicago: University of Chicago Press, 1988.

---

[21] One anonymous critic has quipped that the largest form of actual assistance provided by the IMF has been the hard currency spent by its staff members in Eastern Europe.

Frankel, J. A., and K. Rockett, "International Macroeconomic Coordination when Policymakers Do Not Agree on the True Model," *American Economic Review* **78** (June 1988), 318–340.

Ghosh, A. R., and P. R. Masson, "International Policy Coordination in a World with Model Uncertainty," *International Monetary Fund Staff Papers* **35** (June 1988), 230–258.

Hamada, K., "A Strategic Analysis of Monetary Interdependence," *Journal of Political Economy* **84** (Aug. 1976), 667–700.

Holtham, G., and A. Hughes-Hallett, "International Policy Cooperation and Model Uncertainty," in *Global Macroeconomics: Policy Conflict and Cooperation*, R. C. Bryant and R. Portes, Eds. New York: St. Martin's Press, 1987.

Kawai, M., "Optimum Currency Areas," in *The New Palgrave Dictionary of Money and Finance*, vol. 3, P. Newman, M. Milgate, and J. Eatwell, Eds. New York: Stockton Press, 1992.

Krugman, P. R., and M. Obstfeld, *International Economics: Theory and Policy*, 3rd ed. New York; Harper Collins, 1994.

Lave, L. "An Empirical Approach to the Prisoners' Dilemma Game," *Quarterly Journal of Economics* **76** (Aug. 1962), 424–436.

McKinnon, R. I., "Optimum Currency Areas," *American Economic Review* **53** (Sept. 1963), 717–725.

Mundell, R. A., "A Theory of Optimum Currency Areas," *American Economic Review* **51** (Sept. 1961), 657–665.

Niehans, J., *International Monetary Economics*. Baltimore, MD: Johns Hopkins University Press, 1984.

Oudiz, G. and J. Sachs, "Macroeconomic Policy Coordination among the Industrial Economies," *Brookings Papers on Economic Activity*, no. 1 (1984), 1–64.

Rogoff, K., "Can International Monetary Policy Cooperation Be Counterproductive?" *Journal of International Economics* **18** (May 1985), 199–217.

Wallich, H. C., "Institutional Cooperation in the World Economy," in *The World Economic System: Performance and Prospects*, J. A. Frenkel and M. L. Mussa, Eds. Dover, MA: Auburn House, 1984.

Problems

1. For an extremely simple algebraic example of potential gains from coordination described in Section 12.3, consider an example in which

$$W = \alpha g - \beta g^2 + \gamma g^*$$
$$W^* = \alpha g^* - \beta g^{*2} + \gamma g,$$

where α, β, and γ are all positive. First, determine the values of g and g^* that would be chosen by the two nations' fiscal authorities acting independently (i.e., taking the other's actions as given). Then, second, determine the values of g and g^* that would be required to maximize the sum $W + W^*$, when chosen jointly.

2. Continuing with the setup in Problem 1, find what values of g and g^* would jointly maximize $\omega W + (1 - \omega)W^*$, where $0 < \omega < 1$. Here ω indexes the "weight" assigned to the home country in the joint welfare maximization problem. Show that for any admissible value of ω, the jointly chosen g, g^* values yield a higher value of $\omega W + (1 - \omega)W^*$ than those chosen independently.

3. In the chapter's discussion of the Plaza Accord, reference is made to "coordinated intervention of the G-5 finance ministries and central banks." Was this intervention of the sterilized or nonsterilized type? What leads you to that judgment, in the absence of definitive data?

4. Would the 12 member nations (as of 1994) of the European Union constitute an optimal currency area? Explain the reasons for your belief.

Index

short-run, 111–23, 140–44
Cooper, R. N., 71n4
Cooperation
  difference from coordination, 248–49
  modes of international, 260–61
  monetary cooperation in Europe,
    227–28
  optimal currency areas, 258–59
  related to monetary system, 248
  role of World Bank in international,
    260–61
Coordination, macroeconomic, 248–49
Coordination, macroeconomic
  attempts, 256–57
  case for, 249–50
  difference from cooperation, 248–49
  objections to, 254–55
  potential benefits of, 252–53
  qualifications, 253–55
Cosiander, P. A., 190
Covered interest parity (CIP), 21, 23,
  107, 189–91
Cumby, R., 45n3
Currencies
  in composition of ECU, 230–32
  country's maintenance of par value
    with fixed exchange rate, 136–37
  in European Monetary System (EMS),
    230–37
  value in actual gold standard, 71
  See also High-powered money
Currency areas, optimal, 258–59
Currency boards, 222
Currency union, 234
Current-account balance. *See* Balance of
  payments (BOP)

Debt crisis, developing nations, 90, 260
Delors, Jacques, 235
Delors Report (1989), 235–36
Density function, 183–85
Distributions, bivariate and univariate,
  184–85
Dornbusch, R., 98, 174
Drazen, A., 221n28

Economic shocks
  assumptions related to floating rates,
    207–8
  oil price shock, 89
  response under fixed and floating
    exchange rates, 211–13
Ecu instruments, private, 243–45
Effective exchange rates, 4
Eichenbaum, M., 199

Eichengreen, B., 71n4, 80n13
Einzig, P., 221n16
European Central Bank (ECB), 236
European Community (EC), 230, 235,
  238
  exchange rate par value bands (the
    snake), 228
European Currency Unit (ECU), 229–31
  role of, 232
  trading of privately-issued deposits and
    securities, 243–45
  United Kingdom alternative form,
    242–45
  See also Ecu instruments, private
European Currency Unit (ECU), hard,
  242–43
European Currency Unit (ECU), hard
  See also Ecu instruments, private
European Economic Community (EEC),
  or Common Market. *See* European
  Community (EC); European Union
  (EU)
European Monetary Agreement
  (1958–72), 228
European Monetary Fund (EMF)
  proposal, 243
European Monetary Institute (EMI),
  236
European Monetary System (EMS)
  creation (1979), 89
  exchange rate bands, 240–41
  exchange rate limits, 10
  exchange rate mechanism, 228–29
  performance of, 233
  regulations, 231–33
European Payments Union (EPU),
  227–28
European Union
  See also European Community
European Union (EU), 10
Evans, M. D. D., 197
Exchange Rate Mechanism (ERM), 229
Exchange rates
  behavior in purchasing power parity
    (PPP) theory, 27, 29–32, 200–2
  behavior like random walk variables,
    121–23
  under Bretton Woods system, 80–83
Exchange rates
  nominal, 26
  with par value bands, 223–24
  as prices of money, 208
  under pure gold standard, 70–71
  real effective, 27
  See also Foreign exchange markets